Lecture Notes in Computer Science 696

Edited by G. Goos and J. Hartmanis

Advisory Board: W. Brauer   D. Gries   J. Stoer

M. Worboys, A. F. Grundy (Eds.)

Advances in Databases

11th British National Conference on Databases
BNCOD 11
Keele, UK, July 7-9 1993
Proceedings

Springer-Verlag
Berlin Heidelberg New York
London Paris Tokyo
Hong Kong Barcelona
Budapest

M. Worboys   A. F. Grundy   (Eds.)

Advances in Databases

11th British National Conference on Databases,
BNCOD 11
Keele, UK, July 7-9, 1993
Proceedings

Springer-Verlag
Berlin Heidelberg New York
London Paris Tokyo
Hong Kong Barcelona
Budapest

Series Editors

Gerhard Goos
Universität Karlsruhe
Postfach 69 80
Vincenz-Priessnitz-Straße 1
D-76131 Karlsruhe, FRG

Juris Hartmanis
Cornell University
Department of Computer Science
4130 Upson Hall
Ithaca, NY 14853, USA

Volume Editors

Michael Frederick Worboys
Anna Frances Grundy
Department of Computer Science, Keele University
Keele, North Staffordshire, ST5 5BG, UK

CR Subject Classification (1991): H.2

ISBN 3-540-56921-9 Springer-Verlag Berlin Heidelberg New York
ISBN 0-387-56921-9 Springer-Verlag New York Berlin Heidelberg

© Springer-Verlag Berlin Heidelberg 1993
Printed in Germany

Typesetting: Camera ready by author
Printing and binding: Druckhaus Beltz, Hemsbach/Bergstr.
45/3140-543210 - Printed on acid-free paper

Foreword

The papers following constitute the written proceedings of the eleventh British National Conference on Databases, held at Keele University in the Midlands of England. As with many other current database conferences, a dominant theme is the provision of the means to enhance the capabilities of databases to handle information that has a rich semantic structure. Such provision is clearly based upon user requirements, since many applications demand it and system configurations call for it. A major research question is how to achieve such a semantic scale-up without sacrificing performance. There are currently two main paradigms within which it is possible to propose answers to this question, deduction-oriented and object-oriented. These two approaches are not disjoint; indeed, some would argue that the object-oriented approach is subsumed within the deductive logic-based approach. Both paradigms are well represented in this collection, with perhaps the balance swinging in the direction of the deductive approach, which is followed by both the invited papers.

It has been an unfortunate consequence of the admitted failure of the Japanese Fifth Generation project to develop an effective logic-based paradigm that all approaches based on logic are seen in some quarters as doomed to failure. Our first invited speaker takes a much more optimistic line. *Michael Freeston*, from the European Computer-Industry Research Centre (ECRC) at Munich has argued that ECRC has achieved more than both the Japanese and American initiatives in this area and that logic-based information systems are far from dead. His paper describes work to provide efficient indexes to support both deductive and object-oriented paradigms.

Both deductive and active databases are based upon rules, yet unification of these two types has not yet been achieved. Our second invited speaker, *Carlo Zaniolo* from the University of California at Los Angeles, discusses the technical problems at the heart of such a unification. He outlines a semantic framework that results in a rule-based language, presently being developed at UCLA, with the potential to integrate deductive and active databases.

Three of the papers following address the theme of semantic enhancement in the context of specific applications. *Goble and Glowinski* discuss the handling of integrity constraints in a medical application, *Fernandes et al.* test a generic unification of deductive and object-oriented approaches with a geographic application, and *Eaglestone et al.* consider how recent research on database support for design activities can extend beyond support for standard engineering and software design to the artistic design process.

Two papers discuss distributed configurations. *Castellanos* considers ways to enrich existing models in constituent databases of a distributed system so as to provide integrated access to the federation. *Cohen and Ringwood* use a logic-based language that supports concurrency to integrate heterogeneous nodes.

Four papers deal directly with the object-oriented approach to databases. *Barclay and Kennedy* incorporate the established database concept of the 'view' into their object-oriented world. *Hohenstein and Odberg* use an extended version of the entity- relationship model to enrich the semantics of databases and provide the basis for a uniform C++ interface to a variety of DBMS. *Carnduff and Gray* consider how function materialisation in object-oriented databases can enhance their use for the engineering design process. *Tagg and Liew* provide an excellent summary of the current state of object-oriented DBMS.

Returning to the deductive theme, *Sunderraman* constructs an extension to definite deductive databases that allows for conditional facts. Model-theoretic and fixpoint semantics are provided for this extension. *Singleton and Brereton* consider some of the practicalities in implementing logic features using a relational database.

There are two other papers in this collection which do not fit so easily into our general theme, yet are very much in the mainstream of current database research. *McBrien* discusses some of the algorithms required for querying and updating an historical relational database. The discussion provides information about what is required of a relational system to support an historical information system. *Reddi's* paper makes a contribution to the theory of functional databases by showing how work on optimisation strategies for integrity constraint enforcement in deductive databases can be transferred to the functional database approach.

Acknowledgements

I am very grateful to the programme committee, whose members are listed on a later page. The programme committee was chaired quietly and effectively by John Hughes at a meeting in February. We selected 13 papers for presentation at the eleventh BNCOD conference from a total of 36 full papers submitted. Other submissions were recommended for presentation in poster form. Each full paper was refereed by at least three members of the programme committee.

I would like to acknowledge the support of the BNCOD steering committee, especially its chair, Alex Gray. Last year's conference organiser, Peter Gray, offered much useful practical advice. At Keele, I am grateful for the help of the conference organising committee, without whose assistance this conference could not have taken place. Frances Grundy was able to contribute the benefit of her experience of organising BNCOD at Keele in 1985. My postgraduate students have done a great deal of work behind the scenes. In particular, Priyantha Jayawardena shared many hours with me in routine tasks. Kendal Allen, the conference administrator, provided a friendly and efficient interface with delegates.

Keele, May 1993   Michael F. Worboys

Conference Committees

Programme Committee

J Hughes (University of Ulster) – Chair
J Bocca (University of Birmingham)
TJ Bourne (SIAM Limited)
R Cooper (University of Glasgow)
SM Deen (Keele University)
B Eaglestone (University of Bradford)
WA Gray (University of Wales, Cardiff)
AF Grundy (Keele University)
KG Jeffery (SERC)
G Kemp (University of Aberdeen)
JB Kennedy (Napier, Edinburgh)
RJ Lucas (Keylink Computers Limited)
Z Kemp (University of Kent)
A Poulovassilis (King's College, London University)
NW Paton (Heriot Watt University)
R Tagg (Independent Consultant)
GCH Sharman (IBM, Hursley)
C Small (Birkbeck College, London University)
MF Worboys (Keele University)

Steering Committee

WA Gray (University of Wales, Cardiff) – Chair
PMD Gray (University of Aberdeen)
MS Jackson (Wolverhampton University)
MH Williams (Heriot Watt University)
MF Worboys (Keele University)

Organising Committee

K Allen (Keele University)
AF Grundy (Keele University)
P Jayawardena (Keele University)
MF Worboys (Keele University)

Contents

Contents

Begriffsverzeichnis: a Concept Index

Michael Freeston

ECRC, Arabellastrasse 17, DW-8000 Munich 81, Germany

Abstract. This paper describes a generalised technique for the indexing of data structures of different complexities. It represents the culmination of a long research effort to devise efficient and well-behaved indexing for the low-level support of persistent programming languages: more specifically, persistent logic programming and object-oriented programming environments, which the author sees as the future of database systems.

1 Introduction

This paper describes a generalised technique for the indexing of data structures of different complexities. It represents the culmination of a long research effort to devise efficient and well-behaved indexing for the low-level support of persistent programming languages: more specifically, persistent logic programming and object-oriented programming environments, which the author sees as the future of database systems.

Both programming paradigms are particularly amenable to persistent implementation. In the author's conception of such systems, the executed code locates the target of the next execution step - whether the target be method, object, rule or ground fact - by indirect reference via an index (i.e. search by structure and value), rather than by direct reference to a compiled-in address location. In persistent logic programming, location via an index acts as a clause pre-unification step. In persistent object-oriented programming, it provides the location of complex objects, and the late binding of method to object.

The relative inefficiency introduced by indirect addressing through an index has to be balanced against the advantage of being able to apply all the conventional DBMS operations to objects or clauses, thereby extending the power of the programming language to the database system, while eliminating the 'impedance mismatch' which exists between every programming language and embedded database language. In deductive systems, the loose coupling between a logic programming language and a (relational) DBMS is transformed into the basis of a true, fully integrated, deductive database system. In the object-oriented paradigm, it is the author's view that, whatever arguments there may be about the precise properties which an object-oriented database system should possess, it is nothing if it is not a persistent object-oriented programming language.

Efficient, generalised indexing of complex structures is thus an essential prerequisite, if not the key, to viable persistent programming. But it has a more fundamental significance: it is 120 years since Frege devised a notation (Begriffsschrift) for the representation of any arbitrary concept. Since we reason by matching the structure of one concept against another, efficient reasoning on large bodies of knowledge in any automated system must require an efficient generalised indexing mechanism, whatever particular representation the knowledge may take.

2 Fundamentals

Classically, data structures in database systems have been restricted to fixed-structure *records* or *tuples*. The *structure* of a tuple is a set of *fields*, or *attributes*. The *types* of the attributes have been restricted to a few simple types, such as real, integer, and string.

In order to build an index to a set of records, it is assumed that all the members of the set have the same structure. A *key* value must be associated with each. This value may or may not be unique to the record. In principle, it may be the direct value of a single attribute, or of several attributes, or it may be generated by some conversion operation on one or more attributes. The unit of memory allocation for the data and the index, in main memory or secondary storage, is a *page*, and this page is almost invariably of fixed size.

The best known and most widely used dynamic method of indexing a set of records in a database is the B-tree. In general, a tree structure is composed of a *root node*, *branch nodes* and *leaf nodes*. By convention, the tree is represented in inverted form i.e. with the root at the top. A traversal path through the tree is defined by the sequence of nodes encountered along the path. The *height* of the tree is the length of the longest direct path traversed from root to leaf. The *fan-out ratio* is the number of branches leading from a node in the direction of the leaves. This ratio usually has a range of allowed values, depending on the details of the design and implementation. The limits of this range are the same for all the index nodes.

The B-tree takes the value of a single attribute in a record, or the lexical concatenation of several attributes, as the index key. Each index node corresponds to a page of memory, and contains an ordered set of index keys. The index is constructed as a hierarchy of index keys: at any particular level of the tree, each node contains an ordered set of key values and, associated with each key, a pointer to a node at the index level below. Each key represents an upper (or lower) bound to the key values stored in the node to which it points. At the lowest index level, the keys point to data pages containing records within the ranges defined by the lowest level index keys.

When the insertion of an additional record causes a *data* page to overflow:

1. the page is split into two pages about the median value of the index key attribute(s).
2. the median key attribute value, together with an additional pointer for the new page, is inserted in the index leaf node which holds the pointer to the original page. An index node thus consists of [key, pointer] pairs, stored in key value order. [Plus one additional pointer, for the extreme upper or lower range partition.]

If an insertion in an *index* node causes it to overflow, then the index node is similarly split about its median key value, which is promoted upwards, together with a pointer to the newly created index page.

In the worst case, a single insertion of a data record can trigger a chain of overflows and insertions up to and including the root of the index tree. When the root splits, a new root is generated and the height of the index tree increases by one. In this way a tree-structured index grows upwards (i.e. an inverted tree) as the number of data pages increases.

If all index pages are the same size, and the maximum number of key entries in each index page is F (the fan-out ratio), then each level of the index has maximally F times as many index pages as the level above, and there will be maximally F times as many data pages as pages in the lowest index level. Since both data and index pages are split at their median values, the worst-case occupancy of a data or index page is 50%. On statistical average, the occupancy is around 69%, but it is possible (although often not realised) that the occupancy of the entire index and data set can sink to 50% in pathological cases.

2.1 Properties of the B-tree

The structure has a number of attractive properties, which is why it has been almost universally adopted for dynamic indexing in database systems. In particular:

1. the tree is always perfectly *balanced* i.e. for a given size of tree, every direct path from root to leaf is the same length;
2. if the full key of any individual record is specified (an *exact-match* query), the record can always be accessed via a direct path from root to leaf. Thus the access time for a single record is constant and predictable, for a given tree size;
3. the length of the direct path from root to leaf increases only logarithmically in the total number of indexed records so that, typically, a five-level index is sufficient to index several Terabytes of data;
4. the maximum update time for the insertion or deletion of a single record is also logarithmic in the total number of indexed records;
5. there is a guaranteed minimum occupancy (50%) of the data and index pages;
6. the maximum size of the index is always directly proportional to the quantity of the data;
7. all the above properties are preserved under deletion as well as insertion. i.e. the performance of the structure does not deteriorate with usage - it is fully *dynamic*.

3 Generalisation to n-dimensions

For twenty years researchers have tried to find a structure which generalises the properties of the B-tree to n dimensions i.e. an index on n attributes of a record instead of one. Ideally, such an index should have the property that, if values are specified for m out of n key attributes (a *partial match* query), then the time taken to find all the records matching this combination should be the same, whichever combination of m from n is chosen.

To achieve this, the index must be symmetrical in n dimensions. There is no longer a directly defined ordering between the individual records according to their (single key) attribute values. Each record must be viewed as a point in an n-dimensional data space, which is the Cartesian product of the domains of the n index attributes.

An n-dimensional generalisation of the B-tree must partition this data space into sub-spaces or *regions* in such a way that the properties of the B-tree as listed above are preserved. Specifically, each region corresponds to a data page, and the index represents a recursive partitioning of the data regions into higher level index regions.

In order to achieve symmetry in the n dimensions, in the sense defined above, the following additional property is needed:

8. the number of recursive partitions of the data space required to define the boundaries of each data region should be (as nearly as possible) the same in each dimension.

It is further important to the efficiency of the index that the following properties are maintained:

9. the spatial distribution of the data regions should correspond as closely as possible to the spatial distribution of the data points;
10. the spatial distribution of the index regions at each level of the index tree should correspond as closely as possible to the spatial distribution at the next lower level, and to that of the data regions;
11. the representation of empty space should be minimised.

Unfortunately, it has proved extremely difficult to reconcile all these requirements. Considerable progress has been made, as shown by the substantial number of designs developed in the last few years. [The appended bibliography has been assembled to give the interested reader some entry points to the main research directions and developments in the field during this period]. But there remains an underlying inflexibility in current designs, and there is still no solution which is provably resistant to pathological cases.

The apparent intractability of the underlying problem is clearly related to the increased topological complexity of the n-dimensional case. The approach described below therefore re-attacks the problem from a topological perspective. This clarifies the basic nature of the problem and, by so doing, reveals how it is possible to overcome a fundamental barrier to the achievement of acceptable and guaranteed performance characteristics.

4 Spatial regions

We begin again at the beginning. What precisely do we mean by partitioning a dataspace into subspaces or regions?

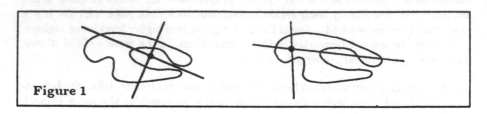

Figure 1

Definition 1. A point X lies *outside* a closed boundary B in a dataspace D iff every straight line of infinite length which passes through X intersects B either zero or an even number of times on each side of X.

Definition 2. A point X lies *inside* a closed boundary B in a dataspace D iff every straight line of infinite length which passes through X intersects B an odd number of times on each side of X.

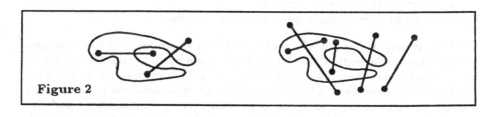

Figure 2

Definition 3. Two points X and Y lie on *opposite* sides of a closed boundary B iff a straight line joining X and Y intersects B an odd number of times.

Definition 4. Two points X and Y lie on *the same* side of a closed boundary B iff a straight line joining X and Y intersects B either zero or an even number of times.

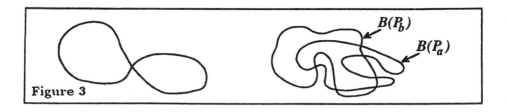

Figure 3

Axiom 1 *No boundary may intersect itself.*

Axiom 2 *No two boundaries may intersect.*

Definition 5. A closed boundary B *encloses* a subspace D_s of a dataspace D iff every point X in D_s lies *inside* boundary B.

Definition 6. A closed boundary B *exclusively encloses* a subspace D_s of a dataspace D iff B encloses D_s and B encloses no point which is not in D_s.

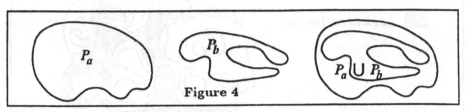

Figure 4

Definition 7. A *partition region* P of a data space D is any subspace D_s which is exclusively enclosed by a finite or infinite closed boundary $B(P)$.

The data space D is itself a partition region, whose closed boundary $B(D)$ is delineated by the finite or infinite upper and lower limits of its data domains or ranges.

Definition 8. A partition region P_a *encloses* a partition region P_b iff every point in P_b also lies within P_a. Thus: $P_a \cap P_b = P_b$ and $P_a \cup P_b = P_a$.

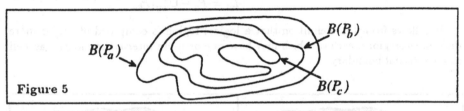

Figure 5

Definition 9. A partition region P_a *directly* encloses a partition region P_b iff P_a encloses P_b and there exists no other partition region P_c which encloses P_b and which is enclosed by P_a.

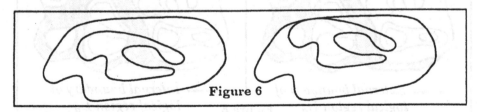

Figure 6

Definition 10. A partition region P_a *strictly* encloses a partition region P_b if P_a encloses P_b and there exists no point which is common to the boundaries of both P_a abd P_b.

Definition 11. A partition region P_a *tangentially* encloses a partition region P_b if P_a encloses P_b but P_a does not strictly enclose P_b i.e. there exists at least one point which is common to $B(P_a)$ and $B(P_b)$.

It follows from axiom 2 that no two partition regions P_a and P_b may intersect, unless one encloses the other: $P_a \cap P_b \in \{\emptyset, P_a, P_b\}$.

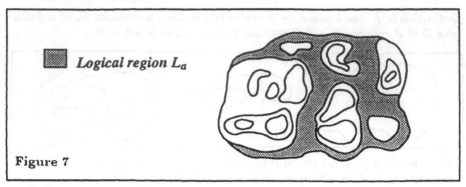

Figure 7

Definition 12. A *logical region* L_a is the difference between a partition region P_a and the set of partition regions $S = \{P_{b_1}, P_{b_2}, \ldots, P_{b_n}\}$ which it directly encloses:

$$P_{b_u} \cap P_{b_v} = \emptyset \; for \; u, v = 1, \ldots, n; u \neq v$$
$$P_a \cup P_{b_u} = P_a \; for \; u = 1 \ldots n$$
$$L_a = P_a - \cup_{u=1}^{n} P_{b_u}$$

It follows from this definition that a logical region is composed of one or more disjoint subregions, each of which may have one or more *internal* boundaries as well as an *external* boundary:

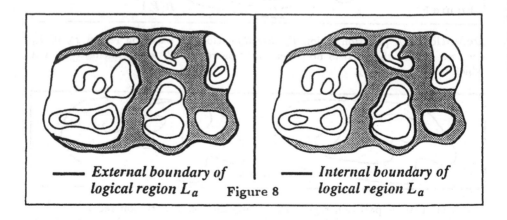

—— *External boundary of logical region* L_a **Figure 8**   —— *Internal boundary of logical region* L_a

Definition 13. The *external boundary* $B_e(L_a)$ of a logical region L_a is the set S_B of boundaries which exclusively enclose the m disjoint subregions $L_{a_u}, u = 1, \ldots, m$ which comprise L_a i.e.:

$$L_a = \cup_{u=1}^{m} L_{a_u}; \qquad B_e = \{B(L_{a_1}), B(L_{a_2}), \ldots, B(L_{a_m})\} \tag{1}$$

Definition 14. The *internal* boundary of a logical region L_a is the set of boundaries of the union of the partition regions which P_a directly and strictly encloses.

Note that, according to these definitions, a logical region always *spans the space* which it encloses i.e. no point which is enclosed by a logical region can at the same time be enclosed by another logical region. In contrast, a partition region does not, in general, span the space which it encloses. Note also that, given two partition regions P_a and P_b such that P_a encloses P_b, it does not necessarily follow that logical region $L_a \equiv P_a - P_b$ will *enclose* $L_b \equiv P_b$.

5 Partitioning the partition regions

Suppose that a data space D is partitioned into a set of n partition regions $S_P = \{P_1, P_2, \ldots, P_n\}$ (figure 9a) according to the definitions and axioms above:

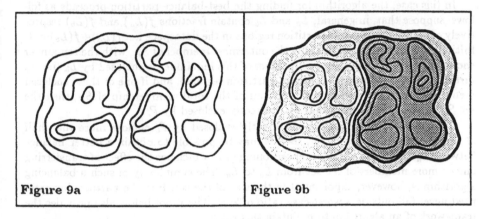

Figure 9a   **Figure 9b**

Suppose further that the set S_P is itself to be partitioned into two sets S_{P_a} and S_{P_b}, such that S_{P_a} and S_{P_b} are enclosed within partition regions P_a and P_b respectively i.e. :

$$P_a \cup P_b \subseteq D; \quad S_{P_a} \cup S_{P_b} = S_P; \quad S_{L_a} \cap S_{L_b} = \emptyset \qquad (2)$$

If all the partition regions are disjoint, then it is always possible to divide the set of partition regions into two halves i.e. to partition S_P so that the cardinalities of S_{P_a} and S_{P_b} do not differ by more than 1 (figure 9b). If, however, some partition regions enclose others, then the situation is not so straightforward. Intuitively, one can see that, the more disjoint partition regions there are, the better the chance of achieving a 1:1 split. The worst case arises when there are *no* disjoint partition regions i.e. every partition region either encloses or is enclosed by another (figure 10a). Since, according to axiom 1, region boundaries may not intersect, the set S_P must be partitioned into two sets, one of which encloses the other (figure 10b) i.e.:

$$P_a \cup P_b = P_a; \quad P_a \cap P_b = P_b; \quad \forall P_i \in S_{P_a}, \forall P_j \in S_{P_b} \ P_i \cup P_j = P_i \qquad (3)$$

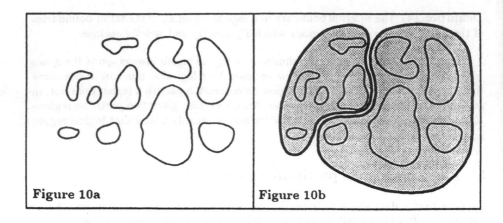

Figure 10a   **Figure 10b**

In this case, the algorithm for finding the best-balance partition proceeds as follows: suppose that, in general, L_a and L_b contain fractions $f(L_a)$ and $f(L_b)$ respectively of the total number of partition regions in the dataspace i.e. $f(L_a)+f(L_b) = 1$. Initially, however, L_a encloses only the outermost member of S_P, with the remainder enclosed by L_b. If more than one member of this remainder is enclosed by L_b (i.e. P_b *directly* encloses a number of disjoint partition regions), and if one of these enclosed members P_i itself encloses more than half of the total membership of S_P, then the set S_P is repositioned such that P_b is directly enclosed by P_i.

If **none** of the partition regions directly enclosed by P_b enclose more than half of the total membership of S_P, then it may be possible to obtain a better balance between L_a and L_b by a further repositioning of P_b which has the effect of transferring one or more members of the set from L_b to L_a. The complexity of such a balancing algorithm is, however, exponential in the size of the set. But the partitioning ratio need never fall outside a worst-case ratio of $2:1$. The proof below also provides the framework of an algorithm to maintain this ratio:

Given that $f(L_a) < 1/3$, then $f(L_b) > 2/3$. Suppose now that P_b is notionally replaced by two arbitrary partition regions P_b' and P_b''. Then two distinct cases arise:

$$(a) \quad f(L_b') \le 2/3 \ and \ f(L_b'') \le 2/3$$
$$(b) \quad f(L_b') > 2/3 \ or \ f(L_b'') > 2/3$$

In both cases, P_b is repositioned to coincide with whichever of the two (notional) partition regions P_b' and P_b'' encloses the larger fraction. Since $f(L_b')+f(L_b'') > 2/3$, this larger fraction must be greater than $1/3$. Therefore, in case (a), $1/3 < f(L_b) \le 2/3$. In case (b), it remains true that $f(L_b) > 2/3$. However, P_b must still directly enclose more than one member of S, because no member which P_b directly encloses can itself comprise a fraction greater than $1/2$. It is therefore possible to repeat the (notional) repartition operation on P_b until case (a) becomes true - which it must eventually do, if only one member remains directly enclosed by P_b.

This is by no means a new result - but we aim here to emphasise that it is a consequence of *topology*, and is quite independent of any particular data model. The proof may not be transparently clear, but the result is almost intuitively obvious. And this intuition relies on topological observation: a superimposed data model usually serves only to obscure it.

6 Partitioning logical regions

If a partition region P_a encloses partition region P_b, and a further partition boundary is introduced between those of the other two, it has no effect on the extent of the dataspaces enclosed by P_a and P_b, because partition regions are completely defined by their (external) boundaries.

In contrast, the *logical* region L_a *is* changed, since it has an internal boundary which is defined by any partition boundaries which it directly encloses. (L_b therefore remains unchanged). In general, if a new partition region P_b is introduced directly inside P_a, then L_a will be split into two logical regions L_a' and L_b, where $L_a = L_a' \cup L_b$.

Our ultimate objective - the construction of an index - requires us to partition a dataspace into a set of non-intersecting subspaces, each of which contains as nearly as possible an equal number of data points. It is therefore clear that, with the definitions given above, these subspaces must be logical regions, since logical regions do not intersect. We note, however, that logical regions are defined in terms of partition regions. It is therefore possible to represent the subspaces of a dataspace either directly, as logical regions, or indirectly as a set of partition regions: a data point which lies in a particular logical region also lies unambiguously in the partition region which *directly* encloses the point. Thus, in the latter case, a search for a target data point simply looks for the smallest partition region which encloses the point.

We do not consider here the problem of representing and indexing a set of objects with spatial extension. However, a fundamental problem which this raises cannot be avoided when we consider a hierarchy of subspaces, since the subspaces themselves have spatial extension.

7 A hierarchy of partition regions

Let us now consider the construction of a hierarchical index to the logical regions of the dataspace. Each branch and leaf node in the tree-structured index represents a logical region, and contains a representation of the set of logical regions which it encloses. Associated with each region is a pointer to an index node at the next level below in the tree structure. The branch nodes contain sets of regions of regions. The pointer associated with a logical region in a leaf node points to a data node which contains a set of data points lying within that logical region of the data space. (If a partition region representation is chosen, then each pointer in the tree is associated with a partition region rather than a logical region. But the index nodes still represent logical regions). We impose no other restrictions on the representation of the index, except that the number of entries in each tree node and data node (the fan-out ratio) has a fixed upper limit F.

Thus, as with a B-tree, the search for a data point in the data space proceeds downwards from the root of the tree, searching at each index level for the logical region which encloses the point, and following the associated pointer down to the next level.

Also, as with a B-tree, the index grows upwards as the data nodes at the bottom of the index hierarchy overflow and split. Provided that all the data points are unique, a partition can always be found which divides an overflowing data node into two half-full nodes. And when an index node overflows, it is always possible to partition the logical regions which it contains in a ratio not worse than $1 : 2$, as proved above. This last property is the general n-dimensional case, contrasting with the $1 : 1$ splitting ratio achieved by the B-tree in the special, one-dimensional case.

However, we have so far ignored a fundamental problem associated with the splitting of index nodes. Although the recursive partitioning procedure described above does not violate any of the axioms or definitions laid down earlier, it nevertheless introduces an ambiguity (the *spanning problem*) when interpreting a logical or partition region as a continuous subspace.

8 The spanning problem

Suppose that a logical region L is to be partitioned into two regions L_a and L_b, such that $L_a \cup L_b = L_a$. If L corresponds to a data node, then the data points lying within L_b can be transferred to the new node representing L_b. But if L is a logical region at a higher index level, then it contains a set of logical regions S_L of the next lower level. In this case, the boundary of P_b cannot be located arbitrarily, since it may easily cross a boundary of one or more of the members of S_L, thereby violating the constraint that no two boundaries may intersect. Nevertheless we know that it is always possible to find a position for the boundary of P_b such that the sizes of S_{L_a} and S_{L_b} do not differ by a ratio greater than $2 : 1$.

But there is no guarantee that the boundary of P_b will not be enclosed by one of the members P_{a_i} of S_{P_a}. (For example, the boundaries of all the members of S_P may be nested one within another). P_{a_i} must then itself be partitioned along the boundary of P_b. If P_{a_i} itself corresponds to an index node, then the same situation may be repeated at the next lower index level, and so on until a data node is reached - which can always be split without invoking any further chain reaction of partitioning.

Note that the partition boundary of the initially invoked partition of L is the boundary used for all subsequent partitions at the lower index levels i.e. only the position of the initial partition can be freely chosen to maintain the $2 : 1$ partition ratio. It can be shown that the basic axioms will not be violated: the partition boundary will never intersect boundaries of regions at the lower index levels. But severe partitioning imbalances may occur at the lower levels. Worse, a lower level node split may trigger overflow in an index node above, which in turn may trigger a further cascade of downward splits.

This is a condition which haunts all multi-dimensional index methods which are based on balanced tree structures. Most of the complexity and ingenuity in their designs is aimed at circumventing or minimising this problem.

9   The solution of the spanning problem

Considering the time and research effort which has been expended on this over the years (not least by the author), it is difficult to believe that there could be a simple and complete solution to the problem. But, when it is examined within the general framework of logical and partition regions developed above, the solution appears almost obvious. It is indeed simple, and complete.

When logical region L is partitioned, the index node which contains the representation of L is modified: the representation of L is replaced by the representation of L_a and L_b. There is *ab initio* no inconsistency within region L_{a_i}, or within any of the regions which it encloses at lower index levels. It only needs to be split in order to ensure the correct behaviour of the search path through the new index branch created by L_b. But there is an alternative strategy: to leave L_{a_i} intact, and modify the search path.

Suppose that L_a and L_b contain the sets of logical regions S_a and S_b respectively. If L_{a_i} is split into L'_{a_i} and L''_{a_i} along the boundary of P_b, then:

$$L_a = \cup_{u=1}^n L_{a_u} \cup L'_{a_i}, \ 1 \le i \le n, \ u \ne i \tag{4}$$

$$L_b = \cup_{v=1}^m L_{b_u} \cup L''_{a_i}, \ 1 \le i \le n \tag{5}$$

But since $L_a \cap L''_{a_i} = \emptyset$ and $L_b \cap L'_{a_i} = \emptyset$ then:

$$\begin{aligned} L_a &= \cup_{u=1}^n L_{a_u} \cup L'_{a_i} \cup L''_{a_i}, 1 \le i \le n, u \ne i \\ &= \cup_{u=1}^n L_{a_u} \cup L_{a_i}, 1 \le i \le n, u \ne i \end{aligned} \tag{6}$$

$$\begin{aligned} L_b &= \cup_{v=1}^m L_{b_u} \cup L''_{a_i} \cup L'_{a_i}, 1 \le i \le n \\ &= \cup_{v=1}^m L_{b_u} \cup L_{a_i}, 1 \le i \le n \end{aligned} \tag{7}$$

This shows that, rather than split L_{a_i}, it can be left intact if the search path can be changed so that L_{a_i} is always searched if the search has failed in L_a or L_b respectively. All that is required is that, before an index node is split according to the partitioning algorithm, the node is searched for an entry which represents a partition boundary P_{a_i} which directly encloses the splitting boundary P_b. If P_{a_i} exists, then it is not split, but *promoted* to the index level above, along with the entries for P_a and P_b. The subtree of P_{a_i} is automatically promoted with it. A marker is attached to the promoted entry, to distinguish it from an entry created by direct partitioning.

The straight-down, exact-match search path through the index is then modified so that, if failure occurs anywhere in the index tree, the search backtracks to the level above. At this level, a search is then made, within the node, among the marked entries only, for an entry which matches the target data point, and which represents a logical region which is *directly enclosed* by the region L in which the search failed. If there is no such entry, then the search is repeated for an entry representing a logical region which *directly encloses* L. If a matching marked entry is found, then the downward search is restarted from this entry. Otherwise, backtracking continues. The entire search terminates unsuccessfully on backtracking from the root of the tree.

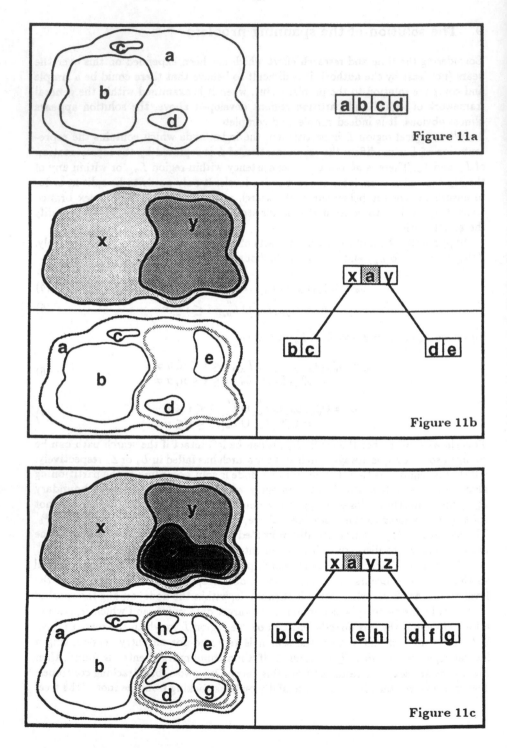

Figure 11a

Figure 11b

Figure 11c

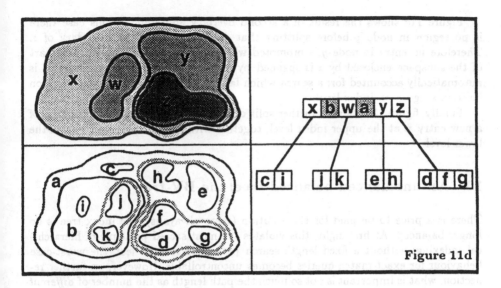

Figure 11d

9.1 An example

In the remainder of this paper, for brevity, *region* means *logical region*, unless explicitly stated otherwise. Often the meaning is not affected if *partition region* is substituted.

Figure 11a above shows a data space partitioned into four subspaces: regions *a*, *b*, *c* and *d*, and the contents of the corresponding index node. Each entry in a node corresponds to the representation of a region and its associated pointer to the level below. For clarity, data nodes are not shown. (Every index entry which does not show a pointer to the level below actually contains a pointer to a data node). The order shown for the entries has no significance: in practice, the particular order chosen depends on the form of the representation of logical regions, and the efficiency of search operations on this representation.

Let us assume, for simplicity, that the fan-out ratio of the index nodes is four. Figure 11b shows the situation after the insertion of an additional region *e* and the consequent overflow of the node. The regions are then partitioned into two regions *x* and *y*, which form the root node of a new, two-level index. The left part of figure 11b shows the partitions represented at the upper and lower levels of the index. (The lightly-shaded boundary shown in the lower left of the figure belongs to the level above - it is only shown at the lower level in order to indicate precisely where the partitioning of the lower level has been made).

The right part of figure 11b shows that the index split has been accompanied by the promotion of region *a* to the level above. This is because the boundary of partition region *a* directly encloses region *y*.(The shading of the index entry for *a* indicates a marked entry). Thus part of logical region *a* lies within the boundary of *y*, and the other part within *x*.

Figure 11c shows the result of a second overflow and split. In this case there is no region in node y before splitting that directly encloses the boundary of z. Therefore no entry in node y is promoted when y is split. Note however that part of the subspace enclosed by z is spanned by region a, as well as by y. But this is automatically accounted for: a search which fails in z may still find a match in a on backtracking up an index level.

Finally, figure 11d shows a further split of region x, which causes the creation of a new entry w at the upper index level, together with the promotion of b from the lower level.

10   An unbalanced balanced tree: the BV-tree

There is a price to be paid for this solution (there always is): the index tree is no longer balanced. At first sight, this violates the most sacred principle of hierarchical indexing: without a fixed length search path from root to leaf, the worst-case behaviour for exact-match queries becomes uncontrollable. However, on further reflection, what is important is not so much the path length as the number of *different* tree branch nodes traversed. These two will be different if a search path involves back-tracking. The total path length must have a predictable upper limit, but it is a reasonable practical assumption that, with standard caching techniques, there will be no extra retrieval cost in re-visiting a node which lies along the direct path from root to leaf.

Let us consider the downward and upward parts of as exact-match search path, according to the search algorithm described above. A downward search will fail if the target location lies within a promoted logical region, and the failure will occur at the level from which the region was originally promoted. But the sum of all the nodes visited during the downward traversal phases of an exact-match search will remain constant for a given tree size. Likewise, although a promoted subtree may be further promoted to any higher level in the tree, and a subtree of a subtree may also be promoted, the total height through which promotion of any logical region can occur cannot be greater than the height of the tree. Therefore:

1. the total path length for an exact-match search cannot be greater than twice the height of the index tree.
2. the number of *different* branch nodes visited in an exact-match search is always equal to the height of the tree.

If any subtree could be arbitrarily promoted to a higher level, a crucially important property of a balanced tree structure would be lost: the logarithmic relationship between the number of data nodes and the path length from root to leaf of the index. This relationship first of all requires that the direct path length from root to leaf is fixed, for a given state of the index tree i.e. that the tree is perfectly balanced. It also requires that the fan-out ratio in every index node (except the root) must never fall below a fixed minimum (which must be at least an order of magnitude greater than 1). The linear relationship between the number of index nodes and the number of data nodes is a further consequence of these requirements.

However, the promotion of a subtree only occurs under the circumstances described above, and only when an index node overflows and splits. Therefore, since every index node except the first is created by splitting, there can be, at most, one promoted (marked) index entry for every unmarked entry.

If a promoted index entry splits, it will create a second entry at the same (promoted) level. It could also cause a further promotion from the level below. Fortunately, it can be proved that it is always possible in such cases to return all but one of the entries resulting from such a split to their originating (unpromoted) positions in the index tree. It is also possible to prove that this requires no more node accesses than would have been necessary if the entries had not been promoted i.e. if the tree had been balanced.

Thus it is possible to prove that there are never more promoted entries than unpromoted entries in an index node. It follows that, if the fan-out ratio in an index node is F, then the fan-out ratio of promoted subtrees is never greater than $F/2$. So, in order to guarantee that the exact-match search path from root to leaf in the BV-tree will be no longer than that of a balanced tree with the same number of data nodes, the index nodes of the BV-tree need to be twice the size of those in the balanced tree. (Note however that the occupancy of the index nodes will still not fall below 33%).

Strictly speaking, since there can be no promoted entries in the leaf nodes of the index, only the higher level index nodes need to be doubled in size, which means that the overall increase in the size of the index is only a few percent. This is the only price which has to be paid for obtaining the characteristics of the B-tree in n-dimensions. The worst-case index node occupancy is only 33%, compared to 50% for the B-tree. But this is a consequence of topological considerations, rather than a limitation of a particular index design. More important is that this occupancy level is guaranteed for every index node under all circumstances, thus guaranteeing a minimum occupancy for the entire index. Note also that this limitation only applies to *index* nodes. There is no fundamental reason why the worst-case occupancy of a *data* node should not remain 50% in the n-dimensional case.

11 Deletion

In any multi-dimensional index design, there are generally two aspects to the problem of deletion of index entries. The first is the result of adopting a representation which imposes severe restrictions on the shape of a logical region. This limits the combinations of regions which can merge, or redistribute their entries, and can lead to deadlock situations.

The second is the spanning problem, in the context of redistribution. If a region drops below an occupancy of less than 1/3, then it can clearly merge with any other region having an occupancy of 2/3 or less, subject to any other merging restrictions. And if the occupancy of the latter is greater than 2/3, then it must be possible to redistribute the entries between the two to restore the balance to 1 : 2 or better. But this redistribution is effectively a re-partitioning of a single, overflowing region, so a solution of the spanning problem is needed just as much for merging on deletion, as for splitting on insertion.

We have not yet addressed the question of what the most suitable representation for a logical region might be, and so we have not yet imposed any restrictions on the shape of regions which might lead to deadlock situations. But the solution of the spanning problem removes the second of the above difficulties entirely.

12 A specific representation

In two dimensions, it would not be out of the question to represent a logical region by the set of vertices of a polygon, although it would be computationally complex to test for enclosure of a data point in such a polygon, and the size of the set of vertices could lead to very large index node entries. The difficulties would be compounded in higher dimensions. So practical multi-dimensional index designs have all adopted a much simpler representation: in almost all cases, the data space is partitioned into *hyper-rectangular* regions, with the sides of the rectangles parallel to the axes of the ranges or domains of the data space. Some, particularly those treating extended spatial objects, have explicitly used a $2n$ coordinates representation, to define a rectangle in n-dimensional space. Others have used repeated division of the ranges or domains of the data space to partition the whole data space.

But almost all have chosen to represent partition regions only, or rather, to draw no distinction between partition and logical regions. There *is* no distinction if no partition boundary is allowed to enclose another. Although this kind of representation is very simple, it offers no flexibility in the shape of logical regions. And since the combination of two rectangles must be a rectangle, it can lead to the deadlock problems mentioned earlier.

It was a consideration of these drawbacks which led the author to a previous multi-dimensional index design, the BANG file [Fre87], which did draw a distinction between logical and partition regions.

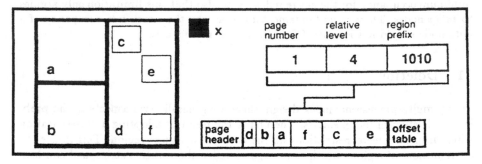

Figure 12

The structure of a BANG index node is shown in figure 12. Each entry in the node contains a representation of a partition region, and a pointer to the index level below. The partition region is represented by a unique binary string, generated by a sequence of strict binary divisions of the domains of the data space, taken in (arbitrary) cyclic order ('Z'-order). Since its identifying binary string is of variable length, it has to be accompanied by a *partition level number*, which indicates the number of bits in the string.

18

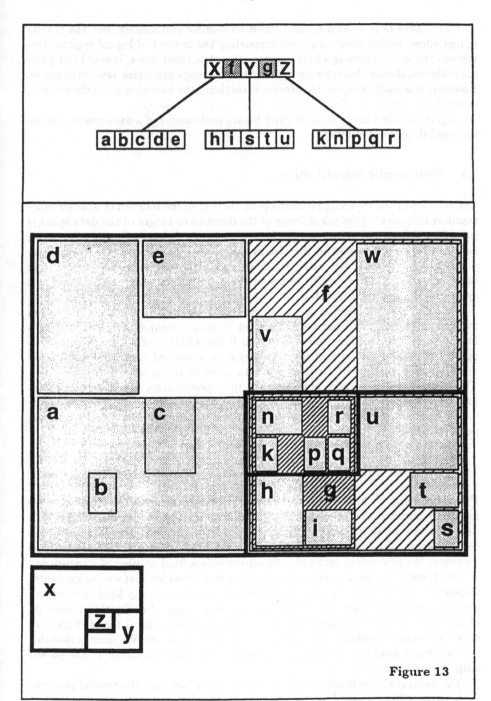

Figure 13

There have been several designs based on Z-order partitioning, but the BANG design allows nested partitions, thus supporting the concept of logical regions. Unfortunately, in maintaining a fully balanced tree-structured index, it could not guarantee the worst-case characteristics offered by the design principles developed above. However, it is easily adapted to accommodate them: the only structural change necessary is the provision of a marker bit within each index entry.

Figure 13 shows an example of strict binary partitioning of a data space, and the corresponding BV-tree index.

13 Non-cyclic partitioning

The solution of the spanning problem opens the way to the solution of another long-standing difficulty: cyclic partitioning of the domains or ranges of the data space is inflexible. When data points are highly non-uniformly distributed, this inflexibility can lead to big differences in the discrimination in each dimension, although the number of partitions is the same (or almost so). In the extreme case, where all the data points lie on a line parallel to one of the domain axes, only one partition in a cycle provides any discrimination.

To solve this problem, it is not necessary to choose the partition dimension at random (which could not be represented in such a compact form as that of a binary partition identifier). What is needed is the addition of a *dimension-hold* to cyclic partitioning i.e. to partition repeatedly on a selected dimension until some discrimination is achieved (at least one data point on either side of the partition). This doubles the size of each index entry in the representation described above, but because the representation is so compact, (typically only one or two per cent of the data), such an overhead can be well worthwhile in terms of more uniform access performance.

14 Variable structure

Up to this point, we have said nothing about the data structures being indexed. We have only assumed that it is always possible to compute a unique mapping from a data structure to an index key, which corresponds to a point in the data space. We have, however, implicitly assumed the indexing of fixed structures, because we have visualised the problem in terms of a dataspace with a fixed number of dimensions.

But there is no reason to be restricted in this way. Provided that we can guarantee to generate a unique key from each different data structure, any kind of structure can be included in the index. Figure 14 indicates a way of doing this (there are other ways). Any data structure can be described in hierarchical terms. Figure 14 shows a predicate *employee*, containing some complex structure. We assume that this information is available in an easily accessible form, most probably as the parsed output from a compiler.

The natural way to index this information is top-down from the general property to the minute factual detail. So the structure is initially treated as one-dimensional: the type of the whole structure is encoded into its index key by a predefined mapping.

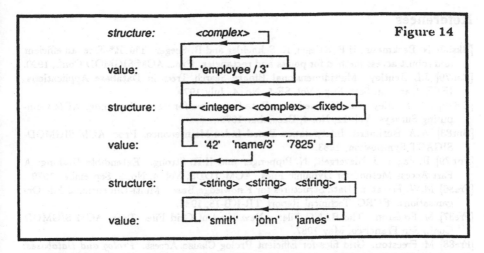

Figure 14

The predicate name and arity are then treated as a point in two-dimensional space, and encoded accordingly, cycling through the two dimensions. This mapping is concatenated to the bit string key as generated so far. Following this, the structure of the predicate is encoded...and so on, alternating structure and value in the encoding, as the bit-string key grows in length.

Conceptually, each step down the structure and value hierarchy transforms a point in one data space - or rather sequence of data spaces - into a new hyper-space. What this means in terms of logical regions in a data space is now beyond visualisation, but the indexing mechanism remains valid.

It might be thought that such a scheme would generate prohibitively long index keys, but this is not the case. A major attraction of strict binary domain partitioning is that only one bit is needed for each partition, in contrast to a full data value for range-based partitioning. Thus every entry representing a partition region in the index is only as long as is necessary to partition the data. Likewise, an exact-match search key is not pre-computed from the source data structure before the index search begins. It is computed *dynamically*, so that no more key bits are generated at any index level than are necessary to perform the search comparisons. Hence, however complex a structure may be, long index keys and search keys will only occur if many structures which are very similar in detail are stored in the index. Even then, the prefix key representation of the BANG file ensures that long common key prefixes are promoted into a single occurence at the top level of the index.

15 Conclusion

We have concentrated, in this paper, on the fundamentals underlying the properties and design problems of multi-dimensional index structures. Although space has not permitted a presentation of all the necessary proofs, we can assert that multi-dimensional indexing can now guarantee acceptable worst-case performance characteristics in the same way that we have in the past only been able to do in the one-dimensional case. We now have to see how to apply these techniques most effectively, wherever the ability to index variable data structures is important - notably in persistent programming languages.

References

[Bks90] N. Beckmann, H.P. Kriegel, R. Schneider and B. Seeger. The R*-Tree: an efficient and robust access method for points and rectangles. Proc. ACM SIGMOD Conf., 1990.

[Ben79] J.L. Bentley. Multidimensional Binary Search Trees in Database Applications. IEEE Trans. on Soft. Eng., Vol. SE-5, No. 4, July 1979.

[Bef79] J.L. Bentley and J.H. Friedman. Data Structures for Range Searching. ACM Computing Surveys, Vol. 11, No. 4, December 1979.

[Bur83] W.A. Burkhard. Interpolation-Based Index Maintenance. Proc. ACM SIGMOD-SIGACT Symposium, 1983.

[Fnp79] R. Fagin, J. Nievergelt, N. Pippenger and H.R. Strong. Extendible Hashing: A Fast Access Method for Dynamic Files. ACM-TODS, Vol. 4, No. 3, September 1979.

[Fre86] M.W. Freeston. Data Structures for Knowledge Bases: Multi-Dimensional File Organisations. ECRC, Technical Report TR-KB-13, 1986.

[Fre87] M. Freeston. The BANG File: a New Kind of Grid File. Proc. ACM SIGMOD Conf., San Francisco, May 1987.

[Fre88] M. Freeston. Grid files for Efficient Prolog Clause Access. *Prolog and Databases: Implementations and Applications*, Ed. Gray P.M.D. and Lucas R.J., Pub. Ellis Horwood.

[Fre89a] M. Freeston. Advances in the design of the BANG File. 3rd International Conference on Foundations of Data Organization and Algoritms (FODO), Paris, June 1989.

[Fre89b] M. Freeston. A Well-Behaved File Structure for the Storage of Spatial Objects. Symposium on the Design and Implementation of Large Spatial Databases, Santa Barbara, California, July 1989, *Lecture Notes in Computer Science No. 409, Springer-Verlag, 1989.*

[Fre92] M. Freeston. The Comparative Performance of BANG Indexing for Spatial Objects. 5th International Symposium on Spatial Data Handling, Charleston, South Carolina, August 1992.

[Fre93a] M. Freeston. On the Generalised Indexing of Complex Structures. ECRC Technical Report ECRC-93-9, May 1993.

[Fre93d] M. Freeston. On the Generalised Application of Spatial Indexing Techniques in Deductive GIS Systems. British Computer Journal, special issue on spatial data, Ed. Freeston and Nievergelt, October 1993 [In preparation].

[Gvv83] G. Gardarin, P. Valduriez, Y. Viemont. Les Arbres de Predicats. INRIA, Rapports de Recherche, No. 203, April 1983.

[Gun88] O. Gunther. The Design of the Cell Tree: an Object-Oriented Index Structure for Geometric Databases. Proc. IEEE 5th Int. Conf. on Data Engineering, Los Angeles, 1989.

[Gut84] A. Guttman. R-trees: a dynamic index structure for spatial searching. Proc. ACM SIGMOD Conf., Boston, 1984.

[Hsw8] A. Henrich, H.-W. Six and P. Widmayer. The LSD-tree: Spatial Access to Multidimensional Point and Non-point Objects. 15th Int. Conf. on Very Large Data Bases (VLDB), 1989.

[Hin85] K.H. Hinrichs. The grid file system: implementation and case studies of applications. Doctoral Thesis Nr. 7734, ETH Zürich, 1985.

[Hsw88] A. Hutflesz, H.-W. Six and P. Widmayer. The Twin Grid File: A Nearly Space Optimal Index Structure. Proc. 1st Int. Conf. on Extending Database Technology (EDBT), Venice, Italy, March 1988, *Lecture Notes in Computer Science No. 303, Springer-Verlag, 1988.*

[Hsw90] A. Hutflesz, H.-W. Six and P. Widmayer. The R-file: An Efficient Access Structure for Proximity Queries. Proc. 6th Int. Conf. on Data Engineering, 1990.

[Kss90] H.P. Kriegel, M. Schiwietz, R. Schneider and B. Seeger. A Performance Comparison of Multidimensional Point and Spatial Access Methods. Proc. Symposium on Large Spatial Databases, Zürich, 1990, *Lecture Notes in Computer Science No. 409, Springer-Verlag, 1990.*

[Lew80] D.T. Lee, C.K. Wong. Quintary Trees: A File Structure for Multidimensional Database Systems. ACM-TODS, Vol. 5, No. 3, September 1980.

[Los89] D.B. Lomet and B. Salzberg. The hB-tree: a Robust Multi-Attribute Indexing Method. ACM Trans. on Database Systems, Vol. 15,4, 1989.

[Nhs81] J. Nievergelt, H. Hintenberger, K.C. Sevcik. The Grid File: an adaptable, symmetric multikey file structure. Internal Report No. 46, Institut für Informatik, ETH Zurich, December 1981.

[Ohs83] Y. Ohsawa and M. Sakauchi. The BD-Tree: a new n-dimensional data structure with highly efficient dynamic characteristics. IFIP 9th World Computer Congress, Paris, 1983.

[Ore86] J.A. Orenstein. Spatial Query Processing in an Object-Oriented Database System. Proc. ACM SIGMOD Conf., 1986.

[Oto85] E.J. Otoo. A Multidimensional Digital Hashing Scheme for Files with Composite Keys. ACM 1985.

[Ous83] M. Ouksel and P. Scheuermann. Storage Mapping for Multidimensional Linear Dynamic Hashing. Proc. of 2nd Symposium on Principles of Database Systems, Atlanta, 1983.

[Ozo85] E.A. Ozkarahan and M. Ouksel. Dynamic and Order Preserving Data Partitioning for Database Machines. Proc. of 11th Int. Conf. on Very Large Data Bases, Stockholm, August 1985.

[Rob81] J.T. Robinson. The K-D-B-Tree: A Search Structure for Large Multidimensional Dynamic Indexes. Proc. ACM SIGMOD Conf., 1981.

[Sam86] H. Samet. Quadtrees and Related Hierarchical Data Structures for Computer Graphics and Image Processing, 1986.

[Sam86] H. Samet. The Design and Analysis of Spatial Data Structures. Pub. Addison Wesley, 1989.

[Sk88] B. Seeger and H.P. Kriegel. Design and Implementation of Spatial Access Methods. Proc. 14th Int. Conf on Very Large Data Bases (VLDB), Long Beach, California, 1988.

[Sk90] B. Seeger and H.P. Kriegel. The Buddy-tree: an Efficient and Robust Access Method for Spatial Data Base Systems. Proc. 16th Int. Conf. on Very Large Data Bases, Brisbane, 1990.

[Srf87] T. Sellis, N. Roussopoulos and C. Faloutsos. The R+ Tree: a Dynamic Index for Multi-dimensional Objects. Proceeding 13th Int. Conf. on Very Large Data Bases, Brighton, 1987.

On the Unification of Active Databases and Deductive Databases

Carlo Zaniolo

Computer Science Department
University of California
Los Angeles, CA 90024
zaniolo@cs.ucla.edu

Abstract. These two rule-oriented paradigms of databases have been the focus of extensive research and are now coming of age in the commercial DBMS world. However, the systems developed so far support well only one of the two paradigms—thus limiting the effectiveness of such systems in many applications that require complete integration of both kinds of rules. In this paper, we discuss the technical problems that make such an integration difficult, and trace their roots to a lack of a unified underlying semantics. Then, we review recent advances in the semantics of non-monotonic logic and show that they can be used to unify the foundations of active databases and deductive databases. Finally, we outline the design a new rule language for databases that integrates a deductive system with a trigger-based DBMS.

1   Introduction

Rules provide the main paradigm for expressing computation in active databases and deductive databases. Yet, there has been little formal work on the unification of these powerful paradigms, although there are many important applications that could benefit from such a marriage. While cultural and historical biases might also have had a role in this chasm, the root of the problem is actually technical and can be traced to certain semantic inadequacies in both approaches.

Several active database languages and systems have been proposed so far: a very incomplete list include [3, 5, 9, 19, 20, 29]. However, there is is no unifying semantic theory for active databases: most of the work done so far has concentrated on explaining operational semantics of particular systems. On the contrary, deductive databases are endowed with extraordinarily rich semantic foundations: not one but three equivalent formal semantics exist for Horn clauses that form the core of deductive database languages [30, 17]. Unfortunately, this elegant semantics is brittle and can not be generalized easily to deal with non-monotonic constructs, such as negation and updates. Similar non-monotonic reasoning problems have emerged in the areas of knowledge representation and of logic programming, and remain the focus of intense research as many difficult problems remain open. While deductive databases encountered early successes in this area (e.g., with the introduction of the concept of stratified negation), recent progress has been very slow. No totally satisfactory semantics currently exist for programs which use non-monotonic constructs such as negation and aggregates in recursion—and the problem of updates in recursion is understood even less.

Given this rather ominous background, the solution presented in this paper is surprisingly simple and general. We introduce the notion of XY-stratified programs that allow non-monotonic constructs in recursive rules. Then, we show that a formal semantics for updates and triggers in databases can be given using XY-stratified programs. The blueprints for the design of a unified rule language for active databases and deductive databases follow from such a solution.

2   Non-Monotonic Constructs

The area of non-monotonic reasoning has benefited significantly from research in deductive databases. The adoption of the fixpoint-based bottom-up approach to define the declarative and constructive semantics of logic programs lead almost immediately to the concept of stratified negation and stratified set aggregates [23]. This concept removes several of the limitations and problems of Prolog's negation-by-failure, and it is conductive to efficient implementation, as demonstrated by systems such as *Glue-Nail*, $\mathcal{LDL}$ and $\mathcal{CORAL}$ [22, 6, 26]. However, experience gained with real-life applications [28] revealed that stratification is too restrictive and there remain many important applications where negation and set aggregates are needed: such applications, range from processing a Bill of Materials to finding the shortest path in a graph [34].

Therefore, during the last five years, a substantial research effort has been devoted to solving the non-stratification issue. This endeavor has produced significant progress on the theoretical front, with the introduction of concepts such as locally stratified programs, well-founded models [13], and the stable models[10], but it has not yet begotten a solution that is both general and practical. Indeed a practical solution must satisfy three difficult requirements, inasmuch as it must

- have a formal logic-based semantics,

- have a simple and intuitive constructive semantics,

- be amenable to efficient implementation.

Thus, in addition to requiring formal semantics and efficient implementation, any practical proposal must also stress the importance of having a simple concrete semantics: i.e., one that can be easily comprehended by the application programmer, without a need to understand abstract formalisms. For instance, a notion such as stratification can be mastered by a programmer, who can make full use of it without having to understand its formal perfect-model semantics. Furthermore, it is simple for a compiler to verify that stratification is satisfied, and then support stratified programs by an efficient bottom-up computation. However, an understanding of the logical formalism is required to understand notions such as well-founded models or stable models. Furthermore, no simple syntactic check exists for deciding whether a program has a well-founded model or a stable model; when such models exist their computation can be very expensive.

The notion of XY-stratified programs was recently proposed to overcome these difficulties [35]. This is a special subclass of locally stratified programs that is easy for a compiler to recognize and implement using the fixpoint-based computation of deductive DBs. It was shown in [35] that classical computational problems such as Floyd's shortest path algorithms, can be expressed naturally by programs in this class using non-stratified negation and aggregates. In this paper, we will build on such a semantics to provide a formal model of updates in deductive databases and triggers in active databases.

The problem of providing a formal semantics to updates in the context of logic also represents a difficult challenge. Several of the approaches proposed deal with the more general problem of modeling revisions of knowledge bases— i.e., including additions, deletions and modifications of rules [4, 7, 33, 14]. As a result, these theories are more complex and less conducive to efficiency than it is desirable in a practical semantics, according to the criteria discussed above. Therefore, we will restrict our attention to the problem of modifying the extensional database only [21]. Most of the work done in this more specific context is based on Dynamic Logic [8]. In particular, the approach given in [31, 18] uses dynamic logic to formalize a concrete semantics where the updates take place according to rule instances—a *tuple-at-a-time* semantics often leading to non-determinism. However, relational databases support a *set-at-a-time* update semantics, where all the applicable updates are fired at once, in parallel. A set-at-a-time semantics based on dynamic logic was adopted and efficiently implemented in $\mathcal{LDL}$ [25, 6]. While the $\mathcal{LDL}$ design has progressed further than other systems toward a complete integration of database-oriented updates into a logic-based language, several problems remain, such as multiple update rules sharing the same heads, and failing goals after update goals [16]. Furthermore, since dynamic logic is quite different from standard logic, the two do not mix well, and, as a result, updates are not allowed in recursive $\mathcal{LDL}$ rules; a special construct, called **forever** had to be introduced to express **do-while** iterations over updates [25]. A further illustration of the difficulties encountered by declarative logic-based languages in dealing with updates is provided by the design of the *Glue-Nail* system [22]. In this second-generation deductive database system, updates were banned from the core declarative language and relegated to the procedural shell that is tightly wrapped around the core [26].

Viewed against the tormented landscape of previous work, the model of updates and active databases proposed in this paper is surprisingly simple. Basically, we define rules with updates in their heads by simply re-writing them into equivalent update-free logic programs that are XY-stratified. The common semantics of active and deductive predicates, so obtained, is the basis for our unification of the active and deductive aspects of databases. This semantics is conducive to the design of a powerful language capable of expressing reasoning, triggers and detection of events as required by the next generation of intelligent database applications.

2.1 XY-Stratification

We begin with a simple example [1] that computes the nodes X of a graph g reachable from a given node a, and the minimum distance of X from this node:

Example 1 *Reachable nodes:*

$$r_0 : \text{delta}(\text{nil}, X, 1) \leftarrow \quad g(a, X).$$
$$r_1 : \text{delta}(s(I), Y, D1) \leftarrow \quad \text{delta}(I, X, D), g(X, Y),$$
$$\neg \text{all}(I, Y, \_), D1 = D + 1.$$
$$r_2 : \text{all}(s(I), Y, D) \leftarrow \quad \text{all}(I, Y, D), \text{delta}(s(I), \_, \_).$$
$$r_3 : \text{all}(I, Y, D) \leftarrow \quad \text{delta}(I, Y, D).$$

This program presents several unusual traits. A most obvious one is the presence of terms such as $\text{nil}, I, s(I)$ in the first argument of the recursive predicates. These arguments will be called *stage arguments*, and their usage is for counting as in the recursive definition of integers: nil stands for zero and $s(I)$ stands for $I+1$.

The intuitive meaning of the program of Example 11 is quite obvious: it implements a seminaive computation of a transitive closure [25], through the use of two predicates: delta contains the new values, and all is the union of all values computed so far. In rule r_1, all is used for checking that no previous (therefore shorter) path exists to this node.

The formal semantics of the program also supports its intuitive semantics. Because of its particular syntactic form, the program is locally stratified, where each stratum corresponds to a different value of the stage argument. The first stratum contains atoms of the form:

$$\text{delta}(\text{nil}, ...), \quad \text{all}(\text{nil}, ...)$$

the next stratum consists of all atoms of the form:

$$\text{delta}(s(\text{nil}), ...), \quad \text{all}(s(\text{nil}), ...)$$

---

[1] We assume our reader familiar with the basic concepts pertaining to Datalog and logic rules, including the concept of locally stratified programs and the *iterated fixpoint procedure* that computes the perfect model of these programs [23, 25]. Given a program P, a set of rules of P defining a maximal set of mutually recursive predicates will be called a *recursive clique* of P.

and so on. As we shall see later, this particular syntactic form of the recursive rules, w.r.t. the stage arguments, makes it simple for a compiler to detect the occurrence of such a locally stratified program. Furthermore, this type of program can be implemented efficiently using a modified fixpoint computation.

It is well-known that the perfect model of such a program is characterized by a transfinite computation called iterated fixpoint [23]. This proceeds as follows: the least fixpoint is first computed for the first (bottom) stratum; then, once the least fixpoint is computed for the n-th stratum, the least fixpoint is computed for the $n + 1$-th stratum. The transfinite computation of perfect models simplifies dramatically for the program at hand. Assume, for now, that the stratification is determined by the values of stage arguments. The fixpoint at the bottom stratum is reached after firing rule r_0 followed by r_3. The fixpoint for the stratum $s(\text{nil})$ is reached by firing rule r_1, followed by firing r_2 and r_3. Then, the higher strata are inductively generated by firing these three rules in the same order. Therefore, the general transfinite procedure to compute perfect models here reduces to the customary fixpoint iteration. Moreover, various improvements can be made to this fixpoint computation to ensure that it executes efficiently. In fact, while rule r_2 seems to suggest that a complete copying of the old relation is needed at each step, no such operation is needed in reality. In fact, the only instances of rules that can produce new atoms are those instantiated with stage values from the current stratum: values from the old strata are not used and can be discarded. Thus, if we keep the values of the stage variable in a separate memory cell, all is needed to perform the copy operation is to increase the value of the integer in this cell by one.

Given a recursive clique, Q, the first arguments of recursive predicates of a rule r (of Q) will be called the *stage arguments* of r (of Q) [2] Then a recursive rule is either an

- **X-rule** if all the stage arguments of r are equal to a simple variable, say J, which does not appear anywhere else in r, or an

- **Y-rule** if (i) some positive goal of r has as stage argument a simple variable J, (ii) the head of r has stage argument $s(J)$, (iii) all the remaining stage arguments are either J or $s(J)$ and (iv) J does not appear anywhere else in r.

In Example 11, r_3 is an X-rule, while r_1 and r_2 are Y-rules. A recursive clique Q such that all its recursive rules are either X-rules or Y-rules, will be said to be a recursive *XY-clique*.

Priming: $p'(...)$ will be called the primed version of an atom $p(...)$. Given an XY-clique, Q, its primed version Q', is constructed by priming certain occurrences of recursive predicates in recursive rules as follows:

- X-rules: all occurrences of recursive predicates are primed,

---

[2]This is only a matter of convention. Alternatively, we could let the last arguments of recursive predicates be our stage arguments.

- Y-rules: the head predicate is primed, and so is every goal with stage argument equal to that of the head.

The primed version of our example is as follows:

$r_0 : \text{delta}(\text{nil}, X, 1) \leftarrow g(a, X).$

$r_1 : \text{delta}'(s(I), Y, D1) \leftarrow \text{delta}(I, X, D), g(X, Y),$
$\qquad\qquad\qquad\qquad\qquad \neg\text{all}(I, Y, \_), D1 = D + 1.$

$r_2 : \text{all}'(s(I), Y, D) \leftarrow \text{all}(I, Y, D), \text{delta}'(s(I), \_, \_).$
$r_3 : \text{all}'(I, Y, D) \leftarrow \text{delta}'(I, Y, D).$

An XY-clique Q is said to be *XY-stratified* when

- The primed version of Q is non-recursive

- All exit rules have as stage argument the same constant.

□

If Q is an XY-stratified clique, then Q is locally stratified, and computable using a simple fixpoint iteration [35].

In fact, observe that the primed dependency graph provides a very simple syntactic test on whether a program is XY-stratified. Furthermore these programs are amenable to very efficient implementation as proven in the following discussion. The primed version Q' of an XY-stratified clique defines a non-recursive program, and thus, it is stratifiable according to the predicate names. In particular, we want to consider a *topological layering* as follows: the bottom layer L_0 contains all the the unprimed predicate names, and the remaining layers $L_1, ..., L_n$ are singleton sets such that, for each rule r in Q', the predicate names of the head of r belongs to layers strictly higher than those of the goals of r. For Example 16, the following is the only topological layering:

$L_0 = \{\text{delta}, \text{all}\}, \quad L_1 = \{\text{delta}'\}, \quad L_2 = \{\text{all}'\}$

The Herbrand Base of a recursive clique Q can now be partitioned into layers, where the atoms of non-recursive predicates form the bottom layer, and recursive atoms with the same predicate name and stage argument form the remaining layers. This partition can be ordered so that each atom with a lower stage argument belongs to lower layer than an atom with a higher stage argument, and if two atoms have the same stage argument, then the atom whose predicate name is first in the topological layering belongs to the lower layer. Now, our clique Q is strictly locally stratified, inasmuch as for each instantiated rule of Q, the goals belong to to layers that are strictly lower than the layer to which the head belongs. It thus follows that, (i) the perfect model of Q can be computed using an iterated fixpoint, and (ii) the fixpoint for each stratum is reached in one step. Therefore the computation of all atoms in the model sharing the same stage value is performed in n steps, where L_n denotes the last layer in the topological layering. Each of these steps involves the firing of all rules with the same head predicate name: thus having computed all the atoms with stage value of J, a *single pass through the rules of Q ordered according to the topological stratification of their heads* computes all the atoms with stage value $s(J)$.

Therefore, if Q is an XY-stratified clique, then (i) Q is locally stratified, and (ii) its perfect model can be constructed by a fixpoint iteration to the first ordinal: the recursive rules in the clique are fired according to the topological layering. In such a computation the stage arguments is projected out from each rule (the notation w.s.a. will denote a rule without its stage argument) [35]:

Perfect Model Computation for XY-stratified Cliques

Step 1. The stage variable is assigned the stage constant from the exit rules.

Step 2. Fire the X-rules (w.s.a), once

Step 3. Fire the recursive rules (w.s.a.) sequentially,

Therefore, the stage argument is updated only once per cycle. XY-stratified programs can express every program expressible under inflationary fixpoint [35].

3 Syntactic Encapsulation

New syntactic constructs introduced to replace frequently used expressions of First Order Logic can yield dramatic benefits in terms of readability and efficient implementation. For instance, the simple idea of encapsulating disjunctive clauses, with no more than one non-negated literal, by the basic rule notation yields the improvements in readability and amenability to efficient implementation that are at root of the popularity of the logic programming paradigm. The same method has be used with remarkable success in other situations. For instance, the choice construct was defined in [12] to capture the notion of don't care non-determinism and encapsulate certain kinds of negative programs amenable to a polynomial-time computation. Two other such constructs are **if-then(-else)** and **min/max** predicates, both used in the XY-stratified program below. This expresses Floyd's classic algorithm for computing the shortest paths in a graph:

Example 2 *Floyd Algorithm.*

```
delta(nil, X, X, 0).
delta(s(J), X, Z, min(< C >)) ←  delta(J, X, Y, C1),
                                  g(Y, Z, C2), C = C1 + C2.
all(s(J), X, Z, C) ←  all(J, X, Z, C).
all(J, X, Z, C) ←     delta(J, X, Z, C),
                      if(all(J, X, Z, C3) then C3 > C).
```

The if-then construct used in the last rule of Example 2, is a construct of $\mathcal{LDL}$ and $\mathcal{LDL}$++ whose formal semantics is defined by its re-writing into a negative program: our rule is equivalent to

$$\text{all}(J, X, Z, C) \leftarrow \text{delta}(J, X, Z, C),$$
$$\text{all}(J, X, Z, C3), \ C3 > C.$$
$$\text{all}(J, X, Z, C) \leftarrow \text{delta}(J, X, Z, C),$$
$$\neg \text{all}(J, X, Z, C3).$$

Thus, programs containing if-then-else constructs are stratified iff their expansion using negation is.

Likewise, the notion of least elements in a set can be defined by the property that no lesser element exists. Take for instance the following rule from Example 2:

$$\text{delta}(s(J), X, Z, \min(< C >)) \leftarrow \text{delta}(J, X, Y, C1),$$
$$g(Y, Z, C2), C = C1 + C2,$$

Here $< C >$ denotes the grouping of C values with respect to the other variables in the head; and $\min$ denotes the least of such values. The meaning of this rule is defined by its equivalent expansion [11].

$$\text{delta}(s(J), X, Z, C) \leftarrow \text{delta}(J, X, Y, C1), \ g(Y, Z, C2), C = C1 + C2,$$
$$\neg \text{lesser}(s(J), X, Z, C).$$
$$\text{lesser}(s(J), X, Z, C) \leftarrow \text{delta}(s(J), X, Z, C'), \ g(Y, Z, C2), C' = C1 + C2,$$
$$C' < C.$$

4 Semantics of Updates

Let us now consider a database language that, in addition to query requests, supports other commands, such as requests to add or delete some extensional facts. As shown in [27], the definition of the semantics of programs with updates need not make use of imperative constructs. Rather, defining the semantics of such a language tantamounts to defining the external behavior of programs written in this language. Neglecting for the moment integrity constraints, we see that the external response to an update command should basically be an acknowledgement of some sort (e.g., a carriage return). Thus, all it is left to do is to define the meaning of queries. However, there is a key difference with respect to standard framework of query-only logic-based semantics [17, 30]: here we must specify the answer to queries *after the database has been modified by a given sequence of updates*. Thus, in our formal model we have (i) a program P containing a set of rules and a schema describing the extensional database, (ii) a set of extensional facts D defining the initial database state (iii) a sequence of update requests R, and (iv) a query Q; then we must define the *meaning function* $M(P, D, R, Q)$. For instance, consider the following example

Example 3 *We assume that our program P contains the declaration of two database relations* std, grad *(describing the majors and the courses and grades of students) and the following rule:*

$$\text{csst}(X, C) \leftarrow \text{std}(X, cs), \text{grad}(X, C, \_).$$

The initial database D contains the following facts:

std(ann, ee).   grad(ann, cs143, 3).
std(tom, cs).

R, the set of update requests, is:

req(1, add, std(marc, ee)).
req(2, del, std(ann, ee)).
req(2, add, std(ann, cs)).

The query is: ?csst(X, Y).

We have represented our sequence of update requests as a relation req; the first argument in req places the particular request in the proper time sequence. Successive requests are given successive integers by the system. However, several requests can be given the same sequence number, to ensure that they are processed in parallel. For instance, the last two entries in R model a user-level request to modify the major of Ann from EE to CS.

We need a logic-based semantics to compute the correct answer to a query such as ?csst(X, Y), given a certain initial database and an arbitrary sequence of updates. Since a query can inquire about the content of any relation after a sequence of such updates, we will have to model the notion of states our database goes through; however, we must avoid destructive assignments in order to remain declarative. To obtain this goal, we use a distinguished predicate quevt that, basically, operates as a queue of events. For now, the quevt predicate can be thought of as performing a copy of the req predicate as follows.

Example 4 *A first attempt at* quevt

$$\text{quevt}(N, \text{Typ}, \text{Atom}, N) \leftarrow \text{req}(N, \text{Typ}, \text{Atom}).$$

The meaning of a program P with external updates is thus defined by generating an equivalent program P'. For each extensional predicate q/n we now define a new intensional predicate q/n + 1 (we assume without loss of generality that there is no q/n + 1 in the original P.) These new intensional predicates are defined recursively, by XY-stratified programs:

Example 5 *From Extensional Predicates to XY-stratified programs.*

$$\text{std}(0, X1, X2) \leftarrow \quad \text{std}(X1, X2).$$
$$\text{std}(J + 1, X1, X2) \leftarrow \quad \text{quevt}(J + 1, \_, \_, \_), \text{std}(J, X1, X2),$$
$$\neg\text{quevt}(J + 1, \text{del}, \text{std}(X1, X2), \_).$$
$$\text{std}(J + 1, X1, X2) \leftarrow \quad \text{std}(J, \_, \_), \text{quevt}(J + 1, \text{add}, \text{std}(X1, X2), \_).$$

$$\text{grad}(0, X1, X2, X3) \leftarrow \quad \text{grad}(X1, X2, X3).$$
$$\text{grad}(J + 1, X1, X2, X3) \leftarrow \quad \text{quevt}(J + 1, \_, \_, \_), \text{grad}(J, X1, X, X3),$$
$$\neg\text{quevt}(J + 1, \text{del}, \text{grad}(X1, X2, X3), \_).$$
$$\text{grad}(J + 1, X1, X2, X3) \leftarrow \quad \text{grad}(J, \_, \_), \text{quevt}(J + 1, \text{add}, \text{grad}(X1, X2, X3), \_).$$

Furthermore, the old rules of P are replaced with new ones, obtained from the old ones by adding a stage argument to every predicate in the rules:

Example 6 *Rewriting the original rules*

$$\text{csst}(J, X, C) \leftarrow \quad \text{std}(J, X, \text{cs}), \text{grad}(J, X, C, \_).$$

The query goal ?sst(S, C) is then modified in an obvious way. To find the proper answer to the query after the first request req(1, add, std(marc, ee)), we pose the query: ?csst(1, S, C). But, the correct answer to the same query after the next two requests have been serviced is produced by ?csst(2, S, C).

Thus, we replaced the old predicates with new ones containing an additional stage argument. For notational convenience we shall represent the stage as a superscript; thus instead of writing std(J, X, cs) we write $\text{std}^J(X, \text{cs})$. Thus a new program P' is constructed from the original one P by replacing the old rules of P with new ones where the predicates are stage-superscripted. Moreover, for each extensional predicate q of P, P' contains the following set of XY-stratified rules:

Example 7 *Intensional Updates*

$$r_1 : q^0(X) \leftarrow \quad q(X).$$
$$\cdot_2 : q^{J+1}(X) \leftarrow \quad \text{quevt}^{J+1}(\_, \_, \_), \ q^J(X),$$
$$\neg\text{quevt}^{J+1}(\text{del}, q(X), \_).$$
$$\cdot_3 : q^{J+1}(X) \leftarrow \quad q^J(X), \ \text{quevt}^{J+1}(\text{add}, q(X), \_).$$

These three rules will be called, respectively as follows: r_1 the *base rule*, r_2 the *copy-delete rule*, and r_3 the *add rule*. Then, the deletion-copy rule copies the old relation into a new one, modulo any deletion that is currently pending on the event queue quevt. The insert rule services the add requests currently pending in quevt. The base rule defines a derived predicate with stage value of zero, for each extensional predicate.[3]

---

[3]We assume that initially our database relations are not empty. Otherwise, an additional exit rule, $p^0(\text{nil}) \leftarrow \neg p(X)$, can be added.

The resulting program P' is XY-stratified and defines the meaning of the original program P. The correct answer to query $?q(X)$ once all the $\mathtt{req}^J$ entries have been serviced is simply the answer to $?q^J(X)$. For instance, with P, D and R defined in Example 4, the perfect model of our modified program P' contains the following derived facts:

Example 8 *The perfect model for P' (derived facts only)*

$$\mathtt{std}^0(\mathtt{tom}, \mathtt{cs}) \qquad \mathtt{grad}^0(\mathtt{ann}, \mathtt{cs143}, 3)$$
$$\mathtt{std}^0(\mathtt{ann}, \mathtt{ee})$$
$$\mathtt{std}^1(\mathtt{tom}, \mathtt{cs}) \qquad \mathtt{grad}^1(\mathtt{ann}, \mathtt{cs143}, 3)$$
$$\mathtt{std}^1(\mathtt{ann}, \mathtt{ee})$$
$$\mathtt{std}^1(\mathtt{marc}, \mathtt{ee})$$
$$\mathtt{std}^2(\mathtt{tom}, \mathtt{cs}) \qquad \mathtt{grad}^2(\mathtt{ann}, \mathtt{cs143}, 3) \qquad \mathtt{csst}^2(\mathtt{ann}, \mathtt{cs143})$$
$$\mathtt{std}^2(\mathtt{marc}, \mathtt{ee})$$
$$\mathtt{std}^2(\mathtt{ann}, \mathtt{cs})$$

A query, such as $?\mathtt{csst}(\mathtt{S}, \mathtt{C})$, is then changed into $?\mathtt{csst}^2(\mathtt{S}, \mathtt{C})$ and answered against such a perfect model.

This simple rendering of the semantics of updates captures one intuitive understanding of these operations. It also is suggestive of efficient operational semantics. In fact, delete-copy rules can be implemented with the update-in-place policy, outlined for XY-programs, whereby records are simply added to, or deleted from, the current copy of the relation. The declarative semantics of these rules is, however, fully retained, as demonstrated by the fact that queries corresponding to update subsequences are also supported: it is also possible to pose queries such as $\mathtt{csst}^0(\mathtt{S}, \mathtt{G})$ or $\mathtt{csst}^1(\mathtt{S}, \mathtt{G})$.

Integrity constraints could also be treated in this framework. If the enforcement policy consists in rejecting any request that violates the constraint (e.g., rejecting a request for insertion of a new tuple violating a key constraint), then the proper checking conditions can be attached to the rule defining $\mathtt{quevt}$. Policies where violations are corrected by additional actions (e.g., elimination of dangling foreign key references) can be supported using the condition-action rules or the event-action rules discussed next.

5 Condition-Action Rules

Say that we want to enforce a rule such as: If a student has taken both cs10 and cs20, then he or she is considered having CS as major. For that, we could write:

$$\mathtt{add}(\mathtt{std}(\mathtt{S}, \mathtt{cs})) \leftarrow \mathtt{grad}(\mathtt{S}, \mathtt{cs10}, \_), \mathtt{grad}(\mathtt{S}, \mathtt{cs20}, \_).$$

Another possible rule could enforce a deletion dependency whereby one will want to delete the classes taken by students that are not longer enrolled. This can be accomplished as follows:

$$\texttt{del(grad(S, C, G))} \leftarrow \quad \texttt{grad(S, C, G)}, \ \neg\texttt{std(S, \_)}.$$

This simple example also illustrates the need for a formal semantics. In fact assume that a request is placed to introduce both a cs20 and a cs10 record for a given student. Then, according to intuition alone, each of the following alternatives appears plausible: (i) an insertion of a new cs student or (ii) the deletion of all the courses this student has taken, or (iii) both such actions, or (iv) neither action, or (v) an infinite loop. After the introduction of a formal semantics, only one of these alternatives will be considered correct (in the semantics discussed next it is iii).

The semantics we propose for active rules, views del and add as built-in derived predicates. Thus these two rules are simply re-written as any other rule:

$$\texttt{add}^J\texttt{(std(S, cs)} \leftarrow \quad \texttt{grad}^J\texttt{(S, cs10, \_)}, \ \texttt{grad}^J\texttt{(S, cs20, \_)}.$$
$$\texttt{del}^J\texttt{(grad(S, C, G)} \leftarrow \quad \texttt{grad}^J\texttt{(S, C, G)}, \ \neg\texttt{std}^J\texttt{(S, \_)}.$$

Furthermore, there is no change in the intensional update rules for the extensional predicates. However, the rules defining quevt must be extended to account for the add and del predicates as follows:

Example 9 *An improved definition for* quevt

$$\texttt{quevt}^{J+1}\texttt{(add, W, N)} \leftarrow \quad \texttt{quevt}^J\texttt{(\_, \_, N)}, \ \texttt{add}^J\texttt{(W)}.$$
$$\texttt{quevt}^{J+1}\texttt{(del, W, N)} \leftarrow \quad \texttt{quevt}^J\texttt{(\_, \_, N)}, \ \texttt{del}^J\texttt{(W)}.$$
$$\texttt{quevt}^{J+1}\texttt{(X, W, N + 1)} \leftarrow \quad \texttt{quevt}^J\texttt{(\_, \_, N)},$$
$$\neg\texttt{add}^J\texttt{(\_)}, \neg\texttt{del}^J\texttt{(\_)},$$
$$\texttt{req}^{N+1}\texttt{(X, W)}.$$

Thus, active rules will add to the quevt table. Once these rules have stopped firing, then new external requests from req can further expand the table.

After a sequence of n requests, the correct answer to query ?q(**X**), is obtained by answering the following three goals

$$?\texttt{quevt}^J\texttt{(\_, \_, n)}, \neg\texttt{quevt}^{J+1}\texttt{(\_, \_, n)}, \texttt{q}^J\texttt{(X)}$$

Thus, one needs to find the highest stage value J reached after input n; the correct answer is derived from predicates $\texttt{p}^J\texttt{(X)}$.

Condition-action rules are very powerful, and can be used in several applications, including constraint maintenance or truth-maintenance support [2]. On the other hand, condition-action rules can be expensive to support since they require the recomputation of the body of each rule every time a new update occurs in the base relations defining such a rule. Thus, every database predicate appearing in the body of an active rule must be monitored for changes; for derived predicates, possibly recursive ones, the derivation tree (dependency graph) must be traced down to the database predicates involved. While differential methods, such as the semi-naive fixpoint and truth-maintenance techniques, can be exploited in this context, it is also clear that condition-action rules tend to be complex and expensive to support. For these reasons, more recent systems favor an alternative approach where the events that can trigger the firing of the rules are stated explicitly in the bodies of the rules.

6 Event-Action Rules

In systems such as Postgres [29], the events upon which a rule fires are stated explicitly. These rules can be easily modeled in our framework. For instance, the previous active rules involving students and courses could be expressed as follows:

Example 10 *Event-driven rules*

$$\text{add}(\text{std}(S, cs)) \leftarrow \text{add}(\text{grad}(S, cs10, \_)), \text{grad}(S, cs20, \_).$$
$$\text{add}(\text{std}(S, cs)) \leftarrow \text{grad}(S, cs10, \_), \text{add}(\text{grad}(S, cs20, \_)).$$
$$\text{del}(\text{grad}(S, \_, \_)) \leftarrow \text{del}(\text{std}(S, \_)).$$

These event-driven rules are easily supported in our framework. We basically interpret event-action rules as stating that, when add or del events are queued in the quevt relation, then, the add or del predicates are enabled (requested). Thus, the meaning of the previous rules is defined by the following re-writing:

Example 11 *Expansion of event-driven rules*

$$\text{add}^J(\text{std}(S, cs)) \leftarrow \text{quevt}^J(\text{add}, \text{grad}(S, cs10, \_), \_), \text{grad}(S, cs20, \_).$$
$$\text{add}^J(\text{std}(S, cs)) \leftarrow \text{grad}(S, cs10, \_)), \text{quevt}^J(\text{add}, \text{grad}(S, cs20, \_), \_).$$
$$\text{del}^J(\text{grad}(S, \_, \_)) \leftarrow \text{quevt}^J(\text{del}, \text{std}(S, \_), \_).$$

By the definition of quevt, these add and del requests queued at stage J will be executed at stage $J + 1$.

7 Event-Based Programming

New events can be defined in addition to the basic add, del ones and used in various roles, including constraint management and application programming. As a (somewhat contrived) example, for instance, say that we want to raise the grades of Ann until her grades are all greater or equal to 4. This will be accomplished by the definition of a new raise event,

Example 12 *Raising the grades of students*

$$\text{del}(\text{grad}(S, C, G)) \leftarrow \text{evt}(\text{raise}(S)), \text{grad}(S, C, G), G < 4.$$
$$\text{add}(\text{grad}(S, C, G')) \leftarrow \text{evt}(\text{raise}(S)), \text{grad}(S, C, G), G < 4, G' = G + 1.$$
$$\text{evt}(\text{raise}(S)) \leftarrow \text{evt}(\text{raise}(S)), \text{grad}(S, C, G), G < 4.$$

followed by the request: `evt(raise(ann))`. These rules, with $S = $ `ann` are now executed in parallel enabling the corresponding set of events. These are then enqueued by the following `quevt` rules:

Example 13 *The final definition of* `quevt`

$$\text{quevt}^{J+1}(\text{add}, W, N) \leftarrow \quad \text{quevt}^J(\_, \_, N), \ \text{add}^J(W).$$
$$\text{quevt}^{J+1}(\text{del}, W, N) \leftarrow \quad \text{quevt}^J(\_, \_, N), \ \text{del}^J(W).$$
$$\text{quevt}^{J+1}(\text{ev}, W, N) \leftarrow \quad \text{quevt}^J(\_, \_, N), \ \text{ev}^J(W).$$
$$\text{quevt}^{J+1}(X, W, N + 1) \leftarrow \quad \text{quevt}^J(\_, \_, N),$$
$$\neg\text{add}^J(\_), \ \neg\text{del}^J(\_), \ \neg\text{evt}^J(\_),$$
$$\text{req}^{N+1}(X, W).$$

Then, event-action rules can be re-written as follows:

Example 14 *Raising the grades of students*

$$\text{del}^J(\text{grad}(S, C, G)) \leftarrow \quad \text{quevt}^J(\text{evt}, \text{raise}(S), \_), \text{grad}^J(S, C, G), G < 4.$$
$$\text{add}^J(\text{grad}(S, C, G1)) \leftarrow \quad \text{quevt}^J(\text{evt}, \text{raise}(S), \_), \text{grad}^J(S, C, G), G < 4, G1 = G$$
$$\text{evt}^J(\text{raise}(S)) \leftarrow \quad \text{quevt}^J(\text{evt}, \text{raise}(S), \_), \text{grad}^J(S, C, G), G < 4.$$

The detection of an event condition `ev(raise(S))` results in the checking of additional conditions and in the setting of a new event, including the re-setting of the old event `ev(raise(S))`, as illustrated by the last rule above. All applicable rules are fired in parallel; it is thus possible to perform recursive programming, whereby the same action is repeated while the body conditions remain true. The action performed at each step can be a basic update, or some other action, including the invocation of a query or the printing of some results.

8 Conclusion

The semantic framework here proposed yields the design of a rule-based language capable of addressing both the active and deductive aspects of programming. For deductive rules, one can keep the basic framework of Horn Clauses, with non-monotonic extensions, including negation and aggregates under the XY-stratification assumption. Active rules can be specified with the same syntax, provided that `add`, `del`, `evt` are built-in predicates. A uniform perfect-model semantics is ensured by the re-writing methods just discussed, which do not rely on meta-level or higher order constructs.

Building on this semantic bedrock, the language designer can consider further improvements and structuring of the language to improve the efficiency and clarity of programs. For instance, practical considerations might suggest that condition-action rules should be disallowed; in this case, the language will only support two kinds of rules. The first kind of rules are deductive ones without any event predicate. The other kind consists of event-action rules: these are defined as having an event predicate in their head, and one or more positive event goals in their bodies. Syntactic sugaring conventions might also be used to improve the expressivity of the language. A simple improvement would allow rules with multiple heads as a short-hand for several rules with similar bodies. The previous example, for instance, could be abbreviated as follows:

Example 15 *A multi-head rule.*

$$
\begin{aligned}
&\text{del}(\text{grad}(\text{ann}, C, G)), \\
&\text{add}(\text{grad}(\text{ann}, C, G1)), \\
&\text{evt}(\text{raise}(S)) \leftarrow \quad \text{evt}(\text{raise}(S)), \\
&\qquad\qquad\qquad\qquad \text{grad}(S, C, G), G < 4, G1 = G + 1.
\end{aligned}
$$

Also observe that that within the power and uniformity provided by such a language, there will be specialized usages. For instance, a system administrator will be predominantly concerned with monitoring events such such as **add** and **del**. However, application programmers will be mostly interested in defining new event types that will be invoked by certain classes of users. Each such application is defined by an event that is invoked by a user request or triggered by other applications. Each application can call itself recursively, or can take various actions, including calling other applications.

A new rule-based language incorporating these principles is currently being designed at UCLA.

References

[1] S. Abiteboul and V. Vianu. Datalog extensions for database queries and updates. *Journal of Comp. and System Sc.*, 43(1):62–124, August 1991.

[2] Apt, K., and J.M. Pugin, "Maintenance of stratified databases viewed as a belief revision system", *ACM PODS*, 1987.

[3] C. Beeri and T. Milo. A model for active object-oriented database. *Seventeenth International Conference on Very Large Data Bases, Barcelona*, pages 337–349, 1991.

[4] Bry, F., Intensional updates: abduction via deduction, in: *Proc. 7th Int. Conf. on Logic Programming*, Jerusalem, 561-575, 1990.

[5] S. Ceri and J. Widom. Deriving production rules for constraint maintenance. *Sixteenth International Conference on Very Large Data Bases, Brisbane*, pages 566–577, 1990.

[6] Chimenti, D. et al., "The $\mathcal{LDL}$ System Prototype," *IEEE Journal on Data and Knowledge Engineering*, vol. 2, no. 1, pp. 76-90, March 1990.

[7] Fagin, R.., Kuper, G., D.Ullman and M.Y.Vardi, "Updating logical databases", *Advances in Comp.Res.*, vol.3, 1-18, JAI Press Inc., 1986.

[8] Harel, D., "Dynamic logic", in *Handbook of Philosophical Logic*, (Gabbay and Guenther, eds.), D.Reidel Publishers, 1983.

38

[9] N.H. Gehani and H.V. Jagadish. Ode as an active database: Constraints and triggers. *Seventeenth International Conference on Very Large Data Bases, Barcelona*, pages 327–336, 1991.

[10] M. Gelfond and V. Lifschitz. The stable model semantics of logic programming. *Proceedings of the Fifth Intern. Conference on Logic Programming*, pages 1070–1080, 1988.

[11] S. Ganguly, S. Greco, and C. Zaniolo. *Minimum and Maximum Predicates in Logic Programming. Proceedings of the Tenth ACM Symposium on Principles of Database Systems*, pp. 154–113, 1991.

[12] F. Giannotti, D. Pedreschi, D. Saccà, and C. Zaniolo. Nondeterminism in deductive databases. *Proc. 2nd Int. Conf. on Deductive and Object-Oriented Databases*, 1991.

[13] A. Van Gelder, K.A. Ross, and J.S. Schlipf. The well-founded semantics for general logic programs. *Journal of ACM*, 38(3):620–650, 1991.

[14] Katzuno, H. and A.O. Mendelzon, Propositional knowledgebase revision and minimal change, *Artificial Intelligence*, 52, 263-294, 1991.

[15] P.G. Kolaitis and C.H. Papadimitriou, Why not negation by fixpoint?, *JCSS*, 43(1), 125-144, 1991.

[16] Krishnamurthy, R., Naqvi, S. and C. Zaniolo, "Database Updates and Transactions in $\mathcal{LDL}$", *Procs. of 1989 North American Conference on Logic Programming*, MIT Press, 1989.

[17] Lloyd, J.W., *Foundations of Logic Programming,*, Springer Verlag, 1977.

[18] Manchanda, S. and D.S. Warren, "Towards a logical theory of database view updates", *Int. Worksh. on Foundations of Deductive databases and Logic Programming*, J.Minker ed., Aug. 1988.

[19] D. McCarty and U. Dayal. The architecture of an active database management system. In *ACM SIGMOD International Conf. on Management of Data*, pages 215–224, 1989.

[20] M. Morgenstern. Active databases as a paradigm for enhanced computing environments. In *Ninth International Conf. on Very Large Data Bases, Florence*, pages 34–42, 1983.

[21] L. Palopoli and R. Torlone. Specifying the dynamics of complex object databases. In *4th Int. Workshop on Foundations of Models and Languages for Data and Objects – Modeling Database Dynamics*, pp. 143–160. Springer-Verlag, 1992.

[22] Phipps, G., M.A., Derr and K. A. Ross, "Glue-Nail: a Deductive Database System," *Proc. 1991 ACM-SIGMOD Conference on Management of Data*, pp. 308-317 (1991).

[23] T. Przymusinski. On the declarative and procedural semantics of stratified deductive databases. In J. Minker, editor, *Foundations of Deductive Databases and Logic Programming*, pages 193–216. Morgan-Kaufman, Los Altos, CA, 1988.

[24] Przymusinski, T.C. "Every logic program has a natural stratification and an iterated fixed point model", in *PODS 1989*.

[25] S. A. Naqvi, S. Tsur *"A Logical Language for Data and Knowledge Bases"*, W. H. Freeman, 1989.

[26] Ramakrishan, R., Srivastava, D. and Sudarshan, S., *"CORAL*: A Deductive Database Programming Language," Proc. VLDB'92 Int. Conf, pp. 238-250, 1992.

[27] Reiter, R., "On Formalizing Database Updates: Preliminary Report," in, *Advances in Database Technology–EDBT'92*, (Pirotte, Delobel, Gottlob, eds.), Springer Verlag, 1992

[28] Tsur S., 'Deductive Databases in Action,' *Proc. 10th, ACM SIGACT-SIGMOD-SIGART Symposium on Principles of Database Systems*, pp. 205-218, 1990.

[29] M.L. Stonebraker, A. Jhingran, J. Goh, and S. Potamianos. On rules, procedure, caching and views in data base systems. In *ACM SIGMOD International Conf. on Management of Data*, pages 281-290, 1990.

[30] van Emden M.H. and R.A. Kowalski, "The Semantics of Predicate Logic as a Programming Language," *J.ACM 23*, 4 (Oct. 76), 67-75.

[31] Warren, D.S., Database Updates in Pure Prolog, *Proc. Int. Conf. on Fifth Generation Computer Systems*, 244-253, 1985.

[32] J. Widom and S. Finkelstein. Set-Oriented production rules in relational database systems. In *ACM SIGMOD International Conf. on Management of Data*, pages 259-270, 1990.

[33] M. Winslett, "A model-theoretic approach to updating logical databases", *ACM PODS*, 1986.

[34] Zaniolo, C., *Intelligent Databases: Old Challenges and New Opportunities*, Journal of Intelligent Information Systems, 1, 271-292 (1992).

[35] Zaniolo, C., N. Arni, K. Ong, "Negation and Aggregates in Recursive Rules: the $\mathcal{LDL}$++ Approach", submitted for publication.

Semantic Constraints in a Medical Information System

Carole A Goble, Andrzej Glowinski

Medical Informatics Group, Department of Computer Science, University of Manchester, Manchester M13 9PL; cag@cs.man.ac.uk

Keith G Jeffery

Systems Engineering Division Informatics Department, Rutherford Appleton Laboratory, Chilton, Didcot, OXON OX11 0QX; kgj@ib.rl.ac.uk

Abstract. Classical constraint handling in data processing systems is concerned with ensuring the integrity of the database. Constraints are usually based on attribute values in a domain, or on syntactic (structural) relationships between the number of values under one attribute related to one under another. In the area of medical informatics, and probably in other application areas, the classical types of constraint are insufficient to ensure the integrity required. A knowledge representation formalism called Structured Meta Knowledge (SMK) is presented which describes conceptual medical terms and their occurrences in individual patient records. The prototype clinical workstation PEN&PAD which uses SMK is introduced. The requirements for constraints in medical informatics are matched against classical constraint types, the extensions defined and compared with those existing in SMK. A scheme for constraints in medical informatics is proposed, and future directions indicated.

1 Introduction

From a computer science point of view, the problem we discuss here concerns the assurance that the database contains a view of the world of interest that is consistent with reality, self-consistent, valid and which has integrity. This can only be achieved by the use of constraints which ensure that updates (input, amendment or deletion) are consistent with some externally defined set of rules. In traditional DBMSs, these rules are more-or-less absent; there may be limited type-checking, and possibly referential integrity enforcement, but little else. Traditionally, scientific DBMSs developed as 'homebrew' systems to handle scientific requirements have had, in addition, existential, enumerative, value-range and referential integrity (attribute-value dependency) checks [1].

The extension of schemas to data dictionaries (or full system dictionaries) will, in time, extend the power of conventional DBMSs not only to encompass those facilities already found in scientific systems, but also to include additional rule-based control of data integrity. In the area of medical informatics, a simple schema and data (or intension and extension) is insufficient. The scientific system schema enhancements are also insufficient. The existing and proposed implementations of system dictionary systems, while certainly going some way to providing a recognisable intension of the database, fall short of these requirements.

The problem is that in Medical Informatics (and probably also in other areas) not only is an extension of base facts sanctioned by an enhanced schema, but the schema itself is sanctioned by a meta-schema, which determines which attribute types, values and relationships may or must exist. Briefly, the problem concerns the sanctioning of a schema by a meta-schema, and the sanctioning of the data by the schema; the interest lies in the increasingly expressive semantics required at the meta-schema level, the representation and interpretation of the meta-schema constraints and the less semantically-rich schema's consistency with the meta-schema. The solution proposed uses a generative representation of medical concepts in a subsumption network implemented with semantic nets called Structured Meta Knowledge (SMK). SMK is the core of a prototype clinical workstation, PEN&PAD, which is a system for intelligent assistance to a medical practitioner entering notes using predictive data entry developed by the Medical Informatics Group at Manchester [2]. SMK unifies the description of the conceptual medical system of concepts and their constraints, the occurrences observed by a clinician for an individual patient and the clinical dialogue. SMK makes use of the object-oriented inheritance mechanism and is expected to act as a platform for deductions.

The rest of the paper is organised as follows: Section 2 presents the problems of the medical domain. Section 3 elaborates the types of constraints required to preserve integrity at all levels and compares the requirement with a recent classification of constraints [3]. Sections 4 and 5 present the SMK approach related to the classification of section 3, highlighting the unsatisfied requirements. Finally, Section 6 discusses the issues, indicates the future direction of the research and concludes.

2 Medical Information Systems

Historically, electronic medical records have focused on supporting the collection of information for aggregated analysis—initially for clinical research, later for audit and financial purposes. The use of electronic records to support *direct clinical patient care* is more recent, and introduces a significantly more complex set of requirements. Let us use an example: Jane Smith who has a severe, spiral non-comminuted fracture of the shaft of the left humerus.

Conventional systems attempt to capture the scale of medicine in a pre-coordinated way using coding and classification systems, usually devised for epidemiological or pathological measurement. The simple mono-axial coding systems such as the Read Clinical Classification [4] define pre hoc all those things that can be said clinically. Such systems are inflexible, restrictive, not comprehensive and prone to combinatorial growth but their terms make medical sense. They also fail to represent the diversity and detail essential to the clinical management of Jane Smith. Multi-axial systems such as SNOMED [5] are highly generative and potentially comprehensive but it is possible to generate a vast number of medically nonsensical combinations.

It is the opinion of a doctor that Jane Smith *may* have fractured her humerus or she may not. The use of a code by itself forces a definite decision which distorts the reality. Recording such uncertainty is essential for litigation purposes and the support of diagnostic systems. The opinion might be directly contradicted by another doctor or by the same doctor at a later date. Such corrections only augment the previous opinion, and do not change it. Medical records should be non-updateable and deletionless. We conclude that the clinical record should:

* be a *faithful* record of the clinicians' observations—what they have heard, seen, thought and done and not force statements that are too certain. This means that conflicting, uncertain and negative statements must be modelled;

* capture in a structured and interpretable form all of the 'clinically significant' information in the narrative notes, such as history and examinations, laboratory tests, procedures and diagnoses, plans, opinions and even speculations The information held must be consistently represented and well formed

The complexity and scale of medicine, the great variation between patients and lack of any neat compartmentalisation of medical practice (for instance, a diabetic patient could have eye, circulatory and skin problems) mean that a medical record system must be truly *comprehensive* for use in direct patient management.

Two further characteristics arise from the sensitive nature of medical information: permanence and attributability [2]. The record can be viewed as a series of observations that cannot be retracted or deleted remaining historically consistent especially when amendments are made to past assertions that are now considered erroneous or false. As a consequence of the need for authenticity, security and data protection, every observation must be attributed to an agent at a particular place and time.

A medical record comprised of atomic observations would offer a faithful yet flexible account. In order to deal with the scale, complexity and variable granularity of the clinical record a *descriptive* model is more promising than a traditional *prescriptive* one since the description of what was actually observed cannot be constrained to fit within a predefined view of what ought to have happened. This descriptive model must be comprehensive but maintainable. Such requirements imply a compact representation that is generative, effectively *evolving a schema* for the patient. A generative schema must be constrained to generate schema statements that are semantically correct within the application domain record—i.e.. medically sensible observations of a patient. A patient can have a fractured bone, but not a fractured eyebrow; a fracture can only occur in one place at a time; there is no such thing as an orange headache; drugs can be prescribed for patients, diseases cannot. The constraints which determine which attribute types, values and relationships can, must or may exist in the schema for the medical record can be termed a meta-schema. This meta-schema is held in a *system of concepts* which represents the semantics of medicine and medical terminology. Its active enforcement is essential for the integrity of the patient record.

Observational descriptions which make up the medical record must be at an arbitrary level of detail and abstraction. These have to be interpreted in the context of the actor making the observation, as what is meant by 'has no respiratory abnormalities' may differ significantly between clinicians. Base clause atomic observations can consequently perform different roles for different applications. All of the information recorded at the end of a consultation must be consistent not only with the system of concepts but also with the model of (medical) tasks and the actors involved. Constraints that apply at the point of committing to the record may be different to ones used during the process of information gathering. For example, gathering data has to be sequential which may lead to some complex constraints being temporarily violated pending the arrival of additional information. As a consequence we are required to include in our information model actors, tasks and time.

In summary we can identify four distinct but integrated components which have semantic constraint requirements (figure 1):

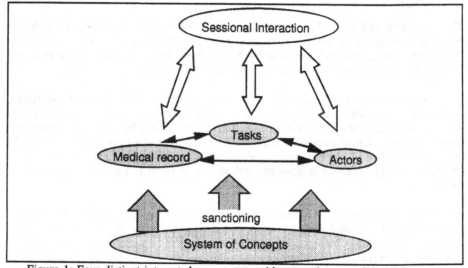

Figure 1: Four distinct integrated components with semantic constraint requirements

- **the system of concepts** – *what can be said or reasoned about*
  the clinical terminology and information model of the medical record and decision-making tasks. This can be divided into static and dynamic ontologies [6], which will have their own specific constraints.

- **the tasks** – *how information may be manipulated*
  this will include models of the process of care—implicit and explicit goals, alternative ways of achieving these, activity models, pre-defined protocols, plans and criteria for making choices. Such information supports clinical audit.

- **the actors involved** – *patients, clinicians and decision making agents*
  this includes models of non-observational information such as preferences and ways in which the actors interact with each other and with other models. Here is defined the assertional applicability of clinical terminology and practice to

the individual—an amputee cannot have an ingrowing toenail in the amputated limb.

- **the medical record** – *observations of what actually occurs*
  essentially the clinical record of the individual patient. Here we may include:

  - temporal and atemporally persistent knowledge about an individual patient inferable from recorded observations;

  - the 'authentic' historical model of the patient (what has been said about the patient by an observer).

Let us give a few concrete examples to illustrate the above points:

System of concepts: amoxycillin is an antimicrobial drug; blood pressure is made up of two values; diseases can be diagnoses; drugs can be treatments;

The model of the medical record: a patient can have repeated measurements of blood pressure; a patient can only have a single blood pressure at one time;

The tasks: how these repeated measurements are entered into the physical record is part of the task of recording information; that patients ought to have their blood pressure taken repeatedly is part of a model of the process of care;

The actors: a particular clinician prefers amoxycillin to other drugs in given circumstances.

The system of concepts constrains what the other models may represent and conversely the other models have requirements for the system of concepts. It is this system of concepts and the control of its semantic constraints that we will discuss further in this paper.

3 The System of Concepts

The system of concepts represents entities found in the universe of discourse, relationships between these entities, rules for combining the entities to form more complex concepts and constraints on the entities, relationships and rules. Here we are primarily concerned with these constraints.

In traditional data processing applications, constraints are encoded within the application programs and are used particularly to validate data input for insert or update operations. Typical constraints are domain-based and cover the range or the enumerated list of permissible values of an attribute. Some systems and applications have inter-attribute constraints of the form 'if $x > a$ then $b < y < c$' where x and y are attributes and a, b and c constants (or variables or even functions over variables). The intention is to ensure that the database maintains integrity; that it is internally self-consistent and that it is sufficiently expressive to be able to faithfully support the universe of discourse.

More formally, the classification of constraints [3], can be extended as follows:

(a)   Uniqueness: no two values of the same attribute can be equal;

(b)   Non-Null: all values of an attribute must be non-null;

(c)   Value Range: all values of an attribute must lie within a defined range (e.g. 0 < x < 100);

(d)   Domain Cardinality: the number of values for an attribute must lie in a defined range (e.g. number of natural parents living: 0, 1 or 2);

(e)   Relationship Range or Relationship Cardinality: the number of values under one attribute that are related to one value under another attribute (e.g. an order entity can be related to one customer entity; a student can take many courses and a course can be taken by many students) ;

(f)   Relationship Participation: the values under one attribute may be optionally or mandatorally related to values under another attribute (e.g.. A child must mandatorily be related through a mother relationship to a person but a person can be optionally related to a child);

(g)   Inclusion: all values of one attribute are also values of another;

(h)   Covering: all values of one attribute are also values of one of a set of attributes (vehicles are cars, boats, planes);

(i)   Disjointedness: the value of an attribute cannot be at the same time for a particular entity more than one value (e.g. male and female);

(j)   Referential: a value under one attribute is guaranteed to exist if there is a corresponding value under another attribute;

(k)   General : more general constraints consisting of a predicate over values under an attribute or across attributes.

The general constraints (which subsume all those classified above) can be stored in a representation of first order logic within a relational DBMS, with associated indexes for speedy access, and interpreted by PROLOG [7]. The enforcement of constraints and the maintenance of database integrity can be costly. For a survey of techniques see [8].

Let us introduce the constraints required to model *Jane Smith's severe, spiral non-comminuted fracture of the shaft of the left humerus*. We will consider these constraints more methodically in section 5. Jane Smith's current fracture is different to another similar fracture she had several years ago. It is also different to Bill Brown's fracture of the same description. Instances of the schema referring to the same medical concepts must be uniquely qualified by a date, place, agent and patient.

All medical concepts must be unique. There should be no tautologies or redundancies. For example, a fracture that is both located in the longbone and located in the humerus is a non-self contradictory tautology because the humerus is a kind of longbone. More complex examples are presented later.

A fracture cannot be located in more than one place, implying a cardinality mechanism. A hand, if it exists, must be part of an arm, but an arm may not have a hand, implying optionality of relationships.

Value-oriented constraints must be expressed. Value ranges are essential for measurements and the representation of typical boundaries to values. Certain concepts are countable (a patient can have more than one fracture) but others are 'mass objects' and cannot be counted (a patient can only have one diabetes).

In the previous section we put the case for a descriptive and generative representation of a system of concepts that constrains the medical model, the tasks and the actors of a clinical system. Such a schema must itself be constrained to only dynamically generate schema statements that are medically sensible observations of a patient. Consequently the semantic constraint mechanism for the system of concepts must be able to use a representation of medical terminology. Every concept must be constrained to be:

- **Grammatically correct.** A disease can be said to be located in any part of the body but not in 'penicillin' or 'left'

- **Semantically correct.** (i.e. medically sensible). A fracture may be located in the humerus but not in the eyebrow, although both are parts of the body.

- **Formally self-consistent.** A fracture of the humerus can be located in the shaft of the humerus but not in the femur.

The traditional domain and inter-domain value-based constraints alone cannot capture the semantics of medicine but must be incorporated into a more sophisticated constraint schema. We propose that such a schema can be represented by a subsumption network. The size of the network can be reduced by the use of inheritance and by combining elemental concepts into complex composite concepts.

4 SMK as an approach

SMK is an experiment in the representation and constraining of some aspects of medical knowledge, in particular medical terminology and some empirical clinical knowledge, and a patient's medical record. Medical concepts are generated, presented to the constraint mechanism and either rejected as semantically incorrect or accepted and absorbed into the constraint base itself. SMK provides the semantics for the individual patient's medical record. All statements in the medical record are observations by an *agent* at a particular *place* and *time* [15,11].

The knowledge representation has a three tiered model, which goes some way to representing the four components of a medical system as introduced in figure 1. The model consists of:

- the **'category' level** which models the system of concepts, constrains the generation of medical concepts and drives the constraint mechanism;

- the **'occurrence' level** which represents specific observations of individuals situated in space and time, and are analogous to instances in other formalisms. This layer models the 'authentic' historical part of the medical record;

- the **'individual' level** which lies between the other two and represents (i) the concrete instances of categories which persist in space and time about the individual patient's medical record such as Jane Smith's Fracture and (ii) the existence of actors and their preferences, such as Jane Smith.

The category level of SMK is one large constraint mechanism controlling the creation of further concepts and sanctioning observational facts in the medical record. The occurrence and individual levels are subject to the constraint controls of the category level in the manner of a strongly typed system. In this paper we only briefly introduce SMK and we concentrate on the system of concepts (category level). For a more detailed account of SMK and the other levels refer to [9,10,11,12].

Absent from the above list is the model of tasks, which is still somewhat 'hard-wired' into the prototype's execution model.

SMK describes subsumption networks consisting of *simple entities, arcs* which connect and describe those entities, *particularization entities* (for a discussion of the issues see [13]). Particularizations (previously called prototypes) are implied descriptions generated in accordance with the arcs between entities. The arc between *Fracture* and *Bone* implies (as *Humerus* inherits the arcs of its parent *Bone*) the existence of the descriptions *Fracture which hasLocation-Humerus* and *Humerus which isLocationOf-Fracture*.

An SMK network has three layers, mirroring the need for a description to be grammatically and semantically correct as well as formally self-consistent (as outlined in section 3). The first consists of grammatical statements; the second consists of statements about medically sense; and the third consists of statements about what is generally thought to be true or has been said to be true in a particular case. Statements in each layer must be sanctioned by the layer above, so all three layers combine with a self-consistency test to define coherence. Each descriptive arc has a qualifier indicating which kind of statement it is.

4.1 Grammatical Correctness

Grammatical statements represent para-linguistic facts, for example that the attribute *hasLocation* must have a *Condition* as its topic and a *BodyPart* as its value. Grammatical statements should not contain significant detailed medical knowledge, do not indicate whether or not any particular statement is medically sensible and are used primarily to guide the process of knowledge acquisition by validating statements such as *Fracture-hasLocation-LongBone* and rejecting statements such as *Fracture-hasLocation-Penicillin*

4.2 Semantic Correctness: the idea of sensible

Sensible statements (previously called possibility statements) represent substantive medical knowledge by determining which of the grammatically correct statements are medically 'sensible', i.e. which statements are semantically correct. However, they contain no information about what is actually true. The sensible statement *Fracture-hasLocation-Humerus:sensible* does not imply that all fractures are located in the humerus, nor that all humeri are fractured. Instead it states that it is semantically correct to talk about fractures of the humerus. The absence of any corresponding sensible statement for eyebrows indicates that it is semantically incorrect to talk about fractures of the eyebrow. Sensible statements are used in PEN&PAD to guide the data entry process.

4.3 Actuality: assertions of fact

Actuality statements represent the assertional knowledge of what is generally believed to be true—the factual knowledge about pathophysiology, medical treatment, and the pragmatics of medical dialogue. The sensible-actual distinction should not be confused with uncertainty about the truth or falsity of a statement. Within SMK, negation and uncertainty are represented by qualifiers attached to all the actuality statements. Actuality statements occur in at least three guises:

Descriptions of asserted concrete relations amongst concepts. A stronger statement than 'it is sensible for hands to be part of arms' is 'it is conventionally true that hands are part of arms'. These are called *necessary* statements and are similar to Brachman and Levesque's 'essential' statements [14]. Such statements are indefeasible and, although they are assertional in nature, they are considered to be part of the system of concepts. The semantics of necessary statements are complex and are discussed further in section 5.2.

General statements corresponding roughly to the 'facts' of many expert systems. They are used primarily in PEN&PAD for describing the user interface, the clinical dialogue and the definition of protocols. These statements provide the concrete information which could be used by other inference engines and cannot be subject to the same reasoning as the terminological and indefeasible concepts presented above [13]. The representation of causality falls into this class of actuality statements.

Facts that record the observations in the medical record. Within the medical record the statement that 'Jane Smith's fracture is located in the humerus' is an actual observation. This statement is sanctioned by the statements that 'the humerus is a sensible location for fractures', which was in turn sanctioned by the grammatical statement that 'conditions are located in body parts'. Every actuality arc in the medical record has a qualifier which may be either *yes* (the default), *no* or *query* (meaning uncertain). It is therefore sensible to represent statements such as 'Jane Smith may have diabetes' or 'Jane Smith does not have diabetes'. These statements make up the occurrence level of the three--tiered SMK model introduced at the beginning of this section.

5 Constraints in SMK

Constraints operate at two levels:

1. Constraints to ensure that the particularizations are medically sensible.

> Prototypes describing the system of concepts are dynamically generated. The particularizations must be constrained such that (like database constraints) integrity is preserved i.e. the database models as closely as possible the real-world of interest. This part of the database is truly meta-knowledge. The constraints are necessarily semantic constraint; even syntactic constraints (such as cardinality) depend on the meaning of the terms in the particularization.

2. Constraints to ensure that the particularization is applicable to the particular patient (given the medical history) and the clinician.

> Once the particularizations are constrained it is necessary to constrain occurrences so that this part of the database also models as closely as possible the universe of discourse. However, this requires additional knowledge concerning the medical history of the patient and the actors involved and the tasks undertaken. This part of the database contains facts (or at least observations). The constraints are therefore closer in kind to those of traditional databases and are of the types discussed in [3] and are not discussed further here.

By using SMK as a concrete experiment for medical constraints we can examine the SMK approach to constraining the system of concepts and relate this to traditional constraints. Elementary entities are asserted to exist and their position in the subsumption hierarchy is explicit and indefeasible. Therefore the semantic constraint mechanism is associated only with the definition of particularizations.

A classifier presented with a particularization attempts to place it in the correct part of the subsumption hierarchy—if a particularization cannot be classified or is not 'well formed' it is rejected as failing the constraints. The classifier only applies to particularizations and then only to the formal definition of those particularizations. In this way classification is the constraint process. In order fully understand the SMK constraints it is necessary to understand the classification process and the definition of particularizations.

A particularization corresponding to a 'comminuted fracture of the humerus' is represented formally in SMK as *Fracture which<hasLocation-Humerus hasForm-comminuted>*. Figure 2 attempts to diagrammatically represent this particularization, some of its sanctioning statements and related entities. The set *<hasLocation-Humerus, hasForm-comminuted>* is referred to as the *criteria set* and the entity Fracture as the *base*; together they make up the definition of the particularization. The particularization is not an instance of its base entity but a *kindOf* its base entity. The criteria set is canonical, .i.e. it is at its most reduced and non-redundant form. The definition of a particularization is indefeasible (so we cannot decide to cancel *hasLocation-Humerus* for the above fracture because then it would not be the same particularization). This is not dissimilar to the notion of entity integrity in a conventional database—the key to an entity cannot be cancelled (i.e. take on a null value).

In addition to its definition, an elementary or particularization entity may have other properties asserted directly or inherited from ancestors. The complete criteria set of an particularization is the full set of all the criteria which belong to an entity whether from its definition, from necessary statements or by inheritance from ancestor entities. The complete criteria set of our example particularization could be *Fracture which<hasLocation-Humerus, hasLocation-LongBone, hasLocation-Bone, hasLocation-BodyPart, hasForm-comminuted, hasForm-FormValueType, hasSeverity-SeverityType>*. We could cancel the *hasSeverity-SeverityType* so that we couldn't give this particularization any severity description. Obviously we cannot cancel any of the others because they are the sanctions that support the defining criteria set. This means that there is a meta-constraint preventing the co-existence of a cancellation and the use of the same criteria in the definition.

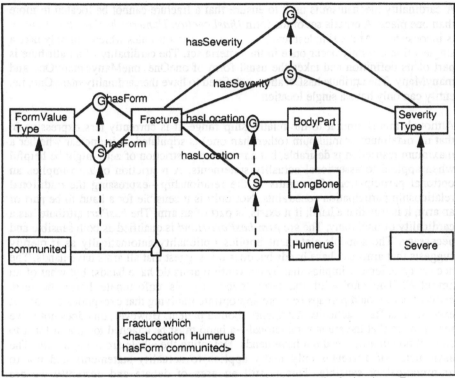

Figure 2: A diagrammatic representation of the particularization *Fracture which<hasLocation-Humerus hasForm-comminuted>*. The broken arrows represent the sanctioning of statements—a (S)ensible statement must be sanctioned by a (G)rammatical statement. The blocked arrows indicate inheritance hierarchies for elementary entities. The ⌂ symbol is a particularization operator.

We can also directly assert a necessary statement *hasSeverity-Severe*. Necessary statements are indefeasible, contribute to the classification of a particularization and are included in the complete criteria set.

This is only a superficial introduction particularizations and classification; for more details refer to [12]. We will now take the taxonomy of traditional constraints introduced in section 4 and relate each in turn to its role in SMK.

5.1 Uniqueness

The definition of a particularization is its unique identity. If particularization A reduces to the same base and criteria set as particularization B then A and B are the same concept and the same particularization. Category level particularizations are unique medical concepts; occurrence level particularizations for referring to the same medical concepts are uniquely qualified by a date, place, agent and patient.

5.2 Relationship Range, Relationship Participation, Referential Integrity and Disjointness

A cardinality mechanism is used to ensure that a fracture cannot be located in more than one place. A criteria set of the form *{hasLocation-Humerus hasLocation-Femur}* is inconsistent. At the simplest level, this means that attributes which can only take a single value can only occur once in the criteria set. The cardinality of an attribute is part of its definition and takes the usual form of oneOne, oneMany, manyOne and manyMany. The attribute hasLocation is defined to have the cardinality manyOne, i.e. entity can only have a single location.

Although this is similar to the relationship range, it is currently less expressive in that no maximum or minimum (other than one) is stipulated. It is unclear whether a maximum restriction is desirable, but a minimum restriction of zero might be helpful when applied to assertional actuality statements. A restriction of zero implies an optional participation of an entity in the relationship—expressing the traditional relationship participation constraints. Not only is it sensible for a hand to be part of an arm, it is true that a hand, if it exists, is part of an arm. The *hasPart* attribute has a cardinality of one:Many. The arc *Arm-hasPart-Hand* is qualified as both sensible and necessary. The sensible statement implies optionality automatically as it merely suggests that arms can have hands but does not suggest that all arms have hands. The necessary statement implies that by convention arms do have hands; but what of an amputee? The choice of the term 'necessary' is unfortunate here; the term *conventional* would perhaps be more appropriate implying that exceptions can occur, expressed as 'fact' actuality statements about a patient. However, this does not solve the problem that the arc is symmetrical—a hand must be attached to an arm for it to exist although arms need not have hands. Defeating the whole arc is too strong. The asymmetry of attributes only really applies to actuality statements and not to grammatical or sensible. This is still an area of debate and currently we are experimenting with the notion of one-sided necessary statements.

Mandatory relationships are also associated with the definition of a particularization. For example, *(Neoplasm which {hasNeoplasticBehaviour-malignant}) name Cancer* is a particularization defining cancer that has been named as such for convenience. Its base entity is *Neoplasm* and its criteria set is *{hasNeoplasticBehaviour-malignant}*. This is a strong statement; it means that it is impossible to express a non-malignant cancer as the criteria set must remain consistent. In an attempt to describe a benign cancer we would generate the criteria set *{hasNeoplasticBehaviour-malignant hasNeoplasticBehaviour-benign}* but as hasNeoplasticBehaviour has a cardinality of manyOne this is a contradiction and forbidden. In this way we can also model the mutual exclusivity of values for objects; i.e. disjointness.

Referential integrity's purpose is to ensure that concepts related in the schema do indeed have their instances related. In particular, all existing relationships must be retained or inherited during the creation of a particularization to ensure that its definition is complete and correct.

52

5.3 Inclusion and Covering

SMK is based upon a inheritance formalism. Either elementary entities are explicitly placed in a multiple inheritance hierarchy or particularizations are classified automatically (or 'formally'). Entities inherit the definitions, properties and sanctioning statements of their ancestors.

Fracture which <hasLocation-Humerus, hasForm-comminuted> inherits all the sanctioning statements (grammatical, sensible and necessary) of Fractures. These are represented in the complete criteria set. The particularization's defining criteria is a canonical subset of the complete criteria set. Thus a subclass entity *includes* all the attributes of its superclass. The superclass *covers* all the values of its subclasses.

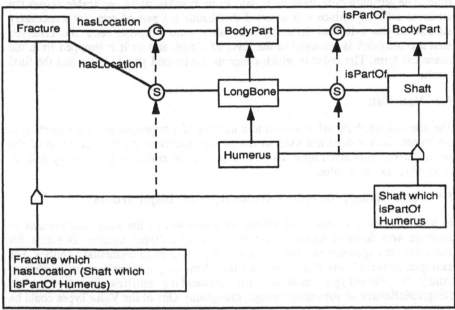

Figure 3: a piece of the SMK subsumption network for bones. BodyPart has been duplicated for clarity. The statements which allow hasLocation to be specialized by isPartOf are discussed in the text and have not been represented in the diagram.

It is important to reduce the defining criteria set to a canonical form without tautologies or redundant concepts. Figure 3 illustrates a piece of SMK which sanctions two particularizations. From this example we can see that the criteria set *<hasLocation-LongBone hasLocation-Humerus>* is a non-self contradictory tautology. LongBone explicitly subsumes Humerus, thus the criterion *hasLocation-LongBone* subsumes the criterion hasLocation-Humerus. Hence this set can be reduced to its non-redundant canonical form {hasLocation-Humerus}. A rule for reducing criteria sets to canonical form is that any criterion that subsumes another in the set is redundant. Similarly, a *Fracture which <hasLocation-Humerus hasLocation-(Shaft which isPartOf-Humerus)>* is reduced to the simpler *Fracture which <hasLocation-(Shaft which isPartOf-Humerus)>*. This is not quite the same as the previous example as a Shaft is not a kind of Humerus, but is part of a Humerus. The values of Humerus include those of LongBone, so the relationship with LongBone can be safely discarded. By reducing redundancy we eliminate synonyms and re-enforce the uniqueness of a concept.

Transitive semantic statements bring their own difficulties. Although *Shaft which {isPartOf-Humerus}* isn't a kind of Humerus, *Fracture which <hasLocation (Shaft which isPartOf-Humerus)>* is a kind of *Fracture which hasLocation-Humerus*. The criterion is subsumed because isPartOf *specializes* the attribute hasLocation. Similarly, the description of the left hand could be expressed either as *Hand which {hasLaterality-left}* or as *Hand which<isPartOf-(Arm which (hasLaterality-left))>*. It is an important function of SMK to ensure that it is the left hand which is a part of the left arm. Clearly the simpler *Hand which <hasLaterality-left>* must be the canonical form. The attribute *hasLaterality* is said to be mandatorially applicable across the attribute *isPartOf*. Since it is asserted that hands are part of arms by a necessary statement, the criterion *isPartOf-Arm* serves no purpose once the criterion *hasLaterality-left* is removed to the level of *Hand*, and so it is dropped from the canonical form. The order in which concepts are refined should not affect the final result.

5.4 Non-Null

The non-null attribute value is open to a number of interpretations. If the attribute is irrelevant, then it does not exist in the particularization. As the definition of the particularization is made up of its criteria set, all the attributes in it are, by default, required to take on a value.

5.5 Value Range, Domain Cardinality and Disjointedness

In SMK the value-oriented constraints are expressed by the same mechanisms of attribute arcs forming particularizations to build a 'type' system. Domains for attributes are expressed as value types at category level as elementary entities. For example, SeverityValueType subsumes the elementary entities [severe, moderate, mild]; SexValueType subsumes the elementary entities [male, female]; NeoplasticBehaviour subsumes [benign, malignant]. One of the ValueTypes could be null.

The attribute hasSeverity has a cardinality of manyOne and is used in the statement *Condition-hasSeverity-SeverityValueType: grammatical sensible*. So the particularization *Fracture which {hasSeverity-Severe}* is using the same arc mechanism to link to domain values, and the cardinality expresses disjointedness in that an attribute can take on severe or mild but not both. Similarly, with the statement *Fracture-hasLocation-Humerus*, Humerus is a domain value in the domain 'set of body parts'. Domain cardinality is only expressed as the enumeration of the elementary entities subsumed by the ValueType. So long as we only deal with enumerated domains we can continue to use the same formalism as before. However, value ranges cannot be expressed using the same mechanism, but are essential for such uses as measurements and the representation of typical boundaries to values. In addition, certain concepts, such as fractures, are countable (a patient can have more that one fracture) but others are 'mass objects' and cannot be counted (a patient can only have one diabetes). Some of this can be expressed through the inheritance and cardinality mechanism.

5.6 General

SMK excludes is any expression using (general) existential quantifiers, unrestricted disjunction, unrestricted negation, or universal quantification over more than a single variable. Inference is restricted to the use of inheritance and defaults. Simple disjunctions can be captured within semantic networks by simple inheritance. Conditional definitions such as "if Drug1 causes Condition & Drug2 causes Condition then Drug1 interacts with Drug2" are currently excluded from the formalism, which is primarily concerned with terminology. This is not a definition of 'interactswith', it is a heuristic rule for determining when two drugs may interact. Such constraints are dealt with by a separate inference mechanism as are recursive definitions, functions on ordered sets and mappings between ordered sets [16].

6 Discussion and Future Work

Developing advanced clinical applications introduces a number of important requirements as a direct consequence of the scale, complexity and diversity of the information that has to be managed. Conventional constraint mechanisms are not powerful enough to ensure the quality of the underlying system of concepts or the statements in the medical record. The experiments with SMK have looked at the ways in which semantic constraints can augment conventional ones in controlling a representation that is sufficiently expressive and flexible to meet the demands of medical informatics, and indicate that there is considerable merit in the approach, and have identified significant areas that require further research.

In general, existing data modelling techniques and representations (such as entity-relationship diagrams) make little provision for semantic constraints; this, allied to strong distinctions between intension and extension make such methods difficult to use in medical informatics. The scale and complexity of the domain has already been mentioned, but it is perhaps the fine-grainedness of regularities that do exist that makes application of general constraints so difficult. Many of the semantic constraints are applicable only locally, and are intimately tied to individual elements of the system of concepts (as distinct to more general constraints that are expressible at the level of the overall schema). For instance, although it may be possible to devise a general model for drugs, to represent all of the required constraints about small groups of (or even individual) drugs would make the schema unmanageable. In a sense, the constraint schema has to become part of the database itself.

Partitioning of the domain has proved vital to the modelling and management of information within applications; the separation of categories, individuals and occurrences has considerably eased the representation of medical records. However, consideration of a wider range of tasks and actors interacting with the same system of concepts (and medical record) introduces multiple roles for knowledge (e.g. a disease may be both the end point for a diagnostic task and the starting point for choice of treatment), each with its own specific data and constraint requirements. This issue is closely related to interoperability, and requires specific consideration. Medical records are complex data structures, subject to a number of safety-critical considerations; complex transactions are needed to maintain their integrity. This combination requires detailed definition of the operations within tasks as well as the data that is being managed.

SMK uses a very restricted set of axioms to limit the complexity of computation; in particular, shared variables and existential quantifiers are excluded, and negation very strictly controlled; all of the statements used in the classificatory inference are indefeasible. The default mechanism essential for real applications is outside the heart of the formalism. These limitations have proved too strong to permit representation of all the information required to support a practical range of applications such as predictive data entry [9], and additional statements have been introduced which are not ranged over by the strictly controlled classificatory inference mechanisms. Adding extra classes of knowledge, particularly support for defeasible assertions, can lead to well-known and very significant computational consequences [14], but appears to be necessary in practice.

Consideration of the demands of medical informatics and the results of the experiments with SMK have highlighted several areas which merit attention. The modelling of a complex domain with significant numbers of semantic constraints needs analytical and representational techniques that considerably extend those currently available. The partitioning of different types of knowledge, inference mechanisms and constraints is promising, but is as yet incomplete. The characterisation of the divisions and the computational properties forms an important part of current and future activities.

7 Acknowledgements

The authors would like to acknowledge the other members of the Medical Informatics Group who have contributed to the work discussed in this paper. Special mention must be made of Anthony Nowlan and Alan Rector who have developed the SMK formalism. This research is supported in part by the United Kingdom Medical Research Council grant number SPG 8800091, the Department of Health, and the European Community under the Advanced Informatics in Medicine (AIM) GALEN project.

References

1. K.G. Jeffery, E.M. Gill: The design philosophy of the G-EXEC system. In: Computers and Geosciences 2, pp. 345-346 (1976)

2. W.A. Nowlan, A.L. Rector: Medical Knowledge Representation and Predictive Data Entry. In: M. Stefanelli, A. Hasman, M. Fieschi, J. Talmon (eds): Proceedings of AIME 91. Lecture Notes in Medical Informatics 44. Berlin: Springer-Verlag 1991, pp 105-116

3   R. Cooper, Z. Qin : A Graphical data Modelling Program with Constraint Specification and Management. In: Proceedings of BNCOD10 Lecture Notes in Computer Science 618. Berlin: Springer-Verlag 1992,.pp 192-208.

4   Computer Aided Medical Systems Ltd (CAMS): Read Clinical Classification developers and user guides. UK: CAMS, Loughborough 1991.

5   College of American Pathologists: Systematized nomenclature of medicine, Edition 1. USA: College of American Pathologists, Skokie, Illinois 1977.

6   J H. Alexander, M.J. Freiling, S.J Shulman, J.L. Staley, S. Rehfuss, S.L. Messick: Knowledge level engineering: ontological analysis. In: Proceedings of AAAI-86 Vol 2 1986, pp 963-968

7   K.G. Jeffery, J.O. Lay, T. Curtis: Logic Programming and Database technology Used for Validation within Transactions. In: Proceedings BNCOD7. Cambridge University Press 1989, pp 71-84

8   S.K. Das, M.H. Williams: Integrity Checking Methods in Deductive Databases: A Comparative Evaluation. In: Proceedings BNCOD7 Cambridge University Press 1989, pp 85-116

9   W.A. Nowlan, A.L. Rector, S. Kay, C.A. Goble, B. Horan, T.J. Howkins, A. Wilson: PEN&PAD: A Doctor's Workstation with Intelligent Data entry and Summaries. In: R.A. Miller (ed) Proceedings of the 14th Annual Symposium on Computer Applications in Medical Care, SCAMC 90, California: IEEE Computer Society Press, Los Alamitos 1990, pp 941-942

10   A.L. Rector, C.A. Goble, B.Horan, T.J. Howkins, S. Kay, W.A. Nowlan, A. Wilson:'Shedding Light on Patients' Problems: Integrating Knowledge Based Systems into Medical Practice. In: L.C. Aiello (ed) Proceedings of the Ninth European Conference on Artifical Intelligence ECAI 90, Stockholm: Pitman Publishing 1990, pp 531-534

11   C.A. Goble, A.J. Glowinski, W.A. Nowlan, A.L. Rector: A Descriptive Semantic Formalism for Medicine. To appear in: Proceedings of The Ninth International Conference on Data Engineering, IEEE Computer Society Press, 1993.

12   A.L. Rector, W.A. Nowlan, A.J. Glowinski, G. Matthews: The Grail Kernal: GALEN Representation and Integration Language version 1. GALEN project deliverable A2012/D6, European Community, Advanced Informatics in Medicine (AIM) (1993).

13   J. Doyle,. R.S. Patil: Two thesis of knowledge representation. In: Artificial Intelligence 48, pp 261-297 (1991)

14   R.J. Brachman, H.J. Levesque: The tractability of subsumption in frame-based description languages. In: Proceedings of AAAI-84 1984, pp.34-37

15   A.L. Rector, W.A. Nowlan, S. Kay: Foundations for an Electronic Medical Record. In: Methods in Information in Medicine 30, F.K. Schattaeur Verlagsgesellscheft mbH publications, pp 179-186 (1991)

16   A.L. Rector, W.A. Nowlan, S. Kay: Conceptual Knowledge: the Core of Medical Information Systems: In: K.C. Lun, P. Degoulet, T.E. Pierre, Reinhoff (eds) MEDINFO '92 Proceedings of the Seventh World Congress on Medical Informatics, Geneva: North-Holland, pp 1420-1426.

A Methodology for Semantically Enriching Interoperable Databases

Malú Castellanos

Dept. de Llenguatges i Sistemes Informàtics
Universitat Politècnica de Catalunya, Spain
castellanos@lsi.upc.es

Abstract. Integrated access to a Federated Database System, whatever its architecture is, requires a deep knowledge about the semantics of its component databases so that interdatabase semantic relationships can be detected. Unfortunately, very often there is a lack of such a knowledge and the local schemas, being semantically poor as a consequence of the limited expressiveness of traditional data models, do not help to acquire it. The solution to overcome this limitation is to upgrade the semantic level of the local schemas through a semantic enrichment process that discovers implicit knowledge and makes it explicit by converting the local schemas to rich schemas expressed in a canonical model. Here we present a methodology for semantic enrichment consisting of two phases. In the knowledge acquisition phase, restrictions in the form of different kinds of identifiers and dependencies are discovered by analysing the intension and the extension of the database. Then, in the conversion phase, the schemas augmented with this knowledge are converted to rich schemas expressed in a canonical object oriented model.

1 Introduction

In Federated Database Systems (FDBS) [16] autonomous databases cooperate sharing their data while at the same time maintaining their autonomy. To access the FDBS in an integrated way, the user is provided with an interface that hides the syntactic and semantic heterogeneities that exist among the component databases. Syntactic heterogeneities, a consequence of the use of different data models, are commonly solved by the use of a *canonical* model to which the local schemas are converted. However, even if all schemas are expressed in the same data model, a single real world concept may be represented in different ways in the component databases, leading to *semantic heterogeneities* that must be identified for accessing the FDBS in an integrated way. Moreover, not only must equivalent concepts be detected, but also any kind of semantic relationship among the concepts of the component databases.

The detection of interdatabase semantic relationships requires a deep knowledge about the meaning of the databases. However, there is often a lack of such a knowledge, specially when there are many different independent databases as in the interoperability context. This problem is augmented by the fact that the database schemas do not help to acquire this knowledge because their semantic content is very poor due to the limited expressiveness of the traditional data models in which they are expressed. A solution to overcome this limitation of the schemas is to upgrade their semantic level through a *semantic enrichment* process where implicit knowledge is discovered and made explicit by converting the schemas to a rich canonical model. This corresponds to the two phases of our methodology described in this paper. In the *knowledge acquisition* phase, implicit knowledge in the form of restrictions, like keys and different kinds of dependencies, is extracted by analyzing the schemas and the extensions of the databases. Since analyzing the extension of the database is a costly operation, emphasis has been put on developing algorithms that eliminate redundant work and minimize the number of disk accesses. The knowledge acquired in this phase is made explicit in the second phase, called *schema conversion,* where the local relational schemas are converted to our rich canonical BLOOM model. The methodology constitutes the basis of a tool that semiautomatizes the enrichment process. Human intervention is required only to resolve some ambiguities when they arise and to confirm the results obtained. At the end of the process, there is the possibility for the user to restructure the final schemas. The enrichment has strong implications on the analysis phase of the integration of databases: the rich abstractions of the BLOOM schemas are used to guide the search in a systematic way and to reduce the number of comparisons of the various aspects of the schemas, as described in [6].

This paper is organized as follows. In section 2 related work is briefly discussed. The BLOOM model is outlined in section 3. Section 4 discusses the knowledge acquisition phase of the enrichment methodology while the conversion of schemas is presented in section 5. Our conclusions and future work are presented in section 7

2 Related Work

The subject of mapping a DB schema from one model to another has been studied by many authors. Most of the work refers to mappings from a more semantic model to a less semantic one, particularly from the Entity-Relationship (ER) model or some extension of it, to the relational model. However, the subject of mapping from a less semantic model to a more semantic one, as is needed for interoperability, has been studied less. In fact, it is more than just a mapping, since knowledge must be acquired in some way in order to upgrade the schema to a higher semantic level. As far as we know all the work on conversion to a richer model uses the relational model as the source data model and the ER model or some extension of it, as the target one. A brief overview of this work is presented in [2]. We do not consider this work adequate for the interoperability context for two reasons. First, the dichotomy (entities versus relationships) of the ER family create problems both, in the conversion and in the integration processes. Second, to acquire the necessary knowledge for upgrading the semantic level of the schemas they either rely entirely on the DBA to obtain all the necessary knowledge interactively [13], or assume that it has been specified in advance ([9], [12]). Furthermore, they consider only partial implicit knowledge, by considering only primary keys ([5]), or by making some candidate key substitutions ([13]), or assume that the schemas are well designed and consider only key-based inclusion dependencies ([12]).

In contrast, we use the BLOOM model described in [3] which is a semantic extension of an O-O model that complies with all the characteristics of suitability in expressiveness and semantic relativism of canonical models reported in [14]. We include a knowledge acquisition phase where the schema and the extension of the database are analysed to discover all the implicit semantics that make our approach more general than previous work. We cover both, well and badly designed schemas, and every candidate key and inclusion dependency (key and non key based) is considered, as well as exclusion and complementariness dependencies.

With respect to dependency inference from the extension of the database, the only work we know is the one reported in [10] where some algorithms for inferring functional dependencies are presented. However, they focus on the number of operations and not on the number of disk accesses, which is the primary factor of the cost in algorithms that analyse the extensions of databases.

3 The BLOOM Model

The choice of the canonical model used for the federated database system is critical in the process of schema integration. It must comply with several characteristics of expressiveness and semantic relativism reported in [14] that make it adequate for this process. In particular it must be rich enough to model the semantics already expressed in the local schemas, as well, as the semantics obtained from a semantic enrichment process.

BLOOM is an extension of an object oriented data model whose main constituents are objects and classes. Classes describe the structure and behaviour of their object members. The description of the structure entails the description of properties and relationships to other object classes. Modeling with BLOOM allows to capture a rich set of semantic relationships (the *construct* and *its inverse* are in parenthesis):

- Classification/Instantiation *(class)*.

- Four kinds of Generalization/Specialization *(generaliz_of / specializ_of)*:
  Disjoint: each object of the superclass belongs *at most* to one subclass.
  Complementary: each object of the superclass belongs *at least* to one subclass.
  Alternative: each object belongs to *one and only one* subclass.
  General: this one has no restrictions.

- Three kinds of Aggregation:

Simple (s_aggreg_of / s_particip(ates)_in): this is the simplest type of aggregation and is employed to express that the attributes involved in it are just properties of the object being described and nothing else. Each attribute takes as domain either a primitive class such as integer, or a user defined class such as department. Attributes can be single valued or multi valued *(set_of)* and *obligatory*, if they don't accept nulls; or not.

Collection (collection_of / collected_in): the collection of some objects of a given class gives rise to a new complex object. This concept introduced in [8] corresponds to the 'cover aggregation' in [4]

Association Aggregation (association_of / associated_in): the aggregate object is formed by aggregating objects from different classes. The component objects are not simply properties of the aggregate, but it is their association what gives rise to it. The aggregate object, in turn, has its own properties specified by the *simple aggregation.*

• Two kinds of specific dependencies (besides those existence dependencies inherent to the other abstractions) to model two different semantic situations:

Interest dependency (has_int_deps / int_dep_on): an object is of interest only as long as another object on which it depends is of interest, like the children of the employees.

Existence dependency (has_exist_deps / exist_dep_on): an object cannot be created if the object on which it depends does not exist, but once created its existence does not depends any more on the other one. For example, orders can only be placed to authorized suppliers, but if an authorization is deleted, the orders that have been put on it are mainlined for historic record

The operational functionality of BLOOM models the dynamic properties which can range from the simple specification of insertion and deletion constraints to the modeling of operations. The insertion and deletion constraints used to maintain the integrity of the semantic database constitutes the behavioural interpretation of the semantics of the model which is specified in the metaclasses corresponding to the different abstractions [3]. Metaclasses in BLOOM do not only specify the behaviour of their class instances, but also that of the instances of their instances. Furthermore, metaclasses permit the model to be adapted for different contexts by extending it with other abstractions.

BLOOM has a whole set of operators for integration, in particular, discriminated operations like discriminated generalization and specialization by attribute are useful for overcoming schematic discrepancies [15] and for building federated schemas that support multiple semantics [7].

4 Knowledge Acquisition

The knowledge acquisition phase takes as input the relational database, the metadatabase that stores its schema, and some information requested to the user when ambiguities arise. In each step of this phase a different aspect of this information is analysed in order to extract some kind of semantic knowledge, and the metadatabase is augmented with it as shown in the figure 1:

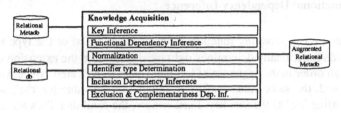

Fig. 1. Knowledge acquisition phase

Since the purpose of the enrichment process is to obtain rich descriptions of the objects, and the semantics of an object is given to a large extent by its semantic relationships to the other ones, the focus of our approach is on discovering the nature of these relationships. The implicit or explicit restrictions imposed on the database in the form of keys and dependencies embody this kind of semantic information, thus, the goal of the knowledge acquisition phase is precisely to discover them through an analysis of the extensions and the schemas of the databases.

Relational DBMSs provide different degrees of support (definition and enforcement) for the different kinds of restrictions. *Direct* support exists as a consequence of special purpose data definition language (DDL) statements to define specific types of restrictions in a straightforward way, while in the *indirect* support these specific statements do not exist but more general ones can be used indirectly for this purpose. In both cases the definitions will be stored as metadata in the catalog. When no DDL statements can be used in any way to define restrictions, we say that there is *no support*. In this case there is no information about restrictions in the catalog and the only way to discover them is by analysing the database extension.

Step 1: Key Inference

In this step we obtain all the keys (simple and composite) for each relation. It is not necessary to obtain their type, primary or secondary, because as will be seen in 2.4 design anomalies covered in our methodology make irrelevant this distinction. Keys can be inferred in various ways depending on the underlying information.

a) *Schema Support*: keys are specified *directly* ('primary key') or *indirectly* ('unique index' or 'unique') when the schema is defined, thus, the corresponding information can be retrieved from the metadata in the catalog.

b) *No Support*: the possibility that some secondary key has not been specified has been considered. Thus, an algorithm for inferring keys from the extensions of the relations has been developed in [1]. Different combinations of attributes are checked for the uniqueness property by comparing its cardinality with the one of the relation. Redundant work is avoided by obtaining only minimal keys.

Step 2: Functional Dependency Inference

Our algorithm for discovering functional dependencies (FDs) of the type lhs $\rightarrow$ rhs (left hand side functionally determines right hand side) from the extension of the DB, establishes an order in the sequence of left hand sides to be tested. Since we must test that tuples with the same value for 'lhs' also agree in the value for 'rhs', we sort the relation by using 'lhs' as the sort key. Furthermore, the candidate lhs's are grouped by the maximal sort key in order to reduce the number of sorts to be performed (for example, a sort by ABCD is used to test the candidate lhs's A, AB, ABC, and ABCD). For every pair of consecutive tuples that are compared, all the lhs's which use the same sort are tested, and for each lhs, all its possible rhs's are compared. The idea is that once two tuples have been retrieved, we test on them everything that we can test. Also, once a FD is discovered, we apply the transitivity rule to obtain derived dependencies and for every FD to be proposed as candidate, we first check if it is not redundant by the augmentation rule. In this way, our algorithm developed in [1] minimizes the number of disk accesses.

Step 3: Normalization

The importance of normalizing the relations for the enrichment process is to obtain relations that describe a unique concept. Furthermore, by normalizing to third normal form, the semantics of the functional dependencies will not be lost. Also, since the classes resulting from the enrichment process will describe unique concepts, this helps in the detection of interdatabase relationships.

Step 4: Determination of the Type of the Identifiers

One of the goals of our methodology is to encompass an as large as possible a class of relational schemas, so it doesn't rely on the assumption that the schemas are well designed. Anomalies like making foreign keys match secondary keys, specially if the secondary key refers to a missing entity (just modelled as an attribute), or choosing as primary key a candidate key that does not correspond to the intention of the relation, are considered in our methodology. These anomalies make it unnecessary to obtain the type of the key when it is discovered. We need a mechanism which adds a more precise semantics to all candidate keys. For this purpose, we introduce two types of identifiers:

a) **Proper identifier** (P_id) .- this is a key whose identification role is adequate according to the intension of the relation.

b) **Extraneous identifier** (E_id) .- it is a key whose identification role is just of a syntactic nature, that is, even though it complies with the uniqueness and minimality properties, it is not an adequate identifier from a semantic point of view because it does not correspond to the intention of the relation.

For example, in a relation 'departments' where the keys could be 'dept_no', 'dept_name' and 'manager', only the first two keys are P_id's, while 'manager' is an E_id. For every key, its type (P_id or E_id) must be disambiguated with the user aid.

Step 5: Inclusion Dependency Inference

Inclusion dependencies (INDs) constitute the basis of the conversion phase, because from their analysis, the nature of the relationships among the objects of the database can be determined. Since the methodology doesn't rely on any convenient good behaviour of schemas, an attribute in a relation R' can reference any kind of attribute in another relation R and not only keys. Thus, INDs in all generality have to be obtained.

a) **Schema Support:** DDL statements are provided to specify INDs *directly* as foreign keys (referential integrity), or *indirectly* as user defined constraints.

b) **No Support:** if INDs have not been defined, then, they have to be inferred by analysing the extensions of the relations. Emphasis must be put on the efficiency of the inference process. The naive method of checking all possible INDs, one by one, is practically impossible for two reasons: one is that for any pair of relations there are (D+d)!/(D!d!)-1 possible non equivalent INDs, and the second one is that in general it is not possible to check the existence of an IND fast. However, we can use some heuristics (A to E) to reduce the set of possible INDs, and to reduce the number of comparisons for the remaining possible INDs (F & G):

A. *The corresponding attributes in the left and right hand side of an IND must be of the same domain or at least of the same type.*

B. *Only those domains/types used for identifying purposes are considered.*
Since INDs constitute the relational mechanism for referencing entities through their identifiers, only syntactic domains used for identification purposes have to be considered, that is, strings of characters and numbers without a decimal part.

C. *A limit must be imposed on the length of INDs considered.*
Typically the INDs that hold in a database are short, so it is not useful to consider INDs of arbitrary length. A limit of three seems rather reasonable.

D. *Start with unary INDs and then disregard all those possible non unary INDs for which there does not exist a unary IND for each pair of the corresponding attributes.*
This heuristic is based on the projection rule of INDs:
if there is an IND: R [a1, a2,..., an] $\subset$ S [b1, b2,..., bn] then

the INDs: R [a1] ⊂ S [b1], R [a2] ⊂ S [b2],..., R [an] ⊂ S [bn] exist.
Thus, unary INDs constitute necessary conditions for the existence of non unary ones. For ternary ones, the heuristic becomes:

E. *Disregard all those possible ternary INDs for which there does not exist a binary IND for each pair of any the corresponding pairs of attributes.*

F. *Compare an attribute (attr) only with those of the same type with greater or equal cardinality.*
   It makes no sense to look for an IND where the attribute on the right hand side (rhs) of the IND has lower cardinality than the one on the left hand side (lhs).

G. *Never compare an attr. Ai with another one Aj with greater (or equal) cardinality before the other attributes with greater cardinality have been compared with Aj.*
   The main idea is to minimize the costly comparison work by comparing the attributes in such an order that only direct INDs are obtained by analysing the extensions, and *all* transitive dependencies are derived by simply applying the transitivity rule.

The algorithm is presented in [1]. The next example illustrates the procedure:

$$C \subset A; \quad D \subset C; \quad D \subset A;$$
$$E \subset D; \quad E \subset C; \quad E \subset B; \quad E \subset O; \quad E \subset F;$$
$$F \subset E; \quad F \subset D; \quad F \subset C; \quad F \subset A; \quad F \subset O;$$

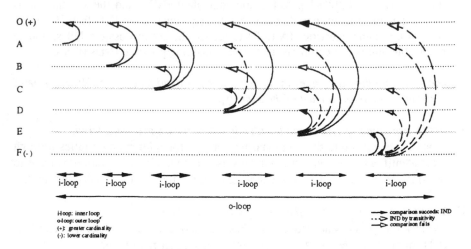

Step 6: Exclusion and Complementariness Dependencies.

An exclusion dependency (EXD) exists when two or more (subsets of) attributes are mutually exclusive, while in a complementary dependency (CD) the union of them gives the extension of the parent.

a) **Schema Support:** when these dependencies can be specified *indirectly* in the schema as user defined constraints, they can be retrieved from the catalog.

b) **No Support:** when they are not specified, then, they can be obtained by analysing the extensions of the relations. These dependencies are only used to determine the kind of specialization (disjoint, alternative, complementary or general). Since a specialization relationship between two relations can exist only when there is an IND between their key attributes, only those key attributes of the relations which have the same parent have to be compared. The problem is to determine the groups of children relations that will be compared. The complexity of the problem is reduced by first testing some conditions on the cardinalities, which gives us the clue about the possible dependencies that may exist. When both kinds of dependencies are satisfied for a group of relations, then, an alternative specialization exist, and these relations are immediately removed from the rest of the analysis. When a certain kind (only one) of dependency exists for a group, this is only an indication of a possible group of sibling relations according to a certain criteria of specialization, but the user has to confirm this.

5 Schema Conversion

Inclusion dependencies (INDs) constitute the core of the conversion phase because they can be interpreted in terms of the general abstraction principles of semantic data models, in particular, of the BLOOM model. Semantic structural relationships conform a network of connexions among the classes and it is the nature of these connexions what must be precisely defined to reflect all the semantics that they embody. In this way, the description of a class embodying the description of *all its interclass connexions* is much richer than its original relational counterpart.

As stated before, one objective of our methodology is to encompass a class of relational schemas as large as possible, that is, we do not assume that schemas have been well designed. In particular, an attribute can reference any kind of attribute in another table, thus, not only key based INDs are considered, but also any other kind, that is, INDs in its whole generality, R.a $\subset$ S.b, as shown in the table 1:

S.b R.a	Simple Key SK	Comp. Key CK	Simple Part CK (s.p.CK)	Composite Part CK (c.p.CK)	Non Key (s.NK)	Non Key (c.NK)
Simple Key (SKI)	S - S	--------	S - s.p.C	S - c.p.C	S - s.N	S - c N
Composite Key (CK)	-------	C - C	--------	C - c.p.C	C -s.N	C - c N
Each Part CK (e.p.CK)	e.p.C - S	e.p.C - C	e.p.C - s.p.C	e.p.C - c.p.C	e.p.C-s.N	e.p.C-c.N
Only Part CK (o.p.CK)	o.p.C - S	o.p.C - C	o.p.C - s.p.C	o.p.C - c.p.C	o.p.C-s.N	o.p.C-c.N
Non Key (NK)	N - S	N - C	N - s.p.C	N - c.p.C	N -s.N	N -c.N

Table 1. Case Analysis of an IND R.a $\subset$ S.b

All the cases of the table (which in turn have subcases) are treated through the different steps of the conversion phase:

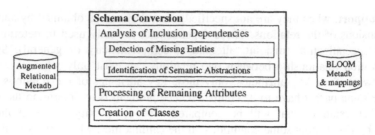

Fig. 2. Schema conversion

Due to space limitations it is not possible to analyze here every case of table 1, only a brief discussion of the main steps of the conversion phase will be presented. Partial descriptions of the classes are given in the examples only to illustrate the semantic abstractions derived from the IND being analysed. In practice the system will ask the user for the detail of description that he wants to see, that is, the depth level in the generalization and in the aggregation hierarchies, as shown in examples 1 and 2. The depth level in each dimension is independent from each other.

Relational Schema:

```
person (ss_num, car_num, name, phone, club)
employee (ss_num, salary, hired, job, dept)
children (emp. name, birth, gender)
department (name, manager, budget)
car (plate, model, owner)
club (name, meet_place, founded)
project_assignment (emp. project, hours, date)
```

BLOOM Schema:

```
class person                    class employee                  class department
   compl_generaliz_of              compl_specializ_of person       s_aggreg_of
      employee, student            generaliz_of manager              set_of employee
   collected_in club               has_int_deps children             manager
   s_particip_in car [as owner]    s_set_particip_in department      budget: float
   s_aggreg_of                     associated_in proj_assignment     id name: char[10]
      name: char[15]               s_aggreg_of                    end_class
      phone: char[8]                  salary: float
      id ss_num: char[10]             hired: date
end_class                            job: char[8]
                                end_class
```

class children
   id name *int_dep_on* employee
   s_aggreg_of
      birth: date
      gender: char[3]
end_class

class project
   associated_in
      proj_assignment
   s_aggreg_of
      p_name: char[8]
end_class

class proj_assignment
   association_of
      employee, project
   s_aggreg_of
      hours: float
      delivery: date
   end_class

class car
   s_aggreg_of
      person [*as* owner]
      plate: char[7]
      model: char[8]
end_class

class manager
   specializ_of employee
   s_particip_in department
   end_class

class club
   collection_of person
   s_aggreg_of
      meet_place: char[15]
      founded: date
      name: char[12]
   end_class

Example 1. Depth level 1 of description in both dimensions

class employee
   compl_specializ_of person
   generaliz_of manager
   collected_in club {inherited}
   s_aggreg_of
      meet_place: char[15]
      founded: date
      name:char[12]
   has_int_deps children
   s_aggreg_of
      birth: date
      gender: char[3]
      name: char[15]
   s_set_particip_in department
   s_aggreg_of
      manager
      budget: float

(cont.)
   associated_in proj_assignment
      associates project (& employee)
   s_aggreg_of
      hours: float
      delivery: date
      s_aggreg_of
         name: char [15] {inherited}
         phone: char[8]   {inherited}
         hire_date: date
         salary: float
         job: char[10]   {inherited}
         id ss_num: char[10] {inherited}
      s_particip [*as* owner] *in* car   {inherited}
      s_aggreg_of
         plate: char[7]
         model: char[8]
   end_class

Example 2. Depth level 2 for class 'employee'

Notice that in example 1, the BLOOM schema includes classes for which there is no corresponding relation, they correspond to missing entities detected in this phase. In example 2, since the interest is on class 'employee' at level 2 in both dimensions, its description in the generalization dimension includes the description inherited from its immediate superclasses, while in the aggregation dimension, the description of its immediate component objects is included, even for those inherited ones.

Step 1: Detection of Missing Entities

In this step all cases of INDs from which missing entities can be detected are analysed through the following substeps:

> Substep 1.1: all INDs on part of key or non key are analyzed here:
> Column 3:   Cases $X \subset$ s.p.CK :   INDs on simple part of a key
> Column 4:   Cases $X \subset$ c.p.CK :   INDs on composite part of a key
> Column 5:   Cases $X \subset$ s. NK: INDs on simple non key
> Column 6:   Cases $X \subset$ c. NK: IND on composite non key

> Substep 1.2: all INDs that involve an extraneous identifiers are considered:
> Cases $X \subset$ E_id
> Cases   E_id $\subset X$

> Substep 1.3: every component of a composite key not involved in any IND is analysed.

A *missing entity* is one that conceptually exists but has not been made explicit as a relation in the relational schema. The solution adopted to overcome this anomaly is to create a *virtual relation* for the missing entity which later will be made explicit in the BLOOM schema as a class. The creation of virtual relations has several effects on the augmented relational schema. Next we summarize the set of actions performed in this step:

1.- Create a virtual relation R' with the name of the (set of) attribute(s) in A. In the original relational schema this missing entity is normally referenced by its name, thus, we simply take this name for naming the new relation. These virtual relations will give rise to new classes in next step and in further steps it will receive the same treatment as the other relations.

2.- The P_id of the virtual relation R' is constituted by the (set of) attribute(s) in A. Each attribute in A is renamed for R' by concatenating the first character of its name in R with the word 'name' if the domain is of character type only with letters, 'num' in any other case.

3.- All INDs (simple if A has only one attribute, composite if A has more than one) whose right hand side is A must be transferred to the new virtual relation R'. This action is very important because it *turns INDs corresponding to cases of columns 3, 4, 5 and 6 into cases of columns 1 and 2* as follows:

$X \subset s.p.CK$ (column 3) $\rightarrow$ $X \subset SKI$ (column 1) where SKI is a P_id
$X \subset c.p.CK$ (column 4) $\rightarrow$ $X \subset CK$ (column 2) where CK is a P_id
$X \subset s.NK$ (column 5) $\rightarrow$ $X \subset SKI$ (column 1) where SKI is a P_id
$X \subset c.NK$ (column 6) $\rightarrow$ $X \subset CK$ (column 2) where CK is a P_id
and INDs corresponding to cases $X \subset E\_id$ into cases $X \subset P\_id$.

4.- All INDs (simple or composite) whose left hand side is A must be transferred to the new virtual relation R'. These INDs will turn into INDs whose left side is a simple or composite P_id respectively.

5.- A new IND: $R.A \subset R'.P\_id$ is added because now R.A has turned into a foreign key referencing the new virtual relation. Also its inverse $R'.P\_id \subset R.A$ is added because R' represents precisely those entities that participate in R, thus, R.A and R'.P_id are the same.

Next, some examples are presented. P_id's appear double underlined, E_id's single underlined and comments between { }.
Example of substep 1.1: rhs of IND is simple part of a key   {⊂ s.p.K}

school (university, s name, head, type);   **private_univ.name ⊂ school.university**
private_univ (name, category, owner);   public_univ.name ⊂ school.university
public_univ (name, category, budget);   univ_building.univ ⊂ school.university
univ_building (univ, blng, address, capacity);

gives rise to:
- virtual relation: university (u name)
    - new IND: school.university ⊂ university.u_name   {⊂ P_id}
               university.u_name ⊂ school.university   {inverse:⊂ p.K}
    - transfer INDs on school.university to INDs on university-u_name:
               private_univ.name ⊂ university.u_name   {⊂ P_id}
               public_univ.name ⊂ university.u_name   {⊂ P_id}
               univ_building.univ⊂ university.u_name   {⊂ P_id}

Notice that there were several INDs on school.university (column 3), but as soon as one of them is considered in this step, the virtual relation 'university' appears and the rest of them are transferred to the new relation. That is, the original INDs disappear and the new ones which have as rhs university.u_name (column 1) will be treated in a later step which considers the cases of INDs on a simple key.

Example of substep 1.2: rhs of IND is and extraneous identifier   {⊂ E_id}
        country (name, currency);   **inflation.currency ⊂ country.currency**
        inflation (currency, year, rate);   available.currency ⊂ country.currency
        available (currency, charge);

gives rise to: - virtual relation: currency (c_name)
- new INDs: country.currency ⊂ currency.c_name {⊂ P_id}
currency.c_name ⊂ country.currency   {inverse: ⊂ E_id}}
- transfer INDs on country.currency to INDs on currency.c_name:
inflation.currency ⊂ currency.c_name   {⊂ P_id}
available.currency ⊂ currency.c_name   {⊂ P_id}

The detection of missing entities is very important not only to make them explicit in the enriched representation, but also for the correct modelling of other classes to which they are connected. If these entities are not detected, then, their relationships with other entities will not be detected either. This leads not only to an incomplete description of a class, but even to an incorrect modelling of the nature of the relationships because a missing IND may lead to a classifying another IND in a case that doesn't correspond to the real semantics, for example, as o.p.CK ⊂ X instead of e.p.CK ⊂ X.

Step 2: Identification of Semantic Abstractions.

In this step all inclusion dependencies on a key are treated:
    Substep 2.1: Case Key ⊂ Key
    Substep 2.2: Case Each Part of Key ⊂ Key
    Substep 2.3: Case Only Part of Key ⊂ Key
    Substep 2.4: Case Non Key ⊂ Key

According to the type of the identifiers, that is, P_id or E_id, of the keys involved in the INDs, different subcases are distinguished in each substep. Moreover, different semantic situations correspond to each subcase depending on whether the inverse IND exists or not, and on other information found in the schema or occasionally asked to the user. Examples of some subcases are given next. As stated before, only partial descriptions of the classes are given to illustrate only the abstraction resulting from the IND being analysed.

The next example illustrates some subcases of case Simple Key ⊂ Simple Key:
    P_id ⊂ P_id without inverse IND,
    E_id ⊂ P_id without inverse IND,
    E_id ⊂ P_id with inverse IND and
    E_id ⊂ E_id without inverse IND.

Relational schema:
    Department (d#, dname, manager)
    Project (p#, pname, responsible)
    Project.responsible ⊂ Department.manager   {manager is E_id}

as it is an IND on an E_id, it has been treated in step 1 (substep 1.2.A where missing entities for E_id's on the right hand side of INDs are detected), giving rise to:

- virtual relation: Manager (m_name)
- new INDs: Department.manager ⊂ Manager.m_name {⊂ P_id}...(1)
  Manager.m_name ⊂ Department.manager {inverse: ⊂ E_id}...(2)
- transference of INDs on/of Department.manager to Manager.m_name:
  Project.responsible ⊂ Manager.m_name {E_id ⊂ P_id}...(3)

the original IND has been transferred to IND (3), which in turn is treated in step I (substep 1.2.B where missing entities for E_id's on the left hand side of INDs are detected), and the user is inquired about the adequacy of creating a new class for the E_id, that is, for project.responsible. Two possible situations can arise depending on the answer of the user:

A) If the user answers 'no' then, INDs 1, 2, 3 are treated in step 2. First, dependency
   (3) is treated in substep 2.1, subcase E_id ⊂ P_id, where it is converted to:

class project	*class* manager
s aggreg of	*s particip in*
manager [as responsible]	project [*as responsible*]
end_class	*end_class*

and then IND (1) is treated in substep 2.1, subcase E_id ⊂ P_id along with its inverse (2) giving rise to:

class department	*class* manager
s aggreg of	*s particip in*
manager	project
end_class	department [*obligatory*]
	end_class

B) However, if the user answers 'yes', then there is a missing entity for the E_id and
   this gives rise to:

- virtual relation: Responsible (r_name)
- new INDs: Project.responsible ⊂ Responsible.r_name {⊂ P_id}..............(4)
  Responsible.r_name ⊂ Project.responsible {inverse: ⊂ E_id}.(5)
- transference of INDs on/of Project.responsible to Responsible.r_name:
  Responsible.r_name ⊂ Manager.m_name {P_id ⊂ P_id}........(6)
  {notice that the original IND has been transferred first to (3) and then to (6)}

then, IND (6) is treated in substep 2.1 (simple key ⊂ simple key), subcase P_id ⊂ P_id resulting in:

class manager
  generaliz of
  responsible
  s aggr of
    m_name
end_class

class responsible
  specializ of
  manager
end_class

and finally IND (4) is analyzed in substep 2.1, subcase E_id $\subset$ P_id along with its inverse (5), as well as, IND (1) and its inverse (2). The result of converting INDs (1) and (2) is the same as in A) while (4) and (5) are converted to:

class project
  s aggr of
  responsible
end_class

class responsible
  specializ of
  manager
  s particip in
    project *[obligatory]*
end_class

To end the discussion of step 2, we illustrate one more substep, merely the 2.4 one where INDs of type non key $\subset$ simple key are analysed, The following examples correspond to two different semantic abstractions for the same type of IND:

i)   department (<u>dept#</u>, name, budget)
      employee (<u>ss#</u>, salary, dept) where dept is non key
      employee.dept $\subset$ department.dept#

  this IND is converted to:

class employee
  s partic as set in department
end_class

class department
  s aggreg of set of employee
end_class

ii) club (<u>c name</u>, foundation, site)
     person (<u>p id</u>, name, club); (in this example a person can be member of only one club)
     club.c_name $\subset$ person.club

  in this case, the corresponding abstraction is the collection aggregation:

class club
  collection of person
end_class

class person
  collected in club
end_class

Step 3: Processing of Remaining Attributes.

All attributes that appear only on the right hand sides of INDs and all attributes not involved in any IND, are treated in this step. They are added to the corresponding classes by connecting them through the *simple aggregation* abstraction. Those attributes that correspond to proper identifiers are distinguished by the construct *id* in the description of the classes.

6. Conclusions.

We have presented here a methodology for upgrading the semantic level of relational database schemas. It comprises not only the conversion of these schemas to richer ones expressed in an adequate canonical model, but also the knowledge acquisition process that analyses both the schema and the extension of the database, to extract implicit semantics. Emphasis has been put on the efficiency aspect because analysing extensions is very costly, and also in minimizing the user intervention so that the methodology can be the basis of a tool that automatizes the whole enrichment process as much as possible. The algorithms to implement the ideas exposed in this paper are implemented in C on a SUN SS-10 workstation.

Since the enrichment process is situated in the context of interoperability, it not only elicites the semantics of the databases, but at the same time it prepares the schemas for being useful in the integration of schemas, in particular, for facilitating the detection of interdatabase semantic relationships [6]. It is part of a methodology for schema integration where semantic enrichment is essential and the semantic abstractions resulting from the enrichment play a central role.

Now we are working on the other phases of the methodology, that is, the detection and merging phases, and plan to build a tool that semiautomatizes the whole integration process. Also we plan to extend the enrichment with additional information extracted from other sources, mainly, of operational kind.

Acknowledgements.

I am undoubtedly grateful to Fèlix Saltor for his invaluable help along the development of this work. Also to Manuel García for his suggestions, and to the reviewers of an earlier version of this paper for his useful comments. This work has been partially supported by the Spanish PRONTIC programme, under project TIC89/0303.

References.

[1]   M.Castellanos, F.Saltor: "Extracting Data Dependencies". Report LSI-93-2-R, Universidad Politécnica de Cataluña (U.P.C), Barcelona.

[2] M.Castellanos, F.Saltor: "Semantic Enrichment of Database Schemas: an Object Oriented Approach". In Proc. First International Workshop on Interoperability in Multidatabase Systems (Kyoto). IEEE-CS Press, 1991.

[3] M.Castellanos, F.Saltor & M.García-Solaco: "The Development of Semantic Concepts in the BLOOM Model using an Object Metamodel". Report LSI-91-22. U.P.C., Barcelona.

[4] E.F.Codd: "Extending the Database Relational Model to Capture More Meaning". ACM TODS vol 4, #4 (Dec 1979).

[5] Davis & Arora: "Converting a Relational Database Model into an ER Model". In [11].

[6] M.García-Solaco, M.Castellanos & F.Saltor: "Discovering Interdatabase Resemblance of Classes for Interoperable Databases". To appear in: Proceedings 2nd Int. Workshop on Interoperability in Multidatabase Systems (RIDE IMS-93, Vienna). IEEE-CS Press.

[7] M.García-Solaco & F.Saltor: "Discriminated Operations in Interoperable Databases". In Proceedings 1st International. Workshop. on Interoperability in Multidatabase. Systems.(Kyoto). IEEE-CS Press, 1991.

[8] Hammer & McLeod: "The Semantic Data Model: a modelling mechanism for database applications". Proc. of ACM SIGMOD Conf. on Management of Data, 1978.

[9] Johannesson & Kalman: "A Method for Translating Relational Schemas into Conceptual Schemas". Proc. 8th Int. ER Conference, Toronto, 1989.

[10] H. Mannila & K.Raiha: "Algorithms for Inferring Functional Dependencies". Report A-1988-3. Department of Computer Science, University of Tampere, april 1988.

[11] S.March (ed.): Proc. 6th Int.Conf. on Entity-Relationship Approach. N.Y, 1987.

[12] Markowitz & Makowsky: "Identifying Extended ER object Structures in Relational Schemas". IEEE Trans. on Software Engineering, Vol.16, No.8 (august 1990).

[13] Navathe & Awong: "Abstracting Relational and Hierarchical Data with a Semantic Data Model". In [11].

[14] F.Saltor, M.G.Castellanos & M.García-Solaco: "Suitability of Data Models as Canonical Models for Federated Databases". ACM SIGMOD Record, Vol.20, No.4 (Dec. 1991)

[15] F.Saltor, M.Castellanos & M.García-Solaco: "Overcoming Schematic Discrepancies in Interoperable Databases". In Hsiao, Neuhold & Sacks-Davis (eds.) Semantics of Interoperable Database Systems (Proc.DS-5 Conf., Lorne). Elsevier N.Holland, 1992.

[16] A.Sheth & J.Larson: "Federated Database Systems for Managing Distributed, Heterogeneous and Autonomous Databases". ACM Computing Surveys, Vol.22, No.3 (Sept. 90).

Distributed Databases Tied with StrIng

Daniel Cohen* and Graem Ringwood

Queen Mary and Westfield College
Department of Computer Science
London, England
dc|gar@dcs.qmw.ac.uk

Abstract. This paper describes work in progress at Queen Mary and Westfield College on integrating heterogeneous distributed knowledge-bases. It advocates the use of concurrent logic programming languages for rapid prototyping distributed database management systems. Concurrent logic languages are identified as generalised decision table languages. As an archetype, the paper describes a stream based interface, StrIng, between the commercial distributed implementation of the concurrent logic programming language **STRAND88** and the commercial relational database Ingres.

1 Introduction

1.1 Distributed Databases

The potential advantages of distributed data, e.g. fault-tolerance; scalability and speedup, have been promoted at great length, e.g. [27]. In practice, these advantages have been difficult to extract because of the complexity of data management required by distributed systems. Issues of distribution such as heterogeneity, replication, partitioning and efficiency combine with concurrency control to form a complex set of simultaneous problems that make the promised benefits difficult to deliver.

1.2 Metadatabase Programming

Howells et al [16] describe metaprogramming techniques to facilitate interoperability of heterogeneous databases. They report an estimate of the time taken to develop an interface between different database systems using traditional approaches (lex and yacc) as six person months. Using Prolog as a metalanguage, they claim to cut the time to twenty four person hours. Their system carries out source to source translation via an intermediate relational algebra tree. For each database system, two translators are required, one source input to tree and one tree to source output. The translators are specified by a source query language BNF (Backus-Naur Form). Such grammars are ideally suited to expression in Prolog.

---

* Funding for this work was provided by SERC grant:GR/G 39167

This work suggests that logic programming might be suitable for meta-database programming. Distributed database systems warrant the use of languages that provide concurrency. While Prolog is ideal for transformational metaprogramming, it is somewhat deficient as a reactive programming language. It is inherently sequential and not, as has been suggested, ideal for parallel implementation [30].

The broad aim of the DTI/SERC STALKS (Department of Trade and Industry, Science and Engineering Research Council, STrAnd for Large Knowledge Bases) project at Queen Mary and Westfield College (QMW) is to provide a platform for the development of large knowledgebases. This paper explains the strategy behind this research. After elaborating the data-mismatch between Prolog and databases, the paper describes a refinement of logic programming, concurrent logic programming, designed to exploit concurrency. The paper explains how concurrent logic languages can be understood as decision table languages. Decision table languages have been used for metadatabase programming since the early 1960s.

The following sections of the paper describe an archetypical stream interface of a commercial concurrent logic language to a commercial relational database. The potential that concurrent logic languages have for programming the management of preexisting relational databases on machines connected by a network is illustrated throughout the paper via examples of code.

2 Prolog and Databases

2.1 Prolog Interfaces to Relational DBMS's

In addition to translators, logic programming has been promoted as a method for rapid prototyping of relational database management systems (DBMS's) [20]. More generally, logic programming has had a significant impact on the database world [13]. The natural affinity between Prolog and databases has resulted in a plethora of research and commercial interfaces (see [5] and [12] for classifications). One of the main problems to be overcome with such an interface is the mismatch between the ways data is handled in the two systems: Prolog deals with individual tuples of a relation while the database deals with entire tables.

There is some confusion in the literature concerning the terminology of language interfaces to databases. Terms such as: loose and tight; static and dynamic; preprocessor access and others are used in confusing and conflicting ways by different authors. One characteristic that will be addressed in this paper is whether the interface permits dynamically generated queries or whether the queries must be present, in some form, in the text of the program. Some interfaces establish access paths for each query at load-time while some embed them in the code or establish them in advance of use, e.g. PRO-SQL [6].

Most Prolog-DBMS interfaces, e.g. [29] [18] [35] [23], involve database predicates which can be called like any Prolog program predicate and which succeed once for each matching tuple in the database. Entire tables are retrieved by failure driven loops, as if the tuples of the relation were part of the Prolog program. This technique is used by nearly all commercial Prolog-DBMS interfaces.

A new approach described by Draxler [12] uses database variants of the Prolog set predicates such as findall/3 (in Prolog and the concurrent logic languages that are described in what follows, each predicate is identified by name/arity) to provide the entire relation at once. The elegance of the interface is an attractive feature, but there are drawbacks: 1) high memory use - if the relation is large then the Prolog system will have to hold a large quantity of data; if the relation is very large this may not be possible. 2) potential wastage - when an application does not necessarily need all the results; for example, the answers may be presented one at a time to a user until just one is selected.

The one-at-a-time approach, however, will be inefficient when the whole relation *is* required; the overheads involved in communication between distributed databases and the Prolog system are likely to be much higher for a large number of small messages. Some Prolog systems overcome this by batching results - retrieving, perhaps, 1000 rows at a time behind the scenes and caching them.

2.2 Stream Based Interfaces

While the use of a backtracking mechanism combined with hidden caching fulfills both efficiency and memory usage requirements, it can be a clumsy mechanism when more than one tuple is required. A better interface might look to combine the single tuple efficiency of one-at-a-time methods with the multiple tuple efficiency of the set method or the cached one-at-a-time.

Parker [28] describes such an interface for a stream data analysis application. Stream processing was introduced by Landin [22] in the context of functional programming. Streams are lists of indefinite, possibly infinite length. They are a natural representation for time series data (especially real time) and provide a declarative mechanism for I/O. Streams must be processed with some sort of coroutining. Parker describes a Prolog coroutining metainterpreter to manage a stream interface with conventional database systems.

This stream based interface provides one answer to the data-mismatch problem for, while the stream is an interpretation of a set, it is also designed to be processed one element at a time. So a stream based interface has the elegance of Draxler's set based interface primitives while retaining the greater practicality of tuple-at-a-time interfaces. The performance of a stream based interface is potentially better than a backtracking interface and can be improved for whole relations by caching.

Streams are a natural way of dealing with the possibility of unlimited amounts of data: "If you don't know how large something will be, assume it will be infinite and try to process the data a bit at a time." The transducers used in stream data analysis generally only refer to a few elements of a stream at a time (see [1] for examples).

3 Concurrent Logic Programming

While, as Parker demonstrates, it is possible to metaprogram coroutining in Prolog, this is inefficient because it has to use busy waiting. Another manifestation of logic programming, the concurrent logic languages, exhibit concurrency in their computational model. The family of concurrent logic languages is reviewed in [31]. It includes Parlog [7], Concurrent Prolog [25], and Guarded Horn Clauses [34] (a product of the Japanese Fifth Generation). Common to them all is the replacement of the Prolog control flow computational model of left to right depth first search by condition synchronisation. For the purposes of illustration the paper will use Flat Guarded Definite Clauses (FGDC) [9] as representative of the family.

The syntax and declarative semantics of FGDC is deceptively similar to Prolog as the following FGDC code implementing two phase commit indicates.

```
transfer_funds( Account1, Account2, Amount ) <- true <-
    resolve( Account1, Bank1 ),
    resolve( Account2, Bank2 ),
    session( [decrease(Account1,Amount,Status1) | Rest1] )@Bank1,
    session( [increase(Account2,Amount,Status2) | Rest2] )@Bank2,
    commit( Status1, Status2, Rest1, Rest2 ).

commit( Status1, Status2, Stream1, Stream2 ) <-
  Status1 == y, Status2 == y <-
    Stream1 := [ commit(_) ],
    Stream2 := [ commit(_) ];
commit( Status1, Status2, Stream1, Stream2 ) <- otherwise <-
    Stream1 := [ rollback(_) ],
    Stream2 := [ rollback(_) ].
```

As with Prolog, program statements are definite clauses. Variable identifiers begin with upper case letters and functors, including constants, begin with lower case letters. Anonymous variables are represented by underscores and lists are denoted with brackets.

The operational semantics of FGDC is, however, very different from Prolog. This is emphasised by the unusual decomposition of definite clauses.

Definition 1. ⟨definite-clause⟩ ::= ⟨guard⟩ ← ⟨body⟩

Definition 2. ⟨guard⟩ ::= ⟨head⟩ ← ⟨conditions⟩

A consequence of this factoring is that the infix implication symbol, ←, is taken to be left associative. (The formula $(A \leftarrow B) \leftarrow C$ is logically equivalent to $A \leftarrow B \wedge C$, the more usual form for a definite clause.)

The computational model of FGDC can be understood in terms of languages very familiar to the database community: decision table languages. The two clauses for commit/4 can be represented as a decision table, Tab. 1.

Table 1. Decision table representation of definite clause procedure

		Rules	
	Conditions	R1	else
C1	Status1	y	
C2	Status2	y	
	Actions		
A1	Stream1:=commit	X	
A2	Stream2:=commit	X	
A3	Stream1:=rollback		X
A4	Stream2:=rollback		X

The clauses of an FGDC procedure (the collection of clauses sharing the same name and arity) correspond to rules of the decision table. Clause guards correspond to the conditions of rules and body goals to actions. The name "guard" comes from Dijkstra's guarded command language [11]. In FGDC, the conditions are restricted to language primitives such as equality and order relations familiar from database selection rules. The predicate **true/0** indicates that there are no conditions for the rule. Anonymous variables can be compared with don't care conditions in decision tables. The clause with the **otherwise/0** predicate as condition corresponds to the else rule of the decision table. As with decision tables, clause guards are compiled into decision trees and graphs.

A concurrent logic programmer would actually write **commit/4** as

```
commit( y, y, Stream1, Stream2 ) <- true <-
    Stream1 := [ commit(_) ],
    Stream2 := [ commit(_) ];
commit( _, _, Stream1, Stream2 ) <- otherwise <-
    Stream1 := [ rollback(_) ],
    Stream2 := [ rollback(_) ].
```

Unlike Prolog, which uses goal/clause-head unification to eliminate clauses with which a goal can be reduced, FGDC only uses pattern matching. Patterns in the head of a clause are compiled into equality conditions. Consequently, the mapping of guarded definite clauses to decision tables is generally more complex than this simple example suggests.

Goals such as **commit(X, Y, S1, S2)** are synchronised by rule conditions. When a condition is satisfied the goal is reduced to the body goals of the clause. Unlike Prolog, but like decision tables, there is no backtracking in FGDC. If more than one set of conditions of a decision table is satisfied simultaneously one rule is chosen arbitrarily. This choice is generally unpredictable because of decision tree compilation. This indeterminism is deemed appropriate for concurrent systems [11]. However, no fairness is guaranteed, and it is the programmer's responsibility to "program" fairness or the appropriate bias. If the guard conditions are satisfied the actions of the body (in correspondence with logic programming called goals) are executed. The goals can be calls to further *decision tables* including recursive goals. As functors are not limited to constants, this decision table language is Turing complete.

Goals, the actions of rules, should be considered as processes, or possibly threads, and are reduced autonomously and concurrently. That is, subject to satisfying the condition of some rule, they may be reduced in any order on a single processor or in parallel on processors at different nodes of a distributed system. The identifier following @ annotations in the only clause for transfer_funds/3 indicates where the goal is to be evaluated. If there is no annotation the default is for each body goal to be evaluated on the same processor as the parent.

If the variables of a goal process are insufficiently instantiated to satisfy any condition of a table, the process suspends. Such processes block until some other goal which shares the same variable instantiates it. If none of the guards can be satisfied the otherwise rule is used for goal reduction.

Variables are bound by the assignment primitive goal :=. Perhaps confusingly, this is not assignment in the usual sense. FGDC is a logic language: variables are referentially transparent. Logic variables can only be assigned once; once instantiated their value may not be changed. In this sense, logical variables are more like messages than shared variables and this analogy is exploited in concurrent logic programming [9]. Single assignment allows lists of variables to be interpreted as message buffers. Because of single assignment and pattern matching, condition synchronisation manifests itself as dataflow synchronisation.

In the bank transaction code above, the nodes on the network where the session goals are to be evaluated are variables. These become instantiated by the resolve/2 predicate which, it is assumed, relates each account number to a particular bank. In this way, the distribution can be determined at run time.

3.1 Layered Streams

With the list structure of logic programming and dataflow synchronisation, stream processing comes for free. A stream is represented as a list with a variable tail. The following code is representative of stream processing. It implements the session/1 predicate from the previous example of two phase commit.

```
session( Stream ) <- true <-
    db_open( Session, Stream ),
    handle_session( Stream, Session ).

handle_session( [query(Query,Results)|Rest], known(State) )
  <- true <-
    query( Query, State, Results, Done ),
    handle_session( Rest, Done );
handle_session( [rollback(Done)|Rest], known(State) )
  <- true <-
    db_rollback( State, Done ),
    handle_session( Rest, Done);
```

```
handle_session( [commit(Done)|Rest], known(State) )
  <- true <-
    db_commit( State, Done ),
    handle_session( Rest, Done );
handle_session( [ready(Ready)|Rest], known(State) )
  <- true <-
    db_ready( State, Ready ),
    handle_session( Rest, Ready );
handle_session( [], known(State) ) <- true <-
    db_close( State ).
```

The code for **session/1** takes the form of an abstract datatype which maintains the state parameters of a database session in the second argument of **handle_session/2**. Each element on the first stream argument can be considered as a message to the database. The alternative clauses of the predicate handle the different messages. An **otherwise/0** clause should be included to handle exceptions. Each clause makes a recursive call to handle subsequent transactions. Another process is invoked to perform the transaction requested by the message. The last clause handles termination of the session.

A stream is ready made for filtering data in time series analysis as described by Parker [28]. An archetypical goal exploiting pipeline parallelism would take the form:

```
<- session( [query(Query, Results1)] ),
    filter1( Results1, Results2 )@node1,
    filter2( Results2, Results3 )@node2,
    filter3( Results3, Results4 )@node3,
    filter4( Results4, Results5 )@node4,
    filter5( Results5, StdOut    )@console.
```

From the point of view of query optimisation, filters that are simple enough to be expressed in the database query language would be applied in selection queries at the database level to minimise the quantity of data retrieved.

3.2   Demand Driven Lists

The eagerness of a database to supply tuples can be controlled by demand driven lists. In demand-driven control, the consumer of the list generates a list structure skeleton with variable elements while the producer instantiates the variables (in the case of databases, with rows retrieved from a database). To illustrate this, suppose a user wants to open a query and display the results on the screen a row at a time. The following code assumes that **session/1** has been modified so that results to queries are returned on a demand-driven list (this requires some additional code to that shown earlier for **handle_session/2**). It further assumes that **StdIn** and **StdOut** will act as normal data-driven streams to the input and output respectively. Two processes can be invoked (concurrently) by the top level goal:

```
<- session( [query(Query, StdOut)] ),
   user( StdIn, StdOut ).
```

Fig. 1. Demand Driven List Communication

In Figure 1, the boxes represent process goals. Links between boxes indicate that the processes communicate via streams. The arrow on the link indicates the direction of flow of data (as opposed to the direction of flow of control). A graphical syntax for FGDC is elaborated in [32].

When the user requires the next row, the **StdOut** variable is instantiated to a list with a variable first element.

```
user( [ "next" | RestStdIn ], StdOut ) <- true <-
    StdOut := [ Row | RestStdOut ],
    user( RestStdIn, RestStdOut ).
```

The **query/4** process referred to in Sec. 3.1 will be implemented as an FGDC predicate that feeds the query to the database and maintains a cursor to retrieve tuples on demand. It will be suspended waiting for a one element list. When the **StdOut** variable shared by the two processes becomes instantiated to a stream the **query/4** process instantiates the variable head of the stream with the next row of data from the database. Thus the flow of control is opposite to the flow of data - the consumer demands data from the producer, which fills orders. This is in contrast to the more usual data-driven communication, in which a producer spews out data as fast as it can and the consumer has to keep up as well as it can.

3.3 Declarations Considered Harmful

Prolog-DBMS interfaces often require declarations which a programmer must be aware of. When such an interface connects to a database a record of each database predicate must be maintained by the Prolog system to mark out those predicates as database predicates. The advantage of the **session/1** predicate is that all information about database connections is maintained in the abstract datatype. Valid queries can be presented as a message to **session/1** at any time while the database connection remains open - nothing need be declared in advance.

The design of **session/1** allows concurrent multiple database connections in a very clean way (no possibility for name-clashes since each query is sent to a specific database session on a specific stream). The tangible advantages of this declarative interface are greater flexibility for queries and the avoidance of cluttering a program with interface predicates.

session/1 utilises the technique of layered streams where streams are embedded within streams. This provides a very neatly packaged protocol. Once the initial connection to the database has been made, a stream variable forms the only point of contact with the database - all communication, both input and output, is fed through this stream (output being produced on sub-streams). Thus only one predicate needs to be exported to the application (or to higher levels of more specialised interfaces), and learning to use the system consists of learning the messages that can be sent to and the responses that may be received from **session/1**. The interface appears to users as protocol-based rather than primitive-based.

4 StrIng

The aim of the STALKS project at QMW is to integrate heterogeneous databases and knowledgebases using a distributed implementation of a concurrent logic programming language. As proof of concept, **StrIng**, a prototypical stream interface between a commercial relational DBMS, Ingres, and a commercial concurrent logic programming system, **STRAND88** has been demonstrated. The interface has been implemented as a set of language primitives (**db_open/2, db_query/4, db_rollback/2, db_commit/2, db_ready/2, db_close/1** used in Section 3.1), combined with some supporting code to package the interface as the abstract datatype: **session/1**.

4.1 StrIng Design and Implementation Considerations

Given the client-server architecture of Ingres version 6, a direct implementation might connect a **STRAND88** system (that is, the Unix process running the **STRAND88** emulator) directly to the various Ingres servers (name server, communications server, and databases) via standard inter-process communication (IPC) facilities. Such an interface would need to "talk" General Communications Facility (GCF) - the protocol used by the Ingres servers to communicate with one another. This protocol is not, however, open and there is the possibility that Ingres could make radical changes to it.

Ruling out direct use of GCF, an indirect alternative would be to pipe queries from **STRAND88** to a SQL terminal monitor. This option was ruled out on efficiency considerations since it involves extraneous IPC. Embedded SQL is the standard way for applications to communicate with Ingres. In general this strategy would involve the construction of two interfaces - one between a C program and Ingres and the other between the Strand program and C. The **STRAND88** environment provides a C interface allowing a programmer to extend the system with additional primitives and datatypes by writing the appropriate functions in C and linking them into the emulator.

A one-at-a-time retrieval mechanism requires the declaration and repeated re-use of cursors which are "presented" to the database when another row is required. At the Strand end, the request for a new row is indicated by the instantiation of a logic variable to a list with a variable first element. Hiding the cursors involves passing a key to each cursor from the C interface code to a Strand **query/4** process handling the query. The Strand query-handling process reacts to the setting of the logic variable by passing the cursor key back to the C interface code. On receiving a tuple from the database the **query/4** process instantiates the variable head of the result stream as described in Section 3.2.

Similar treatment for the session number of any particular query is avoided by using a table of such state information with the key retrieving all the appropriate parameters. The **StrIng** interface as currently implemented can cope with multiple concurrent database connections and multiple concurrent active queries on each connection. Further details of the implementation of **StrIng** may be found in [10].

The **StrIng** interface is intended to be archetypical. Other interfaces to other databases could be constructed in a similar vein. This strategy to heterogeneity is the same as that used by Howells et al [16].

5 Distributed Databases

The metadatabase approach to implementing distributed databases is not new - a metadatabase is at the heart of the ANSI/SPARC (American National Standards Institute, Standards Planning And Requirements Committee) architecture used as a reference model for distributed database systems [33]. The approach taken in the STALKS project combines the use of a metadatabase with the use of the concurrent logic programming language as a metalanguage, both to implement the metadatabase and to provide a flexible and powerful means to express complex relationships between data.

The STALKS metadatabase holds and provides information for the Strand program to break down distributed queries, direct them to the appropriate database and combine results. The metadatabase describes the mapping from each virtual table either to a set of virtual tables or to a real table. The range of the map is sets of *virtual* tables rather than real tables so that nesting is possible. The structure of a prototype distributed database built using **StrIng** is illustrated in Figure 2.

In the figure, "data" refers to demand-driven streams of Strand data representing sets; "IF" refers to some internal format for queries; "SQL" refers to queries and commands in Structured Query Language and "C-data" is used to refer to the raw output from the databases. The details of the internal format of queries are not important - any format suitable for symbolic processing will do, for example, the format used by Howells et al in [16] would be appropriate. Queries passed through **StrIng** are represented explicitly as such - there is no attempt to package queries as logic language goals like most Prolog interfaces

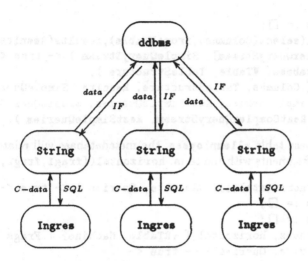

Fig. 2. StrIng based distributed database scheme

do. This is a more suitable form of interface for developing distributed database systems since less translation is required.

5.1 Distributed Query Processing

The processing of queries of a distributed database can be expressed in FGDC as shown below. The code shown would not be used in STALKS since the use of individual database sessions for each query precludes any use of the system for database management (there can be no concurrency control or transaction processing). However, it does serve to illustrate query processing:

```
ddb_session( ComplexQueryStream ) <- true <-
    split( ComplexQueryStream, SimpleQueryStream ),
    distribute( SimpleQueryStream ).

distribute( [] ) <- true <- true;
distribute( [ {Query, Machine} | Queries ] ) <- true <-
    session( Query )@Machine,
    distribute( Queries ).
```

In this outline, the predicate **split/2** uses a metadatabase to break down a complex query into a stream of simple-query, machine pairs. As an illustration, consider a query to a horizontally fragmented virtual table:
select name from allemployees (where allemployees is a table fragmented horizontally across departments). With the SQL query represented as a term, two of the clauses for **split/2** would be:

```
split( [], Queries) <- true <-
```

```
    Queries := [];
split( [sql(select(Columns),from(VTable),results(Results)) |
  RestComplexQueryStream], SimpleQueryStream ) <- true <-
    metadatabase( VTable, TableStructure ),
    split1( Columns, TableStructure, Results, SimpleQueries ),
    merge(SimpleQueries, RestSimpleQueries, SimpleQueryStream );
    split( RestComplexQueryStream, RestSimpleQueries ).
```

For database table **allemployees**, the metadatabase will relate the virtual table to the fragments with the term: **horizontal([frag1,frag2,frag3])**.

```
split1( _, horizontal([]), Results, Queries ) <- true <-
    Results := [],
    Queries := [];
split1( Columns, horizontal([ {RTable, Machine} | Frags ] ),
        Results, Queries ) <- true <-
    Queries :=
      [{sql(select(Columns),from(RTable),results(Results1)),
        Machine} | MoreQueries ],
    merge( Results1, RestResults, Results ),
    split1( Columns, horizontal(Frags),
            RestResults, MoreQueries ).
```

Note the use throughout of layered streams; the results to each query are embedded in the term encoding the query, making the code very compact. The **split/2** predicate and its auxiliaries invoke processes to merge the results of the simple queries at the same time as they produce the queries. The condition synchronisation mechanisms of FGDC ensure that these processes remain idle until results start to appear on the output streams of the simple queries.

5.2   Replicated Databases

Replication schemas for tables can be accommodated in the previous representation by adding a new type of entry to the metadatabase. This allows arbitrarily complex replication schemas to be mixed with fragmentation. The processing of queries of such nested fragmented and replicated tables is made tractable by liberal use of recursion so that only the basic constructions (vertical fragmentation, horizontal fragmentation, replication, etc.) need to be programmed. Of course, optimised performance would require more sophisticated processing than the simple recursive approach illustrated above.

6   From Database to Knowledgebase

6.1   Iterative Queries

The transitive closure of a database relation is often provided by iterative queries [15], [21]. In concurrent logic languages, as with Prolog, transitive closure is coded naturally (though not efficiently) by recursion. Illustrative FGDC code for a stream based ancestor relation formed from a parent database relation follows:

```
ancestors(Children, Ancestors) <- true <-
    ancestors1( Children, DBStream, Ancestors ),
    ddb_session( DBStream ).

ancestors1( [], DBStream, Ancestors ) <- true <-
    DBStream  := [],
    Ancestors := [];
ancestors1( [Child|Children], DBStream, Ancestors ) <- true <-
    DBStream :=
        [ sql(select(parent),from(table),where(child=Child),
                results(Parents)) | RestDBStream ],
    ancestors1( Parents, RestDBStream, RestAncestors ),
    merge( Parents, RestAncestors, Ancestors ).
```

This code is longer than one would expect with a Prolog-DBMS interface, but it uses no implicit state information and can be run in parallel with potential speedups. The use (not shown) of demand driven lists would enable the code to fetch exactly as many ancestors as are required in a lazy fashion, exploiting any parallelism available when querying distributed databases.

6.2 Alerters, Triggers, and Demons

Alerters [4], triggers [2], and other forms of active rules are also easily implemented in a concurrent logic language because condition synchronisation is a part of the computational model. The metadatabase can be extended to include flag variables for tables to which alerters are to be attached. Alerters would take the form of dormant FGDC processes (suspended on the flag variable) that enter a query when the variable is set. Triggers would use the same mechanism, and enter commands when wakened. If the semantics desired of alerters and triggers demands a specific serialisation then the actions of the trigger and the triggering operation can be synchronised appropriately by the simple method of placing them in the right order in a sequence of operation/queries for the database.

Commercially available expert system shells and knowledge representation tools (e.g. KEE) based on frames [26] or objects often provide a battery of such active rules that can placed inside a knowledge base and be used to do much of the work that would otherwise have to be coded in each application that uses the data. KEE's facets and procedural attachments (methods and active values) are used to provide integrity and other constraints, control over inheritance and cardinality, type-checking (important for a weakly typed system), as well as generalised equivalents of the alerters and triggers found in DBMS's. In the AI literature such active rules are often referred to as demons [36] and they would make a useful addition to many DBMS's. Such facilities are as easily programmed in concurrent logic languages.

7 Efficiency Issues

Given the nature of the STALKS project and the small team working on it, little effort has been expended on efficiency considerations. Nevertheless, there are many efficiency improvements that could be envisaged. The **StrIng** interface could be speeded up greatly by implementing a buffering system to prefetch multiple rows for a query and hold them in memory. The **ddbms** module in Fig. 2 is open to all the usual optimisations employed in distributed database systems and it provides a good platform for investigating new query optimisations.

Very little use has been made even of standard relational database features to improve efficiency, such as views, and no use has been made so far of parallel processing for the more cpu intensive operations. The **STRAND88** system being used for this work runs on a variety of systems including some multiprocessors and can also run on a network of workstations treating such as a multiprocessor. As described in Section 3, annotations must be added to goals to run on different nodes of a multiple computer system (multiprocessor or network) but the semantics of the programs themselves do not change with distribution.

There are, however, some problems involved in using **STRAND88** in its current form, notably the static configuration of multiple computer sessions. This is not an inherent drawback of concurrent logic languages but a feature of the **STRAND88** implementation. It would be possible to implement Strand using the Internet demon to allow dynamic reconfiguration. This would allow **STRAND88** sessions to be started when appropriate as with Ingres sessions. Despite this drawback, the system has proved capable of running significant parallel computations across networks and seems to cope with data throughput from Ingres databases.

The **STRAND88** system is the first commercial implementation of a concurrent logic language so it should not be seen as the be all and end all of such systems. With **STRAND88** the concurrent logic language is compiled to an abstract machine code which is then interpreted. That improvements are possible is illustrated by jc, an experimental compiler (compiles to C) for the concurrent logic language Janus. Janus programs run at a third the speed of the equivalent C code [14]. But the speed of a distributed database system has so far proved to be bound by the speed of the underlying databases. The use of demand-driven streams has not yet shown to be a significant effect on the speed of the overall system.

8 Conclusion

The STALKS project aims to demonstrate the rapid prototyping of distributed knowledgebases using concurrent logic languages. In this paper it was argued that concurrent logic languages can be viewed as generalised decision table languages. The use of decision table languages to manage databases has a long pedigree. In the early 1960's The Insurance Company of North America produced a decision table system to manage a large complex file system [3]. In

1962 the Systems Group of CODASYL introduced the decision table language DETAB-X [8]. It was intended for programming file management and was designed to supplement and be compiled into COBOL. The language was never implemented, but a subset called DETAB/65 became the most widely successful decision table language. More of the history of decision table languages can be found in [24]

There is a multitude of possibilities to extend the scope of the system so far developed under the STALKS project. For example, there is no need for the data repositories used by the system to be restricted to relational DBMS's. Interfaces to other forms of database, including deductive and object-oriented databases, could be provided in much the same vein as the work of Howells et al. If the databases underneath a STALKS system are sufficiently complex to justify the term "knowledge base" then the knowledge of the STALKS system will constitute a form of metaknowledge. Thus the STALKS project could be expanded to include multiagent system technology. For example, the metaknowledgebase could constitute an arbitration mechanism such as a contract-net for different expert systems.

It must be acknowledged that advances in information systems science, particularly the rapid rise in networking facilities, has resulted in many projects designed to provide information across local area, and even wide area, networks. Systems such as WAIS [19], and gopher [17] are designed to allow world-wide access to data. Concurrent logic languages appear to offer the potential of introducing reactive AI capability at the metadatabase level. That is, AI techniques for database decision making on the fly can easily be developed. At the very least, what the STALKS project provides is a platform for prototyping multi-knowledgebase management systems with relatively little programming effort.

References

1. H. Abelson and G. Sussman. *The Structure and Interpretation of Computer Programs.* MIT Press, 1985.

2. M. M. Astrahan, M. W. Blasgen, D. D. Chamberlin, K. P. Eswaran, J. N. Gray, P. P. Griffiths, W. F. King, R. A. Lorie, P. R. McJones, J. W. Mehl, G. R. Putzolu, I. L. Traiger, B. W. Wade, and V. Watson. System R: Relational approach to Database Management. *ACM TODS*, 1(2):97–137, June 1976.

3. L. M. Brown. Decision table experience on a file maintainance system. In *Proceedings of the Decision Tables Symposium*, pages 75–80. ACM, 1962.

4. P. Bunemann and E. Clemons. Efficiently monitoring relational databases. *ACM TODS*, September 1979.

5. S. Ceri, G. Gottlob, and L. Tanca. *Logic Programming and Databases.* Surveys in Computer Science. Springer Verlag, 1990.

6. S. Ceri, G. Gottlob, and G. Weiderhold. Efficient database access through Prolog. *IEEE Transactions on Software Engineering*, February 1989.

7. K. L. Clark and S. Gregory. Parlog: Parallel programming in logic. *ACM TOPLAS*, 8:1–49, 1986.

8. CODASYL Systems Group. *Preliminary Specifications for a Decision Table Structured Language*, 1962.

9. D. Cohen, M. M. Huntbach, and G. A. Ringwood. Logical Occam. In P. Kacsuk and M. Wise, editors, *Implementations of Distributed Prolog*. Wiley, 1992.

10. D. Cohen and G. A. Ringwood. Stalks reports 1-4 - the first two years. Technical Report 614, QMW Department of Computer Science, August 1992.

11. E. W. Dijkstra. Cooperating sequential processes. In F. Genuys, editor, *Programming Languages*, pages 43–112. Academic Press, 1968.

12. C. Draxler. *Accessing Relational and Higher Databases Through Database Set Predicates in Logic Programming Languages*. PhD thesis, Universität Zürich, 1991.

13. J. Grant and J. Minker. The impact of logic programming on databases. *Communications of the ACM*, 35(3):66–81, March 1992.

14. D. Gudeman, K. De Bosschere, and S. K. Debray. jc: An efficient and portable sequential implementation of janus. In K. Apt, editor, *Proceedings of the Joint International Conference and Symposium on Logic Programming*, pages 399–413, Washington, USA, 1992. The MIT Press.

15. A. Guttman. R-trees: A dynamic index structure for spatial searching. *SIGMOD Record*, 14(2):47–57, 1984.

16. D. I. Howells, N. J. Fiddian, and W. A. Gray. A source-to-source meta-translation system for database query languages - implementation in Prolog. In P. M. D. Gray and R. J. Lucas, editors, *Prolog and Databases*. Ellis Horwood, 1988.

17. Interop. The Internet Gopher. *ConneXions*, July 1992.

18. T. Irving. A generalized interface between Prolog and relational databases. In P. M. D. Gray and R. J. Lucas, editors, *Prolog and Databases*. Ellis Horwood, 1988.

19. B. Kahle. An information system for corporate users: Wide Area Information Servers. Technical Report TMC-199, Thinking Machines, April 1991. Available via anonymous ftp: /pub/wais/doc/wais-corp.txt@quake.think.com
Also in ONLINE Magazine, August 1991.

20. T. Kazic, E. Lusk, R. Olson, R. Overbeek, and S. Tuecke. Prototyping databases in Prolog. In L. S. Sterling, editor, *The Practice of Prolog*. MIT Press, 1990.

21. R.-M. Kung, E. Hanson, Y. Ioannidis, T. Sellis, L. Shapiro, and M. Stonebraker. Heuristic search in database systems. In L. Kerschberg, editor, *Expert Database Systems*. Benjamin/Cummings, 1984. Proceedings of the 1st International Workshop on Expert Database Systems, Kiowah, SC, October 1984.

22. P. J. Landin. A correspondence betweeen Algol 60 and Church's Lambda-Notation, Parts i and ii. *Communications of the ACM*, 8(2 and 3), 1965.

23. R. Lucas. *Database Applications using Prolog*. Ellis Horwood, 1988.

24. J. R. Metzner and B. H. Barnes. *Decision Table Languages and Systems*. Academic Press, 1977.

25. C. Mierowsky, S. Taylor, E. Shapiro, J. Levy, and M. Safra. The design and implementation of Flat Concurrent Prolog. Technical Report CS85-09, Weizmann Institute, 1985.

26. M. Minsky. A framework for representing knowledge. In P. H. Winston, editor, *The Psychology of Computer Vision*. McGraw-Hill, New York, 1975.

27. M. T. Ozsu and P. Valduriez. *Principles of Distributed Database Systems.*

Prentice-Hall, 1991.

28. D. S. Parker. Stream data analysis in Prolog. In L. S. Sterling, editor, *The Practice of Prolog*. MIT Press, 1990.

29. Quintus Computer Systems Inc. *ProDBI Users' Guide and Reference Manual*.

30. G. A. Ringwood. Metalogic machines: a retrospective rationale for the Japanese fifth generation. *The Knowledge Engineering Review*, 3(3):303–320, 1988.

31. G. A. Ringwood. A comparative exploration of concurrent logic languages. *The Knowledge Engineering Review*, 4(4):305–332, 1989.

32. G. A. Ringwood. Predicates and pixels. *New Generation Computing*, 7:59–80, 1989.

33. D. C. Tsichritzis and A. Klug. The ANSI/X3/SPARC DBMS framework report of the study group on database management systems. *Information Systems*, 1:173–191, 1978.

34. K. Ueda. *Guarded Horn Clauses*. DEng dissertation, University of Tokyo, 1986.

35. R. Venken and A. Mulkers. The interaction between BIM-Prolog and relational databases. In P. M. D. Gray and R. J. Lucas, editors, *Prolog and Databases*. Ellis Horwood, 1988.

36. P. H. Winston. *Artificial Intelligence*. Addison-Wesley, 1977.

Viewing Objects

Peter J Barclay and Jessie B Kennedy

Computer Studies Dept., Napier University
219 Colinton Road, Edinburgh EH14 1DJ

Abstract. This paper examines the incorporation of database views into an object oriented conceptual model. An approach is presented where views are themselves objects, instances of view classes. These view objects provide new ways of interacting with preexisting data; no new objects are required to populate the view. Although this approach requires no new concepts to be added to the object oriented data model, a large category of views may be realised. These views allow (parameterisable) specification of their populations, and may be arranged in hierarchies; the objects they contain may be decomposed or combined, and may have properties added or hidden. The views presented maintain the integrity of the underlying object model, and allow updating where appropriate. A prototype implementation of a data management system supporting such views is described briefly.

1 Introduction

This paper presents an approach to database views consistent with a generic object oriented data model. Section 2 reviews database views, and their incorporation in object oriented approaches. Section 3 overviews the object oriented data model used. Section 4 shows how a wide category of views can be realised without need of new modelling constructs. Section 5 addresses the use and maintenance of views, describing briefly one implementation. Section 6 concludes with a discussion, a comparison with related work, and some directions for future research.

2 Background

2.1 Database Views

ANSI/SPARC have defined a three-level architecture of database description [Jar76] where the topmost 'external' level represents a collection of subschemata[1] appropriate for particular database users. The central 'conceptual' level provides a comprehensive overall déscription of the enterprise modelled. Since some users may work at this conceptual level directly, it might be considered a special case of a view of the data — the most complete view. The views at the external level are abstractions over this base.

Views help manage the intellectual complexity of interacting with the data, by hiding unnecessary detail and presenting information in the most appropriate format;

---

[1] More accurately, these are alternative schemata which may be derived from the conceptual schema or some subset of it.

further, they may provide a level of security where only the information allowable to certain users will be present in the views which they use.

A view is sometimes defined as a query, but is perhaps better thought of simply as a database schema and its extension. Since for the user of a view, the view schema provides the most comprehensive overall description of the data as she knows it, the term 'notional (conceptual) schema' will be used here to mean a schema describing the data as if the view it represents were the central conceptual level. The term 'implementing schema' will be used for the schema which shows how the notional view schema is abstracted from the base conceptual schema. This implementing schema corresponds to the queries in the 'view as query' perspective.

2.2 Views in an Object Oriented Context

Views have been well investigated in the relational context (*eg* [Dat87, chapter 8]). However, developments such as object oriented database systems [Dit88], [Oxb88], [ABD+89], [GJ89], [Kho90], [ZM90b], [ZM90a] and database programming languages [Atk78], [Bun84] (including persistent programming languages [ABC+83], [ABC+84], [Coc82], [Coo90]) require development of the concept of a view beyond that found in the relational model.

Programming languages have incorporated various notions of data abstraction [Gut77], [MP88] which have been realised in constructs such as the packages of Ada [Bar82], [alr83]. Data abstraction is central in the class concept of object oriented programming languages [SB85], [Sau89] such as Simula [BDMN79], Smalltalk [GR83] and C++ [Str87], [BG93]. Although some object oriented database systems such as Postgres have been based on extensions of the relational model [pos90], [Sto87], others such as Gemstone [BMO+89] and ONTOS [ont90] have been based closely on such object oriented programming languages. However, the programming language notions of data abstraction are often insufficient for database views since the latter requires the notions of population — a subset of preexisting objects are to participate in the view. Further, databases frequently require multiple coexisting abstractions over the same data.

So far, views have been little supported in object oriented database systems (some exceptions are reviewed in section 6.2). Whereas relational views may hide or create attributes in tables, objected oriented views must hide or create behaviour as well as structure. Further, they should not violate encapsulation, and should interact felicitously with the inheritance graph and the composition graph of the underlying model. Some approaches to object oriented views (*eg* [HZ90]) have involved the creation of new objects to populate the view; this gives rise to various problems in assigning identity [KC86] to these 'imaginary' objects.

3 NOM — The Napier Object Model

This section reviews briefly the object oriented modelling context within which views will be explored.

3.1 A Conceptual Object Oriented Model

NOM (the Napier Object Model) is an object oriented data model based on the modelling approach described by the authors in [BK91]. The basic aim of NOM is to provide a simple, 'vanilla' object data model for the investigation of issues in object oriented modelling. The model is more biased towards expressivity for semantics capture than towards efficient implementation.

NOM has been used for the analysis of novel database application areas [BK92a], and for the investigation of specific modelling issues such as declarative integrity constraints and activeness in object oriented data models [BK92b].

3.2 NOODL — the Napier Object Oriented Data Definition Language

NOODL (Napier Object Oriented Data Definition Language) is a data definition and manipulation language based on the textual notation used in [BK91]. A brief summary only is given here; further detail will be introduced later through examples. A complete description of NOODL may be found in [Bar93].

A NOODL schema consists of a collection of class definitions; each definition pertains to one particular class of object appearing in the domain modelled. Each class is named, and its ancestors (superclasses) cited. The properties of the class are named and defined, and their sorts given. NOM blurs any distinction between 'attributes' and 'methods'; the term 'property' is intended to cover both. Properties declared without definition represent stored values, those declared with definition represent computed values. The definition of a property may be an arbitrary query.

The names of properties may serve as messages to get and set the corresponding values; such messages are called *gettors* and *settors* respectively, and are distinguished simply by the absence or presence of the new value. For example, the expression x.name returns the name of the object x, and x.name("Inyan Hoksi") sets the value of the name property of x to be "Inyan Hoksi".

Operations[2] which may be suffered by instances of the class, and integrity constraints to which they are subject, are also specified in each class definition. A simple example of a NOODL schema is shown in figure 1.

4 Object Oriented Views

4.1 An Approach to Object Oriented Views

The basic technique used here to create any desired view is to create a class of objects, instances of which represent the view itself. The operations of this class provide a site for the various queries defining how the view is derived from the base. No new objects are created to populate the view; the same populations are simply viewed differently, through the new operations. This approach circumvents the problems of assigning identity to imaginary view objects, and facilitates updatability.

---

[2] Properties are simple characteristics of an object, representing a (notionally) stored value; operations represent the more complex behaviour of an object, are parameterisable and represented by arbitrarily long sequences of query expressions.

In the following sections, three classes of views are treated separately: selection-views, projection-views, and join-views[3]. Any general view may be a combination of these three categories, which are treated separately for clarity of exposition.

A selection-view does not change the 'shape' of the data, but hides the existence of those instances which do not meet the selection criterion ; the selection criterion thus specifies the *population* of the view. A projection-view reshapes instances of individual classes; objects may lose some properties they possess in the base, and (despite the name 'projection') may also gain new properties not specified in the base. A join-view may aggregate together objects which are separate in the base, or disaggregate single base objects into fragments in the view.

Such views can be specified (and implemented) entirely at the conceptual level, using NOODL. For simplicity of exposition, the example base schema shows only properties; operations can be treated similarly. (Operations are however used extensively in the *implementation* of the example views).

4.2 Example

In this section an example of a NOODL schema is presented which will serve as the base for the views developed subsequently (figure 1). This schema corresponds to the 'conceptual level' of the ANSI/SPARC architecture. Exact NOODL syntax is sometimes altered slightly for clarity of exposition.

This schema describes a fragment of an enterprise involving employees and other people, and the departments the former work for. The domain declaration introduces Location as an enumerated domain, containing only the values specified. These are taken to be all the locations with which this enterprise is concerned.

The schema shows that a person has a name, of sort Text (an arbitrary collection of alphanumeric and formatting characters), and a date of birth (dob) of sort Date[4]. An integrity constraint is that any living person must have been born after the beginning of 1880 and not later than the current date.

An employee is a sort of person, having the properties of a person above, together with its own direct properties wage, of sort Money, and dept, of sort Department. The line \ staff means that staff, defined in the Department class, is the obverse[5] property to dept defined in the Employee class.

Finally, a department is shown to have a name (of sort Text), a location (of the enumerated sort Location), and some staff; the sort of the staff property is a set of Employees, denoted # Employee.

4.3 Selection Views

In order to create a selection-view, it is necessary to hide the existence of any objects which do not meet the selection criteria. Such objects must not be found when

---

[3] Although these names follow relational terminology, there are some differences between these categories and the relational equivalents; these are indicated as they arise.

[4] This is essentially an abstract data type (defined elsewhere) with appropriate operators to support date arithmetic.

[5] By 'obverse' is meant the intuitive inverse of a set-valued property — see [BK91] or [Bar93].

```
domain Location is ("Edinburgh", "Paris", "Athens", "Reykjavik")

class Person
properties
   name : Text ;;
   dob  : Date ;;
constraint
   reasonable_age  is
      "1-Jan-1880" < self.dob and self.dob <= Today.date ;;

class Employee
ISA Person
properties
   wage : Money       ;;
   dept : Department
        \ staff       ;;

class Department
properties
   name     : Text         ;;
   location : Location      ;;
   staff    : # Employee
            \ dept          ;;
```

Fig. 1. Example NOODL Schema (Base)

traversing class extents, must not be returned by queries, and must not be created by database updates.

This is achieved by defining operations on the view which represent these filtered extents; these can be thought of as virtual classes, but do not introduce new sorts into the model. Then operations are defined on the view to represent the properties as in the base, but which hide the existence of any unwanted objects. The necessary steps are itemised below.

- Create a class to represent the selection-view itself.
- Define operations on the view class to return the extents of the data classes in the base, filtered by the selection criterion.
- Define operations to represent all properties returning objects not affected by the selection criterion; these are (trivially) defined as in the base.
- Define operations representing those properties returning objects affected by the selection criterion; these evaluate the properties as defined in the base, and then either return the result or a substituted fail value, depending on whether the selection criterion is met.
- Define operations to represent settors for properties not affected by the selection criterion; these are (trivially) defined as in the base.
- Define operations to represent settors for properties affected by the selection criteria; these invoke the settors defined in the base if the criteria are met, otherwise abort.

For example, consider a selection-view which limits the population of the viewed data to only those departments located in Edinburgh or Reykjavik, and only those persons born after the beginning of 1960. A notional conceptual schema for such a view is shown in figure 2; The NOODL schema which actually implements this view in terms of the base is shown in figures 3 and 4.

```
domain Location is ("Edinburgh", "Reykjavik")

class Person
properties
   name : Text ;;
   dob  : Date ;;
constraint
   valid_age is
      "1-Jan-1960" < self.dob and self.dob <= Today.date ;;


class Employee
ISA Person
properties
   wage : Money       ;;
   dept : Department ;;
        \ staff        ;;

class Department
properties
   name     : Text         ;;
   location : Location     ;;
   staff    : # Employee
            \ dept          ;;
```

Fig. 2. Notional Schema for Selection View

Figure 3 shows the definition of the virtual classes. These are defined using the NOODL where-clause, which returns a set containing those values of the specified set meeting the specified condition. The virtual classes SV_person, SV_employee and SV_department will generally have smaller extents than the corresponding real classes Person, Employee and Department in the base.

Note that parameterised view extents as described in [AB91] are easily implemented in this approach. For example, if the extent of class Person had been defined in the view by:

```
SV_person Date d : # Person is
   Person where its.dob > d          ;;
```

99

then all persons born after the beginning of 1960 would be represented by
SV_person("1-Jan-60"); similarly, all persons born after, say, the beginning of
1940, would be SV_person("1-Jan-40"). This parameterisation produces an infinite number of virtual classes, although of course only finitely many of them will be
populated. Figure 3 also shows gettors for the selection-view; where a gettor would
return a value not meeting the selection criteria, it is substituted for a fail value.

```
domain Namable is Person or Department

class SV { selection-view }
operations

   { class extents }

   SV_person     : # Person is
     Person      where its.dob > "1-Jan-60"                    ;;
   SV_employee   : # Employee is
     Employee    where its.dob > "1-Jan-60"                    ;;
   SV_department : # Department is
     Department where its.location in ("Edinburgh", "Reykjavik") ;;

   { gettors }

   SV_name Namable pd : Text is pd.name  ;;
   SV_dob  Person p : Date is
      if p.dob > "1-Jan-60" then
         p.dob
      else
         bottom { fail value }          ;;
   SV_wage Employee e : Money is e.wage  ;;
   SV_dept Employee e : Department is
      if e.dept.location in ("Edinburgh", "Reykjavik") then
         e.dept
      else
         bottom { fail value }          ;;
   SV_location Department d : Text is
      if dept.location in ("Edinburgh", "Reykjavik") then
         dept.location
      else
         "error - I don't exist!"       ;;
   SV_staff Department d : # Employee is
      d.staff where its.dob > "1-Jan-60" ;;

{ bottom is NOODL universal fail value }
```

Fig. 3. Implementing Schema for Selection View (Extents and Gettors)

```
{ selection view settors }

SV_set_name Namable pd, Text n is pd.name(n)      ;;
SV_set_dob Person p, Date d is
    if d > "1-Jan-60" then
        p.dob(d)
    else
        error("selection view update violation")  ;;
SV_set_wage Employee e, Money w is e.wage(w)      ;;
SV_set_dept Employee e, Department d is
    if d.location in ("Edinburgh", "Reykjavik") then
        e.dept(d)
    else
        error("selection view update violation")  ;;
SV_set_location Department d, Location l is
    if l in ("Edinburgh", "Reykjavik") then
        d.location(l)
    else
        error("selection view update violation") ;;
SV_set_staff Department d, # Employee se is
    d.staff(se where its.dob > "1-Jan-60")        ;;
```

Fig. 4. Implementing Schema for Selection View (Settors)

Figure 4 shows the definition of settors appropriate to the view; it is the responsibility of the view designer to ensure that they maintain value-closure [HZ90]; that is, that they do not create objects which cannot exist in the view.

4.4 Projection Views

In a projection-view, the shapes of the data objects are altered; they may gain or lose properties.

For example, consider a view where class Person is hidden, as are the wage and dob properties of an employee. To show how a class may also gain properties not defined for it in the base[6] the class Employee gains a property age derived from the hidden base property dob. The location property of class Department is hidden.

Figure 5 shows the notional conceptual schema which would describe this projection-view. The schema actually implementing this view over the base (as defined in figure 1) is given in figure 6. The steps to create a projection-view are itemised below.

- Create a class to represent the projection-view itself.
- Define operations to return the (full) extents of those data classes in the base which appear in the view.
- Define operations to represent gettors for all properties in the base appearing in the view. No gettors are defined for those properties which are to be hidden.

---

[6] This could be termed an 'accretion-view'

```
class Employee
properties
   name : Text    ;;
   age  : Number  ;;
   dept : Department
       \ staff   ;;

class Department
properties
   name      : Text  ;;
   staff     : # Employee
             \ dept  ;;
```

Fig. 5. Notional Schema for Projection View

(For consistency, any properties which return objects belonging to classes which are hidden in the view should themselves be hidden).
- Define operations representing those gettors for properties defined in the view but not present in the base.
- Define operations to represent settors for properties present in both the base and the view; these are (trivially) defined as in the base.
- Define operations to represent settors for properties present in the view but not the base (where possible).

Where classes or properties are hidden in a view, it is the responsibility of the view designer to ensure that type-closure is maintained [HZ90]; that is, all the sorts mentioned in operation signatures appearing in the view schema must be provided in the view.

4.5 Join Views

A 'join-view' is a view in which separate base objects may be aggregated into single view objects, or single base objects may be disaggregated into separate view objects. Despite the name, relational-style join operations will often be unnecessary since links between objects will be encoded in the schema; that is, finding them requires navigations rather than searches (see [Bar93, chapter3]). The steps necessary to construct a join-view are itemised below:

- Create a class to represent the join-view itself.
- Define operations to return the extents of those data classes which appear in the view. Where objects of several base classes are aggregated, a virtual class derived from the extent of one of these will serve to represent the aggregation. Where base objects are disaggregated, several virtual classes derived from the same base class will be used.
- Define operations to represent gettors for properties of data classes appearing in the view without (dis)aggregation; these are (trivially) defined as in the base.

```
class PV { projection-view }
operations

   { class extents }

   PV_employee   is Employee   ;;
   PV_department is Department ;;

   { gettors }

   PV_name Namable pd    : Text is pd.name                          ;;
   PV_age Employee e     : Number is (Today.date - e.dob) div 365 ;;
   PV_dept Employee e    : Department is e.dept                     ;;
   PV_staff Department d : # Employee is d.staff                    ;;

   { settors }

   PV_set_name Namable pd, Text n pd.name(n)                        ;;
   PV_set_dept Employee e, Department d is e.dept(d)                ;;
   PV Department d, #.Employee se is d.staff(se)                    ;;
```

Fig. 6. Implementing Schema for Projection View

- Define operations to represent gettors for properties of objects suffering (dis)aggregation in the view; these gettors will incorporate queries containing the necessary navigational or search expression.
- Define operations to represent settors for properties of data classes appearing in the view without (dis)aggregation; these are (trivially) defined as in the base.
- Define operations to represent settors for properties of objects suffering (dis)aggregation in the view; this will involve inverting the query expressions to update the correct object in the base.

As an example, imagine that some users have a view in which person and department objects are not present; instead, each employee has as a direct property the name, size and location of the department for which she works. The notional schema describing this view is shown in figure 7. The schema actually implementing this view is shown in figure 8.

The properties dept_name, dept_size and location of an employee are implemented by delegation to the appropriate associated instance; this is similar to the technique Neuhold and Schrefl calls 'message-forwarding' [NS88]. Note that it is possible to update the dept_name and location properties, but not the dept_size property.

Since in an object oriented model information will often be contained in navigation paths which in the relational model would require a join, it may be expected that a wider class of views will be updatable. However, updatability still relies on being able to invert the derivation function, so for example 'statistical summary' views will not in general be updatable.

```
class Employee
properties
   name       : Text   ;;
   dob        : Date   ;;
   wage       : Money  ;;
   dept_name  : Text   ;;
   dept_size  : Number ;;
   location   : Text   ;;
```

Fig. 7. Notional Schema for Join View

```
class JV { join-view }
operations

   { class extents }

   PV_employee is Employee                          ;;

   { gettors }

   PV_name      Employee e : Text   is e.name                ;;
   PV_dob       Employee e : Date   is e.dob                 ;;
   PV_wage      Employee e : money  is e.wage                ;;
   PV_dept_name Employee e : Text   is e.dept.name           ;;
   PV_dept_size Employee e : Number is e.dept.staff.cardinality ;;
   PV_location  Employee e : Text   is e.dept.location        ;;

   { settors }

   PV_set_name      Employee e, Text n   is e.name(n)              ;;
   PV_set_dob       Employee e, Date d   is e.dob(d)               ;;
   PV_set_wage      Employee e, Money m  is e.wage(m)              ;;
   PV_set_dept_name Employee e, Text n   is e.dept.name(n)         ;;
   { department size not updatable since it is a "statistical" function }
   PV_set_location  Employee e, Text l   is e.dept.location(l)     ;;
```

Fig. 8. Implementing Schema for Join View

The semantics represented are that changing the department name of an employee represents a change in name of the department; all others employees of the department will 'see' the change, since the one object to which they all delegate the get-name message is the only object actually modified. If updating the department name of an employee were to mean transferring the employee to a different department, then the gettor could still be defined appropriately. The view designer must establish the intended semantics of such an update.

In general, it is the responsibility of the view designer to ensure that update operations provide equivalence-preservation [HZ90]; that is, that they provide the correct changes in the base to provide the intended update in the view.

If objects in the base are to be disaggregated in the view (*ie* really it is an 'unjoin-view'), this may be accomplished in a similar manner. If a class Lorry has properties representing information both about the motor and the trailer of the lorry, two new classes Motor and Trailer may be defined if these are to be disaggregated in the view. In fact, both classes have the same extent, the same as the extent of Lorry, but properties relating to the motor or the trailer specifically are defined only on the appropriate virtual class in the view. In this way one class in the base is split into two virtual classes in the view.

5 Using and Maintaining Views

5.1 Interacting with Data Through a View

Another way of thinking of a view is as an interface between some data and some programs; even the interactive manipulation of viewed data by a user requires some program (a browser or query engine) to access the data, and so may be considered in the same way.

To use a view, an instance of the view class must be created; let it be called myview. Then the extent of class Person under this view is represented by the NOODL expression myview.MV_person(), and the name of object x under the view by myview.MV_name(x). Instead of sending the message to the data object as in the base (x.name), the message is sent to the view itself, with the data object as parameter. The tag MV_ shows in which view these messages are defined. Of course, if desired, any program accessing these view operations may rename them, eliminating the view identifier tag so that in the local name space of the program these names correspond to those in the base; for clarity the tagged forms will be used here. (Similarly, the operations could be locally redefined to be applied to the data objects themselves rather than to the view).

Calling the place where a program looks for the persistent data to which it binds a *binding space*, then to use a view a single instance of the view-class is created and placed in this binding space. The operations on persistent objects under this view are then available as the operations, parameterised by these objects, on the view object itself.

5.2 View Evolution

Views should provide logical data independence; this enforces a separation of an individual's view of the data from the community view. The alteration of one view of the data should not impact on any other view of the data (unless of course the latter is a higher level view based on the changed view). Since views are represented as objects defined within the enterprise schema, alteration of a view may be considered as a schema evolution [BCG+87]. In general, where preexistent instances of persistent classes do not require to be modified, evolution may be supported relatively easily;

where instances do require modification, techniques such as conversion, screening [BMO+89], lazy evolution [Owo84] or partial evolution [Bar93] are required. However, since views as presented here do not require the creation of any new database objects other than the ones representing the views themselves, in any implementation the modifications required by a view evolution should be only of the former, more straightforward kind.

5.3 GNOME — a Generic Napier Object Model Environment

GNOME (Generic Napier Object Model Environment) is a software system to support the construction of data intensive applications in the persistent programming language Napier88 [DCBM89], [MBCD89]. GNOME is based on the software construction approach described in [Bar93]. GNOME contains a schema compiler which allows the automatic generation of the Napier88 structures necessary to represent data described in NOODL, providing an active interface to the data [Day88] and enforcing integrity constraints. Although Napier88 is not an object oriented programming language, GNOME supports the development of applications in Napier88 based on an object oriented data design. Data modelling [Mul92], [Gol92] and *ad hoc* querying tools are under construction, and facilities of management of data evolution are planned.

GNOME created the necessary infrastructure to represent an enterprise described in NOODL. Collections representing class extents and procedures, the application[7] of which represent sending messages to objects, are made available to applications which interact with the data. The actual physical data structures are hidden behind this interface, providing first order information hiding [CW85]. These access procedures are placed in a Napier88 environment [Dea88], which constitutes the binding space between the persistent data and the applications. The automatically created binding space contains a complete realisation of the conceptual level description of the data.

This presentation of object oriented views has focussed on their incorporation into a conceptual model. However, since no new constructs are required for the realisation of the object oriented views described in section 4, GNOME immediately provides an implementation for these views without need for modification; similarly, the use of such views adds flexibility and usability to GNOME. The semantic checking which GNOME provides for NOODL schemata ensures that these views are well-formed. It is planned to experiment with some substantial case studies of view-implementation.

6 Conclusion

6.1 Discussion

An approach has been described where views themselves are represented as objects. There is not a general class 'View'; rather, a class is defined for each view required, showing how the view is derived from the base schema. An instance of this view

---

[7] Despatching over class to execute the correct local code is handled by the GNOME infrastructure.

class then is an object which can mediate access to the database, presenting the underlying data as required by the view.

Views can be used in the construction of other, higher level views. One interesting possibility arising from the representation of views as objects is the construction of view hierarchies. This would be particularly useful where a number of views are in use, corresponding to varying levels of detail, or varying levels of security.

The main disadvantage of this approach is the need to introduce a class for each view which has but a single instance, which may seem contrived from a conceptual viewpoint. On the other hand, such one-instance classes can provide other useful functions such as providing structure for enterprise models [Bar93, chapter 4].

6.2 Related Work

Connor *et al* have presented a technique for using the existential types [MP88] of Napier88 to construct strongly typed multiple coexisting abstractions over the same persistent data [CDMB90]. This provides a mechanism similar to database views, although it focuses only on what are here termed projection-views. Since there is no notion of inheritance in Napier88, these views are not object oriented. Connor *et al*'s work develops a particular way of using Napier88, in contrast with the work reported here which uses Napier88 as the implementation vehicle for a particular semantic model.

Neuhold and Schrefl have described a system based on message forwarding [NS88] where a knowledge base management system attempts to deduce and construct a personalised view of data based on a user's attempts to query it. This work focuses on techniques to realise such a personalised view, rather than on basic issues of view definition.

Shilling and Sweeney have described extensions to the conventional object oriented paradigm which support the construction of views in a software development environment [SS89]. Multiple copies of instance variables are available to support versioning, and a system implemented in C++ resolves references to these by methods. Unlike in the work reported here, a 'view instance' is taken to signify a particular activation of a view with a corresponding set of values of the instance variables.

Views in an object oriented database are outlined by Mariani in [Mar92]. These views have a relational flavour; a mechanism is shown where views can be represented by classes defined using selective inheritance.

Mamou and Medeiros describe 'hyperviews' [MM91]. A software system constructs a view, given the schema which defines it and a query which establishes its population; a graphical interface to the view can then be constructed. Mamou and Medeiros's focuses on the presentation and manipulation of data through views, rather than on view definition.

Abiteboul and Bonner present an approach to views which centres on specifying the populations of the view [AB91]; this work focuses heavily on type-inference, relieving the user of the need to specify the position of the view classes within the class hierarchy (view classes are virtual classes integrated into the conceptual level description, rather than a self-contained alternative description). Since the approach used involves creating new objects, fixing the identity of these is problematical.

Heiler and Zdonik present the only work aimed at realising views without the need for new constructs in the data model. Data abstraction through views is examined [HZ88], the important criteria of value-closure, type-closure and equivalence-preservation are introduced, and the use of views to support the federation of heterogeneous databases is discussed [HZ90].

Richardson and Schwartz introduce 'aspects', which provide a convincing solution to allowing objects to have multiple, independent rôles within a strongly typed model [RS91]. Aspects provide new interfaces to existing objects, and hence could be adapted as a view mechanism. However, providing a new view of a schema would involve creating a new aspect instance for each object populating that schema.

None of the above have emphasised investigation of the extent to which the potential to support views is inherent in a representative 'vanilla' object model. The work reported in [AB91] and [HZ90] is the most similar to that reported in this paper. However, the approach of both of these papers allows the creation of new objects to populate views, raising problems of fixing identity. Neither has represented views themselves as objects, which not only integrates views well into the basic object model but also allows the construction of hierarchies of views (see section 6.1). None of the other work has identified and treated the three issues of populating a view, restructuring objects in a view, and aggregating or disaggregating objects in a view respectively through the (extended) concepts of a selection-view, projection-view and join-view.

6.3 Further Work

Some case studies of view-implementation in real-world applications remain to be investigated.

By careful construction of settors it has often been possible to create updatable views; a detailed investigation of updatability in object oriented views is merited (including object creation within views, which for brevity is not discussed in this paper). Such an investigation might identify useful standard approaches to updatability, guaranteeing equivalence-preservation, and relieving the designer of some of the effort of crafting the settors.

An interesting and unexplored area is the automatic derivation of views, in the sense of generating the implementing schema from the notional view schema and the base schema. It is hoped that a GNOME tool will be developed from exploration of this idea.

7 Summary

A proposal for the representation of views in an object context has been presented; the approach followed should be possible in any objected oriented model or system which allows the definition of parameterisable operations on user-defined classes. Since no constructs are added to the model used specifically for the support of views, this work demonstrates that the potentiality for views of useful sophistication is inherent in many object oriented models and systems.

Examples have been given of how view populations may be specified, how objects gain and lose properties in the view as compared to in the base, of how base objects may be aggregated or disaggregated in the view, and of how appropriate update operations may often be defined. Multiple views may be defined over the same base, and views may be arranged into hierarchies.

No new objects are created in view populations, obviating problems of assigning identity. Views of objects interact safely with the generalisation and aggregation structures of the model, and with explicit integrity constraints. A system supporting such views is briefly described.

References

[AB91]   S Abiteboul and A Bonner. Objects and Views. In *proc ACM SIGMOD conference (SIGMOD Record)*, pages 238 – 247, June 1991.

[ABC⁺83] MP Atkinson, PJ Bailey, KJ Chisholm, WP Cockshott, and R Morrison. An Approach to Persistent Programming. *Computer Journal*, 26(4), 1983.

[ABC⁺84] MP Atkinson, P Bailey, WP Cockshott, et al. Progress with Persistent Programming. In Stocker, editor, *Databases - Role and Structure*. Cambridge University Press, 1984.

[ABD⁺89] M Atkinson, F Bancilhon, D DeWitt, K Dittrich, D Maier, and S Zdonik. The Object Oriented Database System Manifesto: (a Political Pamphlet). In *proc DOOD*, Kyoto, Dec 1989.

[alr83]   *A Reference Manual for the Ada Programming Language*. US Government (ANSI/MIL-STD 1815 A), 1983.

[Atk78]   Malcolm P Atkinson. Programming Languages and Databases. In *proc VLDB 4*, pages 408 – 419, Berlin, Sep 1978.

[Bar82]   John GP Barnes. *Programming in Ada*. Addison Wesley, 1982.

[Bar93]   Peter J Barclay. *Object Oriented Modelling of Complex Data with Automatic Generation of a Persistent Representation*. PhD thesis, Napier University, Edinburgh, 1993.

[BCG⁺87] J Banerjee, H-T Chou, JF Garza, W Kim, D Woelk, and N Ballou. Data Model Issues in Object Oriented Applications. *ACM Transactions on Office Information Systems*, 5(1):3 – 26, Jan 1987.

[BDMN79] GM Birtwistle, O-J Dahl, B Myhrhaug, and K Nygaard. *Simula Begin*. Van Nostrand Reinhold, New York, 1979.

[BG93]   Kenneth Barclay and Brian Gordon. *Developing Object Oriented Software in C++*. Prentice Hall, 1993.

[BK91]   Peter J Barclay and Jessie B Kennedy. Regaining the Conceptual Level in Object Oriented Data Modelling. In *proc BNCOD-9*, Wolverhampton, Jun 1991. Butterworths.

[BK92a]   Peter J Barclay and Jessie B Kennedy. Modelling Ecological Data. In *proc 6th International Working Conference on Scientific and Statistical Database Management*, Ascona, Switzerland, Jun 1992. Eidgenossische Technische Hochschule, Zurich.

[BK92b]   Peter J Barclay and Jessie B Kennedy. Semantic Integrity for Persistent Objects. *Information and Software Technology*, 34(8):533 – 541, August 1992.

[BMO⁺89] R Bretl, D Maier, A Otis, J Penney, B Schuchardt, and J Stein. The Gemstone Data Management System. In W Kim and FH Lochovsky, editors, *Object-Oriented Concepts, Databases, and Applications*, 1989.

[Bun84]   P Buneman. Can We Reconcile Programming Languages and Databases? In Stocker, editor, *Databases - Role and Structure*. Cambridge University Press, 1984.

[CDMB90] Richard Connor, Alan Dearle, Ron Morrison, and Fred Brown. Existentially Quantified Types as a Database Viewing Mechanism. Technical report, University of St Andrews, 1990.

[Coc82] W Paul Cockshott. *Orthogonal Persistence*. PhD thesis, University of Edinburgh, 1982.

[Coo90] Richard Cooper. *On The Utilisation of Persistent Programming Environments*. PhD thesis, University of Glasgow, 1990.

[CW85] Luca Cardelli and Peter Wegner. On Understanding Types, Data Abstraction, and Polymorphism. *Computing Surveys*, 17(4), Dec 1985.

[Dat87] CJ Date. *An Introduction to Database Systems*. Addison-Wesley, 1987.

[Day88] Umeshwar Dayal. Active Database Management Systems. In *proc 3rd International Conference on Data and Knowledge Bases*, pages 150 – 169, Jerusalem, Jun 1988.

[DCBM89] Alan Dearle, Richard Connor, Fred Brown, and Ron Morrison. Napier88 - A Database Programming Language? In *proc DBPL 2*, 1989.

[Dea88] Alan Dearle. Environments: A Flexible Binding Mechanism to Support System Evolution. *22nd International Conference on Systems Sciences*, 1988.

[Dit88] KR Dittrich. Advances in Object Oriented Database Systems. *Lecture Notes in Computer Science*, 334, 1988.

[GJ89] MA Garvey and Michael S Jackson. Introduction to Object Oriented Databases. *Information and Software Technology*, 31(10), Dec 1989.

[Gol92] Craig Goldie. An Object Oriented Schema Compiler. Technical report, Napier University, Edinburgh, 1992.

[GR83] A Goldberg and D Robson. *Smalltalk-80: the Language and its Implementation*. Addison-Wesley, May 1983.

[Gut77] John Guttag. Abstract Data Types and the Development of Data Structures. *CACM*, 20(6), Jun 1977.

[HZ88] Sandra Heiler and Stanley Zdonik. Views, Data Abstraction and Inheritance in the FUGUE Data Model. In *proc 2nd Workshop on Object Oriented Database Systems*, pages 225 – 241. Springer Verlag, 1988.

[HZ90] S Heiler and S Zdonik. Object Views: Extending the Vision. In *proc 6th International Conference on Data Engineering*, pages 86 – 93. IEEE Computer Society Press, 1990.

[Jar76] DA Jardine. *The ANSI/SPARC DBMS Model*. North-Holland Pub. Co., 1976.

[KC86] S Khosafian and GC Copeland. Object Identity. In Norman Meyrowitz, editor, *proc OOPSLA*, pages 406 – 416, Portland, Oregon, September 1986.

[Kho90] S Khoshafian. Insight into Object Oriented Databases. *Information and Software Technology*, 32(4):274 – 289, 1990.

[Mar92] John A Mariani. Realising Relational-Style Operators and Views in the Oggetto Object Oriented Database. Technical report, Lancaster University, Lancaster, 1992.

[MBCD89] R Morrison, F Brown, R Connor, and A Dearle. The Napier88 Reference Manual. Technical report, Universities of Glasgow and St Andrews, Jul 1989.

[MM91] J-C Mamou and CB Medeiros. Interactive Manipulation of Object Oriented Views. In *proc 7th International Conference on Data Engineering*, pages 60 – 69. IEEE Computer Society Press, 1991.

[MP88] John C Mitchell and Gordon D Plotkin. Abstract Types Have Existential Type. *ACM TOPLAS*, 10(3):470 – 502, Jul 1988.

[Mul92] Anthony Mullen. An Object Oriented Modelling Tool. Technical report, Napier University, Edinburgh, 1992.

[NS88]   EJ Neuhold and M Schrefl. Dynamic Derivation of Personalised Views. In *proc 14th International Conference on Very Large Data Bases*, Long Beach, California, 1988.

[ont90]   ONTOS SQL User's Guide. *(ONTOS documentation)*, 12 Dec 1990.

[Owo84]   GO Owoso. *Data Description and Manipulation in Persistent Programming Languages*. PhD thesis, University of Edinburgh, 1984.

[Oxb88]   EA Oxborrow. Object Oriented Database Systems: What are they and what is their Future? *Database Technology*, Jun 1988.

[pos90]   *Postgres Reference Manual (version 2.0)*. University of California, 1990.

[RS91]   Joel Richardson and Peter Schwartz. Aspects: Extending Objects to Support Multiple, Independent Roles. In *proc annual SIGMOD conference*, pages 298 – 307. ACM Press, 1991.

[Sau89]   John H Saunders. A Survey of Object Oriented Programming Languages. *Journal of Object Oriented Programming*, Mar/Apr 1989.

[SB85]   M Stefik and DG Bobrow. Object Oriented Programming: Themes and Variations. *the AI Magazine*, 1985.

[SS89]   John J Shilling and Peter F Sweeney. Three Steps to Views: Extending the Object Oriented Paradigm. In Norman Meyrowitz, editor, *proc OOPSLA*, pages 353 – 361, October 1989.

[Sto87]   Michael R Stonebraker. Extending a Relational Database System with Procedures. In *ACM TODS*, Sep 1987.

[Str87]   Bjarne Stroustrup. *The C++ Programming Language*. Addison-Wesley, 1987.

[ZM90a]   S Zdonik and D Maier. Fundamentals of Object Oriented Databases. In SB Zdonik, editor, *Readings in Object Oriented Database Systems*, San Mateo, Ca, 1990. Morgan Kaufmann.

[ZM90b]   SB Zdonik and D Maier, editors. *Readings in Object Oriented Database Systems*. Morgan Kaufmann, San Mateo, Ca, 1990.

Function Materialization Through Object Versioning in Object-Oriented Databases

T W Carnduff[a], W A Gray[b]

[a] Cardiff Institute of Higher Education and University of Wales College of Cardiff

[b] University of Wales College of Cardiff

Abstract. This paper discusses function materialization for features of objects in object-oriented databases, and identifies its role in design databases. Drawbacks with the present approaches are discussed and a new approach to this materialization is presented, which has been implemented in prototype form. In a tentative and iterative engineering design environment, function materialization is seen as a useful optimization technique for designers. As design artefacts develop, they evolve through a succession of versions. Our new approach to materialization involves creating a function materialization object to hold a pre-computed set of results for a function. Dependencies between function materialization objects and component objects are represented, so that changes to component objects will cause new versions of dependent function materialization objects to be created. A configuration manager maintains consistent groupings of complex design objects and their corresponding materialized function objects in dereferenced monolithic versions.

1 Introduction

We have been investigating the application of object-oriented database systems to a particular area of engineering design, namely ship design [CAR92]. Most published work on advanced database support for CAD seems to concentrate on VLSI design which, although sharing much in common with other engineering design applications, is unrepresentative in some ways. One prominent characteristic of the classes developed for our ship design class library is that class features are predominantly behavioural, that is to say that the majority of the features are implemented as functions. Some class function implementations in our application library entail substantial processing involving, for example, repeated polynomial function integration and complex geometrical analysis. Computational re-evaluation of such functions can be avoided by storing result values.

The engineering design process is both iterative and tentative, and during the early stages of a design, the engineer will be "feeling his way", exploring alternatives and establishing the general suitablity of design fragments by means of coarse boundary condition parameter evaluation. When the calculated boundary conditions for a design fragment are found to be within acceptable limits, the next iteration of the "design spiral" (figure 1) may take place. As the designer moves closer to the centre of this spiral (the completed design), he/she is less likely to accept time penalties associated with complex functional evaluation, particularily if these calculations have not been invalidated by changes in the design. The approach presented in this paper as a means of overcoming the processing bottleneck that can result from such re-evaluation, is function materialization associated with object versioning.

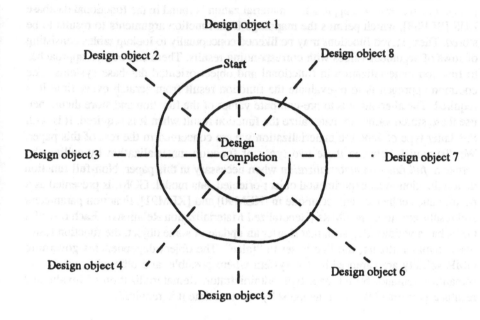

Fig. 1. Design Spiral after [BUX72]

2.1 A Review of Materialization in Databases

In a database, materialization is the process by which a predefined computation on the data such as a view or a function, is carried out before or when a user requires it. In relational systems this was primarily carried out for views. References to the materialization of relational views have appeared with some frequency in recent database literature and in [ADI80], "snapshots" were described. A database snapshot captures on disk 'the state of a database at a particular time instant. The content of a snapshot may be defined in terms of a database query in a manner similar to view definition, except that the snapshot so defined, does not reflect a dynamic situation. Instead a snapshot captures a static copy of the database. Later papers [BLA86, HAN87, BLA89] explore the initial materialization and subsequent update of frequently accessed relational views. Extended relational models have been developed which support procedural attributes. For efficient access, these query attribute results may be materialized (caching) and [STO87, HAN88, JHI88] describe storage and update considerations in these situations.

The POSTGRES database system is a well-developed example of an extended relational data model in which a rules system permits, amongst other things, an alternative and more powerful means for expressing views and procedural data types. Caching of the action part of rules may be used as a performance enhancement for view materialization and precomputation of procedural data items in such a system [STO90]. An alternative approach to materialization is found in the functional database IRIS [BEE88], which permits the mappings from function arguments to results to be stored. These stored functions may be likened conceptually to lookup tables consisting of rows of argument values with corresponding results. There can be two approaches to function materialization in functional and object-oriented database systems. The common approach is to re-evaluate the function result from scratch every time it is required. The alternative is to pre-compute values of the function and store them, then use these stored values to materialize the function result when it is required. It is with this latter type of function materialization we are concerned in the rest of this paper. We distinguish between these two types of function materialization by calling the former a *full function materialization* when necessary in this paper. Non-full function materialization in an experimental object-oriented data model, GOM, is presented as a performance enhancement technique in [KEM90] and [KEM91]. Function parameters and results are stored in GMRs (Generalized Materialization Relations). Each row of a GMR has a validity flag such that if after an update of some object, the function result needs rematerializing, the flag is set to "false". The object dependencies governing GMR validity are captured by the system where possible, and otherwise, where the semantics demand, by the data type administrator. Rematerialization of invalidated results is performed lazily, at the latest by the next time it is required.

2.2 Function Materialization and CAD Databases

The materialization of a function in GOM, provides for only one set of results to be held. If these results are invalidated by an update to the database, the subsequent rematerialization will cause a new set of calculated results to replace the previous set. This situation is inappropriate to an engineering CAD environment where the evolution of design objects is managed through versioning, since if a design object is updated in some way, then this change is reflected in a new version of the object. If this update invalidates the materialized results of a function encapsulated within a design object, then provided this function is still required in materialized form, the results must be recalculated. However, versioning can mean the original design object maintains its reference to the original materialized function object and the new design object version uses the new materialization. Thus both versions of the materialized result are required, and in a real design situation, many versions may be required. This situation is not supported by the GOM approach.

3 Function Materialization in the Design Environment

This section explores the purpose and use of function materialization in a design environment where the design objects (artefacts) produced, pertain to engineering design as characterised in CAE (computer-aided engineering).

3.1 Functions in the Object-Oriented Paradigm

In this paper an object type consists of both attributes and routines. Attributes are references to objects and routines include both procedures and functions, where a procedure is a special form of function which does not return a value. A function returns a value of either basic type, e.g. boolean, integer, real, or an instance of any type, that is an object or at least a reference to an object. Functions may or may not have input parameters, of basic or user-defined type.

3.2 Function Materialization

Function materialization is the means by which pre-calculated function results may be stored and accessed in a database. Thus the result from a materialized function is returned through access to its pre-stored results. The motive for function materialization is to reduce the time taken to return the result after a function call compared with a full function materialization. This is particularily relevant if repeated calls are made with the same parameter values. However, there will inevitably be a storage cost and an access cost. If, for example, we materialize a function with several input parameters, each of which has a large number of potential values, the resulting materialization object will occupy a large amount of store, and gains will only occur if the function is evaluated more than once with the same parameter values. The database user (a design engineer), must be aware of this overhead and should weigh up the relative storage(cost) *vs* time(benefit) before undertaking function materialization. Relative time gains to the user may occur if lazy evaluation is used in the materialization.

3.3 Engineering Design Information Modelling and Environment

The particular focus of our research is on MCAD (mechanical computer-aided design) as opposed to ECAD (electrical computer-aided design). MCAD spans realms as diverse as civil engineering [KAO91, REE91], architecture and structural engineering [ANN91, FEN90, FOR89, GAR87, MIL88], mechanical engineering [KUT83] heavy engineering [BAN75, BIR86, BRO89, OOR88, XIA85, XUE89], and aerospace [JOH84]. It is apparent that there are many common functional areas between the various branches of MCAD, for example structural analysis, geometrical modelling and the determination of statical and dynamic factors, most of which involve the undertaking of substantial design calculations.

Engineering design is a tentative process involving experimentation, during which alternative versions of design components evolve and develop. Many design calculations occur in the formative initial analysis stage of the design lifecycle, when successive versions of the design fragments under analysis are frequently produced. It is these function results that are often reused in the later stages as the designer iteratively generates new versions. Thus within such a design process, there is a need to be able to access and recover different versions of the design fragments in a reasonable time frame.

Engineering design components are necessarily complex in terms of both structure and semantics. This complexity can lead to substantial processing overheads for object function evaluation. Consider, for example, a three-dimensional geometric object which consists of a set of disjoint, recursively-defined, three-dimensional geometric objects. A function returning the volume of such a design object must determine the sum of the volumes of each of its constituent subobjects. If the lowest level subobjects are irregular in shape and the calculation of their volume requires for example, repeated polynomial integration using an algorithm such as Romberg's integration method [PRE86], the processing task can be substantial. We can add an extra level of semantic complexity to this situation by considering a function which returns the volume of the object up to a certain vertical distance above its base, i.e. *volume_to_depth(d)*, where *d* is the input parameter expressing the required depth. This function would be defined recursively in much the same manner as that described for the volume function, except that in this case, the actual parameter for depth must be locally translated for each of the constituent subobjects.

An experienced design engineer would have some feel for the critical values of this depth parameter and would, in examining various alternative object versions, evaluate the *volume_to_depth* function for coarse boundary values of the actual parameter for each of the alternative design objects in the initial design analysis. Having decided upon an acceptable design version from the alternatives based on the *volume_to_depth* function results and other factors, he/she would then proceed into the next iteration of the design spiral. However, although such a designer would be willing to pay the processing cost of function evaluation in the outer iterations of the design spiral, he/she would expect much better response in subsequent iterations, particularily if this required reuse of previous function evaluation. This is not unreasonable once a design version has been chosen for further development. The means of supporting this expectation is function materialization where, for our example, a re-implemented *volume_to_depth* function would reference an object containing function results tabulated against values of the *depth* parameter ranging between minimum and maximum boundaries. Even if there are minor changes in the parameters, such users want reasonably fast responses, and this is best supported by using techniques within the function materialization such as, for example, interpolation and extrapolation in the case of continuous functions.

4 Design Object Versioning

Various schemes for design object versioning within an object-oriented database have been proposed [AHM91, BEE88, BIL90, CHO86, ECK87, KAT90, KIM90, ZDO86]. Our version model is based on an amalgam of the schemes described in [AHM91, KAT87 and KIM90], and assumes that versioning and complex object configuration should not be part of the kernel object management system, but should be added via a class library. This position is defended in [FON91] on the grounds that change management is not appropriate to all applications, and it follows, that through the extendibility offered by the object-oriented paradigm, the application implementor may modify the functionality supplied by this class library as required.

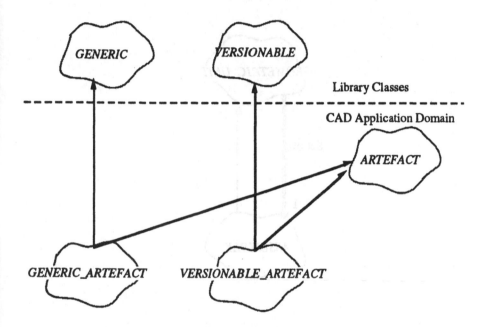

Fig. 2. Class Inheritance Graph for Design Object Versioning

Figure 2 shows the class inheritance graph used to achieve design object versioning. The *GENERIC* class provides a version history mechanism and a means of referencing each version within a design object version set. Access to each version object (instances of the class *VERSIONABLE_ARTEFACT*) can be made by direct reference, a so-called statically bound reference, or via the generic object (instance of the class *GENERIC_ARTEFACT*) for a design object, as a dynamically bound reference. For each of the design object versions the generic or abstract design object contains information on version numbers, for example a count of versions and a default version number to be used to resolve dynamically bound references. A version tree in the generic object maintains the version history and required binding to individual object versions.

In addition to describing the structural and behavioural features of a design artefact, every design object version contains a version number, the version number of its parent version and the object identifier of its generic object. Design objects are usually complex in structure, consisting of versioned component objects, which may in turn be complex objects. This necessitates the identification of design object configurations, where a configuration is a complex versioned object whose components are specific versions. In our model, configuration identifiers are represented in both generic and versioned objects.

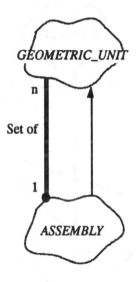

Fig. 3. Class Relationship Graph for *ASSEMBLY*

Figure 3 shows a class relationship graph for the classes defining a three-dimensional geometric object (notation according to Booch [BOO91]). We can see that this object, which will be referred to as the assembly object (instance of the class *ASSEMBLY*), consists of a set of geometric units (instances of the class *GEOMETRIC_UNIT*). To limit the complexity of the example we will assume that each of the geometric objects is a direct instance of the class *GEOMETRIC_UNIT*, although as can be seen in figure 3, the class *ASSEMBLY* is recursively defined. Figure 4 shows the class relationship graph extended to permit versioned geometrical units and assemblies for this design situation.

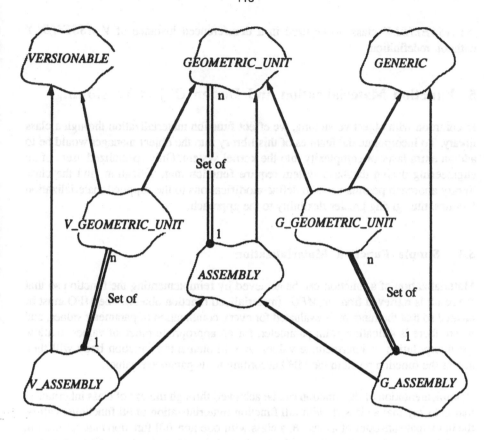

Fig. 4. Class Relationship Graph for Versioned Assembly

If we have several versions of the assembly and several versions of each of the
geometric units, we require configuration management facilities to group a single
assembly version with a set of identified, versioned, geometric unit objects. Thus
assembly version 1 could be grouped in a configuration (number 1) of geometric units
such as version 3 of a spheroid object, version 2 of a prismatic object and version 1 of
a cylinder object. Each of these four objects has a configuration attribute value of 1.
However, the versioned assembly in the configuration is dynamically bound to its
constituent versioned geometric units via an attribute with a set of references to
generic geometric objects as its value, that is a set of dynamically bound references. It
is necessary to remove this extra level of indirection in a configuration in order to
make it useful to the designer. The outcome of this operation is what we call a
composite configuration, or *monolithic version.* The monolithic version of the
assembly contains a corresponding attribute whose value has been transformed into a
set of statically bound references to versioned geometric units. This dereferencing
operation allows the implementation of functions such as *volume_to_depth,* defined in

the *ASSEMBLY* class, to be used in a dereferenced instance of *V_ASSEMBLY* without redefinition.

5 Function Materialization and Design Object Versioning

In common with object versioning, we effect function materialization through a class library. To incorporate the features of this library into the object manager would be to add an extra layer of complexity into the kernel system. Only specialized users of an engineering design database system require function materialization, and the class library approach permits users to define modifications to the supplied materialization facilties, thus giving greater flexibility to the approach.

5.1 Simple Function Materialization

Materialization of a function can be achieved by reimplementing the function so that the result is retrieved from an *MFO* (materialized function object). The MFO must be created so that the function is evaluated for every combination of parameter values, and where there is a floating point parameter, for an appropriate range of values to allow for interpolation of intermediate values. A reimplemented function body will then access the function result in the MFO according to its parameter values.

Reimplementation of the function can be achieved through the use of class inheritance, that is to say that a class *A* with full function materialization of all functions, will be the immediate ancestor of a class *B*, a class with one non-full function materialization, which has an unchanged public interface and a redefined function body. Given the class *B*, should we wish to non-fully materialize a further function then we need only define a new subclass of *B* with a redefined function implementation. An instance of class *B* is a version of an instance of class *A*, as versions can be defined [CHO86] as objects that share the same interface but have different implementations.

5.2 Change Management and Rematerialization

A function result will be dependent on the function's parameter values (which may be objects), and other objects referenced within the body of the function. We contend that the generic dependencies should be specified explicitly by the user (e.g. that the volume of a sphere is dependent on its radius), rather than attempting to have the database system automatically record them, upon first materialization of a function. The reason for this is that we wish to avoid the redundant representation of non-existent dependencies which may have been inferred by the system (e.g. that the volume of a sphere is dependent on its colour). The intended user of the function materialization features presented in this paper, is a computerate design engineer, who understands very well the underlying generic dependencies which exist between and within the artefacts in the design domain.

To continue with our geometrical example, if we assume that the volume of a prismatic (box-shaped) object is defined by the three orthogonal dimensions length, breadth and height, then the function *volume_to_depth* and hence its MFO, is dependent upon *length*, *breadth*, and *depth*. The *volume_to_depth* MFO is called the *dependent* and the two dimensions *length* and *breadth* are known as *components*. The function parameter *depth* is not treated as a component as its actual value is variable for a single prism object. An MFO depends on its components. The example given above is a direct dependency, but other dependencies may be transitive. For example, to materialize another function *weight_to_depth(d)*, where *d* is the input parameter expressing the required depth, the function is implemented in its fully materialized form by the expression:

```
volume_to_depth(d) * substance.density
```

Here *substance* is an attribute of the prism which represents the material from which the prism is made. The *weight_to_depth* MFO is transitively dependent on the *volume_to_depth* MFO. The system resolves this dependency into a direct dependency between *weight_to_depth* and the components of *volume_to_depth*, namely *length* and *breadth*. The *weight_to_depth* MFO is also directly dependent on the *substance* component.

It is necessary to express these dependent-component relationships to effect change management. If the value of a component in a dependent-component relationship changes, then its dependent MFO becomes invalid and must be rematerialized. However, the context of our treatment of function materialization is that of design object evolution through versions. If we change the value of the *length* component in our prismatic artefact, we do not discard the old artefact, rather we derive a new version from it and hold both versions in the database. The consequence of this is that the previous version of the artefact should use its own MFO for function evaluation and the new version of the artefact should access the newly materialized MFO. This type of situation can be accommodated relatively easily by arranging that the MFOs are versionable, i.e. descendants of class *VERSIONABLE*, so that when a component change results in MFO invalidation, the resulting rematerialization invokes an MFO version derivation.

This facility is achieved by implementing the materialized function so that it refers to a generic version of the MFO, by means of a dynamic reference. The generic version of the MFO for a particular function maintains, in common with every generic version, a version history and a default version identifier. To avoid every artefact version referring to the same MFO version (the default version) at any given instant, the dynamically bound references to MFOs must be replaced by statically bound references. This can be achieved through the facilities of version configuration management, where each MFO is identified with an artefact configuration and may be statically bound to the configuration as part of a monolithic version.

We will now evolve the 3-dimensional assembly object described in section 4 as consisting of spheroid, prismatic and cylindrical geometric units. Figure 5 documents this evolution through several versions of this object, where new versions have resulted from function materialization. If we refer to the assembly object as the *assembly* and its constituent geometric units as the *units* then, considering the assembly functions *volume_to_depth* and *weight_to_depth*, the dependencies are as follows. The volume_to_depth MFO is directly dependent on the dimensions of each of the units and their z (vertical) coordinates. The weight_to_depth MFO is transitively dependent on the volume_to_depth MFO and on the *substance* attribute of each of the units. Figure 5 details the evolution of new versions of both the assembly and the MFOs for volume_to_depth and weight_to_depth. It should be noted that for simplicity, the only unit explicitly named in the figure is the spheroid object. This changes its size between assembly version 2 and assembly version 3. Sphere 1 and sphere 2 are, of course, different versions of the same spheroid unit, however, our simplified diagram does not show the version or configuration identities of units. In fact, we contend that changes in subobjects should not automatically generate new versions in a parent, complex object. The decision as to whether a change resulting in a new version of a subobject should filter upwards to the next level in the component hierarchy should be left to the design engineer. In our example a new version has resulted, not as a direct result of the change to the spheroid unit, but because of the invalidation of its volume_to_depth MFO, which has brought about a rematerialization.

Dependent-component relationships are represented by instances of a *MAT_TRIPLE* class, which groups a dependent MFO and a component object with the version number of the materialized artefact to which they belong. Every materialized versionable object and its associated generic version inherit the features of the *MATERIALIZABLE* class, which includes an attribute of type *CHANGE_MANAGER*. The purpose of a *CHANGE_MANAGER* object is:

  * to maintain a set of materialization dependencies (*MAT_TRIPLE* objects),
  * to maintain a set of components that have changed, so that
  * a set of references to dependent MFOs requiring rematerialization, can be built.

Each materialized, versioned artefact maintains its own set of dependency relationship occurences, reflected in the corresponding generic version *CHANGE_MANAGER* attribute, which maintains a set of *MAT_TRIPLE* objects which are the union of the dependency sets for each of the versions referred to in the version history tree. This ensures that all dependency, change management and rematerialization information for a particular artefact version evolution history is maintained centrally, through the generic version for the artefact. Figure 6 shows the set of triples for version 4 of the assembly object represented in Figure 5. This set is combined in the generic assembly version with the corresponding sets of triples for all of the assembly object versions. When the substance in version 4 of the assembly (s′) is changed (to s″), the weight_to_depth MFO (version 1) is invalidated, resulting in a rematerialization with a consequent new MFO version.

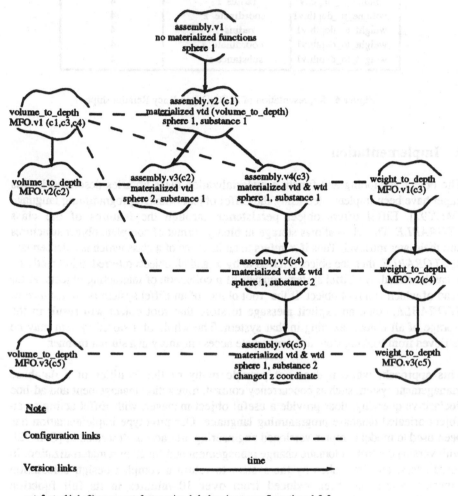

Note

Configuration links − − − − − − − − − −

Version links ⟶ time

artefact.v1(c1,c2) means artefact version 1, belonging to configurations 1 & 2

Configuration 4 of the assembly consists of:
assembly.v5+volume_to_depth_MFO.v1+weight_to_depth_MFO.v2

The assembly objects and their respective MFOs are dereferenced configurations, i.e. monolithic versions.

Sphere 1 & sphere 2 have different radii. Substance 1 & substance 2 have different densities

Fig. 5. Evolution of Complex Object with Materialized Functions

Set of MAT_TRIPLEs for Assembly Version 4

MFO Reference	Reference to Component (attributes of sphere)	Version Number
volume_to_depth.v1	radius r'	4
volume_to_depth.v1	coordinate z'	4
weight_to_depth.v1	radius r'	4
weight_to_depth.v1	coordinate z'	4
weight_to_depth.v1	substance s'	4

Figure 6. Representation of MFO Dependency Relationships

6 Implementation

The object versioning and function materialization class libraries described in this paper have been implemented using the Eiffel object-oriented programming language [MEY92]. Eiffel offers object persistence through the features of the class *STORABLE*. This class allows storage in binary format of complete object structures and their later retrieval. Thus if x refers to an instance of a class which is a descendant of *STORABLE*, then the object referred to by x and all objects referred to indirectly by x can be stored. An Eiffel system consists of a collection of interacting objects, at the head of which is a root object. If the root object of an Eiffel system is an instance of *STORABLE*, then an explicit message to store that root object will result in the storage of all objects existing in that system. The whole of a stored system may be retrieved from backing store into immediate access memory in a similar manner.

This approach, while it does not provide many of the facilities of a database management system such as concurrency control, transaction management and ad-hoc declaritive querying, does provide a useful object manager, with Eiffel acting as an object-oriented database programming language. Our prototype implementation has been used to model complex versioned engineering artefacts as described in [CAR92], with version control, automatic change management and function rematerialization. In some cases, the time taken by the system to return a complex design calculation function result, has been reduced from over 10 minutes in its full function materialization form, to microseconds for the non-full function materialization version of the function implementation.

7 Conclusions

In this paper we have presented function materialization as an optimization technique for use in object-oriented engineering design databases. Non-full function materialization involves the reimplementation of function bodies to access precomputed results stored in materialized function objects. Dependencies between function results and objects used to determine these results or components, are captured so that should one of these components change, a rematerialization of dependent functions can be instigated.

Our approach to rematerialization is fundamentally different to that presented in the GOM system [KEM90, KEM91], due to the context in which we see function materialization being used. Engineering design artefacts evolve through discrete versions, such that a version set represents the complete development history of an artefact. Each artefact version containing one or more materialized functions has its own MFO(s). If an artefact is changed, this will result in a new version of the artefact, and, if appropriate, a rematerialization of the relevant functions. These new MFOs will be versions of the predecessor artefact version MFOs. MFO versions are statically bound to their corresponding artefact versions via a configuration management operation which produces monolithic versions of the artefact. The GOM approach allows for only one version of a generalized materialization relation (the equivalent of our MFO), and a great deal of effort is involved in representing and dealing with the invalidation of this relation.

Initial function materialization and subsequent rematerialization can be eager (immediate) or lazy (deferred), according to the needs of the designer. If eager materialization is not itself to cause a processing bottleneck similar to that which it was designed to cure, it should be carried out as a background task, but it should be borne in mind that the resulting MFO will not be available until the calculation of function results is complete. Alternatively, lazy materialization may be preferred and could take place when calls on the database system are few. As highlighted in section 3.2, there is a considerable storage penalty associated with our approach, both as a result of object versioning and storage of precalculated function results. Ultimately, the choice of whether or not to materialize a function, and whether this materialization and subsequent rematerialization is carried out immediately or is deferred, must lie with the user.

We believe that function materialization and object versioning are best represented using class libraries so that database system users who do not require these particular features are spared the complexity and overhead that may be introduced by incorporating function materialization and object versioning in the kernel database system. The class library approach, also permits the user to modify and extend the facilities presented in these libraries.

References

ADI80
Adiba, M E; Lindsay, B G; Database Snapshots, *Proc. Conf. on Very Large Data Bases (VLDB)*, IEEE, 1980, pp 86-91.

AHM91
Ahmed, Rafi; Navathe, Shamkant; Version Management Of Composite Objects In CAD Databases, Clifford & King, *Proc. of Int. Conf. On Management Of Data (SIGMOD 91)*, ACM, Denver, 1991, pp 218-227.

ANN91
An-Nashif, H N; Powell, G H; An Object-Oriented Algorithm for Automatic Modelling of Frame Structures: Stiffness Modelling, *Engineering With Computers*, 1991, 7, pp 121-128.

BAN75
Bandurski, A E; Jefferson, D K; Enhancements To The DBTG Model For Computer Aided Ship Design, *Proc. ACM Workshop on Databases for Interactive Design*, ACM, 1975, pp 17-25.

BEE88
Beech, D; Mahbod, B; Generalized Version Control In An Object-Oriented Database, *Proc. 4th Int. Conf. on Data Engineering*, IEEE, 1988, pp 14-22.

BIL90
Biliris, Alexandros; Modelling Design Object Relationships In Pegasus, *IEEE Int. Conf. on Data Engineering*, IEEE, 1990, pp 228-236.

BIR86
Biran, A; Kantorowitz, E; vShip Design System Integrated Around a Relational Database, Eds. Keramidas & Murthy, *Computer-Aided Design of Marine and Offshore Structures (CADMO 86)*, Springer-Verlag, Berlin, 1986, pp 85-94.

BLA86
Blakely, J A; Larson, P et al; Efficiently Updating Materialized Views, Ed. Zaniolo, *Proc. ACM SIGMOD 86 Conf.*, ACM, 1986, pp 61-71.

BLA89
Blakely, J A; Coburn, N et al; Updating Derived Relations: Detecting Irrelevant and Autonomously Computable Updates, *ACM Transactions on Database Systems*, 1989, 14, 3, pp 369-400.

BOO91
Booch, Grady; Object-Oriented Design With Applications, Benjamin/Cummings, Redwood City, Ca, 1991.

BRO89
Bronsart, R; Lehmann, E; A Datamodel for Ship Steel Structures, Eds. Lin, Wang, & Kuo, *Proc. of Int. Conf. on Computer Applications in the Automation of Shipyard Operation and Ship Design (ICCAS VI)*, North-Holland,1989, pp 237-246.

BUX72
Buxton, I L; Engineering Economics Applied to Ship Design, *Transactions RINA*, 1972, 114, pp 409-428.

CAR92
Carnduff, T W; Gray, W A; An Eiffel Class Library for Ship Design, Eds. Heeg, Magnusson & Meyer, *Proc. of Int. Conf. Technology of Object-Oriented Languages and Systems (TOOLS 7)*, Prentice-Hall, 1992, pp 233-245.

CHO86
Chou, H T; Kim, W; A Unifying Framework for Versions in a CAD Environment, Eds. Chu, Gardarin & Ohsuga, *Proceedings Int. Conf. on Very Large Data Bases (VLDB)*, 1986, pp 336-344.

ECK87
Ecklund, Denise J; Ecklund, Earl F et al; DVSS: A Distributed Version Storage Server for CAD Applications, Eds. Stocker & Kent, *Proc. 13th Int. Conf. on Very Large Data Bases (VLDB 13)*, Morgan Kauffmann, Brighton, 1987, pp 443-454.

FEN90
Fenves, Gregory L; Object-Oriented Programming for Engineering Software Development, *Journal of Engineering with Computers*, 1990, 6, pp 1-15.

FON91
Fong, Elizabeth; Kent, William et al ; X3/SPARC/DBSSG/OODBTG= Final Report, Object-Oriented Database Task Group, 1991.

FOR89
Forde, Bruce W R; Stiemer, Siegfried F; Knowledge-Based Control for Finite Element Analysis, *Engineering with Computers*, 1989, 5, pp 195-204.

GAR87
Garrett, James H; Fenves, Steven J; A Knowledge-Based Standards Processor for Structural Component Design, *Engineering with Computers*, 1987, 2, pp 219-238.

HAN87
Hanson, Eric N; A Performance Analysis of View Materialization Strategies, Eds.
Dayal & Traiger, *Proc. ACM SIGMOD '87 Conf.*, ACM , 1987, pp 440-453.

HAN88
Hanson, Eric N; Processing Queries Against Database Procedures: a Performance
Analysis, *Proc. ACM SIGMOD '88 Conf.*, ACM, 1988, pp 295-302.

JHI88
Jhingran, Anant; A Performance Study of Query Optimization Algorithms on a
Database System Supporting Procedures, Eds. Bancilhon & De Witt, *Proc. 14th Int.
Conf. on Very Large Databases (VLDB 14)*, 1988, pp 88-99.

JOH84
Johnson, H R; Engineering Data Management Activities within the IPAD Project,
Database Engineering, IEEE Computer Society, 1984, 7, 1, pp 91-99.

KAO91
Kao, Jehng-Jung; Object-Oriented Database for Wastewater Treatment Plant Design,
Eds. Cohn & Rasdorf, *Computing In Civil Engineering and Symposium on
Databases*, American Society Of Civil Engineers, New York, 1991, pp 259-267.

KAT90
Katz, Randy H; Toward a Unified Framework For Version Modeling In Engineering
Databases, *ACM Computing Surveys*, 1990, 22, 4, pp 375-408.

KEM90
Kemper, Alfons; Kilger, Cristoph et al; Function Materialization In Object Bases,
Universitat Karlsruhe, Fakultat Fur Informatik, Karlsruhe, Germany, 1990.

KEM91
Kemper, Alfons; Kilger, Christof et al; Function Materialization In Object Bases, Eds.
Clifford & King, *Proc. Int. Conf. on Management of Data (SIGMOD 91)*, ACM,
Denver, 1991, pp 258-267.

KIM90
Kim, Won; Introduction To Object-Oriented Databases, MIT Press, Cambridge, MA,
1990.

KUT83
Kutay, Ali R; Eastman, Charles M; Transaction Management in Engineering
Databases, *Proc. Engineering Design Applications*, IEEE, 1983, pp 73-80.

128

MEY92
Meyer, Bertrand; *Eiffel the Language*, Prentice Hall, Hemel Hempstead, 1992.

MIL88
Miller, G R; A Lisp-Based Object-Oriented Approach to Structural Analysis, *Engineering with Computers*, 1988, 4, pp 197-203.

OOR88
Van Oortmerssen, G; Van Oossanen, P; A New CAD System for the Design of Ships, Eds. Murthy, Dern and Goodrich, *Marine and Offshore Computer Applications*, Computational Mechanics-Springer Verlag, Southampton, 1988, pp 105-129.

PRE86
Press, William H; Flannery, Brian P et al; Numerical Recipes, Cambridge University Press, Cambridge, 1986.

REE91
Reed, D A; Naeher, F et al; An Object-Oriented Approach to Wind Safety Analysis, Eds. Cohn & Rasdorf, *Computing in Civil Engineering and Symposium on Databases*, American Society Of Civil Engineers, New York, 1991, pp 150-158.

STO87
Stonebraker, Michael; Anton, Jeff et al; Extending a Database System with Procedures, *ACM Transactions on Database Systems*, 1987, 12, 3, pp 350-376.

STO90
Stonebraker, Michael; Jhingran, Anant et al; On Rules, Procedures, Caching and Views in Data Base Systems, *ACM SIGMOD*, 1990, 0, pp 281-290.

XIA85
Xia, Daozhong; An Approach of Integrated DBMS for CAD/CAM and MIS, Eds. Banda & Kuo, *Proc. of Int. Conf. on Computer Applications in the Automation of Shipyard Operation and Ship Design (ICCAS V)*, Elsevier Science, Amsterdam, 1985, pp 265-271.

XUE89
Xue, Zengfeng; Xu, Gang; CAD Databases for Shipbuilding CAD/CAM Integrated Systems, Eds. Lin, Wang & Kuo, *Proc. of Int. Conf. on Computer Applications in the Automation of Shipyard Operation and Ship Design (ICCAS VI)*, North-Holland, 1989, pp 289-293.

ZDO86
Zdonik, S B; Version Management in an Object-Oriented Database, *Proc. of Intl. Workshop on Advanced Programming Environments*, Trondheim, Norway, 1986, pp 405-422.

A C++ Database Interface Based on the Entity-Relationship Approach

Uwe Hohenstein[1] and Erik Odberg[2] *

[1] Siemens AG, ZFE BT SE 33, Otto-Hahn-Ring 6, D-8000 München 83, Germany
[2] Division of Computer Systems and Telematics (DCST), Norwegian Institute of Technology (NTH), N-7034 Trondheim, Norway

Abstract. This paper presents a database interface for C++ that provides an adequate and uniform coupling to different kinds of database management systems. An extended Entity-Relationship approach which is married to object-oriented features is used to provide a common modelling basis. The concepts of the data model are directly reflected by the interface thereby providing an abstract view of data even in the context of access and manipulation. The functionality of the interface ressembles much of current object-oriented database systems.

The essential aspects of the implementation of the interface are elucidated. A layered architecture has been chosen that abstracts from system-specific peculiarities and consequently facilitates putting the interface on several database platforms. The overall architecture convinces by its simplicity and ease of implementation.

1 Introduction

Object-orientation is a recent buzzword, which has successfully conquered several areas in computer science, like programming languages, user interfaces, and database management systems (DBMSs) [20]. Object-oriented programming languages generally provide useful concepts like methods and inheritance, which enables one to profit greatly from encapsulation and late binding. In spite of a large variety of existing languages, C++ [30] has been elevated to de-facto standard, even if it possesses lots of unpleasant properties due to its close relation to C. The relevance of C++ in the field of object-oriented programming languages has also been splashed over to object-oriented DBMSs, which attempt to merge the concepts of object-oriented languages with database capabilities [1]. Although there are some systems like Gemstone [23], which extends Smalltalk, or O_2 [10], which pursues a multilingual interface, the mainstream can be characterized as "persistent C++". This is not meant pejoratively, but actually a lot of systems (cf. [21, 22]) essentially extend the programming language C++ with persistence features.

On the other hand, industry frequently uses conventional DBMSs like hierarchical or network systems. Even relational systems, which undoubtedly mark a milestone in database technology, are employed still rather rarely. This is remarkable because relational systems have reached maturity in the meantime;

---

* The work is partially funded by the EEC's Esprit II program and the Research Council of Norway (NFR-NTNF).

robustness and reliablity are widely accepted in the community. In contrast, object-oriented systems are comparitively in their infancies, and since they do not achieve the same degree of trustworthiness, it is not to be expected that object-oriented systems will supersede all the classical systems entirely. Hence, many companies will not replace their old system with object-oriented ones for the forseeable future. Conventional DBMSs will not lose relevance, they will keep themselves alive even in the era of object-oriented technology.

In this paper, we attempt to accomodate ourselves to the significance of classical DBMSs and C++. We suggest an interface for C++ that allows C++ programs to invoke database functionality given by hierarchical, network, or relational DBMSs. We will call these types of DBMSs *classical* or *platform* systems in the following. Our approach can be seen as a first step to introduce object-oriented technology in classical database systems. With the intention to provide a uniform C++ database interface for classical systems, several points must be taken into account:

- A first problem results from the fact that the platform systems are based upon different data models having quite a dissimilar nature. Furthermore, the systems prefer different kinds of coupling originally. In general, hierarchical and network systems provide couplings to old-fashioned languages like COBOL. Relational systems are more flexible owing to a so-called cursor concept, which could easily be extended to C++. Nevertheless, it is no use providing individual solutions for each type of system. An integrated solution is indispensable.

- Next the systems rely on dissimilar query and manipulation philosophies. Hierarchical and network systems provide navigational access by using some fixed, predefined access paths, while relational systems prefer a descriptive and powerful way of querying and manipulating data. Consequently, different degrees of functionality must be reconciled.

We propose a flexible coupling of C++ with classical systems that does not retain the specific coupling mechanism of the individual platform systems. The above mentioned problems are tackled in the following way. We reap the benefits of the Entity-Relationship (ER) approach. The ER model was invented by Chen [9] in order to provide a meta-model for classical data models. It has successfully been used for describing requirements of later database users during the conceptual design because of its ease of understanding and its convenience in representation. Moreover, it supports a conceptual modelling that does not depend on concrete DBMSs but can easily be mapped to them. All these properties are very useful in our context. One additional advantage is given by the fact that further modelling concepts can be integrated simply (e.g., [13, 14]) without giving up the above nice properties. Following these approaches, we add object-oriented modelling concepts to the original ER model.

We then pass on the modelling concepts to the access and manipulation level thus retaining the higher degree of abstraction. Manipulating and accessing data is completely done on a more abstract level in terms of ER concepts, handling entities and relationships. Moreover, a uniform access to all platform systems is provided that completely abstracts from the platform.

The coupling is done smoothly and entirely fits to C++. We pick up ideas developed for object-oriented systems and adopt them into our approach. The strength of the program interface essentially lies in the fact that handling both persistent and transient data is done only in C++. The overall result behaves like an object-oriented DBMS that has been implemented on top of a platform system. But in contrast to them, we ease the implementation by neither modifying the C++ compiler (as object-oriented systems in general do), nor building a C++ precompiler. We let the C++ compiler do the work as much as possible, for instance, handling aspects like inheritance. Ordinary C++ compilers can be used for coupling.

In the following, we present the essential concepts of the database interface. To lay the foundations for our approach, we first present our extension of Chen's ER model in section 2. The ER model is married with concepts from the object-oriented paradigm [1] like object identity, subtyping and complex objects in the sense of [19].

Section 3 is mainly concerned with the database interface. We present an abstract object-oriented data manipulation facility that corresponds to the data model and provides a comfortable and C++ conforming way to handle data. Essentially, the class concept of C++ is used for a simple but elegant coupling. The database access is provided in terms of methods, called member functions in C++. In addition to features for navigating through the database, the associative query access can be tuned from no support up to powerful associative access known from relational languages. In fact we present two proposals: The first one was implemented in an Esprit project called REBOOT [24] and describes a simple functional approach. The second one is dedicated to relational systems and relies on an SQL-like ER query language passing on the full power of relational SQL to the ER level.

We lay particular stress on easing the implementation effort and flexibility. Section 4 outlines the most important parts of the implementation elucidating the efficiency and simplicity of the approach. Emphasizing the main benefits, there is no need for modifying the C++ compiler. A well-structured and layered architecture makes the database interface portable so that it could easily be coupled with other platform systems. On the other hand, we are relieved of implementing basic functionality for the most part, e.g., concurrency control, recovery mechanisms, and transaction handling, because the architecture takes profit by the platform. Besides the classical systems, a coupling to NF^2 [25, 29], ER, or even object-oriented systems is also possible with low effort owing to the powerful ER approach subsuming their data models. Furthermore, the architecture opens the door to adapt the interface for other programming languages.

We conclude the paper with some remarks about possible improvements and future research topics in section 5.

2 The Data Model

The Entity-Relationship (ER) model [9], since originally proposed as a meta-model for classical data models, is a good starting point to bring these standard models under a common roof. Moreover, several extensions have been proposed enhancing the classical ER model with additional modelling primitives [13, 14]. Most of them also show how to map their ER variant onto the classical data models – investigations we can use for free.

We pick up these ideas and present an extension of the ER model similar to [14, 18, 26, 5]. Particularly we introduce the notions of object-identity, (single) inheritance, set-valued attributes and complex objects, making the data model "structurally" object-oriented [12].

Figure 1 gives an example of a simple schema in a diagrammatic form. The schema models parts of a (reusable) software component and its facet-based classification, i.e., describing a component by several values related to certain classification facets.

132

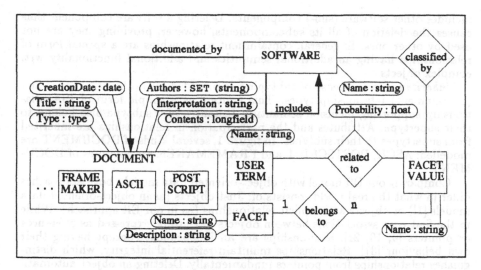

Figure. 1. *Sample ER Schema*

Entity types like SOFTWARE correspond to object types in the object-oriented world. Every object of an entity type possesses an *identity* that is independent of any properties and globally unique in the database.

Properties of objects are described by attributes. In addition to some predefined domains like int and string, *complex domains* are also available for attributes. For example, the entity type DOCUMENT possesses a 'CreationDate' of domain date, a 'Type' denoting the type of a document in form of an enumeration, and a set of 'Authors' given as SET(string). The domain longfield is used for the database representation of a file in the sense of 'binary large objects'.

Associations between objects are represented by relationship types. Relationships are symmetrical and may have attributes. In contrast to objects, relationships do not possess an identity of their own. As there must be at most one relationship (of a given type) between two entities, the identity of relationships can be derived from the objects involved in a relationship. The entity types participating in a relationship type can be given rolenames and cardinalities. Cardinalities restrict the number of maximal instances involved in a relationship, distinguishing between 1:1, 1:n, and n:m relationships in the usual sense. For example, 'belongs_to' denotes a 1:n relationship, requiring every facet value to belong to at most one facet.

Special relationship types called *containment relationship types* support a notion of *complex objects*, i.e., objects that are composed of other (sub-)objects thus getting a complex structure. Containment relationships are very similar to the "owner references" of EXODUS [8]: They are directed from a parent *container* type to a *contained* child entity type, and model a stronger form of association, having a special "propagation" semantics: If an object of a container type is deleted, all the related instances of the contained type are also deleted if not contained by other objects. Sharing on type and instance level is possible. Hence several entity types can share a common contained type, just as several instances (of the same or different types) may refer to the same instance of a contained type. For example, 'includes' is a containment relationship type, graphically represented by a broad arrow. Every object of type SOFTWARE includes other software (sub-) components. Deleting a software component thus causes the deletion of all its subcomponents, however, providing they are not used by other ones. In general, containment relationships are a special form of relationships having an additional semantics and additional functionality wrt. complex objects.

Inheritance in the sense of subtyping is provided for both entity types and (containment) relationship types. This concept is a simple form of ISA relationship supporting inclusion semantics: Instances of a subtype also belong to their supertype. Attributes and the participation in relationships are inherited from supertypes to their subtypes. In figure 1, several kinds of DOCUMENT are modelled: ASCII, POSTSCRIPT and FRAMEMAKER are subtypes of DOCUMENT.

Comparing our ER model with object-oriented data models, both approaches differ in what the real world consists of: Just objects (as in object-oriented data models [1]) or objects and explicit relationships (as in our ER approach). While in the first case associations between objects have to be expressed as references or pointers [4, 10, 21], relationships are an independent concept having their own behaviour [31]. Relationships maintain referential integrity, which distinguishes relationships from pointers fundamentally. Deleting an object automatically deletes all the relationships the object participates in. Dangling pointers are thus avoided. In this regard we agree with [28, 3] who argue that relationships are conceptually higher than just references and should be supported directly.

Naturally, a DDL (*Data Definition Language*) exists that provides a C++-like syntax for defining database schemas. As in object-oriented DBMSs, user-defined methods for entity types can be added to the schema definitions. Implementing the methods must naturally be done in C++. As usual, methods can make use of predefined generic operations described in the next section. For instance, there are elementary functions to insert or delete entities and to establish or remove relationships. Supporting containment relationships furthermore implies to make deep or shallow copies and to propagate the delete operation along the complex objects's structure.

3 The C++ Database Interface

3.1 Basic Idea

The data model provides an abstract view to the data stored in the database. Corresponding to this data model, a database interface has been defined that provides a coupling of C++ programs with classical database systems. C++ programs can use platform database functionality in a comfortable way that smoothly fits to C++. The interface directly reflects the ER view of information on the one hand, and abstracts from the underlying platform on the other hand.

In fact, we have to struggle with the "impedance mismatch", because our data model provides more concepts to model data than can be done in C++. In particular, we attach importance to an explicit relationship concept, while C++ only offers ordinary pointers without any support for referential integrity. Other issues concern complex attribute domains like longfield or set-valued attributes. However, we avoid the impedance mismatch to a large degree, since we directly reflect the ER modelling concepts in C++ by using the class concept.

The simple but fundamental principle of our approach is called *generative* [24]: Given a database schema, several C++ classes are automatically generated, the methods (called member functions in C++) of which yield the database functionality. The resulting classes are called *DML* (*D*ata *M*anipulation *L*anguage) *classes*, because their (generic) functions provide the data manipulation facilities. Each entity type ET and each relationship type RT thus have a corresponding *entity class* ET and *relationship class* RT in C++, respectively. The type hierarchy of the database schema can directly be transferred to the C++ inheritance hierarchy.

As already mentioned before, the entity classes can be enhanced with user-defined methods by using those predefined functions. Those methods will automatically be included in these classes.

Attributes having a domain int or float are directly represented by C++ attributes of their related class. Other attribute domains like string, date, or longfield are mapped to special C++ classes String etc., because these domains are not available in C++. Similarly, set-valued attributes like SET(int) are handled. However, we can use the C++ template concept [30] here that provides parameterized classes SetOf<...>. Instantiating such template classes with a domain like float or an entity type ET yields a corresponding SetOf<float> or SetOf<ET> class.

A C++ class corresponding to the entity type DOCUMENT looks as follows:

```
class DOCUMENT : TYPE
    { Date*          CreationDate; // attributes of DOCUMENT
      Longfield*     Contents;
      SetOf<String>* Authors; ...
      "generic functions (methods) for manipulation"   }
```

Here, the class TYPE is predefined; it works as the common root of all entity types. In case of a subtype, the corresponding supertype replaces TYPE.

The predefined classes like Longfield or templates like SetOf<...> also obtain functions to provide related functionality, e.g., to store a file as a Longfield-value or to iterate over a set. Consequently, all the data manipulation is done through these DML classes.

3.2 Data Manipulation

The generated DML classes, more precisely their generic functions (methods), provide the C++ database interface. We shall explain these functions now in more detail.

The following code gives a short sketch showing usage of the DML interface. Obviously, application programs are not aware of an explicit database language, since all the manipulation is done in pure C++. Hence, no extensions of C++ are made in contrast to as object-oriented DBMSs. The code correctly runs through any commercial C++ compiler.

```
SOFTWARE *sw = new SOFTWARE;            // C++ object            (1)
  sw->Name = new String("MyComponent"); // set attribute value
  sw->MakePersist();                    // insert object into DB

POSTSCRIPT *ps = new POSTSCRIPT;
  ps->Authors = new SetOf<String>;      // insertion into
  ps->Authors->Insert("Uwe");           // set-valued attribute
  ps->Authors->Insert("Erik");          //    'Authors'
```

```
                                              // copy file into Longfield:
ps->Contents->CopyIn("/home/hackers/filename.ps");
ps->MakePersist();

SOFTWARE_documented_by::Insert(sw,ps);   // establish relationship (2)

FACET_VALUE *value = NULL;                // navigation :          (3)
classified_by cursor (sw,value);         // cursor for 'classified_by'
for (cursor.First(); !cursor::EOS(); cursor.Next())
    { cout << cursor.FACET_VALUE->Name;
      SetOf<FACET> *fset =
             belongs_to::Get_Facet(cursor.FACET_VALUE);
      FACET *f = fset->First();          // first (single) element of set
      cout << "for facet " << f->Name << endl;   };
```

The C++ classes corresponding to entity types like SOFTWARE represent the structural properties (attributes) as well as providing the functionality to manipulate persistent objects by means of predefined functions. C++ objects that are C++ placeholders for database objects can be created by applying the C++ operator new. (1) creates two C++ objects, one of type resp. class SOFTWARE and another one of type POSTSRCIPT, and let two corresponding pointer variables sw and ps refer to them. The C++ objects are now transient, they are just containers for database objects and are consequently not stored in the database yet. But objects may be stored in the database by explicitly invoking the MakePersist function. Any persistent object gets a unique object identifier automatically, which is also held in the C++ object for identification. Storing an already existing object can thus be recognized. No identifier is then created, and the object is overwritten in the database.

An entity type can consequently possess both persistent and transient objects at the same time. Ordinary C++ capabilities can be used to handle both. Hence, attribute values can be set, e.g., by applying the C++ dereference operator '->'. Some of the attribute domains like int and float are already available in C++ so that no special treatment is necessary. On the other hand, complex attribute domains are represented by corresponding C++ classes providing the related functionality. For instance, the classes SetOf<domain> possess predefined functions that can be used to insert values into or delete values from such a set-valued attribute. In our example, two authors are inserted into the set-valued attribute 'Authors' by means of Insert. Inheritance takes place the same way as in C++. Hence 'CreationDate' and 'Authors', which both are actually attributes of the supertype DOCUMENT, can be accessed. The class Longfield essentially provides functions to copy a file into an attribute (CopyIn), to copy out into a file (CopyOut), and to check whether an associated file exists (Exist).

Further functions for entity classes are Delete and copy. sw->Delete() deletes the object referred to by sw from the database. However, the C++ representation of the object will still exist, but could be destroyed afterwards by invoking the C++ operator delete. Deleting an object implies the deletion of all relationships it is involved in. Moreover, Delete is a propagating operation, deleting all subobjects in the sense of containment relationships (complex objects). Similarly, operations to produce a DeepCopy (i.e. all the objects building a complex object are copied) and to make a ShallowCopy (copying the object and establishing references to the direct subobjects [1]) are given.

Similar to entity classes, relationship classes reflect the facilities associated with relationship types, mainly to establish and delete relationships between objects. Containment relationship types are handled as ordinary relationship types, but they must be prefixed with the name of the container type in order to avoid ambiguities. (2) inserts a relationship (instance) between the two now persistent objects sw and ps. The participating objects as well as possible attribute values are given as parameters. We are again confronted with inheritance, because the relationship type 'documented_by' really expects the second role to be of type DOCUMENT rather than POSTSCRIPT.

The navigational principle also relies on the concept of relationship classes. In this context, it becomes obvious that relationships are quite different from objects in the model. Although they are also handled through generated C++ classes, the individual relationships are not treated as C++ objects. An instance of a relationship class is not a relationship, but rather a non-persistent *cursor* related to the set of relationship instances in the type extent. The cursor can then be used for navigation. The piece of code (3) demonstrates the principle, printing out the classification of a software component, i.e., its classifying facet values and the facets they belong to. The initialization of a cursor defines what relationships in a type should be traversed: If none of the roles is set, i.e., if the parameters refer to the null pointer NULL, then all the relationships (instances) of the relationship type are fetched. If one role refers to a given object, then all the relationships related with this object are retrieved. And if both roles are set, one relationship (if there is one at all) will be the result. The cursor only contains the first relationship including the participating objects just as the attribute values of the relationship. An access to them is possible, e.g., cursor.FACET_VALUE yields the participating facet value. Cursors can be moved on to the next relationship by the function Next. If the relationship type is exhausted, a special flag EOS is set. For each relationship type, several cursors can be defined.

Instead of navigating through relationships in the aforementioned way, a simpler way is provided by using Get_Role functions. For instance, the function belongs_to::Get_Facet yields all the FACET objects that are related to a given FACET_VALUE object via the relationship type 'belongs_to'. Even more comfort is provided in case of containment relationship types. Here all the contained or containing objects can directly be accessed. As the result consists of a set of objects, the parameterized SetOf<ET> classes are used to handle the resulting objects.

The SetOf<...> templates can be instantiated with attribute domains or entity types. These templates provide the usual set functionality. The ordinary set operations are possible, e.g., compatible sets can be merged or intersected, and the number of instances in a set can be determined by Count. New objects, no matter whether database objects or C++ objects, can be inserted into a set. Existing elements can be deleted, however, not deleting the object itself but only its occurrence in the set. In contrast to ObjectStore [21] or O_2 [10], we do not introduce iterators like 'for each' or 'for x in ...' for traversing sets, because these constructs require a new compiler. We only rely on C++ by just providing a First or Next function to traverse through a set object by object. Exhausted sets are again indicated by the flag EOS.

Comparing the achieved functionality with the one of object-oriented systems, we obtain quite a similar manipulation of data. But we do not rely on the data model of C++ providing a form of "persistent C++", but rather an extended ER approach. In particular, our approach has an advantage by supporting complex objects in the sense of [19], which in spite of being a well-known feature is rather rarely provided. On the other hand, we lose some flexibility because the persistence of objects is strictly related to entity types; it is not possible to make any other C++ objects persistent.

3.3 Querying

It is recognized that both navigational and associative access to the database are important. This complies with experience from systems, where large complex databases are to be handled, e.g., [15]. Our interface provides very flexible functionality to navigate through relationships, returning individual relationships or (sets of) objects which are related to a specific object.

For querying objects from the database, the ET classes possess a Find function. A single parameter of type char* denotes a character sequence that describes a formula being subject to an associative language. This formula specifies a selection condition that restricts the occurrences of the extent of the entity type to all instances satisfying this condition. The actual parameter can be a variable that contains a query specification, thus allowing for dynamic queries that are evaluated at run-time. The result will be a set of instances represented by the class SetOf<ET>.

In the following we are presenting two different proposals for an associative query language. The first one [24] uses a functional and compact notation, which has a more navigational flavour. It only provides some basic functionality. The second approach pays special attention to make extensive use of the capabilities of relational query languages. It follows the SQL style in the sense of ER extensions [17]. Due to an open architecture, further associative query languages can be designed having different degrees of functionality or just different syntactical forms. Generally, the associative capabilities should be brought into line with those of the platform system. The platform naturally should do as much selection work as possible, but otherwise its capabilities should not be exceeded too much.

3.3.1 A Functional Query Approach

We propose an associative language that attempts to adopt the style of C++. This will let the programmer become quickly familiar with the associative language. We have given preference to only basic functionality and a short and compact notation, however, not neglecting readability. Indeed, simplicity is one main characteristic of the first associative language.

We do not provide for aggregate functions like the computation of the minimum or average. Similarly, no arithmetic functions like '+' and '*' are supported. The platform used for implementation in [24] does support neither of them directly. The same would hold for hierarchical or network systems. Thus it would be hard to efficiently implement such functionality. On the other hand, the corresponding computations could anyway be implemented in C++ application programs themselves. Consequently this approach cannot (and does not want to) compete with high-level query languages proposed for the ER model or object-oriented models, like GORDAS [14], O_2 [10], and EXCESS [8].

Some restrictions are obvious due to the embedding of the language in the used C++ frame: There are no join capabilities, because the result of a query is always a set of objects belonging to exactly one entity type. For similar reasons, no projection is provided, but can easily be done in the program by using C++ facilities, as we have seen before.

Let us start with the main principle of the associative language. Each query possesses a natural starting point given by the type associated with the Find statement, i.e., the type whose instances are to be selected. Starting from this type, any relationship that is related to that type can be followed.

Example 1. *Give me all the software components that are documented by a design document written with Framemaker*

```
char* query1 = "documented_by[Interpretation == 'Design' &&
                            Type           == Framemaker ]";

SetOf<SOFTWARE> *result = SOFTWARE::Find(query1);
```

The relationship type 'documented_by' is used to reach DOCUMENT. Given a reusable component, several instances of DOCUMENT are related to it in general. The part within '[...]' then specifies that there must exist at least one related instance of DOCUMENT satisfying the condition "Interpretation == 'Design' && Type == Framemaker". Please note the difference to the syntactically quite similar query

```
"documented_by[Interpretation == 'Design'] &&
documented_by[Type == Framemaker]"
```

which computes *"the set of software components that are documented by both a design document and (another) one written with Framemaker"*.

The result of such an associative query constitutes a set of objects, here represented by the variable **result** of type SetOf<SOFTWARE>. By declaring SOFTWARE *sw and using sw = result->Next(), all objects in the set can be accessed. It is worth mentioning that each entity of the result can be used for further manipulation, for instance to access the 'CreationDate' attribute in the usual way sw->Name.

The square brackets have the purpose of an existential quantifier: One related instance has to satisfy the condition. Similarly, universal quantification is provided by replacing the square brackets with curly brackets '{ ... }': Now every instance has to fulfill the condition.

Comparisons of the form *"attribute Θ value"* are the simplest form of conditions. Indeed the attribute must belong to the corresponding type or to a supertype of it. If the square brackets only contain one such formula, we can replace the square brackets with a dot notation, e.g., documented_by.Type == Framemaker.

Possible comparison operators Θ are '==', '>', '<=', etc. possessing the usual C++ semantics. Special predicates IN (element of) and CONTAINS (subset of) are dedicated to set-valued attributes to compare any two sets. Furthermore, the equality '==' is extended to cover sets. Consequently we are able to distinguish between "documented_by.Authors == {'Erik'}" and "documented_by.Authors CONTAINS {'Erik'}" : The first formula requires exactly one value 'Erik' in the set of authors related to the desired document, while the second condition is satisfied if that set contains at least one author 'Erik'. The typical logical C++ operators like '&&' (And), '||' (Or), and '!' (Negation) can be used to build complex formulas.

Even more complicated formulas can be built by nesting '[...]' and '{ ... }' in any depth. The entity type reached so far defines the scope of a sub-formula. The next query demonstrates the use of nested formulas:

Example 2. *Give me all the reusable components that are classified by a 'Facet1' value that is related to 'userterm' with a probability of 70 %*

```
SetOf<SOFTWARE> *result =
SOFTWARE::Find("classified_by[belongs_to.Name == 'Facet1' &&
                            related_to[Name == 'userterm' &&
                                      Probability > 70 ]]");
```

Here 'classified_by' relates to FACET_VALUE. There should be at least one value that belongs to a facet with the name 'Facet1' and that is related to a USER_TERM 'userterm', the latter relationship having a probability value of 70. Here, attributes of relationship types are involved, too.

A special constant NULL can be used in equations in order to detect NULL values. A similar situation occurs in case of relationship types. Here it may be the case that there does not exist a related object. Again, we use NULL to detect whether there exists a relationship or not.

3.3.2 An SQL-like Query Approach

Our second approach is especially dedicated to relational platform systems. Having an underlying relational DBMS, we would commit a sin by not taking advantage of the relational query mechanism. Consequently, we emphasize associative query facilities passing on the full use of relational SQL to the interface. Deficiencies of querying, often recognized in object-oriented systems, could thus be avoided.

The essential principle of querying given by the Find function is kept. However, the string passed as parameter to Find follows quite a different syntax belonging to a SQL-like associative query language providing the power of SQL at the ER level. To this end, we essentially use the ER query language SQL/EER defined in [17], however, slightly modified and adapted to our data model. Similar to other SQL extensions, like HDBL [25] proposed for a NF^2 data model, this query language supports all the modelling concepts like set-valued attributes and subtyping with inheritance in an adequate manner. Furthermore, concepts like aggregate functions or nesting/unnesting are orthogonally integrated. For instance, we can use the aggregate function cnt in formulas, e.g., we could now select in example 1 only documents having exactly two authors, which is not possible in the functional approach.

Nevertheless, the usage of Find implies that the result of an associative query still constitutes a *set* of objects of a given entity type. This naturally restricts the form of SQL/EER queries to those having a form select x from x in ρ where ϕ, i.e., selecting whole entities. Hence the query possibilities are artificially reduced. Neither projections nor joins are possible.

In order to pass on the full functionality of relational SQL to the querying facility, an extended query mechanism that is more flexible and allows formulating arbitrary queries, is provided:

Example 3. *Select the classification of the software 'my_sw', i.e., for each facet the set of classifying facet values*

```
class Query3 { FACET* facet;                          (1)
               SetOf<FACET_VALUE> *vset; };

char* query3 = "select f , (select fv                 (2)
                    from   fv in FACET_VALUE
                    where  sw classified_by fv
                    and    fv belongs_to f )
               from   sw in SOFTWARE , f in FACET
               where  sw.Name = 'my_sw' "

SetOf<Query3> *result = new SetOf<Query3> (query3);    (3)
```

```
Query3 *tuple = result->First();                            (4)
cout << tuple->facet->Name << endl;
```

Similar to O_2 [10], the first step (1) consists of defining a class Query3 that specifies the structure of each tuple of the result. The C++ class may refer to other classes. Here, each tuple of the result should have two parts, a part facet conatining a facet object and a part vset comprising a set of facet values.

(2) then specifies a query as a string in query3 following an SQL-like ER query language. This query computes the classification of 'my_sw' selecting *"for each facet f and for each software sw a tuple consisting of f and a set of values belonging to the facet f and classifying sw"*. Technically, variables are bound to entity types, e.g., sw in SOFTWARE. However, relationship types and select-from-where blocks are also valid variable ranges. Those declared variables can then be used in terms and formulas. Relationship types can be used as predicates. Indeed, sw classified_by fv requires the component sw be related to the facet value fv via a relationship of type 'classified_by'. Furthermore (sub-) queries of the form select-from-where are special kinds of terms. Thus, they can be used as target terms. This makes the query result *nested* in the sense of NF^2 models ([25, 29]).

Afterwards, invoking the new operator with the parameter query3 starts execution of the query (3). Again, the result of such an associative query constitutes a set of objects (here pairs of values), each now belonging to the class Query3. Owing to the SetOf-template, the resulting set can be represented by the class SetOf<Query3>, yielding the necessary functionality to handle sets. Hence, the result can be accessed via result and handled in the usual way by applying the iterators first and next (4). Please note that we put up with the obvious gap due to a lack of "closeness": The structure of a query result is defined by a C++ class, rather than an entity type following the ER rules. Consequently the result does not consist of entities; it contains several tuples, the parts of which can certainly be entities. The result classes are generally not DML classes and consequently cannot be stored in the database. However, our main goal providing a powerful query facility justifies this disadvantage for the moment.

The structure of the result, given by Query3, must be determined at compile-time. However, the query itself can dynamically be composed at run-time. The correctness of the query, i.e., whether the result of the query matches the class structure can only be checked at run-time due to the dynamic execution of queries. However, it is important that no precompiler is necessary to check the consistency of both owing to the use of the Meta Information Protocol [6]: This tool provides type information about C++ classes at run-time so that a check can easily be done.

4 Implementational Aspects

The design of the database interface presented in the previous section is guided by the overall goal to make the implementation easy and applicable to several platform database systems.

The main strategy is to avoid building a precompiler or extending the C++ compiler for achieving the coupling; just an ordinary C++ compiler is used and is made do as much of the work as possible. This leads to the principle of automatically generating C++ classes to provide the database functionality. Even the extended associative capabilities given by an SQL-like query language and the opportunity to define the structure of query results in form of C++ classes can be integrated in this framework.

In the remainder of this section, we want to investigate the most important aspects of the implementation in more detail elaborating the advantages of the general approach. Subsection 4.1 discusses the generative process, while 4.2 elucidates on how aiming at portability leads to a layered architecture. Figure 2 gives a survey of the architecture and describes the basic constituents needed to be implemented: The *DDL compiler* that generates the DML classes (the interface), and the *Basic Access layer* that performs the mapping onto the platform system and attends to portability. Finally, the openness of the approach is clarified (subsection 4.3).

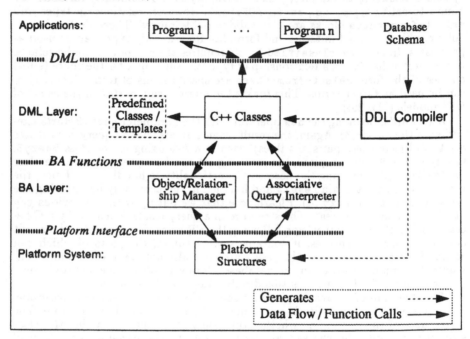

Figure. 2. *Database Architecture*

4.1 Generative Approach

The substantial principle of our approach is given by a mechanism to generate C++ classes for a given database schema. These DML classes represent the structural properties of entity types and relationship types as well as providing the DML functionality associated with them. The task of generation is done by a so-called *DDL compiler*. The generation is based on a mixture of macro instantiation, C++ templates, and direct output of C++ code. C++ templates are very useful since they allow defining one single SetOf-template so that the corresponding set functionality can be used for any instatiation SetOf<ET> of the template. Producing direct output is necessary to include the code of user-defined methods into entity classes. Given a database schema, the generated output consists of C++ *header files* (".h"), which contains the C++ class definitions including the signatures of the member functions, and *implementation files*

("`.cc`") implementing the member functions. Some other files are predefined as they contain C++ templates (producing generic **SetOf** classes) and classes like **Longfield** and **Date** that are independent of the schema. All these files (i.e., C++ classes) are compiled and linked into application programs. The ordinary C++ compiler is used as much as possible, especially for type checking and inheritance. The main database task is hidden in the code generated by the DDL compiler.

The generation of the header files is quite easy and fairly straightforward due to the close correspondence between the ER schema definitions and C++ classes. The implementation of the member functions must call the platform interface in order to establish the connection. Before doing that, an equivalent platform schema must be established, mapping ER concepts onto platform ones, i.e., entity types and relationship types onto hierarchies, networks, or relations. The DDL compiler thus has to perform a *model transformation* mapping the ER model to the platform model, and installing the equivalent resulting schema on the system. Afterwards the DML functions must be transformed into corresponding platform functions in dependence on the model transformation.

4.2 Layering of Implementation

The code of the implementation files (implementing the functions of the DML classes) must use the interface given by the platform system. However, we put another layer, called the *Basic Access (BA) layer*, between the platform system and the DML classes. The advantages are obvious: First, the implementation of the DML functions uses BA functions, which eventually are implemented by using platform features. Consequently the code to be generated becomes shorter, since the handling of platform operations is extracted into this additional layer. Second, the BA layer abstracts from the physical storage platform and concentrates the platform dependence on as small as possible parts of the implementation. Moreover, the new BA layer allows the environment to connect to several platforms without changing the implementation of the DML since the BA functions are platform-independent. Hence the implementation consists of a three-level architecture building two layers upon the platform system (cf. figure 2): The *DML layer*, generated by the DDL compiler, implements the data manipulation interface to the application programs, i.e., C++ classes for manipulating objects and relationships. This layer invokes the BA functions, which are the same for any platform system. The BA functions themselves are implemented in the *BA layer*, which consequently hides platform peculiarities from the DML layer. In contrast to the DML layer, the BA layer does not need to be generated by the DDL compiler, as the layer is independent of the schema. However, each platform system needs its own BA layer. Finally, the *Platform System* is used as a persistent storage server providing the basic functionality like concurrency control, transaction mechanisms, and recovery.

Let us now discuss the layers by addressing some special problems in more detail.

The DML layer implements the DML for the programs, i.e., C++ DML classes that allow manipulating entities and relationships in C++. The implementation of the DML on top of the BA layer is very straightforward. The member functions can directly be mapped onto corresponding BA function calls. Furthermore, the DML is responsible for some specific points:

- One application may have *different* C++ variables pointing to the *same* database object, e.g., if this object is fetched into several C++ objects. Hence, synchronisation of modifications is necessary. This is achieved by an in-memory *object cache* that maintains consistent updates of objects in an application.

- Management of complex objects is based on *lazy* retrieval, i.e., having an object, the contained objects are fetched when explicitly requested. This is more efficient since not all parts of a complex structure are generally interesting. In the same way, set traversal is also performed in a lazy manner.

- Generally, DML functions related to complex objects are handled here, e.g., deleting complex objects and making deep or shallow copies, because platform systems generally offer only elementary (record-based) operations.

The Basic Access layer provides functionality for communicating objects (including sets/longfields) and relationships between C++ object representations and the platform system.

- It operates as an *Object Manager* and a *Relationship Manager* providing functions to cater for storage and retrieval of objects and relationships. In fact, both perform the task of transforming DML functions onto platform operations. Consequently, the implementation of the BA functions is obviously dependent on the model transformation. However, these functions are independent of the schema and furthermore do not rely on the model transformation. The interface is always the same for any kind of transformation.

- Another functional component is dedicated to the query evaluation. Associative queries are communicated to the *Associative Query Interpreter (AQI)* for evaluation to take advantage of special platform capabilities. The associative language is mapped onto a corresponding language in the platform, i.e., each associative (ER) query will be translated into a query of the platform system. The implementation of the associative language, the AQI, is dependent on the platform capabilities. The AQI makes use of two important features. First, the Meta Information Protocol (MIP) [6] is used to check whether the result of an associative query matches the definition of the Query class that describe the structure of the result. This requires that type information about those query classes is available, which exactly is the information provided by the MIP. Second, we use the templates of the C++ version 3.0 one more time to use generic SetOf classes. Consequently, the SetOf<Query> C++ classes containing query results are automatically made available by the C++ compiler.

4.3 Openness

The layered architecture separates functionality in such a way that both extensibility *downwards* (towards other DBMS platforms) as well as *upwards* (towards other programming languages) is facilitated. No components of the architecture put special requirements on platform functionality.

Establishing a C++ coupling to another platform system requires a modification of the model transformation. The other parts of the DDL compiler, especially the generation of DML classes, are not affected. Furthermore, a reimplementation of the Basic Access layer is necessary. This layer is essentially just a storage server, and the transition to any reasonable platform is fairly straightforward for the transformation of DML functions. The associative query *languages* are platform independent, but their *implementations* (the Associative Query Interpreter AQI) are dependent on the platform capabilities. Thus, this mapping needs to be changed. On the other hand, having a module AQI allows for especially tailor-made query interfaces that take into account the capabilities of the platform system. Upward extensibility concerns the desire to access a database from *different* programming languages – [32] states that the DBMS should support persistent X for a variety of programming languages X. Making the DML connectable to multiple programming languages is facilitated by modifying the DDL compiler to emit code for another language, rather than C++ code. Similarly, the predefined classes must be rewritten in the new programming language. In fact, specifying user-defined methods must then be done in the new programming language.

5 Conclusions

In this paper, we have described a C++ database interface for classical database management systems like hierarchical, network, and relational ones. The work was strongly influenced by current object-oriented database systems. However, our approach rely on the concept of explicit relationships, which are believed to provide valuable modelling capabilities. Few comparable database systems use relationship types in the same way, many provides a notion of pointers (possibly with automatically maintained inverses) only.

The coupling of C++ with database functionality is reasonably easy and simple to implement causing only low expenses. In particular, there is no need for developing a new C++ compiler or precompiler due to a simple generative approach. We just need a DDL compiler to install a conceptual schema on the platform system and to create some C++ classes. The remaining work is done by ordinary C++ compilers. We make intensive use of the C++ compiler of AT&T, version 3.0, which provides so-called "templates" in the sense of parameterized classes. Using the Meta Information Protocol which provides meta information about classes used in a C++ program, helps doing without a precompiler approach even for powerful querying.

The presented database interface has been implemented on SUN4 workstations in AT&T C++ on top of an ER-like configuration management system called ADELE. For the time being, implementations on PCTE [16], and C-ISAM are under development. All this work was part of a project called RE-BOOT ("*RE*use *B*ased on *O*bject-*O*riented *T*echniques"), which is funded by the European Community's Esprit II program. Furthermore, a next version will be built on top of a relational DBMS at Siemens AG. While all the implementations done in REBOOT use the functional associative language (cf. subsection 3.3.1) due to limited platform capabilities, we are then able to utilize the full associative power of an SQL-like ER query language.

Up to now, we have only designed a uniform manipulation mechanism for different types of DBMSs. What is still needed is a possibility to use the interface for already *existing* databases. Since the database interface is based upon the ER model, we have to remodel existing data in terms of the ER model. Therefore, it is necessary to have some kind of re-engineering, a "backward" mapping from the classical platform data models to the ER model in order to be able to manipulate data with the interface. This is the price we have to pay for uniformity. This point will be tackled next.

Furthermore, some future improvements could be done in the following directions:

- The data model should be enhanced with further modelling concepts. Problems might arise due to their representation in C++. In particular, a *version-*

145

ing mechanism as part of the data model seems to be indispensable. Corresponding support in the search and manipulation process must be provided.

- *Dynamic schema modifications* should be possible. As a first step, incremental schema extensions will be supported, allowing to extend a schema step by step.
- Support for *(local) subdatabases/workspaces*, i.e. some protection mechanism on type and instance level. This also relates to access right mechanisms.
- The current implementation is oriented towards rather large-grained objects, however some requirements for handling more *fine-grained* information (e.g. C++ working structures) have been raised. This requirement could possibly be satisfied by having a two-level object model along the lines of Eclipse [7]. Thus, the database may be used as storage for working images or communication between application programs.

Finally, we may envisage improving the use of several physical platforms *at the same time* by releasing the application programs from the task of determining the DBMS. However, it will be a long way to achieve this goal requiring a lot of investigations.

References

1. M. Atkinson, F. Bancilhon, D. DeWitt, K. Dittrich, D. Maier, St. Zdonik: *The Object-Oriented Database System Manifesto.* In: Proc. of DOOD '89, Kyoto (Japan) 1989.
2. S. Abiteboul, P.C. Fischer, H.-J. Schek (eds.): *Nested relations and Complex Objects in Databases.* Springer Verlag, 1989. Lecture Notes in Computer Science No. 361.
3. A. Albano, G. Ghelli, R. Orsini: *A Relationship Mechanism for a Strongly Typed Object-Oriented Database Programming Language.* In: Proc. of 16th Int. Conf. on Very Large Databases, Barcelona, Spain (VLDB '91) 1991 (565–575)
4. D. Beech: *A Foundation for Evolutions from Relational to Object Databases.* In J.W. Schmidt, S. Ceri, M. Missikoff: Advances in Database Technology – EDBT '88, Venice 1988
5. S.-E. Bratsberg, E. Odberg: *Relation Refinement in Object-Relation Data Models.* In: Nordic Workshop on Programming Environment Research - NWPER '92, Tampere (Finland), January 1992.
6. F. Buschmann, K. Kiefer, M. Stal: *A Runtime Type System for C++.* In G. Heeg, B. Magnusson, B. Meyer (eds.): Technology of Object-Oriented Languages and Systems – TOOLS Europe 92, Dortmund 1992
7. J. Cartmell, A. Alderson: *The Eclipse Two-Tier Database Interface.* In: ESEC '87, 1st European Software Engineering Conference, September 1987 (139–147)
8. M.J. Carey, D. DeWitt, S.L. Vandenberg: *A Data Model and Query Language for EXODUS.* Proc. of the ACM SIGMOD Int. Conf. on Management of Data 1988, Chicago
9. P.P. Chen: *The Entity-Relationship Model - Towards a Unified View of Data.* ACM Transactions on Database Systems 1976, Vol. 1, No. 1 (9 – 36)
10. O. Deux et al: *The Story of O_2.* IEEE Transactions on Knowledge and Data Engineering, Vol. 2, No. 1, 1990
11. O. Diaz, P. Gray: *Semantic-Rich User-Defined Relationship as a Main Constructor in Object-Oriented Databases.* In: IFIP TC-2 Working Conference on Database Semantics in Windermere (U.K.) 1990.

12. K. Dittrich: *Advances in Object-Oriented Database Systems.* In: Proc. of the 2nd Int. Workshop on Object-Oriented Systems 1988, Springer LNCS No. 334.
13. G. Engels, M. Gogolla, U. Hohenstein, K. Hülsmann, P. Löhr-Richter, G. Saake, H.-D. Ehrich: *Conceptual Modelling of Database Applications.* In: Data & Knowledge Engineering 1992.
14. R. Elmasri, J. Weeldreyer, A. Hevner: *The Category Concept: An Extension to the Entity-Relationship Model.* Data & Knowledge Engineering 1985, Vol. 1
15. M. Fuller, A. Kent, R. Sacks-Davis, J. Thom, R. Wilkinson, J. Zobel: *Querying in a Large Hyperbase.* In: Database and Expert Systems Applications - DEXA '91, Berlin, (Germany), August 1991 (455–458).
16. F. Gallo, R. Minot, I. Thomas: *The Object Management System of PCTE as a Software Engineering Database Management System.* In: Proceedings of the 2nd ACM Software Engineering Symposium on Practical Software Development Environments, Palo Alto 1986 (12–15).
17. U. Hohenstein, G. Engels: *SQL/EER : Syntax and Semantics of an Entity-Relationship Based Query Language.* Information Systems 1992, 17 (3)
18. M.Gogolla, U. Hohenstein: *Towards a Semantic View of an Extended Entity-Relationship Model.* ACM Transactions on Database Systems 16 (3), 1991
19. W. Kim, E. Bertino, J. Garcia: *Composite Objects Revised.* In J. Clifford / B. Lindsay, D. Maier (eds.): Proc. of the 1989 ACM SIGMOD Int. Conf. on the Management of Data, Portland 1989. SIGMOD RECORD 1989, 18(2) (337 – 347)
20. S. Khoshafian, R. Abnous: *Object-Orientation: Concepts, Languages, Databases, and User Interfaces.* Villey & Sons Inc. 1990
21. Ch. Lamb, G. Landis, J. Orenstein, D. Weinreb: *The ObjectStore Database System.* Communications of ACM, 34(10), October 1991 (50–63)
22. M. Loomis: *Client-Server Architecture.* Object-Oriented Programming, February 1992.
23. D. Maier, J. Stein, A. Otis, A. Purdy: *Development of an Object-Oriented Database Management System.* Proc. OOPSLA 1986, Portland (Oregon)
24. E. Odberg, U. Hohenstein: *Data Model and Database Interface Specification.* Technical Report (Deliverable D1.2.B1 No. REBOOT-7046.7), December 1991.
25. P. Pistor, P. Dadam: *The Advanced Information Management Prototype.* In: [2]
26. C. Parent, H. Rolin, K. Yetongon, S. Spaccapietra: *An ER Calculus for the Entity-Relationship Complex Model.* In F. Lochovski (ed.): Proc. of the 8th Int. Conference on Entity-Relationship Approach. Toronto (Canada) 1989
27. L.A. Rowe, M.R. Stonebraker: *The POSTGRES Data Model.* In: Proceedings of the 13th International Conference on Very Large Databases, Brighton 1987
28. J. Rumbaugh: *Relations as Semantic Constructs in an Object-Oriented Language.* In: Proceedings of the Conf. on Object-Oriented Systems, Languages and Applications (OOPSLA), Orlando (Florida), 1987 (466–481)
29. H.-J. Schek, M.H. Scholl: *The Two Roles of Nested Relations in the DASDBS Project.* In: [2]
30. B. Stroustrup: *The C++ Programming Language.* Addison-Wesley 1985
31. A.V. Shah, J.E. Rumbaugh, J.H. Hamel, R.A. Borsari: *DSM: An Object-Relationship Modelling Language.* In: Proc. of the Conf. on Object-Oriented Systems, Languages and Applications (OOPSLA), New Orleans (Lousiana), 1989
32. M. Stonebraker (The Committee for Advanced DBMS Function). *Third-Generation Database System Manifesto.* SIGMOD RECORD 1990, 19(3).
Also in Proc. from IFIP 4th TC2 Conf. on Database Semantics; Object-Oriented Databases: Analysis, Design and Construction. Windermere (U.K.)

Object-Oriented Database Methodology
- State of the Art

Roger Tagg and Benny Liew

School of Mathematical and Information Sciences, Massey University,
Palmerston North, New Zealand

Abstract. Not far behind the leaders in the object-oriented revolution, the advocates of object-oriented databases and methodologies have been rushing into print to establish their commercial positions - or academic reputations. Yet there are doubts about the ability of the proposed methodologies to meet both the needs of the database approach and the opportunities of an evolutionary software engineering approach based on re-usable components. This paper reviews a range of available and proposed methodologies, and suggests requirements to be met by any methodology claiming to offer an advance on existing techniques. It also suggests what might be fruitful areas for further research.

1   Introduction

In practical use of database technology, formal methodology has become a vital ingredient for successful implementation, especially on larger projects with a high level of sharing of data. Although any application development methodology must address the full life-cycle from Planning and Feasibility through to Testing and Implementation, a large part of what differentiates the various methodologies is their approach to modelling the structure and behaviour of the application domain. Traditionally, most methodologies rely on a strict distinction between "procedure" and "data", eg [MAR 91, OLL 92].

The object-oriented (OO) paradigm, on the other hand, requires encapsulation of both data and procedure into objects. Methodologies based on a strict "procedure on data" dualism do not fit naturally into this approach. Meanwhile, many real-time applications have found the common data-oriented approaches unsuitable, and a number of alternative methodologies carrying the "object-oriented" flag have been proposed, geared to languages such as ADA (pre-object-oriented) and C++, eg [BOO 90, ROB 89].

More recently, further OO methodologies have been proposed which incorporate database-oriented concepts such as Entity or Semantic modelling, extended to capture behavioural aspects, eg [COA 91, RUM 91, ROL 92].

UK contact address: 6 Beechwood Avenue, Little Chalfont, Bucks HP6 6PH, England
Telephone (+ 44) 494 762645   email rtagg@cix.compulink.co.ok

While these newer methodologies all bring some advantage when developing OO databases, there are several questions which need answering before the user community gains confidence enough to make the costly switch from current methodologies.

1 - Is "object-oriented database" a sensible concept in the first place?

This may sound facile, but a database is something that is shared by several users or functions. If object orientation requires that data and procedures are encapsulated, what is left in the system that is not already in the "object base"? Should one not talk about "object system" rather than "database"? On the other hand, ad-hoc queries provide a counter-example of a class of procedures that it might make no sense to encapsulate. This suggests a need for "loose encapsulation" - where only predefinable procedures are encapsulated - as opposed to "strict encapsulation" where, for example, queries are messages from user interface objects to query handler objects. Any methodology has to take a view on this issue.

2 - Can one methodology be suitable for all target environments?

OO database still lacks adequate, generally-accepted standards, and the current range of potential target OODBMS environments contains large variations in concepts included or excluded. Examples are ONTOS [ONT 91], which is closely linked to C++ - a language fairly relaxed in its object orientation; GEMSTONE [OTI 91], which is linked to a strict OOPL, ie Smalltalk; and POSTGRES [STO 86], which is an "extended Relational" DBMS, where a main program or free queries are still required. While one cannot foresee all future OODBMS developments, a methodology must settle on a sufficiently expressive and flexible model of constructs, and include mapping guidelines for each target.

3 - Can users evolve from their current methodologies, or is a 'big bang" culture
    change needed?

Many users will not react favourably to the suggestion that all those Data Flow Diagrams (DFDs) and Entity Models, which they have sometimes just got used to, are now obsolete. However, it is difficult to see how they can be preserved if the full benefits of object orientation are to be achieved. Most of the proposed methods do include some extended Object Modelling approach, which allows relatively easily evolution from Entity Modelling. But the behavioural side is very variable - the use made of DFDs, for example, varies from "essential" through "optional" to "not used at all".

4 - What are the fruitful - and less fruitful - areas for further research'?

The OO database methodology area, in spite of a high level of literary output, has by no means reached a steady state. Some research efforts seem better directed than others at solving the more critical outstanding problems. Some suggestions are given in the conclusions to this paper.

2   Review of the Current Scene

Methodologies may be grouped into a number of recognisable categories, although there will always be some borderline cases.

2.1   Classic Functional Decomposition

This includes the methods of Constantine, De Marco, Myers, Yourdon and Gane & Sarson - the latter being known as STRADIS. These methodologies concentrate on functional Analysis and Design, and depend heavily on a hierarchical structure of Data Flow Diagrams. They contain little or no database design, and do not appear to offer an easy evolution path towards OO systems. Also related to this group is Jackson Structured Design [JAC 83].

2.2   Mainstream Database Oriented

This includes Information Engineering [MAR 91], SSADM and MERISE (all discussed in [OLL 92]. These methodologies are more data-oriented than the above group, some form of Entity or Semantic modelling being a significant aspect of the work. They often cover the stages before and after the Analysis and Design stages, and are usually well supported by CASE tools and Generators. The data aspects are relatively easy to extend for object orientation, but on the behavioural side different methodologies start from very different models, eg MERISE uses Petri nets; the IEF CASE tool uses "Process Dependency"; while IEW, SSADM and others preserve the use of Data Flow Diagrams.

2.3   Mainstream Object Oriented

This includes Booch's methodology [BOO 90], the European Space Agency's HOOD [ROB 89], Jacobson's ObjectOry [JAC 90] and Meyer's methodology for EIFFEL [MEY 88]. These methodologies concentrate on the Design stage, with variable coverage of Analysis. They are usually geared to a target of an OOPL, but usually without an OODBMS. Although they may be associated with CASE tools, they may not offer the same productivity gains as the previous group for Commercial TP applications, which tend today to use databases and 4GLs.

2.4   Object Oriented with Database Flavour

This includes Coad & Yourdon [COA 91], OMT [RUM 91], Shlaer & Mellor [SHL 89] and O* [ROL 92]. These methodologies all include some element of Object Modelling which is evolved from Data Modelling. However, behavioural aspects are still very variable from product to product. For example, O* does not use DFDs, but Coad & Yourdon and OMT still keep them for use "as needed". Shlaer & Mellor's method is the basis for the TEAMWORK OOA and OOD CASE products. O* is designed specifically for use with the O2 OODBMS [BAN 92]. So far, these methodologies have concentrated on Analysis (OOA) and Design (OOD), rather than the full development life cycle.

2.5 Service Based Approaches

One or two recent proposals have tackled the difficulties on the behavioural side of OO methodologies by incorporating concepts such as Actor Models, Responsibility Models [WIR 90] and "Client-Server" architecture. Jacobson, and Henderson-Sellers [HEN 90] have included some elements of this in their proposals. These approaches put prime importance on identifying objects in terms of the services they require and render. This category seems to offer the most promising hope so far to overcoming the problems of different behavioural models.

2.6 New Approaches to the Development Life Cycle

However truly object-oriented the above methods may aspire to be, most are still very much tied to a relatively "waterfall" view of the development process. In particular, they concentrate on the stages of Analysis and Design, and assume a traditional, largely top-down, progression from stage to stage. But the OO approach is supposed to be justified, to a greater or lesser extent, from the gains achievable by "engineering of re-usable components". This suggests quite a different view of the development life cycle, possibly including stages such as the following:

* Characterisation of the system in terms of Goals and Requirements
* Analysis of the application's processing pattern and "system type"
* Identifying existing systems or frameworks which could provide reusable software components
* Designing software structures incorporating tailored pre-existing objects and newly-created ones
* Tailoring and newly coding objects
* Massaging new objects into suitable form for Class Libraries.

This also has some relation to prototyping approaches, in which simple, generalised parts of the system are generated quickly, to be tailored later on to meet precise requirements.

Prototyping methodologies have tended to be informal, but have recently been linked with Information Engineering [MAR 91a] and the CorVision CASE tool [BAT 88]. Among the OOP fraternity, informal evolutionary development, without formal Analysis and Design, is often practised [DRA 90, HOD 90]. In some methods, the Analysis/Design and Design/Implementation boundaries become blurred as interaction takes place.

Methodologies that adapt the development life cycle to take conscious consideration of re-usability and use of Class Libraries are so far rare in current literature. A recent proposal in this area is that of Henderson-Sellers [HEN 90] who combines top-down and bottom-up approaches. Tsichritzis et al [TSI 92] discuss a component-oriented approach based on Generic Application Frames (GAFs) stored in a repository.

2.7 ORCA

This UK project was described at BNCOD-10 by David Gradwell [GRA 92]. It proposes a series of meta-models which provide a new architecture for OO methodology. The approach takes a wide view of "systems", including "extrinsic" Goals and Purposes. It adopts a "context analysis" approach which leads to a Client-Server view of systems. So far it seems more oriented to modelling than to development procedures, but it looks to be a promising architectural approach to the next generation of methodologies.

ORCA also appears to lean partly towards the concept of Soft Systems Methodology (SSM) as proposed by Checkland and others [CHE 90].

2.8 Summary of the Current State of the Art

In spite of many attempts to preach a "definitive" methodology for OODB, it seems clear that the area is in anything but a steady state. Structural object modelling conventions have been proposed that have yet to be exposed to trials in practice. The behavioural side (or "dynamic modelling") has lagged behind the structural, many of the thornier problems of concurrency having still to be faced [SOL 90]. Old methods such as DFDs are often retained without a very clear idea as to their purpose. And little has been done in re-examining the overall stage structure of the methodologies in the light of prototyping or reuse.

3   Requirements for Better OODB Methodologies

3.1   New Approach to the Whole Development Life Cycle

Many of the methodologies proposed so far are little more than Analysis and design techniques. As well as the need to cater for prototyping and re-usability (which are addressed later), there is a need to give more guidance at the Feasibility stage. Gilb [GIL 88] proposes metricised statements of requirement in terms of performance and failure conditions/rates. Especially where prototyping is to be used, clear statements of required functionality and interface, with agreement of the level of tailoring to be achieved within each development timebox, should be documented.

An alternative approach to the whole life cycle is a "differential" one (see 2.6 above). Instead of analysing each new application from square one, the technique is to compare the application being developed with a standard or skeleton one, for which software elements may be available in a Library (eg Tsichritzis's GAF mentioned earlier). The implementation task is reduced to one of tailoring or "specialisation", while the comparison is made between high level model constructs.

The challenge here is to develop a new macro structure for the methodology which takes into account these new activities, without throwing out the established benefits of a staged development approach.

3.2 Aids to Identifying Object Classes

The idea that the Objects in a system, like Entity Types, can be put into Classes just by underlining nouns in a text statement of requirements, is simplistic and somewhat dangerous. Many people have observed that entity models can be subjective, and that different personal modelling styles often lead to quite different resulting systems (eg "snapshot" versus "time series" views of the state of Entities). The scope for this variation in OO systems, where behavioural aspects are included as well, is an order of magnitude higher.

It would seem theoretically possible for an initial class identification tool to be built, providing a check list of classes expected in most systems:

a) of any type
b) with a given processing pattern (eg batch, TP, real-time control)
c) of a given application type (eg sales, inventory, robotics).

This would ideally be provided within a CASE tool, and could also link to Class Libraries. Assistance could also be envisaged for the task of enhancing and refining the Object Classes. The idea could also be combined with that of "Generalised Application Frameworks" as mentioned elsewhere in this paper.

3.3 Consistent Approach to Relationships, Constraints and Rules

The treatment of Relationships in OODB methodologies (and in the OODBMS themselves) is an area of great inconsistency. The OODBMS do tend to have more support for relationships than Relational DBMS, eg "References" and compound object structures; but these involve making design choices. Some methodologies attempt to capture both Relationships and Constraints (some of the latter of which may overlap with the former).

Fundamentalist OO designers tend to forget about the old-style "association" Relationships, and to draw instead on their diagrams only the "is-a" (and sometimes "part-of") lines. These two types of Relationship are "specials" in that they may have distinctive treatment in the target OODBMS - although they may not be the only ones (eg also "is-instance-of" and "requests-service-from"). It is obviously a problem to show all potential inter-object Relationships on one diagram at once, so any new OO CASE tools need a mechanism for showing only certain types of Relationship on one display - or colour coding!

Since Relationships form a natural concept that is now imprinted on many database designers' minds, methodologies must take a clear position on whether or not they are to be formally recorded. If they are, then mapping guidelines for representing them in OODBMS terms are needed; if not, then suitable substitute constructs have to be provided in the Analysis and Design modelling methods.

Similar comments apply to Constraints and Rules - see for example [DIA 91].

3.4   Adequate Coverage of Behavioural Modelling

Current methodologies are nearly all weak in this area. There is a tendency to suppose that one can put in a few Methods for each Object Class and the job is done. The problem seems to be that in the rush to encapsulate, inter-object dynamics are forgotten. There are plenty of Object Life Histories or State Transitions, but only for one Object Class at a time. Hence, the weakest subarea is that of modelling concurrency and synchronisation where multiple objects are involved.

The most useful behaviour model diagrams seem to be:

- Object Communications Diagram (Booch's "Object Diagram")

- State Transition Diagrams (for each important, active Object Class)

- Event Trace Diagrams (for each key scenario, with multiple Objects)

We look briefly at each of these, after which the use of Data Flow Diagrams will also be commented on.

3.4.1   Object Communications Diagram

This aims to show which Object Classes send messages to, or serve, other Classes. An example using Booch's notation is shown in Fig 1. Extra annotation can be added - Booch has conventions to represent 5 types of concurrency.

It is usually necessary to choose an Object (either a Requesting Object or a special Controller Object) to be controller of any synchronisation situation - ie to await messages indicating completion of the concurrent tasks and executing a method to resolve the next activity to be started.

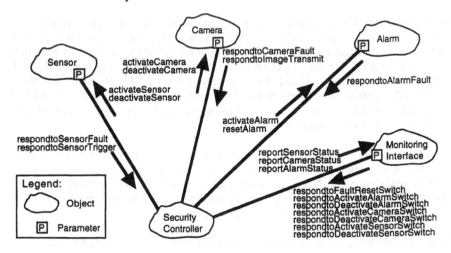

Fig. 1. Example Object Communications Diagram

Object Communication Diagrams can also form hierarchies as with DFDs, the top level Object (the system) being termed the Context Object (eg Fig 2).

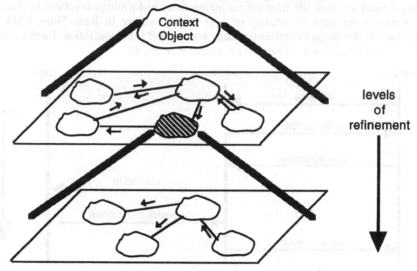

Fig. 2. Hierarchy of Object Communications Diagrams

3.4.2 State Transition Diagram

This is useful for analysing Classes of Active Objects, and those based on key Entity Types, that can take any of a finite number of states. It shows as lines the processing that is needed to move from one state to another (eg Fig 3). It is comparable to the "Entity Life History" of some data-oriented traditional methodologies. However, this primarily captures "intra-object" behaviour, and there is a separate diagram for each Object Class.

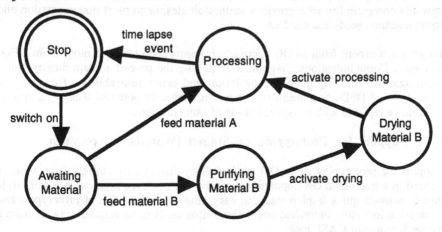

Fig. 3. Example State Transition Diagram

3.4.3 Event Trace Diagram

This is used to detail the inter-object interactions and timings involved in the most important sequences of activity of a system - mainly in Real-Time, CIM and Robotics. It also helps to capture dynamic aspects and synchronisation. Each sequence or "Scenario" has its own diagram (see example in Fig 4).

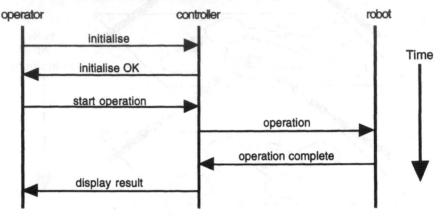

Fig. 4. Example Event Trace Diagram

3.4.4 Data Flow Diagrams - and why not?

The DFD essentially indicates the interaction between procedure and data in a system, rather than pure behaviour. It does not contribute to considerations of concurrency and synchronisation. Most authors seem to feel that DFDs do not add anything to the other diagrams that the designer is required to use, primarily the Object Structure Model and the Object Communications Diagram(s). However they often retain the use of DFDs, possibly as a tool for comparison with existing systems, or to provide upwards compatibility with previous methodologies, or to meet documentation and communication needs and standards.

To get good benefit from an OO approach, it seems appropriate to move from DFDs to Object Communications Diagrams. Retaining the procedure/data duality could work against achieving good encapsulation and hence re-usability. However the current use of DFDs as a means of communication with potential users of a system needs to be replaced with an equivalent use of other diagrams.

3.5 Support for Prototyping or Staged (Waterfall) Approach

Support for prototyping in an OO methodology differs only slightly from what is needed in a traditional development approach. The main requirement is a 4GL-style tool to provide quick implementation, easy amendment/revision of prototypes, and generation into more optimised code. There also needs to be suitable support from a Repository and/or CASE tool.

However, some designers prefer to maintain the formal "sign-off" structure of Analysis, Design and Implementation. even when prototyping is used. But it seems tiresome to have multiple sets of concepts (eg "Process". "Procedure", "Module"). Instead, the methodology should deal with "Objects" at all the stages, distinguishing one stage from another by the level of detail to which Object Class characteristics must be defined.

3.6 Orientation to Engineering of Re-usable Components

Given that this is one of the chief justifications of an OO approach, it is probably the one least well supported by today's methodologies. A problem for the top-down design advocates is that this requirement takes the designer into "engineering" quite early on, since the availability or unavailability of re-usable software components must have an effect on the choice of how the system is designed.

The questions that be answered by any intelligent aid to identifying available components (or cataloguing new ones) include:

- are there any existing components that meet the same or similar requirement?
- what interfaces do the components have (message names, parameters)?
- is the underlying software compatible/portable (language, OS, DBMS)?

The first of these requires something not too different from a bibliographic retrieval system, with searching on the basis of matching of descriptive words between the requirement and the Class Library catalogue.

Libraries of application frameworks [TSI 92], which have already been mentioned, could also be used in an intelligent component retrieval and cataloguing tool.

3.7 Facilities for Detailed Systems Design and Implementation

Also at the "engineering" level, one of the important development tasks is to map relatively conceptual objects to more physical things like:

- code module structures
- storage structures
- processor structures (eg parallel processors, client/server)

However, this will normally be largely OODBMS-dependent.

User interfaces, which could also be included here, are however one area where use of re-usable components is most advanced, and libraries for windowing and other graphical interfaces are available with many OOPLs.

3.8   Evolution or Migration from Current Methodologies

This has been discussed briefly earlier, to the effect that it is "nice to have" a development of existing concepts rather than totally new ones. It is also "nice to have" re-engineering tools which can preserve as much of the semantics as possible from a traditional repository and convert it into a new structure.

However, it is inevitable that new OO systems will have to continue to communicate with non-OO systems (as well as different OO systems), and here the work of the OMG (Object Management Group) is likely to be valuable [OMG 91].

4   Tools Needed to Support the Methodologies

The complexity of an OO system is likely to be high, and manual methods of development may be too laborious to enable systems to be delivered to acceptable timescales or cost. Primarily this means CASE Tools - to the level of those being used currently, and preferably - since not all comment on CASE-based development has been favourable - better.

The originators of the current group of database-oriented OO methodologies are generally still developing their CASE products. Although Coad and Yourdon have announced products to support their methodology, experience in using it is still limited.

The basic facilities of the target OODBMS or ERDBMS (Extended Relational) obviously have a very large influence on how easy a methodology is to use, especially with prototyping. An OODBMS which is closely tied to an OOPL (eg ONTOS with C++) can only be easy to prototype if there are generators to produce a lot of "default" code in the methods ("member functions").

Some prototyping of user interfaces is usually required, in which case some sort of 4GL with screen form generation, preferably in a WINDOWS-style GUI, is needed. Today such tools have virtually always been developed for a specific OODBMS, eg

- GeODE with GEMSTONE

- DBDesigner, Studio and Shorthand with ONTOS

- O2look, O2C(4GL) with O2

For searching and browsing in Class Libraries for available components, an intelligent search facility is desirable. However, very few examples are known of at the time of writing [HEL 91, PIE 91]. No examples have been heard of to date of intelligent aids to initial Object Class identification or mapping of Relationships, Constraints or Rules. Other possible tools are Testing Aids and Portability/Re-engineering Aids for Class Libraries and Repositories, but nothing has been heard of in a specifically OODB context.

5   Conclusions

We should first examine whether or not our original questions can be answered.

   1 - Is object-oriented database a sensible concept in the first place?

With strict encapsulation, the answer is probably no. In practice, encapsulation is likely to be fairly loose in whatever OODBMS or ERDBMS is the target. This leaves users with the cultural conversion from "procedure *on* data" to "ad hoc queries as messages *on* active database with predefinable behaviour built in".

   2 - Can one methodology be suitable for all target environments?

This has certainly not been proved, and with the methodology being very dependent on the OODBMS and related tools, it seems quite possible that insufficient common concepts exist at present to justify a rush into target-independent methodologies.

   3 - Can users evolve from current methodologies, or is a "big bang" culture
       change needed?

The answer seems to depend on where the user is starting. An Information Engineering user with experience of design for Relational DBMS with Database Procedures (eg SYBASE or ORACLE Version 7) may well stand a chance to evolve. For those relying mainly on Data Flow Diagrams, the half-way house of some methodologies is not recommended, and the move to Object Communication Diagrams is inevitably going to cause a fairly big bang.

   4 - What are the fruitful - and less fruitful - areas for further research?

The following list arises from the earlier discussion:

1 -   alternative approaches to incorporating the Actor Model and Wirfs-Brock
      Responsibility Model into a general methodology.

2 -   a fuller examination of the Feasibility stage in an OO context: formalisation and
      metricisation of requirements, and looking to business modelling and
      objectives/CSF analysis, possibly in conjunction with the ORCA approach.

3 -   approaches to "differential" analysis of application requirements, including the
      encoding of domain knowledge and the automation of the difference analysis
      procedure.

4 -   a tool to assist in the identification of Object Classes, possibly based on skeleton
      application frameworks.

5 -   meta-models for Class Libraries/Repositories in an OO context.

6 - resolution of the treatment of Relationships, Constraints and Rules in an Object Model, and intelligent help for mapping them to target constructs.

7 - review of the adequacy of behvioural modelling constructs in OO methodologies. Do they cover all cases? Are any constructs or diagrams redundant? [SOL 90]

8 - project management level control of separate Analysis, Design and Implementation stages using a single set of constructs around an OO repository.

9 - Class Library searching and browsing - reviewing published ideas and building a prototype for a target environment, including use of Application Frameworks.

10 - facilities for mapping an OO database design onto a variable hardware/software structure with parallelism and client/server architecture.

11 - portability and re-engineering of Class Libraries and OO Repositories.

12 - review of OO CASE tools, 4GLs and other aids.

The major task which is probably less fruitful, yet still attracts research effort, is the proposing of yet more Object Structure Modelling conventions. However, it would admittedly be convenient if some latter-day Codd were to settle the current confused Tower of Babel!

6   Acknowledgements

This paper is partly based on an M.Sc thesis carried out by Benny Liew at Massey University during 1992, and supervised by Roger Tagg who was a visiting academic. We would like to thank Prof. Mark Apperley, Head of the School of Mathematical and Information Sciences, Dr Daniela Mehandjiska-Stavreva, who was additional supervisor for the research, and the staff of the School who helped with laboratory work.

References

BAT 88   Batezael, Daniel. *Du Pont RIPP Presentation* Information Engineering Associates 1988.

BAN 92   Bancilhon, Francois & Delobel, Claude & Kanellakis, Paris. *Building an Object-Oriented Database System. the Story of O~* Morgan Kaufmann *1992*.

BOO 90   Booch, Grady. *Object-Oriented Design with Applications.* Benjamin /Cummings 1990.

CHE 90   Checkland, Peter and Scholes, Jim. *Soft Systems Methodology in Action* John Wiley 1990.

COA 91   Coad, Peter & Yourdon, Edward. *Object-Oriented Analysis* and *Object-Oriented Design* Prentice-Hall 1991 (2 volumes).

DIA 91   Diaz, Oscar; Paton, Norman & Gray, Peter. *Rule Management in Object-Oriented Databases: a Uniform Approach* Proc Conf on VLDB, Barcelona 1991.

DRA 90   Drake, Richard. *Object Oriented Programming and Evolutionary Delivery* Blenheim Online Seminar on Object Oriented Techniques, London 1990.

GIL 88   Gilb, Tom. *Principles of Software Engineering Management.* Addison-Wesley 1988.

GRA 92   Gradwell, David. Invited paper in *Advanced Database Systems* Proc BNCOD- 10 Lecture Notes in Comp. Sci. no 618, Springer Verlag 1992.

HEL 91   Helm, R & Maarek, Y.S. *Integrating Information Retrieval and Domain-Specific Approaches for Browsing and Retrieval in Object-Oriented Class Libraries* Proc OOPSLA 1991.

HEN 90   Henderson-Sellers, Brian & Edwards, Julian. *The Object-Oriented Systems Lifecycle.* CACM, Vol 33 no 9, 1990, pp 142-159

HOD 90   Hodgson, Ralph. *Placing Object-Orientation within a Wider Methods Context.* Blenheim Online Seminar on Object Oriented Techniques, London 1990.

JAC 83   Jackson Michael. *System Development.* Prentice-Hall 1983.

JAC 90   Jacobson, Ivar. *Object Oriented Development in an Industrial Environment.* Blenheim Online Seminar on Object Oriented Techniques, London 1990.

MAR 91 Martin, James & Palmer, Ian. *An Introduction to Information Engineering Methodology* James Martin & Company 1991.

MAR 91a Martin, James. *Rapid Application Development* Macmillan 1991.

MEY 88 Meyer,Bertrand. *Object-Oriented Software Construction* Prentice-Hall 1988.

OLL 92 Olle,T.William. *Information Systems Methodologies: a framework of understanding* Addison-Wesley 1992.

OMG 91 Object Management Group Inc. *Object Management Architecture Guide* and *The Common Object Request Broker: Architecture and Specification* OMG 1991.

OTI 91 Otis, Allen & Stein, Jacob & Butterworth, Paul. *The GEMSTONE Object Database Management System*. CACM vol 34 no 9, Oct 1991 pp 65-77.

PIE 91 Pietro-Diaz, R. *Implementing Faceted Classification for Software Reuse* CACM vol34, no5, May 1991.

ROB 89 Robinson, Peter et al. *Hierarchical Object Oriented Design (HOOD), Tutorials and Demonstrations* Unicom Seminars Ltd, Nov 1989

ROL 92 Rolland, Colette & Brunet, Joel. *Object Database Design*. In *Object Management,* Proc BCS DMSG Conference, 1992 pp 97-108.

RUM 91 Rumbaugh, James; Blaha, Michael; Premerlani, William; Eddy, Frederick & Lorensen, William. *Object-Oriented Modelling and Design* Prentice Hall 1991.

SHL 89 Shlaer, Sally & Mellor, Stephen. *An OO Approach to Domain Analysis* ACM SIGSOFT Software Eng Notes Vol 14 no 5, Jul 1989, pp 66-77.

SOL 90 Sol, H.G. & Van Hee, K.M., eds. *International/ Working Conference on Dynamic Modelling of Information.Systems* North Holland 1990.

STO 86 Stonebraker, Mike and Rowe, Lawrence. *The Design of POSTGRES* Proc ACM SIGMOD Conf June 1986.

TSI 92 Tsichritzis, Dennis; Nierstrasz, Oscar & Gibbs, Simon. *Beyond Objects: Objects* in *Object Frameworks* Research report of CUI Geneva 1992.

WIR 90 Wirfs-Brock, Rebecca & Johnson, Ralph. *Surveying Current Research in Object Oriented Design*. CACM Sept 1990 vol 33 no 9 pp 104-124.

Deductive Databases with Conditional Facts

Rajshekhar Sunderraman

Department of Computer Science
The Wichita State University
Wichita, Kansas 67260-0083, USA
e-mail: raj@cs.twsu.edu

Abstract. We introduce the notion of conditional facts in deductive databases. The language used to express the conditions in the basic facts does not involve constructs used to describe the database and is motivated by its potential usefulness in expressing disjunctive facts and answering queries in disjunctive deductive databases. We present a bottom-up procedure that uses tabular structures to represent the conditional facts and computes the intended meaning of conditional deductive databases. We show how this procedure can be used to answer queries in a subclass of disjunctive deductive databases which involves disjunctive facts but only definite rules.

1 Introduction

In recent years, the field of deductive databases has been the focus of intense research and there has been a dramatic advance in the understanding of the theoretical and practical issues involved. A substantial amount of effort has gone into definite deductive databases, a subclass of deductive databases in which only Horn clauses are allowed. The semantics of such databases are fully understood and there has been a great deal of research dealing with implementation issues, particularly in query optimization in the presence of recursive rules. This research has culminated in various experimental systems such as NAIL! [12], glue-NAIL! [15], LDL [1, 14], Aditi [19], EKS-V1 [20], CORAL [16], and Starburst SQL [13], the utility of which have been successfully demonstrated. Therefore, it is not unreasonable to assume that within the next decade, commercial systems with deductive capabilities will become available.

In the presence of a large number of facts and relatively few rules, as is the case with definite deductive databases, the bottom-up evaluation of rules (with optimization techniques like magic sets) performs much more efficiently than top-down evaluation. Moreover, the bottom-up evaluation using the relational algebra can take advantage of the efficient database access techniques involving joins that are a part of modern day relational database management systems. For these and other reasons the successful experimental systems like LDL, NAIL!, and some of the others mentioned earlier have opted for the bottom-up evaluation model.

In this paper, we introduce the concept of conditional facts in deductive databases. We envision many applications where the basic facts obtained can only be confirmed if certain conditions were true. For example, most scientific experiments involve collection of data under certain wide-ranging conditions. These data can be expressed as conditional facts. The language used to express these conditions could depend on the application and may or may not involve constructs of the language used to describe the facts and the rules of a deductive database. We consider a simplified language for the conditions that does not involve constructs of the deductive database language. The model-theoretic and fixpoint semantics for deductive databases with conditional facts are presented. We then describe an operational procedure which computes the intended meaning of the database. This procedure uses a bottom-up strategy involving tabular structures to evaluate the rules against the conditional facts. Finally, we show how to use the tabular structures to represent ground disjunctive facts and how to use the bottom-up procedure developed to answer queries in a subclass of disjunctive deductive databases. We have omitted the proofs of the theorems stated in this paper for space reasons. For a detailed version of this paper see [17].

2 Conditional Deductive Databases

This section describes the syntax of conditional deductive databases. Then, the model-theoretic and fixpoint semantics are introduced. Finally, an operational procedure to compute the meaning of the database is presented.

2.1 Syntax

Let P_{DB} be a finite set of symbols called *predicates*, V_{DB} be a set of symbols called *constants*, and V_{DB} be a set of symbols called *variables*. With each predicate, we associate a number (greater than or equal to 0), called the *arity*. A *term* is either a constant or a variable. An *atomic formula* or simply an *atom* is of the form $p(t_1, \ldots, t_n)$, where $p \in P_{DB}$ is a predicate of arity n and $t_1, \ldots, t_n$ are terms. Let L_{DB} be the set of all possible atoms.

Let V_{CON} be a countably infinite set of symbols called *conditional variables* and C_{CON} be a countably infinite set of symbols called *conditional constants* containing a distinguished constant which we shall refer to as *other*. We shall assume that $V_{DB}, V_{DB}, P_{DB}, V_{CON}$, and C_{CON} are all disjoint. A *conditional atomic formula* or simply a *conditional atom* is either of the form *true*, or of the form *false*, or of the form $v = a$, where $v \in V_{CON}$ and $a \in C_{CON}$. A *conditional formula* or simply a *condition* is either a conditional atom or is of one of the following three forms: $(F_1 \vee F_2)$, $(F_1 \wedge F_2)$, or $\neg F_1$, where F_1 and F_2 are conditions. Let L_{CON} be the set of all conditions that can be formed using the conditional variables of V_{CON} and the conditional constants of C_{CON}.

A *conditional fact* over L_{DB} and L_{CON} is of the form:

$$p \leftarrow C,$$

where p is an element of L_{DB} and C is an element of L_{CON}.

A *rule* over L_{DB} is of the form:

$$p \leftarrow q_1, \ldots, q_k$$

where $p, q_1, \ldots, q_k$ are members of L_{DB}. All the variables appearing in the rule are assumed to be universally quantified.

A *database* over the sets L_{DB} and L_{CON} consists of two components: an *extensional* part (called the Extensional Database or EDB for short) consisting of a finite set of conditional facts over L_{DB} and L_{CON}, and an *intensional* part (called the Intensional Database or IDB for short) consisting of a finite set of rules over L_{DB}.

Example 1. Let P_{DB} contain the predicates p, q, r, and s with arities 2, 1, 1, and 2 respectively, V_{DB} contain the constants a, b, c, d, and e, V_{DB} contain the variables X, Y, and Z, C_{CON} contain the conditional constants a_1, a_2, and *other*, and V_{CON} contain the conditional variables v_1 and v_2. A database instance over L_{DB} and L_{CON} is shown in Fig. 1.

EDB:

$$p(a,b) \leftarrow (v_1 = a_1).$$
$$p(a,c) \leftarrow \neg(v_1 = a_1).$$
$$r(c) \leftarrow (v_2 = a_1).$$
$$r(d) \leftarrow (v_2 = a_2).$$
$$r(e) \leftarrow \neg(v_2 = a_1) \wedge \neg(v_2 = a_2).$$

IDB:

$$q(Y) \leftarrow p(X, Y).$$
$$s(X, Y) \leftarrow q(X), r(Y).$$

Fig. 1. An example database

2.2 Model-Theoretic and Fixpoint Semantics

Model-theoretic Semantics. Consider a database $DB = EDB \cup IDB$ defined over L_{DB} and L_{CON}. Let ρ be an assignment of constant symbols from C_{CON} to the variables that appear in the condition part of the conditions of the EDB. This assignment will be referred to as a *valuation*. We now define the application of a valuation to EDB as follows:

$$\rho(EDB) = \{p | (p \leftarrow C) \in EDB \text{ and } C \text{ evaluates to true under } \rho\}$$

Finally, we define the model-theoretic semantics of the database as follows:

$$REP(DB) = \{\text{minimal-model}(\rho(EDB) \cup IDB) | \rho \text{ is a valuation}\}$$

Example 2. REP(DB) for the database of Fig. 1 is shown in Fig. 2. Along with each minimal-model we have shown the corresponding valuation.

Valuation	Minimal-Model
$v_1 = a_1$ and $v_2 = a_1$	{ p(a,b), r(c), q(b), s(b,c) }
$v_1 = a_1$ and $v_2 = a_2$	{ p(a,b), r(d), q(b), s(b,d) }
$v_1 = a_1$ and $v_2 = other$	{ p(a,b), r(e), q(b), s(b,e) }
$v_1 = other$ and $v_2 = a_1$	{ p(a,c), r(c), q(c), s(c,c) }
$v_1 = other$ and $v_2 = a_2$	{ p(a,c), r(d), q(c), s(c,d) }
$v_1 = other$ and $v_2 = other$	{ p(a,c), r(e), q(c), s(c,e) }

Fig. 2. Minimal-model semantics for example database

Fixpoint Semantics. Consider the database DB = EDB $\cup$ IDB defined over L_{DB} and L_{CON}. Let HB_{DB} be the set of all ground atoms (atoms with no variables) in L_{DB}. Define EHB_{DB}, the extended Herbrand Base, as follows:

$$EHB_{DB} = \{(p \leftarrow C)|(p \in HB_{DB}) \text{ and } (C \in L_{CON})\}$$

We now define a fixpoint operator, T_{DB} : power-set(EHB_{DB}) $\rightarrow$ power-set(EHB_{DB}). Let $S \subseteq EHB_{DB}$. Then,

$$T_{DB}(S) = \{p \leftarrow (C_1 \wedge \cdots \wedge C_n) \mid p \leftarrow q_1, \ldots, q_n \text{ is a ground instance of a rule of DB}$$
$$\text{and } (\forall i)(1 \leq i \leq n \rightarrow (q_i \leftarrow C_i) \in S)\}$$

Define the powers of T_{DB} as follows:

$$T_{DB} \uparrow 0 = EDB$$
$$T_{DB} \uparrow (i+1) = T_{DB}(T_{DB} \uparrow (i))$$
$$T_{DB} \uparrow \omega = \text{lub}\{T_{DB} \uparrow (i)|i < \omega\}$$

Essentially, $T_{DB} \uparrow \omega$ is the set of all conditional facts that can be deduced from the database.

Example 3. Consider the database of Fig. 1. The powers of T_{DB} are shown in Fig. 3.

The equivalence of the model-theoretic semantics and the fixpoint semantics is illustrated in the following theorem:

Theorem 1. *Let* DB *be a database. Then,* REP(DB) = REP($T_{DB} \uparrow \omega$).

The theorem states that the conditional deductive database DB = EDB $\cup$ IDB and the set of conditional facts in $T_{DB} \uparrow \omega$ have the same valuations and under each valuation ρ, the minimal model of ρ(EDB) $\cup$ IDB is the same as the set of facts in $\rho(T_{DB} \uparrow \omega)$.

$$T_{DB}^0 = \{\, p(a,b) \leftarrow (v_1 = a_1),$$
$$p(a,c) \leftarrow \neg(v_1 = a_1),$$
$$r(c) \leftarrow (v_2 = a_1),$$
$$r(d) \leftarrow (v_2 = a_2),$$
$$r(e) \leftarrow \neg(v_2 = a_1) \wedge \neg(v_2 = a_2)\,\}$$

$$T_{DB}^1 = \{\, q(b) \leftarrow (v_1 = a_1),$$
$$q(c) \leftarrow \neg(v_1 = a_1)\,\} \cup T_{DB}^0$$

$$T_{DB}^2 = \{\, s(b,c) \leftarrow (v_1 = a_1) \wedge (v_2 = a_1),$$
$$s(b,d) \leftarrow (v_1 = a_1) \wedge (v_2 = a_2),$$
$$s(b,e) \leftarrow (v_1 = a_1) \wedge \neg(v_2 = a_1) \wedge \neg(v_2 = a_2),$$
$$s(c,c) \leftarrow \neg(v_1 = a_1) \wedge (v_2 = a_1),$$
$$s(c,d) \leftarrow \neg(v_1 = a_1) \wedge (v_2 = a_2),$$
$$s(c,e) \leftarrow \neg(v_1 = a_1) \wedge \neg(v_2 = a_1) \wedge \neg(v_2 = a_2)\,\} \cup T_{DB}^1$$

$$T_{DB}^3 = T_{DB}^2.$$

Fig. 3. Powers of T_{DB}

2.3 Operational Semantics

We shall use the *C-table* structure of [5] to represent the conditional facts of the database. We shall then show that the extended relational algebra on C-tables can be effectively used to evaluate the rules of the database. The operational meaning of the database will be shown to be equivalent to the fixpoint semantics defined earlier. We shall now define C-tables and its algebra.

A *domain* is a set of values, usually finite. A *relation scheme* is a list of attribute names, $(A_1, \ldots, A_n)$. We associate a domain with each attribute. Let $D_1, \ldots, D_n$ be the domains associated with the attributes $A_1, \ldots, A_n$ respectively. We shall associate L_{CON} with a special attribute COND. A *C-table* T over the scheme (R,COND), where $R = (A_1, \ldots, A_n)$, consists of tuples (t, c) where $t \in D_1 \times \cdots \times D_n$ and $c \in L_{CON}$. The tuple (t, c) belonging to the C-table T can be interpreted as the logical formula

$$T(t) \leftarrow c$$

where T is the predicate symbol associated with the C-table T. If the condition c were true then the tuple t belongs to the relation T.

Example 4. The C-table in Fig. 4 represents conditional facts about blood groups of individuals:

A C-table is said to be *normalized* if

1. it does not contain two tuples (t_1, c_1) and (t_2, c_2) with $t_1 = t_2$ and

BG

NAME	BGROUP	COND
John	A	true
Tom	A	$(x = a)$
Tom	B	$\neg(x = a)$
Gary	A	$(y = a)$
Gary	B	$(y = b)$
Gary	O	$\neg(y = a) \wedge \neg(y = b)$

Fig. 4. C-table Bloodgroup

2. it does not contain a tuple of the form (t, c), where c is a contradiction.

To normalize a C-table, we simple delete all tuples of the form (t, c), where c is a contradiction. and combine the tuples $(t, c_1), \ldots, (t, c_k)$ into one tuple $(t, c_1 \vee \cdots \vee c_k)$ (It can be easily observed that the logical formula $(c_1 \rightarrow T(t)) \wedge \cdots \wedge (c_k \rightarrow T(t))$ is logically equivalent to $(c_1 \vee \cdots \vee c_k \rightarrow T(t))$). We shall assume that all C-tables are normalized. Often, we shall replace tuple (t, c) by (t, c') where c and c' are equivalent. If T were a C-table then we denote its normalized form by T^*.

We now present the relevant extended relational algebraic operations for C-tables.

Selection Let T be a C-table defined on the scheme (R,COND) and let F be a selection formula involving the attributes of R. Then,

$$\sigma_F(T) = \{t | (\exists t_1)(t_1 \in T \wedge t[R] = t_1[R] \wedge t[\text{COND}] = (t_1[\text{COND}] \wedge F(t_1))\}^*$$

where $F(t_1)$ is F with all occurrences of attribute A replaced by $t[A]$.

Projection Let T be a C-table defined on the scheme (R,COND) and let Y be a list of attributes of R. Then,

$$\Pi_Y(T) = \{t | (\exists t_1)(t_1 \in T \wedge t[Y] = t_1[Y] \wedge t[\text{COND}] = t_1[\text{COND}])\}^*$$

Join Let T and W be two C-tables defined on the schemes (R,COND) and (S,COND) respectively. Then,

$$T \bowtie W = \{t \mid (\exists t_1)(\exists t_2)(t_1 \in T \wedge t_2 \in W \wedge t[R] = t_1[R] \wedge t[S - R] = t_2[S - R] \wedge$$

$$t[\text{COND}] = (t_1[\text{COND}] \wedge t_2[\text{COND}] \wedge \bigwedge_{A \in R \cap S} (t_1[A] = t_2[A])))\}^*$$

Union Let T_1 and T_2 be two C-tables defined on the scheme (R,COND). Then,

$$T_1 \cup T_2 = \{t | t \in T_1 \vee t \in T_2\}^*$$

IDB Equations and their Solution. Let DB = EDB ∪ IDB be a database. We shall represent the conditional facts of the EDB in C-tables which we shall refer to as EDB C-tables. Assuming that a predicate symbol can either be in the EDB or in the IDB but not both, we can use the algorithm presented in Chapter 3 of [18] to obtain IDB equations for each IDB predicate symbol. The solution to these equations will be C-tables for the IDB predicates, which we shall refer to as IDB C-tables.

Example 5. Consider the following IDB:

$$a(X,Y) \leftarrow p(X,Y)$$
$$a(X,Y) \leftarrow p(X,Z), a(Z,Y)$$

The IDB equation for the IDB predicate a is

$$\text{A(X,Y,COND)} = \text{P(X,Y,COND)} \cup \Pi_{X,Y}(\text{P(X,Z,COND)} \bowtie \text{A(Z,Y,COND)})$$

where P is the C-table for the IDB predicate p and A is the C-table for the IDB predicate a.

Let $R_1, \ldots, R_n$ be the EDB C-tables and $P_1, \ldots, P_m$ be the IDB C-Tables. We shall denote the IDB equation for IDB predicate p_i as

$$P_i = \text{EVAL}(p_i, P_1, \ldots, P_m, R_1, \ldots, R_n).$$

A *fixpoint* of the IDB equations with respect to $R_1, \ldots, R_n$ is a solution for the C-tables corresponding to the IDB predicates of those equations. Given a solution S, we can reconvert the C-tables in S back to conditional facts. Let us denote the set of conditional facts obtained from solution S by DB(S).

The information content of two databases can be compared using the following definition: $\text{DB}_1 \leq \text{DB}_2$ if and only if for every $M_2 \in \text{REP}(\text{DB}_2)$ there exists a $M_1 \in \text{REP}(\text{DB}_1)$ such that $M_1 \subseteq M_2$. Intuitively, this definition states that the information content of DB_2 is greater than the information-content of DB_1.

Example 6. Let $\text{DB}_1 = \{p \leftarrow (v_1 = a_1), q \leftarrow \neg(v_1 = a_1), r \leftarrow true, s \leftarrow (v_2 = a_1), t \leftarrow \neg(v_2 = a_1)\}$ and $\text{DB}_2 = \{u \leftarrow true, p \leftarrow true, r \leftarrow true, s \leftarrow (v_2 = a_1), t \leftarrow \neg(v_2 = a_1)\}$. Then, $\text{REP}(\text{DB}_1) = \{\{p, r, s\}, \{p, r, t\}, \{q, r, s\}, \{q, r, t\}\}$ and $\text{REP}(\text{DB}_2) = \{\{u, p, r, s\}, \{u, p, r, t\}\}$. It can be easily verified that $\text{DB}_1 \leq \text{DB}_2$.

Let S_1 and S_2 be two solutions to a set of IDB equations. Then, we say that $S_1 \leq S_2$ if $\text{DB}(S_1) \leq \text{DB}(S_2)$. S_0 is said to be the *least fixpoint solution* of a set of IDB equations if for any solution S, $S_0 \leq S$.

Theorem 2. *Let* DB *be a database and let* S *be the least fixpoint solution to the* IDB *equations of* DB. *Then,* $\text{REP}(\text{DB(S)}) = \text{REP}(T_{\text{DB}} \uparrow \omega)$.

The above theorem relates the least fixpoint solution of the IDB equations to the fixpoint semantics of the database. The set of conditional facts represented in the least fixpoint solution and the set of conditional facts in $T_{\text{DB}} \uparrow \omega$ have the same valuations and under each valuation have the same minimal model. The significance of this theorem is that it provides a bridge between the more abstract semantics of conditional deductive databases and the computational method to compute the meaning of the database.

We now present an algorithm to compute the least fixpoint solution for a set of IDB equations. This algorithm is a bottom-up procedure which starts with the EDB and evaluates the right-hand side algebraic expression of each IDB equation and assigns the value obtained to the IDB C-table variable on the left-hand side of the equation. This process is repeated until no more new entries are added to the C-tables. The algorithm is shown in Fig. 5.

$$
\begin{aligned}
&\textbf{for } i \leftarrow 1 \textbf{ to } m \textbf{ do } P_i = \emptyset \\
&\textbf{repeat} \\
&\quad \textbf{for } i \leftarrow 1 \textbf{ to } m \textbf{ do } Q_i = P_i \\
&\quad P_i \leftarrow \text{EVAL}(p_i, Q_1, \ldots, Q_m, R_1, \ldots, R_n) \\
&\textbf{until } Q_i = P_i, \text{ for all } i, 1 \le i \le m \\
&\textbf{output } Q_1, \ldots, Q_m
\end{aligned}
$$

Fig. 5. Algorithm to Solve IDB Equations

The following theorem establishes the correctness of the bottom-up algorithm of Fig. 5 with respect to the model-theoretic and fixpoint semantics defined earlier.

Theorem 3. *Let DB be a database. Then, Algorithm of Fig. 5 correctly computes the least fixpoint solution to the IDB equations of DB.*

3 Application

In this section, we show how the C-table data structure and the bottom-up procedure can be used to answer queries in a subclass of disjunctive deductive databases. The subclass we are interested is a disjunctive deductive database consisting of disjunctive facts and definite rules.

3.1 Representing Disjunctive Facts in C-tables

The C-table data structure can be used to represent ground disjunctive facts. For example, the ground disjunctive fact $r(t_1) \vee r(t_2)$ can be represented by the two tuples $(t_1, x = a)$ and $(t_2, \neg(x = a))$ in the C-table R for predicate r. The justification for this is the fact that

$$
((x = a) \rightarrow R(t_1)) \wedge (\neg(x = a) \rightarrow R(t_2))
$$

logically implies $R(t_1) \vee R(t_2)$. In general, a ground disjunctive fact

$$
r_1(t_1) \vee \cdots \vee r_n(t_n)
$$

will be represented by $(n-1)$ tuples of the form $(t_i, x = a_i)$ in the C-table R_i for predicate r_i, $1 \leq i \leq n-1$ and a tuple of the form $(t_n, \neg(x = a_1) \wedge \cdots \wedge \neg(x = a_{n-1}))$ in the C-table R_n for predicate r_n. Conversely, if there are n tuples of the form (t_i, c_i) in C-table R_i, $1 \leq i \leq n$, such that $c_1 \vee \cdots \vee c_n$ is a tautology, then we say that the ground disjunctive fact $r_1(t_1) \vee \cdots \vee r_n(t_n)$ is represented in the C-tables, where R_i is the C-table for the predicate r_i.

Example 7. The C-table of Example 4 represents the following disjunctive facts:

$$bg(\text{John,A})$$
$$bg(\text{Tom,A}) \vee bg(\text{Tom,B})$$
$$bg(\text{Gary,A}) \vee bg(\text{Gary,B}) \vee bg(\text{Gary,O})$$

3.2 Answering Queries in Disjunctive Deductive Databases

Example 8. Consider the following disjunctive deductive database:

Facts: father(jim,chris).
mother(liz,chris).
father(chris,tom) ∨ mother(chris,tom).
father(tom,pat).
father(pat,john) ∨ mother(pat,john).

Rules: male_ancestor $(X,Y) \leftarrow$ father(X,Y).
male_ancestor $(X,Y) \leftarrow$ father(X,Z), male_ancestor (Z,Y).
male_ancestor$(X,Y) \leftarrow$ father(X,Z), female_ancestor(Z,Y).
female_ancestor$(X,Y) \leftarrow$ mother(X,Y).
female_ancestor$(X,Y) \leftarrow$ mother(X,Z), male_ancestor(Z,Y).
female_ancestor$(X,Y) \leftarrow$ mother(X,Z), female_ancestor(Z,Y).

where father(X,Y) denotes the fact that X is the father of Y, mother(X,Y) denotes the fact that X is the mother of Y, male_ancestor (X,Y) denotes the fact that X is the male ancestor of Y, and female_ancestor (X,Y) denotes the fact that X is the female ancestor of Y. Consider the query "Find all male ancestors of *john*". The definite answers to this query are *tom* and *jim*. There is also a possibility of *pat* and *chris* being answers, but this is not certain. We shall refer to such answers as *maybe* answers.

The disjunctive facts can be represented in the following C-tables:

F

FATHER	SON	COND
jim	chris	true
chris	tom	$(v_1 = a_1)$
tom	pat	true
pat	john	$(v_2 = a_1)$

M

MOTHER	SON	COND
liz	chris	true
chris	tom	$\neg(v_1 = a_1)$
pat	john	$\neg(v_2 = a_1)$

The IDB equations for the rules are:

$$MA(X,Y,COND) = F(X,Y,COND) \cup$$
$$\Pi_{X,Y}(F(X,Z,COND) \bowtie MA(Z,Y,COND)) \cup$$
$$\Pi_{X,Y}(F(X,Z,COND) \bowtie FA(Z,Y,COND))$$

$$FA(X,Y,COND) = M(X,Y,COND) \cup$$
$$\Pi_{X,Y}(M(X,Z,COND) \bowtie MA(Z,Y,COND)) \cup$$
$$\Pi_{X,Y}(M(X,Z,COND) \bowtie FA(Z,Y,COND))$$

where F, M, MA, and FA are the C-tables for the predicates *father, mother, male_ancestor* , and *female_ancestor* respectively. Applying the bottom-up procedure of Fig. 5, we obtain the C-tables FA and MA shown below:

MA

M_ANC	PERSON	COND
jim	chris	true
chris	tom	$(v_1 = a_1)$
tom	pat	true
pat	john	$(v_2 = a_1)$
jim	tom	true
chris	pat	$(v_1 = a_1)$
tom	john	true
jim	pat	true
chris	john	$(v_1 = a_1)$
jim	john	true

FA

F_ANC	PERSON	COND
liz	chris	true
chris	tom	$\neg(v_1 = a_1)$
pat	john	$\neg(v_2 = a_1)$
liz	tom	true
chris	pat	$\neg(v_1 = a_1)$
liz	pat	true
chris	john	$\neg(v_1 = a_1)$
liz	john	true

Returning to the query of finding all of *john's* male ancestors, we can use the algebraic expression:

$$ANSWER(X,COND) = \Pi_X(\sigma_{Y=john}(MA(X,Y,COND)))$$

to answer the query. Evaluating this expression, we get

ANSWER

M_ANC	COND
pat	$(v_2 = a_1)$
tom	true
chris	$(v_1 = a_1)$
jim	true

which corresponds to the definite and maybe answers of the query.

3.3 Correctness of Bottom-Up Procedure

In this section, we relate the approach used to answer queries in the subclass of disjunctive deductive databases with the semantics of disjunctive deductive databases as presented in [11]. First, we present some of the relevant definitions and results for disjunctive deductive databases.

A disjunctive deductive database consists of a set of clauses of the form

$$A_1, \ldots, A_n \leftarrow B_1, \ldots, B_m$$

where A_is and B_is are atomic formulas that do not contain function symbols and all the variables appearing on the left-hand side of $\leftarrow$ also appear on the right-hand side of $\leftarrow$.

The *declarative* semantics of disjunctive deductive databases is based on Herbrand models. Such databases do not possess a unique smallest Herbrand model, but instead have a collection of minimal Herbrand models [10]. The following theorem illustrates the declarative semantics:

Theorem 4 (Minker 1982). *For a disjunctive deductive database* P *and for every positive clause* E, $P \models E$ *if and only if* E *is true in every minimal model of* P.

The *fixpoint* semantics of disjunctive deductive databases is based on the immediate consequence operator T_P^I defined in [11]. For this, we need the notion of the *extended Herbrand Base*, EHB_P for database P, which is defined to be the set of all finite disjunctions of different atoms of the Herbrand Base HB_P. T_P^I is defined as follows:

$$T_P^I(S) = \{C \in EHB_P \mid C' \leftarrow B_1, \ldots, B_n \text{ is a ground instance of a program}$$
$$\text{clause in P and } B_1 \vee C_1, \ldots, B_n \vee C_n \text{ are in S and}$$
$$C'' = C' \vee C_1 \vee \cdots \vee C_n, \text{ where } \forall i, 1 \leq i \leq n, C_i \text{ can be}$$
$$\text{null, and } C \text{ is the smallest factor of } C''\}.$$

Define the powers of T_P^I as follows:

$$T_P^I \uparrow 0 = \emptyset$$
$$T_P^I \uparrow (i+1) = T_P^I(T_P^I \uparrow (i))$$
$$T_P^I \uparrow \omega = \text{lub}\{T_P^I \uparrow (i) \mid i < \omega\}$$

The following theorem illustrates the fixpoint semantics of disjunctive deductive databases:

Theorem 5 (Minker and Rajasekar, 1989). *For a disjunctive deductive database* P *and a positive clause* E, $P \models E$ *if and only if* $T_P^I \uparrow \omega \models E$ *if and only if* E *is true in every minimal model of* P.

Essentially, $T_P^I \uparrow \omega$ is equivalent to the set of all disjunctions that are true in each minimal model. The bottom-up algebraic method presented in this paper will essentially capture all the disjuncts in $T_P^I \uparrow \omega$.

We now relate the bottom-up procedure presented in this paper to the fixpoint semantics of disjunctive deductive databases.

Theorem 6. *Let* DB *be a disjunctive deductive database consisting of ground disjunctive facts and definite rules and let* $p_1, \ldots, p_n$ *be the IDB predicates of* DB. *Let* $S = P_1, \ldots, P_n$ *be the fixpoint solution returned by the bottom-up procedure of Fig. 5, where* P_i *is the C-table for predicate* p_i. *Then,* $(p_1(t_1) \vee \cdots \vee p_k(t_k)) \in T_P^I \uparrow \omega$ *if and only if for all* i, $1 \leq i \leq k$, $(t_i, C_i) \in P_i$ *and* $(C_1 \vee \cdots \vee C_k)$ *is a tautology.*

The above theorem states that the fixpoint solution returned by the bottom-up procedure of Fig. 5 captures exactly those disjuncts that are present in $T_P^I \uparrow \omega$.

4 Related Work

As has been noted earlier, most of the research on implementation issues of deductive databases has concentrated on definite deductive databases. A comprehensive discussion of these results can be found in [18]. As far as disjunctive deductive databases and their implementations are concerned, one can find relatively few scattered work. We shall mention some of the bottom-up methods for disjunctive deductive databases.

Henschen and Park [4] provide results with respect to yes/no answers to queries posed over disjunctive deductive databases. They handle negation by using the Generalized Closed World Assumption (GCWA). They present several fundamental results on compiling the GCWA in disjunctive deductive databases. They also present three representation schemes which separate the rules from the facts. Using these schemes, they isolate the deduction part in answering queries from the retrieval part. Several effective ways for compiling the GCWA inference on the rules and evaluating it through the facts are presented for non-recursive databases. Recursive rules are not adequately treated.

Grant and Minker [3] have developed algorithms to answer arbitrary queries in disjunctive databases. They provide algorithms to check if a candidate answer is indeed an answer to the query. Using this algorithm, they present an algorithm to find all minimal answers to queries. Although this paper does not deal with rules, queries can be answered by straightforward extensions to the algorithms.

Imielinski's C-tables [5] are capable of representing disjunctive facts. The extended relational algebra can be used to answer queries in disjunctive databases without rules.

Liu and Sunderraman [8] present a generalization to the relational model to represent disjunctive facts in tabular structures called M-tables. Queries can be answered using the generalized relational algebra. In [7], they apply the generalized model to disjunctive deductive databases. This method is sound but not complete. In contrast, the approach taken in this paper is both sound and complete for the subclass of disjunctive deductive databases considered.

Recently, there has been some research in identifying tractable classes of disjunctive databases in which query processing is efficient and in identifying classes of queries which can be answered efficiently given some syntactic information about the database. Lobo, Yu, and Wang ([9]) show that the computation of sets of pairs in the transitive closure of an acyclic relation with disjunctive description is polynomial. Dalal ([2]) defines a parameter called *cryptness* and uses the measure of cryptness to identify classes of disjunctive databases that can be queried in polynomial time. Khandaker, Fernandez, and Minker ([6]) identify a class of disjunctive databases in which at most two atoms are allowed in a disjunction and in which there are no rules. They present a polynomial time algorithm to compute answers to queries in this class.

5 Concluding Remarks

We have presented the notion of conditional facts in deductive databases and have shown their utility in answering queries in a subclass of disjunctive deductive databases. We envision that by increasing the expressibility of the language used to represent the conditions, we can model various other situations such as temporal deductive databases and incompletely specified databases. Of course, one has to redefine the semantics and design suitable data structures to represent these kinds of basic facts.

One important aspect that needs to be studied is how to extract disjunctive facts from a collection of C-tables efficiently. Indexing the conditional facts on the conditional variables would speed up the extraction process. Further study is required to solve this problem.

We are currently studying the possibility of extending the approach presented in this paper to answer queries in general disjunctive databases. One needs to consider additional operations on the C-tables to be able to account for multiple atoms in the head of the rules.

References

1. D. Chimenti, R. Gamboa, S. Naqvi R. Krishnamurthy, S. Tsur, and C. Zaniola. The ldl system prototype. *IEEE Transactions on Knowledge and Data Engineering*, 2(1):76–90, 1990.

2. M. Dalal. Some tractable classes of disjunctive logic programs. Technical Report, Department of Computer Science, Rutgers University, 1992.

3. John Grant and Jack Minker. Answering queries in indefinite databases and the null value problem. In *Advances in Computing Research, Volume 3*, pages 247–267. JAI Press Inc., 1986.

4. Lawrence Henschen and Hyuing-Sik Park. Compiling the GCWA in indefinite deductive databases. In Jack Minker, editor, *Foundations of Deductive Databases and Logic Programming*, pages 395–438. Morgan Kaufmann, Los Altos, CA, 1988.

5. Tomasz Imieliński and Witold Lipski Jr. On representing incomplete information in a relational database. In *Proceedings of the 7th International Conference on Very Large Data Bases, Cannes, France*, pages 389–397, New York, September 1981. IEEE.

6. Zahidul A. Khandaker, Jose Alberto Fernandez, and Jack Minker. A tractable class of disjunctive deductive databases. In *Proceedings of the Joint International Conference and Symposium on Logic Programming, Washington D.C.,,* 1992.

7. Ken-Chih Liu and Rajshekhar Sunderraman. An algebraic approach to indefinite deductive databases. In *Proceedings of the 5th International Symposium on Methodologies for Intelligent Systems, Knoxville, Tennessee*, New York, October 1990. Elsevier Press.

8. Ken-Chih Liu and Rajshekhar Sunderraman. A generalized relational model for indefinite and maybe information. *IEEE Transactions on Knowledge and Data Engineering*, 3(1):65–77, 1991.

9. Jorge Lobo, C. Yu, and G. Wang. Computing the transitive closure in disjunctive databases. Technical Report, University of Illinois at Chicago, Department of Electrical Engineering and Computer Science, 1992.

10. Jack Minker. On indefinite databases and the closed world assumption. In *Lecture Notes in Computer Science, N138*, pages 292–308. Springer-Verlag, 1982.

11. Jack Minker and Arcot Rajasekar. A fixpoint semantics for disjunctive logic programs. *Journal of Logic Programming*, 9:45–74, 1990.

12. K. Morris, J.D. Ullman, and A. Van Gelder. Design overview of the NAIL! system. In E. Shapiro, editor, *Proceedings of the Third International Conference on Logic Programming*, pages 554–568. Springer-Verlag, New York, 1986.

13. Inderpal S. Mumick, Hamid Pirahesh, and Raghu Ramakrishnan. Duplicates and aggregates in deductive databases. In *Proceedings of the 16th VLDB Conference*, 1990.

14. Shamim Naqvi and Shalom Tsur. *A Logic Language for Data and Knowledge Bases*. Computer Science Press, Rockville, MD, 1988.

15. Geoffrey Phipps, Marcia A. Derr, and Kenneth A. Ross. Glue-nail!: A deductive database system. In *Proceedings of the ACM SIGMOD Conference on Management of Data*, 1991.

16. Raghu Ramakrishnan, Divesh Srivastava, and S. Sudarshan. Coral – control, relations and logic. In *Proceedings of the 18th VLDB Conference, Vancouver, British Columbia, Canada*, 1992.

17. Rajshekhar Sunderraman. Deductive databases with conditional facts. Manuscript, 1992.

18. Jeffrey D. Ullman. *Principles of Database and Knowledge-Base Systems*, volume I and II. Computer Science Press, Rockville, Maryland, 1988.

19. Jayen Vaghani, Kotagiri Ramamohanarao, David Kemp, Zoltan Somogyi, and Peter Stuckey. The Aditi deductive database system. In *Proceedings of the NACLP'90 Workshop on Deductive Database Systems, Available as TR-CS-90-14, Dept. of Computing and Information Sciences, Kansas State University, Manhattan, Kansas*, 1990.

20. L. Vielle, P. Bayer, V. Kuchenhoff, and A. Lefebvre. Eks-v1, a short overview. In *Proceedings of the AAAI Workshop on Knowledge Base Management Systems*, 1990.

A Deductive Object-Oriented Database For Data Intensive Application Development

Alvaro A.A. Fernandes, Maria L. Barja, Norman W. Paton,
and M. Howard Williams

Department of Computing and Electrical Engineering,
Heriot-Watt University
Riccarton, Edinburgh EH14 4AS, Scotland, UK
e-mail: < alvaro,marisa,norm,howard>@cee.hw.ac.uk
phone: +44-31-449-5111 ; fax: +44-31-451-3431

Abstract. This paper outlines an approach to the development of a deductive object-oriented database system. The approach presented uses a formally defined object-oriented data model as the starting point for the development of a logic query language and an imperative database programming language. These languages can be used independently – the logic language for expressing queries or defining rule-based applications, the imperative language for manipulating the database – or together to support a flexible system for data-intensive application development.

1 Introduction

This paper presents the architecture of a deductive object-oriented database system (DOOD) currently under development at Heriot-Watt University, and indicates how such an architecture supports the development of large-scale data-intensive applications.

The software development life-cycle traditionally involves a sequence of steps which take the development team through problem analysis, high-level design, detailed design, and implementation. Regardless of the tools and techniques which are used within a particular organisation to support analysis and design, it is likely that implementation using conventional database systems will not follow naturally from the documents which emerge from the design process. The database system often fails to integrate smoothly with the design process in two major areas. Firstly, the structural features of the application, which are described during design using a semantic data model such as the E/R model, have to be mapped into the less expressive structure representation facilities of the data model. Secondly, the behavioural features of the application, which are described using a process modelling system such as data flow diagrams, have to be mapped onto the constructs of a conventional programming language which embeds calls to the database system.

Database researchers have adopted a number of approaches which seek to ease the development of applications which make use of database systems. For example, database programming languages [7] remove the dichotomy between the constructs of a database system and the language used to program the application, and object-oriented databases [20] provide database support for certain modelling constructs which are reminiscent of those supported by semantic data models. However, database programming languages such as PS-algol [8] and its descendants lack high-level data modelling facilities. Furthermore, most commercial object-oriented database systems are based upon object-oriented programming languages such as C++, and thus support low-level data description mechanisms instead of the more abstract models associated with database design tools. Thus while such systems ease the implementation phase of certain data-intensive applications, they do not significantly reduce the dichotomy between database design and implementation tools. A broader review of recent proposals for database systems, such as that given in section 2, indicates that it is normal to find at least one area of compromise concerning the accessibility of the data, the richness of the data model, or the expressive power of the data manipulation language.

This paper describes an approach to the development of a deductive object-oriented database system which includes an object-oriented data model which is appropriate for use as a semantic data model. This data model is fully integrated with both an imperative database programming language and a logic query language, and thus helps to bridge the gap between the design and implementation processes. The object management facilities which are supported by the data model of [15] and the manipulation language of [9] are collectively known as ROCK (Rule Object Computational Kernel). The logic language, which can either be used interactively or in an embedded form, is known as ROLL (Rule Object Logic Language).

This paper outlines an architecture in which a semantically rich data model can be fully integrated with a computationally complete programming language and a logical query language. The strategy is outlined in section 3, and an overview of the associated components is presented in section 4. Section 5 describes the consequences of the architecture for the development of large-scale, data-intensive applications, and section 6 presents some general conclusions. In section 4 acquaintance with object-oriented and deductive notions is assumed at the level of [20] and [12], respectively.

2   Related Work

This section compares a number of alternative approaches to the development of database systems which are intended to support application development, and in particular those approaches which utilise some form of object-oriented data model. One of the major goals of the DOOD project at Heriot-Watt is to integrate within a uniform formalism a range of facilities which have traditionally been supported by distinct systems. These distinct systems – semantic data models, database programming languages, and query languages – have been the focus of considerable attention by database researchers in recent years, as has their integration. However, an examination of the literature shows that many of the most prominent proposals for third generation database systems provide solutions which fail to cleanly integrate the three categories of system mentioned above. Figure 1 presents a classification of a number of systems according to the three categories introduced above, and identifies key areas of overlap which have been addressed by particular proposals. Such a classification process is clearly inexact, but should serve to identify different areas of emphasis among various research groups. The classification has been restricted to two systems in each category for reasons of limited space. The different assignments of systems to areas in the diagram are discussed in what follows.

Query Language Emphasis: Such systems, e.g. POSTGRES [29], GEM [30], are likely to operate on a data model which is either not independently defined, or which is lacking in certain modelling facilities commonly supported by semantic data models. The implementation of data-intensive applications is likely to require the embedding of the query language in a conventional programming language, thereby introducing an impedance mismatch. POSTGRES is considered to belong to this category because its principal advocate adheres to the manifesto suggestion that all access to the database is obtained through the query language [29], and because it is hard to imagine using the POSTGRES data model as a stand-alone modelling formalism.

Semantic Data Model Emphasis: Such systems, e.g. IFO [4], SDM [21], major on the description of the static properties of an application, and as such are amenable to use for conceptual modelling, independent of a particular implementation platform. There may be few, if any, behaviour description mechanisms.

Programming Language Emphasis: Such systems commonly start with an existing programming language, and minimise modifications to the language by making persistence orthogonal to the type of data being processed. Facilities for structuring data are thus directly descended from programming language mechanisms, and are often at a lower level than those of semantic data models. Typical examples are PS-Algol [8], Ontos [6] and GemStone [24], which are descended from S-Algol, C++ and Smalltalk respectively.

Programming Language plus Query Language: Such systems can result either from embedding a query formalism within a programming language (e.g. deductive query statements within the functional language PFL [26]), or by merging a data manipulation language with an existing query language (e.g. Glue/Nail [25]).

Programming Language plus Semantic Data Model: Where the type system of a database programming language includes data modelling constructs akin to those of a semantic data model, rather than lower level structuring mechanisms, systems in this category result. Galileo [5] is included in this category, while GemStone and Ontos are not, because certain abstractions are explicit in

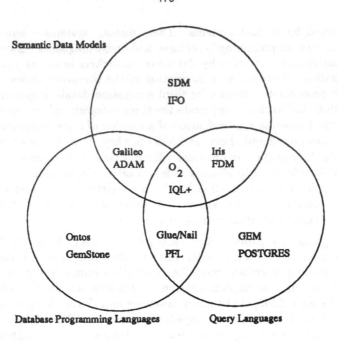

Figure 1: A Classification of Recent Database Systems

the Galileo type system which have to be implemented by programmers in Gem-Stone or Ontos. ADAM [20] is included because it supports a computationally complete programming language and has a data model which has been extended to support semantic modelling facilities.

Semantic Data Model plus Query Language: The addition of a query language to a semantic data model permits the structures of the model to be directly accessed and manipulated. However, such languages are not normally computationally complete, and thus have to be embedded in some imperative programming language for application development. Examples in this category include the query languages DAPLEX [28] and OSQL [11], which have been proposed for use with the Functional Data Model and Iris respectively.

Fully Combined Approach: Few systems smoothly integrate all three categories mentioned above. The O_2 [14] database system supports an independently specified data model, a number of programming language interfaces, and a query language. The approach described in this paper aims to yield a more expressive data model, a more powerful deductive query language, and a smoother integration of the three components. The system referred to as IQL+ [3] is an alternative approach to providing a deductive object-oriented database, by successively extending Datalog with concepts such as identity and inheritance for structuring the database, and explicit control to support updates. The principal limitations of IQL+ are the limited power of its data model, and the rather basic database programming facilities. The approach outlined in this paper does not introduce procedural mechanisms into the logic as in IQL+, but rather uses distinct languages for expressing deductive rules and for manipulating data, following in the footsteps of Glue/Nail [25]. This should result in much more standard and powerful data manipulation facilities, without complicating the semantics of the logic component by introducing extra-logical features.

The IQL+ approach to extending Datalog with object-oriented facilities is typical of a number of approaches summarised by [18]. An alternative approach adopted by [22] is to develop new logics, although current proposals in this area are a long way from yielding implemented systems. A summary of approaches to the development of DOODs is given in [17].

3 Architecture

The architecture we propose is built upon the data model defined in [15]. Conceptually, the model is defined as a formalism which specifies a mathematical structure corresponding to the database schema and which, for reasoning with such structures, provides:

- *Modelling axioms* which formalise the semantics of the abstraction mechanisms used in the model. When combined with the structures, these yield a logic theory of objects.

- *Operation axioms* which formalise the semantics of the operations which act on structures defined by the model. When taken with the structures, these yield an algebraic theory of objects.

Differentiating between the logical and algebraic theories gives rise to two design strands: the first combines the logic theory of objects with a proof procedure to yield an object-oriented logic language; the second associates the syntax and type system of a data manipulation language with the algebraic theory to yield an object-oriented database programming-language.

In this context, a deductive object-oriented database system can be envisaged which allows a user to interact with an object database through the two languages mentioned above. Crucially, in this approach the same set of objects determining a database must be taken as the Herbrand universe in the logical context, and as the carriers of the algebraic theory, as shown in Figure 2.

Some important shortcomings of DOOD proposals that have appeared so far can be explained by the fact that their sets of objects cannot be taken in both the above ways. Further, we have argued elsewhere [17] that an independently-defined data model is instrumental in achieving this.

The motivation for postulating the design of two languages is to keep the deductive language as pure as possible, leaving state-transition and control as the

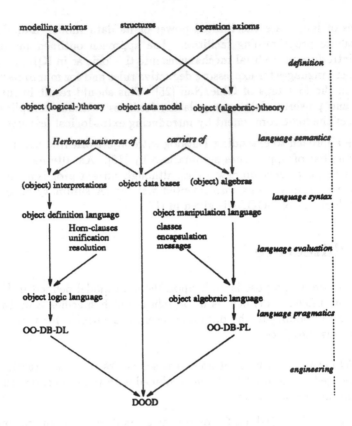

Figure 2: An Approach to DOODs

province of the imperative language. This simplifies the formal treatment of properties of logically-expressed queries, integrity constraints and derived data, while not necessarily imposing any mismatch in the embedding of the deductive language in the imperative one (as demonstrated by [25]). The logic language can be used in an interactive mode for expressing queries, for defining methods stored in the database, or as individual statements embedded within the imperative programming language. The resulting system can thus be placed in the intersection of all three categories in Figure 1, without the need to compromise on any of the three aspects.

4 Model and Languages

The previous section presented a strategy for the integration of an object-oriented data model with a logic query language and an imperative manipulation language without describing any of the individual components. This section introduces the data model and its associated languages.

4.1 The Data Model

A brief informal account of the model is now given with the purpose of providing an introduction to the terminology used later in the paper. Both atomic values and whatever abstractions are used to model a particular application domain are considered as *objects*. Atomic values are called *primary objects*, and all other abstractions are called *secondary objects*. Each object is assigned to an *object type*, and thereby conforms to the structure associated with the object type. Every object has a unique, immutable *identifier* the existence of which is completely detached from its *state*.

Structures comprise references of two kinds. The first kind of reference is used to model the *properties* of the object. This results, for each object, in a possibly empty set of pairs of the form ⟨*object-type, object-identifier*⟩. The second kind of reference is used when the object is complex, to model its *construction* from other objects. The result of this, for each such object, is a structure that takes one of three forms: a set of object identifiers, or a set of pairs of the form ⟨*index, object identifier*⟩, or a set of pairs of the form ⟨*object-type, object-identifier*⟩, which are the representations of abstraction mechanisms referred to as *association* (or set), *sequentiation* (or list) and *aggregation* (or tuple), respectively.

The *behaviour* of an object is determined by its response to *requests* for *operations* to be performed. Such operations are defined on an object class. From the point of view of users, an operation is viewed in terms of its *interface*, i.e. the *operation name* to be invoked in a request and the *operation signature* which dictates the types of the arguments and result which a request must carry. Designers are concerned, in addition, with *operation implementations*, generally called *methods*. Operations *encapsulate* the state of an object.

Invariants in the model are of two different kinds: domain-independent and domain-dependent. The first kind is established by means of *modelling axioms* and *operation axioms* which are embodied in any management system implementing the model. The second kind is handled within the rule-based language introduced in section 4.2. To give a flavour of the model, an example schema is given in Figure 3. The diagramming notation is as follows:

Nodes A **horizontal oval** represents an object type whose instances are primary objects. A **full-line rectangle** represents an object type whose instances are secondary objects. A **round-cornered rectangle** represents an operation. A **vertical oval** represents the source of the identifiers in the grounding of an object type.

Directed Edges An **unlabelled directed edge** represents the grounding of an object type by pointing to a primitive type, to the set of proper oids or to another object type. Note that some groundings have not been indicated (e.g. all those into integer) to keep the diagram less cluttered.

A **labelled directed edge** has one of seven symbols as its label: a directed edge labelled with a $\bigcirc$-*symbol* indicates an *attribution*; a directed edge labelled with a $\ominus$-*symbol* indicates a *generalisation*; a directed edge labelled with a $\odot$-*symbol* indicates a *partition*; a directed edge labelled with a $\oslash$-*symbol* indicates a *specialisation*; a directed edge labelled with a $\otimes$-*symbol* indicates an *aggregation*; a directed edge labelled with a $\circledast$-*symbol* indicates an *association*; a directed edge labelled with a $\circledcirc$-*symbol* indicates a *sequentiation*;

The last three have a *cohesive* version in which the characteristic symbol is enclosed within a square, instead of a circle, as described in 4.3.1.

Constraint Arrows in Constructive Edges A **double-headed arrow** represents the fact that multiple references to the same object of the type that is pointed to are admissible in the constructed objects. A **single-headed arrow** represents the fact that an object cannot be referenced more than once.

A **dashed-line arrow** represents the fact that some object of the type that is pointed to may not be referenced by any of the constructed objects. A **full-line arrow** represents the fact that every object of the type pointed to must be referenced.

4.2   The Logic Language

This section describes the logic language (ROLL) which can be used to query databases described by the model presented in the previous subsection. The syntax presented here bears some resemblance to that of the Stony Brook object logics [22], but is likely to be revised in the light of experience, and to ease its integration with the programming language introduced in the next section.

A ROLL **term** is either a variable, a constant or a keyword. There are no function symbols, so a term is *ground* iff it is a constant or a keyword. The set of all terms is $Term = Cons \cup Kwords \cup Var$. The set of all ground terms is called the *Herbrand universe*, denoted by H_U. Since both $Cons$ and $Kwords$ are finite, it follows that so is H_U.

The general form of a ROLL **atom** is $\ulcorner \alpha \,[\beta(\gamma) \; \Rightarrow \; \delta] \urcorner$, where the Greek letters are place holders as follows: α is a ROLL term which represents an object; β is a ROLL term which represents the name of an operation defined on the class of α; γ is a sequence of terms which represent the arguments of β; δ is a term which represents the result of applying the operation β with arguments γ to the object α. If β requires no arguments or if it returns no results then $\ulcorner(\gamma)\urcorner$ can dropped or $\ulcorner \Rightarrow \delta \urcorner$ can be dropped or both. An atom is *ground* iff α and β are ground, and γ and δ are either ground or missing.

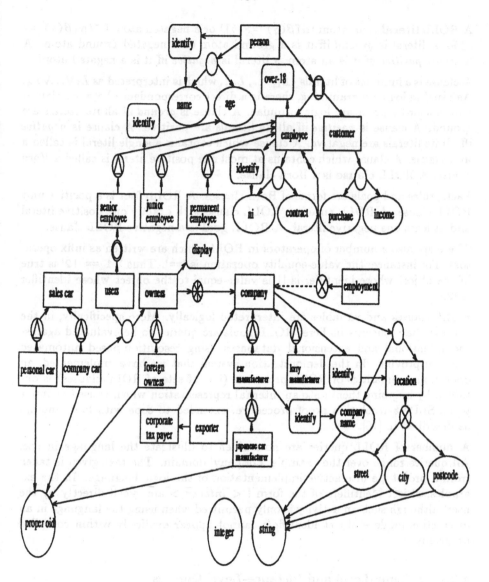

Figure 3: Company schema diagram

A ROLL **literal** is an atom $\ulcorner\alpha[\beta(\gamma) \Rightarrow \delta]\urcorner$ or a negated atom $\ulcorner \neg(\alpha[\beta(\gamma) \Rightarrow \delta])\urcorner$. A literal is *ground* iff it is a ground atom or a negated ground atom. A literal is *positive* iff it is an atom, a literal is *negative* iff it is a negated atom.

A clause is a finite set of literals $\{L_1, \ldots, L_n\}$, which is interpreted as $L_1 \vee \ldots \vee L_n$. As usual in logic programming, there is a direct correspondence between clauses and first-order predicate logic formulae. A clause is *ground* iff all its literals are ground. A clause is *positive* iff all its literals are positive. A clause is *negative* iff all its literals are negative. A clause which contains a single literal is called a *unit clause*. A clause which contains at most one positive literal is called a *Horn clause*. A ROLL **clause** is a Horn clause.

Facts, rules and goals are forms of Horn clauses. A ROLL **fact** is a positive unit ROLL clause. A ROLL **rule** is a ROLL clause with exactly one positive literal and at least one negative literal. A ROLL **goal** is a negative ROLL clause.

There are also a number of operators in ROLL which are written as infix operators. For instance, the value-equality operation is '=='. Thus '!1 == !2' is true iff the object whose identifier is !1 is value-equal to the object whose identifier is !2.

ROLL clauses and variables are interpreted logically. More specifically, in the context that concerns us here, ROLL goals are queries to be evaluated against the intensional and extensional databases using resolution-based automated theorem-proving. In the demonstration system that we have implemented, an operational semantics of ROLL programs (i.e. of sets of ROLL clauses) is obtained by mapping them onto an internal representation which is used as input to an SLDNF-resolution proof procedure, extended to cope with late binding, as described in [16].

A number of ROLL queries are now given to illustrate the language in use. All queries range over the example 'company' domain. The text given is taken from a prototype interactive implementation of the logic language. In the examples, object identifiers of the form ! < *integer* > are typed directly by the user, although such an activity is only permitted when using the language in an interactive mode – object identifiers cannot appear explicitly within compiled programs.

4.2.1 Schema-Level and Instance-Level Queries

The following are example schema-level ROLL queries:

```
roll ?- employee[isa => person].
yes
roll ?- city[ipo => location].
yes
roll ?- company[ici => X].
[X = owners] ;
[X = foreignOwners] ;
no
roll ?- seniorEmployee[ici => X].
```

```
[X = users] ;
no
roll ?- X[has => name].
[X = customer] ;
...
no
```

The first query returns true iff the object-type whose name is 'employee' is a subtype of the object-type whose name is 'person'. Intuitively, the object-type name 'person' is the result of sending the message 'isa' to the object-type name 'employee'.

The second query is analogous, but sends the message corresponding to the *is-part-of* relationship rather than *is-a* as in the first. The third and fourth use the messages corresponding to the *is-collected-in* relationship, which is applicable to association and sequentiation abstractions, to find object-types which are collections of companies (in the case of the third) and of senior employees (in the case of the fourth). Finally, the fifth query uses the message corresponding to the *has-a* relationship to retrieve all object-types which have a 'name' property.

The following are example instance level queries:

```
roll ?- !4[iof => employee].
yes
roll ?- Y[ith(city) => "edinburgh"].
[Y = !2] ;
[Y = !14] ;
no
roll ?- X[iin => !16].
[X = !18] ;
[X = !21] ;
no
roll ?- !4[.age => Y], Y :>= 18.
[Y = 25] ;
no
roll ?- !4[.name => Y], !13[.name => Z], Y :@> Z.
[Y = mary, Z = john] ;
no
roll ?- all !4[.X => Y].
[X = age, Y = 25]
[X = contract, Y = permanent]
[X = name, Y = mary]
[X = ni, Y = 12345]
yes
```

The first query returns true iff the object whose name is '!4' is an instance of the object-type whose name is 'employee'. Intuitively, this is done by sending the message 'iof' to the instance '!4'.

The second and third queries uses two other message names. The second query uses the *is-the* relationship between an object, the numeral or object-type-name that indexes a reference to an object in its construction (by sequentiation or aggregation) and the referenced object. Thus, the second query returns as 'Y' the names of aggregate objects which have the object named "**edinburgh**" in their 'city' component. The message in the third query corresponds to the *is-in* relationship between an object and the association to which it belongs. Thus, the third query returns the names of the objects which are referenced in the construction by association of the object whose name is '!16'.

The three remaining queries use the message '.<propertyname>' (which is simply a shorthand for 'get(<propertyname>)') to gain access to objects referenced as properties of the addressee. The fourth query demonstrates the use of an arithmetical comparison operator ':>=', and the fifth that of a term comparison operator':@>'. Finally, the sixth returns as property('X')-value('Y') pairs all property references of the object with name '!4'.

```
roll ?- !2[..street => Y].
[Y = grassmarket] ;
no
roll ?- !7[.. 1 => X].
[X = !4] ;
no
roll ?- all !2[..X => Y].
[X = street, Y = grassmarket]
[X = city, Y = edinburgh]
[X = postcode, Y = eh12hj]
yes
```

The three queries above illustrate how the elements in the construction of objects built by sequentiation and aggregation can be manipulated in ROLL. Analogously to 'get' and '.', '..' is synonymous with 'ith'. The first query returns the 'street' coordinate of the object whose name is '!2' as the instantiation of 'Y'. The second query returns the first element in the construction by sequentiation of the object whose name is '!7'. Finally, the third query returns as coordinate('X')-value('Y') pairs all construction references of the object (in this case built by aggregation) with name '!2'.

4.2.2 Overloading, Overriding and Late-Binding Methods

It is difficult to claim that a formalism falls under the object-oriented paradigm if the phenomena known as overloading, overriding and late-binding of methods are not accounted for in a clearly recognisable way. At present, this is a point where most ongoing research in the area of deductive object-oriented databases runs into problems. The following three groups of queries illustrate how these features are present in ROLL, and how the account given to them is intuitive from both the deductive and the object-oriented perspectives. We begin with overloading.

```
roll ?- !1[iof => X], !1[identify => Y], Y[iof => Z].
[X = company, Y = scotcars, Z = companyName] .
yes
roll ?- !4[iof => X], !4[identify => Y], Y[iof => Z].
```

```
[X = seniorEmployee, Y = 12345, Z = ni] .
yes
```

In the examples above, '!1' is an instance of 'company', and '!4' is an instance of 'seniorEmployee'. The crucial point to notice is that the operation 'identify' associated with 'company' objects is different from that associated with 'seniorEmployee' objects, and thus the name 'identify' is overloaded – its implementation in class 'company' is different from that in class 'seniorEmployee'.

At this point it is important to have a closer look at ROLL methods. As already pointed out, methods are an integral part of a domain definition, in that they are used in building the intensional database. The ROLL program that implements a method must be assigned to a pair $\langle \mu, t \rangle$, where μ is a method name and t is an object type name, so that overloading, overriding and late-binding can be catered for.

The available methods in a particular class are determined by the computed operation set of the class, which supports inheritance as described in [15]. For instance, in the example domain (see Figure 3) the operation name 'identify' appears in five $\langle \mu, t \rangle$ pairs, viz. $\langle$ identify, company $\rangle$, $\langle$ identify, carManufacturer $\rangle$, $\langle$ identify, person $\rangle$, $\langle$ identify, employee $\rangle$, $\langle$ identify, juniorEmployee $\rangle$. To each of these pairs there corresponds a method implementation, two of which are given below:

```
method(identify,person,
        {
X as person[identify => Y] <- X[.name => Y]
        }).
method(identify,employee,
        {
X as employee[identify => Y] <- X[.ni => Y]
        }).
```

The first of these can be read as: the method 'identify' attached to the class 'person' has as result 'X' as defined by the clause 'person[identify => Y] <- X[.name => Y]'. Thus the ROLL program which gives a definition to the method is enclosed in curly brackets. Some features present in the above ROLL programs are explained later in this document.

In order to cater for late-binding, the proof procedure must be extended to select that implementation of *identify* that best suits the addressee. The precise definition of what it is that best suits an addressee can be found in [15], and roughly amounts to selecting the implementation associated with the most specific class of the addressee. The absence of conflicting implementations at a given class is a well-definedness property of domain-definitions [15].

Recall that *identify* is defined for *juniorEmployee*, *employee* and *person*. These three classes are ordered from the most to the least specific as follows:

juniorEmployee ⊑ *employee* ⊑ *person* [15]. The following two queries illustrate how overriding takes place with respect to instances of *employee* and *person*.

```
roll ?- !3[identify => X].
[X = john] .
yes
roll ?- !4[identify => X].
[X = 12345] .
yes
```

In the above cases the (rather contrived) *identify* operation name has been late-bound to its implementation in the most specific class of the addressee for which the operation is available, viz. *person* for '!3', and *employee* for '!4'. The prototype implementation does not cater for static type checking, and hence the differing result types of *identify* in the examples above are permitted.

4.3 The Programming Language

The logic language described in the previous section can be considered to be the query language of the database system. Its role differs from that of SQL in relational databases in two important senses – it has no statements which support data manipulation, and it enables rule-based applications to be built within the database system itself.

The role of the DBPL in the DOOD architecture is to support data definition and manipulation at both the schema and the data levels, and to enable complete applications to be implemented without the hindrance of the impedance mismatch. This can be achieved by developing a programming language which shares the same type system as the logic language – in our case derived from the data model described in section 4.1, in accordance with the architecture given in Figure 2. This section gives a flavour of the programming language through a number of examples of data definition and manipulation statements.

The language is defined as a strongly typed imperative language with the intention of adopting static type-checking whenever possible. To relieve the user of the burden of having to specify the types of all variables and expressions, a type inferencing mechanism is used.

4.3.1 Object type declarations

Each object in the system can be categorised as belonging to either the set of primary or the set of secondary objects. Primary objects are instances of primitive types and secondary objects are instances of classes each of which has a structure that conforms to that given by an *object type* definition. The primitive types supported by the language are *int, real, string* and *bool*. Each of these primitive types is associated with a number of standard operators for manipulating objects of that type.

The programmer can define new types by renaming existing types or by aggregating a number of primitive and/or user defined types to build an object type declaration. An object type declaration consists of a name (the name of the object type being defined) and an object type definition.

An object type definition may consist of up to six components, namely a *grounding expression*, an *inheritance expression*, an *attributive expression*, a *constructive expression*, a *construction constraints expression*, and an *interface expression*.

The **grounding expression** determines whether the objects conforming to this type are primary objects or secondary ones. A type definition can have at most one grounding expression – if no grounding expression is present, the objects conforming to the type are secondary objects. If the objects in the grounding set are defined to be primary objects then the definition of the type includes only a grounding expression (the grounding set of an object-type contains the set of objects that conform to that object-type). Alternatively, the grounding set of the object type may be the same as that of another object type (objects may have the same structure, but the operations which determine their behaviour may be different). As an example of a grounding expression, *type name:string* indicates that *name* is grounded on *string*.

The **inheritance expression** allows for the specification of relationships between the grounding set of the object type being defined and that of other object types. A type may *specialise, generalise* or be *partitioned-by* other types.

The **attributive expression** declares the properties of the objects of the type being defined.

The **constructive expression** determines the mode of construction for complex objects. Three constructors exist, namely *association* (which builds a set), *sequentiation* (which builds a list) and *aggregation* (which builds a tuple). These constructors may be *non-cohesive* (in which case they are denoted by { }, [ ] and < > respectively) or *cohesive* (in which case they are denoted by {{ }}, [[ ]], and << >> respectively). A type definition can have at most one constructive expression and cannot both specify and inherit a constructive expression. The removal of an object from a collection of objects defined using a *cohesive* constructor leads to the deletion of the cohesively constructed object. As an example, the object type *location* in Figure 4 has a constructive expression which is an *aggregation* (see also Figure 3).

A **construction constraint** may be defined for object types involved in the construction and is composed of a *membership constraint* and a *correlation constraint*. The membership constraint determines whether or not it is required that every object of the constituent type occurs in the construction of some object of the type being defined. A membership constraint can take as value one of *exhaustive* or *sparse*. Correlation constraints allow the specification of whether or not any particular object of the constituent type can have one or more references to it. The value taken by a correlation constraint is one of *exclusive* or *shared*. The update semantics for cohesive constructors follow a similar approach to that

of [23] with respect to the semantics of references to composite objects, where
properties model *weak references*, non-cohesive constructors model *independent
composite references* and cohesive constructors model *dependent composite references*. If we wish further to express whether any of these references is *exclusive*
or *shared*, this is accomplished by defining *correlation constraints*.

```
type person:
   generalises: employee, customer;
   properties :
        name, age;
   interface :
        identify: name;
end-type
type employee:
   properties:
        ni, contract, salary;
   interface :
        identify: ni;
        increment_salary(incr: salary);
end-type
type customer:
   properties:
        purchase, income;
end-type
type location:
   construction: < street, city, code >;
end-type
type company:
   properties:
        location, company_name;
   interface :
        identify: location;
end-type
type employment:
   < (employee,exhaustive,shared),
        (company, sparse, exclusive) >;
end-type
```

Figure 4: Object type declaration examples

The **interface expression** defines the set of operation interfaces of the operations which are publicly available. An operation interface consists of a name and
a signature. The signature specifies the formal input parameters, their types,
and optionally the type of the result that might be returned when the operation is invoked. An implementation for each one of the interfaces defined on
an object type definition is given in the *class* declaration associated with each

type declaration for which the interface expression is not empty. If no interface expression is given in an object type declaration a class is declared implicitly, and objects of this class can only be accessed and manipulated using the default behaviour.

A **method** is the code specifying the implementation of an operation. Objects of different classes may have different methods for the same operation. The choice of the method to be executed as a consequence of a request for an operation is performed by binding the operation to an actual implementation taking into account overriding and late binding.

Types are declared as a means of defining the structure of classes. A class is determined by (and has the same name as) the type which specifies its structure. Two kinds of method can be defined for a class: private methods and public methods. A private method can only be called from other methods attached to its class, or subclasses thereof. For private methods, both the interface and the implementation are specified within the class definition. Figure 5 presents class definitions corresponding to the object type definitions in Figure 4. The data manipulation language described below is the language used for method implementation.

4.3.2 Data Manipulation

The Data Manipulation Language is a language for specifying operations. It provides a syntax for defining operations on objects and for requesting that operations be performed on objects. The model of computation adopted is the messaging one according to [19] that is, the recipient of the message is a distinguished parameter within the request. The message sending operator is @. The message recipient is an object and a message can also be sent to *self* or to *super*.

The constructs supported by the Data Manipulation Language are roughly the ones supported by most imperative programming languages, i.e. assignment, control structures such as *while* and *if then else*, and I/O statements. A further control statement is the *foreach* construct which may be used to iterate over the elements of a set or a sequence, or over the instances of a class. All these constructs have a mode of operation in which they may return an object (or a set of objects in the case of *foreach*) and can therefore be assigned to an *object name*. In general, the language offers two main types of syntactic classes namely *object expressions* and *statements*. Object expressions return an object when they are executed, while statements do not return an object but instead provoke a change in the state of computation.

The system provides a set of built-in methods to manipulate objects i.e. their properties and construction. In order to ease the programmer's task by offering a simpler syntax to express computations, most of the built-in methods need not be written in a message sending style. Ultimately, all these expressions can be recast in the message sending style, and in fact their associated meaning is defined using

```
    class person:
      public:
        identify: name begin get_name@self end
    end-class
    class employee:
      public:
        identify: ni begin get_ni@self end
        begin
                put_salary((get_salary@self) * (1 + incr / 100))@self;
        end
    end-class
    class company:
      public:
        identify: location begin get_company_name@self end
    end-class
```

Figure 5: Class declaration examples

this form. For example, each class whose construction is an association has a method *add_member* which takes as parameter an object which is to be added to the association. Such an operation can be invoked by (*add_member(a)@b*), or using the simpler and more intuitive syntax *b ++ a*.

For each property the system generates a pair of methods whose names are formed from the name of the respective property with the prefixes *get_* and *put_*. These methods allow the object referenced by a property to be retrieved or replaced, and can be made public or redefined in the public part of a class definition.

A class can be assigned to a persistent environment, and if so the type associated with the class, its methods and its instances are made to persist. A persistent class is only allowed to reference other persistent classes. Examples of how to make class and object type definitions persist and how to manipulate them are given in Figures 6 and 7 respectively. Figure 6 shows how an environment, which is a parameter to a program, can be associated with a class by naming the environment in the definition of the class. Figure 7 shows how such an environment is subsequently accessed, and includes an example of a *foreach* statement which awards a salary increase to all employees older than *18*.

4.4 Integrating The Languages

The logic language and the DBPL can be fully integrated in the following sense – the logic language can call any method written in the DBPL as long as that

```
program employees_schema(ENV)
begin
   ...
   class ENV.person:
      public:
         identify: name begin get_name@self end
   end-class
   ...
end
```

Figure 6: Defining a persistent class

```
program employees_management(ENV)
begin
   ...
   foreach y in employee do
      if get_age@y > 18 then increment_salary(5)@y;
   ...
end
```

Figure 7: Manipulation of a persistent environment

method does not (directly or indirectly) change any global data; the DBPL can invoke any logic language expression for which an appropriate type can be inferred. This latter restriction on the calling of a logic expression from the DBPL applies because it is not possible to infer a single result type for a number of different goal categories – for example, goals in which the method name is a variable.

The exact syntax to be used for embedding the logic language within the DBPL has yet to be finalised. However, the nature of the integration can be illustrated using the example in Figure 8, in which the program in Figure 7 has been modified to iterate over a set specified using the logic language.

```
    program employees_management(ENV)
    begin
        ...
        foreach y in [E | E[iof => employee], E[.age => A], A :> 18] do
            increment_salary(5)@y;
        ...
    end
```

Figure 8: Integrating a logic query with the DBPL

5 Summary

5.1 Current Position and Future Plans

The data model and DBPL are fully specified in [15] and [9], and a prototype of the logic language has been implemented using MegaLog, as described in [16]. The data model and DBPL are currently being implemented using EX-ODUS [27], which will then be used to re-implement the logic language. The formalisation of the logic language is underway.

A central aim of the project is to evaluate the resulting system using an application in the area of geographic information systems. To this end work has been done to identify key areas of Geographic Data Management where the power of a DOOD yields significant benefits over conventional techniques [1, 2, 32].

5.2 Conclusions

This paper has presented an approach to the development of a deductive object-oriented database system in which a semantically rich object-oriented data model is used to underpin a logic query language and an imperative data manipulation language. The resulting system provides comprehensive support for semantic data modelling, user queries and application development. This integration of facilities provides improved database support for the software development process based upon an object-oriented view of design. The data model presented in section 4.1 supports the classical abstraction mechanisms supported by many semantic data models, and as such can be used during both design and implementation. Furthermore, method interfaces specified during the design phase can be directly implemented using the database programming language presented in section 4.3, and rule-based solutions specified using the logic language described in section 4.2.

To summarise, the principal benefits of the approach presented here are:

- There is no longer an emphasis on the data model, the query language or the programming language at the expense of other components, a feature of many other proposals identified in section 2.

- The database system provides facilities which reduce the size of the step which must be taken when moving from design to implementation.

- The logic language is powerful enough to support the expression of complete rule-based applications or components of applications, and is not limited to straightforward retrieval operations.

- The envisaged advantages of deductive object-oriented databases are supported – a theoretical foundation for object-oriented modelling and querying; rule-based applications are freed from the limitations of the relational model; OODBs can be queried using a rule-based language.

Acknowledgements The work that resulted in this paper has been funded by the Science and Engineering Research Council through the IEATP programme, and their support is duly acknowledged. We would also like to thank our colleague Alia Abdelmoty, and Dr. Keith G. Jeffery of Rutherford Appleton Laboratory for useful discussions on the subject of this paper, and Dr. J.M.P. Quinn representing ICL and Mr Neil Smith of Ordnance Survey as the industrial partners in the project.

References

[1] Alia Abdelmoty, M. Howard Williams, and Michael Quinn. A Rule-Based Approach to Computerized Map Reading to be published in *Information and Software Technology*, 1993.

[2] Alia Abdelmoty, M. Howard Williams, and Norman W. Paton. Deduction and Deductive Databases for Geographic Data Handling, to be published in *3rd Symposium on Spatial Databases (SSD)*, Springer-Verlag, 1993.

[3] Serge Abiteboul. Towards a Deductive Object-Oriented Database Language. *Data & Knowledge Engineering*, 5:263–287, 1990.

[4] Serge Abiteboul and Richard Hull. IFO: A Formal Semantic Database Model. *ACM Transactions on Database Systems*, 12(4):525–565, December 1987.

[5] Antonio Albano, Giorgio Ghelli, and Renzo Orsini. A Relationship Mechanism for a Strongly Typed Object-Oriented Database Programming Language. In G.M. Lohman et al., editor, *Proceedings of 17th VLDB*, pages 565–575, 1991.

[6] T. Andrews and C. Harris. *The Ontos Object Database*. Ontologic Corp., 1989.

[7] Malcolm Atkinson, and Peter Buneman. Types and Persistence in Database Programming Languages. *ACM Computing Surveys*, 19(2):105–190, 1988.

[8] M.P. Atkinson, K.J. Chisholm, and W.P. Cockshott. PS-algol: An Algol with a Persistent Heap. *ACM SIGPLAN Notices*, 17, 1981.

[9] Maria L. Barja. Design of a Database Programming Language for a DOOD Technical Report TR92016, Department of Computing and Electrical Engineering, Heriot-Watt University, Riccarton, Edinburgh EH14 4AS, Scotland, 1992.

[10] François Bancilhon and Peter Buneman, editors. *Advances in Database Programming Languages.* Frontier Series. ACM Press/Addison-Wesley Publ. Co., New York, NY, 1990.

[11] David Beech. A Foundation for Evolution from Relational to Object Databases. In M. Missikoff J.W.Schmidt, S. Ceri, editor, *Proceedings of EDBT '88*, LNCS 303, pages 251–270, March 1988. Springer-Verlag.

[12] Subrata Das. Deductive Databases and Logic Programming. Addison-Wesley, 1992.

[13] Claude Delobel, Michael Kifer, and Yoshifumi Masunaga. *Deductive and Object-Oriented Databases (Second International Conference DOOD'91, Munich).* Springer-Verlag, Berlin, 1991.

[14] O. Deux et al. The Story of O_2. *IEEE Transactions on Knowledge and Data Engineering*, 2(1), March 1990.

[15] Alvaro A.A. Fernandes, M. Howard Williams, and Norman W. Paton. A Formal Abstract Definition of Objects as a Data Modelling Primitive. Technical Report TR92003, Department of Computing and Electrical Engineering, Heriot-Watt University, Riccarton, Edinburgh EH14 4AS, Scotland. June 1992.

[16] Alvaro A.A. Fernandes. An Object-Oriented Logic by Examples Technical Report, Department of Computing and Electrical Engineering, Heriot-Watt University, Riccarton, Edinburgh EH14 4AS, Scotland, September 1992.

[17] Alvaro A.A. Fernandes, M. Howard Williams, Norman W. Paton, and Andrew Bowles. Approaches to Deductive Object-Oriented Databases. *Information and Software Technology*, Vol 34, No 12, 787-803, 1992.

[18] Georges Gardarin. Rule Languages for Relational and Object-Oriented Databases. *Proc. 9th BNCOD*, M.S. Jackson and A.E. Robinson (eds), 1–16, 1991.

[19] Elizabeth Fong, William Kent, Ken Moore and Craig Thompson X3/ SPARC/ DBSSG/ OODBTG Final Report, September, 1991.

[20] Peter M.D. Gray, Krishna G. Kulkarni, and Norman W. Paton. Object-Oriented Databases: A Semantic Data Model Approach. Prentice-Hall, 1992.

[21] Michael Hammer and Dennis McLeod. Database Description with SDM: A Semantic Database Model. *ACM Transactions on Database Systems*, 6(3):351–386, September 1981.

[22] Michael Kifer and Georg Lausen. F-logic: A Higher-Order Language for Reasoning about Objects, Inheritance and Scheme. In James Clifford, Bruce Lindsay, and David Maier, editors, *Proceedings ACM SIGMOD Conference*, 134–146, 1989.

[23] Won Kim, Elisa Bertino, Jorge F. Garza. Composite Objects Revisited. In James Clifford, Bruce Lindsay, and David Maier, editors, *Proceedings of ACM SIGMOD Conference* , 337–347, 1989.

[24] D. Maier, J. Stein, A. Otis, and A. Purdy. Development of an Object-Oriented DBMS. In *OOPSLA '86*, pages 472–482, 1986. ACM Press.

[25] Geoffrey Phipps, Marcia A. Derr, and Kenneth A. Ross. Glue-Nail: A Deductive Database System. In James Clifford and Roger King, editors, *Proceedings of ACM SIGMOD Conference*, pages 308–317, 1991. ACM Press.

[26] Alexandra Poulovassilis and Peter King. Extending the Functional Data Model to Computational Completeness. In C. Thanos F. Bancilhon and D. Tsichritzis, editors, *EDBT '90*, pages 75–91. Springer-Verlag, March 1990.

[27] Joel E. Richardson and Michael J. Carey. Implementeing Persistence in E. In John Rosenberg and David Koch (eds), *Persistent Object Systems*, pages 175–199. Springer-Verlag, 1989.

[28] David W. Shipman. The Functional Data Model and the Data Language DAPLEX. *ACM Transactions on Database Systems*, 6(1):140–173, 1981.

[29] The Comittee for Advanced DBMS Function. Database Systems: Achievements and Opportunities. *ACM SIGMOD Record*, 19(3):31–44, September 1990. The *Committee* is composed of Michael Stonebraker, Lawrence A. Rowe, Bruce Lindsay, James Gray, Michael Brodie, Philip Bernstein, and David Beech.

[30] Carlo Zaniolo. The Database Language GEM. In *Proceedings of the 1983 ACM SIGMOD International Conference on the Management of Data*. ACM Press, 207–218, 1983.

[31] Peter Wegner Concepts and Paradigms of Object-Oriented Programming *OOPS Messenger*, 1(1):7–87, August 1990.

[32] M. Howard Williams, Norman W. Paton, Alia Abdelmoty, Alvaro A.A. Fernandes, Maria L. Barja. Applying Advanced Database Techniques to Geographic Information Systems. *JFIT Technical Conference*, Keele, March, 1993.

Storage and Retrieval of First-order Terms Using a Relational Database

Paul Singleton
Pearl Brereton

Department of Computer Science, Keele University,
Keele, Newcastle, Staffs ST5 5BG, UK

Abstract. We present several practical techniques for storing first-order terms (e.g. clauses) in a relational database, and for mechanically constructing SQL *select* queries which retrieve all terms matching a given pattern. First we outline the deductive database application which prompted us to develop the techniques, then we present our approach to clause storage and indexing, and consider three variants of the *unifiability* retrieval condition. We discuss several issues in interfacing Prolog to a RDBMS, including caching and re-entrancy. We then present four techniques: one for storing and retrieving general terms; a specialisation of this for storing ground terms; another specialisation for storing finite maps; and a quite different technique for ground terms. We comment on the complexity of some of the generated SQL queries.

1 Introduction

This paper describes several practical techniques for storing Prolog terms in a SQL-compliant relational database. These techniques were developed in the course of a project (***DERIVE*** [26]) which can be summarised as follows:

The problem. We sought to automate and control the construction of deliverable software products by mechanically transforming and combining source files (and other primitive components) which have unlimited independent dimensions of variance.

The solution. We chose to construct a deductive database in which primitive configuration items are *facts*, composition and derivation tools are *relations*, configurations are described by *rules*, and products are derived by evaluation of *queries* (either concretely, partially or abstractly).

The implementation. We built this database from a combination of Prolog (which provides meta-programming and deductive capabilities) and a proprietary RDBMS (which provides robust, persistent, high-capacity, shareable storage for configuration data).

We needed to meta-program the evaluation of queries so as to exploit the following techniques:

- *memoisation* [16] of deductions: in order to support minimal recompilation [27] of large systems after small changes;

- *abstract interpretation* of build deductions, to discover which components (or variants thereof) are used, whether they are available, whether they are compatible, etc., without the expense of invoking compilers;

- *partial evaluation* of builds, to leave some parameterisation unspecified in a deliverable generic product configuration of which the customer will perform the final stages of building.

We built this deductive database around two main components:

- a proprietary Prolog system (Quintus V3), with which we programmed a stateless front-end to the database;

- a proprietary RDBMS kernel (ORACLE V6), which provided a distributed, robust and high-capacity repository for simple data in tabular form.

DERIVE needs a clause base which is

- *persistent*: changes to the database must persist beyond the end of each session;

- *shareable*: many concurrent users must be able to add configuration items and derive products;

- *scalable*: not limited in its capacity for configuration data by the size of primary or virtual memory (as is Prolog's built-in database).

Prolog is famously supportive of meta-programming, but (in its conventional implementations) its database lacks persistence, shareability and high capacity.

We therefore designed a schema (for the RDBMS) and developed algorithms (implemented in Prolog) for storing arbitrary terms (e.g. clauses) in the RDBMS, and for retrieving them according to their unifiability with arbitrary query terms.

This combination of Prolog and an RDBMS combines the strengths of each component system. Its main weakness is in the bandwidth of the interface between the two, but strategic caching of data within Prolog can reduce the impact of this bottleneck.

1.1 Structure of the Paper

The remainder of this paper has three main sections.

[§2 Analysis] presents an analysis of the term storage problem in terms of representation, indexing and retrieval. It considers some interesting special cases, some variants of the *unifiability* retrieval condition, and some implementation approaches.

[§3 Coupling Prolog to a RDBMS] considers two strategic and seven tactical aspects of the problem of interfacing Prolog applications to an RDBMS, and then classifies and describes the interface which we adopted.

[§4 Practical Techniques for Term Indexing and Retrieval] presents four assorted techniques for retrieving stored terms for an RDBMS according to their unifiability with an arbitrary query term.

Finally, we present a concise summary and some conclusions.

2 Analysis

In this section we define *clause* and *term*; we consider the independence of *storage*, *indexing* and *retrieval*; we briefly review the storage and retrieval models of Prolog and the RDBMS; and finally we consider some special cases of retrieval, some alternative retrieval criteria and some alternative retrieval strategies.

2.1 Data Models and Representations

A typical RDBMS stores tables of records, whose fields are either character strings or numbers (plus a few other special cases like dates).

A Prolog database, however, stores *clauses*, whose arguments are first order *terms* [Fig. 1.], i.e. labelled trees whose nodes are labelled with strings (*atoms*), and whose leaves may be strings, numbers or logical unknowns (*variables*). The terms manipulated by a Prolog application may be of arbitrary size and structure, neither of which is known at compile time.

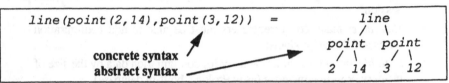

Fig. 1. Illustrating the concrete and abstract syntax of Prolog terms.

Clauses (i.e. the facts and rules of a program) are instances of terms [Fig. 2.]:

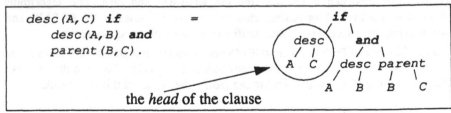

Fig. 2. In Prolog, a *clause* is an instance of a *term*.

The general problem of providing persistent storage for Prolog applications is thus one of storing *terms*, and our solutions also satisfy the *clause storage* requirement.

2.2 Storage, Indexing and Retrieval

Conventionally, a Prolog clause is indexed only by its head [Fig. 2.]. This is because Prolog uses a backward-chaining search strategy, which only ever retrieves a rule according to the unifiability of its head with the current goal. Other search strategies are possible (and can readily be programmed in Prolog, as was done for **DERIVE**), so we therefore implement a generalisation of this retrieval scheme, in which term *storage* and *indexing* are handled separately: a term is stored in such a way that it can be reconstructed (cheaply and accurately) within Prolog after retrieval; it is indexed in whatever way suits the application (e.g. on its entire structure, on only part of it, or on a different but related term).

The difficulties of implementing a term store over a RDBMS lie not in representing the terms so as to permit their reconstruction, but in indexing them so that they can be retrieved according to their unifiability ("matching") with arbitrary patterns. To store a term, it is only necessary to encode it as a character or byte string from which the original term (strictly, an *alphabetic variant* of that term) can be reconstructed. The traditional *write* and *read* procedures of Prolog achieve this (although they do not give the most compact representation).

General term indexing is non-trivial: there is, for example, no total ordering [26] of stored terms such that all those which match each given query term are adjacent, and indexed sequential access storage is inapplicable. Nor can we (nor wish we to) rely on simplifying assumptions about likely patterns of access or about likely structures of stored terms: we want a completely general mechanism which allows *any* term to be stored, and *any* term to be uttered as a query term.

A typical RDBMS evaluates expressions in relational algebra (*unite, select, project, join*) augmented by some higher-order operations (aggregate functions and correlated subqueries). Ultimately, attribute values in an expression match attribute values in tables by:

- equality and inequality ('=' and '!=');
- arithmetic and lexicographic comparison ('<', '<=', '>' and '>=');
- wild-card string matching (a small subset of *regular expression* matching [13]).

Prolog, however, retrieves clauses from its database by attempting to unify a query term with each stored term (sequentially, upon backtracking). Unification of two terms instantiates each to their *most general unifier* (hereafter, just *unifier*), i.e. the most general term which is an instance of each [Fig. 3.].

These terms *unify*:	`point(X,9,Z) = point(14,Y,Z)`
This is their *unifier*:	`point(14,9,Z)`

Fig. 3. The most general *unifier* of two terms (example)

2.3 Special Cases of Term Storage

Despite the disclaimers of [§2.2 Storage, Indexing and Retrieval], we *are* interested in certain special cases of term storage. In particular, we consider the cases where either the query terms or the stored terms are known (at the application design stage) to be *ground* (i.e. free of variables). In these circumstances, it is possible to exploit simplified storage and indexing algorithms, with better performance than the completely general scheme.

We consider the four combinations of general or ground query terms used to retrieve unifiable general or ground stored terms.

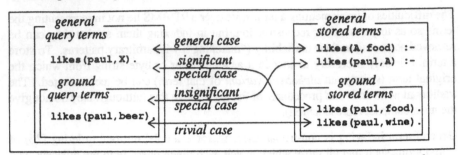

Fig. 4. Four combinations of general/ground query terms matching general/ground stored terms

Of these cases:

- *general* ↔ *general* is indeed the general case, and any implementation of this would serve (albeit sub-optimally) for *all* circumstances;

- *general* ↔ *ground* is significantly likely to arise in real applications (e.g. in RDB applications, all stored data is ground), and may be worth implementing separately (e.g. for savings in time, space or complexity);

- *ground* ↔ *general* is an artificial and insignificant case (in our experience and judgement);

- *ground* ↔ *ground* is trivial.

Since the latter two cases are of no interest, we give no special consideration to ground query terms. Later in this paper we shall present four techniques for matching general query terms with different classes of stored terms:

- general stored terms [§4.1 Technique T1a: Retrieval of General Terms];

- ground stored terms [§4.2 Technique T1b: Retrieval of Ground Terms] by a simplification of technique T1a;

- finite maps (a specialised data structure of particular importance to *DERIVE*) [§4.3 Technique T2(a,b): Storage and Retrieval of Maps];

- ground stored terms [§4.4 Technique T3: Wild-card Retrieval of Ground Terms] by a technique quite different to T1a and T1b.

2.4 Term Retrieval Conditions

In addition to the *unifiability* retrieval condition discussed above, there are three variants [Fig. 5.] which are useful in meta-programmed applications such as *DERIVE*. An application may wish to retrieve exactly those stored terms which:

- are *specialisations* of (i.e. are subsumed by) the query term;

- are *generalisations* of (i.e. which subsume) the query term;

- are *alphabetic variants* of (i.e. are identical to, except for renaming of variables) the query term.

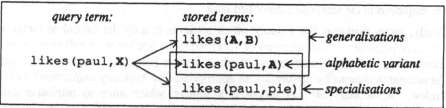

Fig. 5. Example of generalised, variant and specialised terms.

We support these three variant conditions by exploiting Prolog's *freeze*[1] operation [22], applied either to the query term, to the stored term, or to both [Fig. 6.].

- unifiability (a) of the (raw) query term with the stored *frozen* term implies that the stored term is a *specialisation* of the query term;

- unifiability (b) of the *frozen* query term with the stored (raw) term implies that the stored term is a *generalisation* of the query term;

- unifiability (c) of the *frozen* query term with the stored *frozen* term implies that the stored term is a *variant* of the query term.

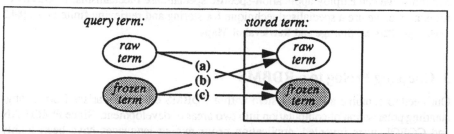

Fig. 6. Implementation of subsumption, variance and supersumption tests using freezing and unification (see text).

If either of the latter two cases is to be supported, it is necessary to anticipate this by indexing *frozen* copies of stored terms (although, due to the independence of storage and indexing, the terms themselves can be stored unfrozen). We can cater for *all* possibilities by indexing in both unfrozen and frozen forms. We envisage, however, that (in this respect at least) retrieval criteria will typically be known at the application design stage.

Furthermore, the application may either need to retrieve the unifier of the query term and the stored term (as is conventional in Prolog), or it may require a copy of that raw stored term which was found to be unifiable. Our techniques therefore retrieve each term as stored: if the application requires the unifier, then this can most efficiently be computed within Prolog (where unification is a primitive and efficient operation).

---

[1] *Freezing* binds each distinct variable in a term to some novel, distinctly numbered ground structure.

2.5 Retrieval Strategies

We consider two strategic options for term retrieval from an RDBMS, both of which are employed in the techniques described later.

Firstly, rather than contrive a query which retrieves exactly the candidate terms, it would be possible to construct an under-specified (complete but unsound) query which retrieves not only the wanted terms but others besides (i.e. "false drops"), then reject the mismatched terms by performing an appropriate test (typically *unification*) within Prolog. Rothermel [24] has proposed a scheme which aims to minimise data manipulation operations within the RDBMS by dispatching under-specified queries and filtering out the false matches after retrieval. The drawback of this tactic is that the extra retrieval traffic must pass through what is already a bottlenéck: the interface between Prolog and the RDBMS, whose bandwidth in delivering the results of a query is rather poor. Compared to the extra transfer costs, the costs of checking the retrieved terms within Prolog is negligible (both costs are proportional to term size, and transfer rate is far lower than unification rate). The wild-card string matching techniques [§4.4 **Technique T3: Wild-card Retrieval of Ground Terms**] employ this strategy, since SQL wild-card matching is not expressive enough to match exactly the required terms. In the other techniques, we aim to minimise false retrievals by emulating unifiability tests within the RDBMS.

Secondly, we can employ application-specific special-case mechanisms: in *DERIVE*, for example, we use a specialised technique for storing and retrieving finite *maps* [§4.3 **Technique T2(a,b): Storage and Retrieval of Maps**].

3 Coupling Prolog to a RDBMS

Our need to combine a Prolog system with a RDBMS essentially arises from a long-standing polarisation of computation into two areas of development. Since FORTRAN and COBOL were invented, application programming languages have been highly developed to support recursive control and data structures and sophisticated type systems; typically, however, they lack well-integrated mechanisms to support *persistence* of data (beyond the lifetime of a program instance), *shareability* of data and functionality (by concurrent users), and *scaleability* to very large data sets (beyond the scope of primary memory). Databases, on the other hand, have computational strengths and weaknesses which are essentially the reverse of the above. The common (and arguable) observation that most applications fall into either one camp or the other does not excuse this state of affairs. Furthermore, considerable research efforts are expended on rediscovering, within one camp, techniques which are well-explored within the other.

Our application required the virtues of both systems: Prolog was almost ideal for building a range of meta-interpreters for *DERIVE*'s configuration description language, but its traditional per-process memory-resident database was quite inadequate for supporting long-term multi-user development of large software configurations. The RDBMS provided good data management facilities, but only a primitive programmability (SQL is not even Turing-complete).

Despite their superficial differences, there is an intriguing overlap of the concepts which underlie Prolog and relational databases, as discussed theoretically in [9], and realistically in [11], and several schemes have been proposed for combining the two mechanisms in practice. We are interested only in the case where Prolog is in control and the RDBMS serves it (indeed, we can find no published proposals to augment a RDBMS by allowing it to invoke Prolog externally, although there are proposals to extend RDBMS functionality to allow it to emulate Prolog internally [7]).

3.1 Strategic Issues

We identify (below) a number of strategic and tactical issues in combining Prolog and RDBMS technology, in terms of which each proposed scheme (our own included) can be classified.

There is one strategic issue to which the others are subordinate: we can

either bolt together a *hybrid* system by interfacing an existing implementation of Prolog to an existing RDBMS;

or implement a single *unified* system, drawing on the technology and development experience of both paradigms.

The latter "unified" approach was discussed in [25], investigated experimentally in [1], and realised in [2].

There have been less ambitious forms of this unified approach: one [4] augments Prolog with a purpose-built external clause database using conventional secondary storage, and others use specialised interface hardware [29] [5] (although such hardware seems doomed to commercial insignificance). "Grid files" [8] have been adapted successfully for clause storage and retrieval, and are used for this purpose in MegaLog [2].

Meanwhile, the "hybrid" approach has been employed in several applications (including *DERIVE*), and implemented in several different ways, as we discuss below.

3.2 Tactical Issues

The first issue is as much one of approach and perspective as of technique: we can

either statically compile an abstract program definition into a hybrid implementation coded both in Prolog and in a RDBMS query language (QL), and with data partly stored within Prolog and partly within the database;

or dynamically couple a Prolog program to a database, allowing it to construct and issue arbitrary queries at run-time.

The first approach can be seen as an attempt to reconcile the PL+DB paradigms into a single virtual programming model; the second approach is more flexible and more pragmatic.

The second issue concerns the choice of shared data model: we can

either merely map the RDBMS' relational data model into Prolog;

or try and support Prolog's more expressive data model within the RDBMS.

The former approach is taken by those who regard Prolog as a useful language for implementing front-ends to traditional RDBMS applications, e.g. [19], and the latter approach is taken by those (ourselves included) whose Prolog applications need one or more of the qualities of *persistence*, *shareability* or *scaleability* of a typical RDBMS.

A third issue concerns the expressiveness of the coupling: we can

> *either* merely support simple searches of RDBMS tables (and perhaps of views, which are virtual tables);

> *or* allow arbitrary queries (e.g. in SQL) to be constructed dynamically within Prolog and evaluated within the RDBMS.

An example of the former approach is described in [17], where a Prolog system is coupled to the tables and views of the relational database Mimer, and [20] describes an instance of the more general second approach where arbitrary Prolog goals are mechanically translated into a relational-algebraic language for evaluation by PEPIN (a research database).

A fourth issue concerns the assertion of retrieved terms as clauses within the Prolog database. Some proposed interfaces do this inescapably, e.g. [30] which extracts the resulting tuples of each RDBMS query into a temporary file, reformats them textually into Prolog clauses, then loads them into Prolog. Others, e.g. [3], recognise (as we do), that this is an orthogonal issue of *caching*: in general, an interface should *not* automatically commit all retrieved data to Prolog's database, but follow an independent per-application caching policy.

Clause caching policies in hybrid systems are discussed in [10], where a "virtual memory" scheme is proposed, in which clauses are clustered according to their likelihood of calling each other (as determined from static call dependency analysis).

[15] considers ways of preserving some of the non-declarative (*assert/retract*) and non-logical (*cut*) semantics of Prolog when clauses are stored in a RDBMS. **DERIVE** is (currently) pure enough not to need these techniques.

A fifth issue: the result relation of a query can be returned

> *either* as a single data structure (a set of tuples);

> *or* tuple-at-a-time upon backtracking.

The latter form of coupling is far more natural to Prolog, since it corresponds to the way that a procedure of Prolog facts would be accessed by a program.

Finally, the sixth and seventh issues concern properties which any tuple-at-a-time interface should have:

- *re-entrancy*: allowing multiple nested accesses to RDBMS data;

- *cuttability*: automatically tidying up whenever retrieval is aborted (by a Prolog *cut*) before the result relation is exhausted.

Not all published proposals consider the last two aspects explicitly.

3.3 RDBMS Term Retrieval in *DERIVE*

Our adopted proprietary interface[2] between (Quintus) Prolog and the (ORACLE) RDBMS [Fig. 7.] maps an SQL query onto its result relation thus:

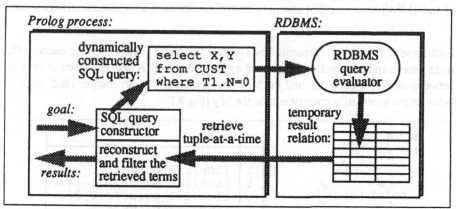

Fig. 7. Operation of *DERIVE*'s adopted hybrid Prolog-RDBMS interface

- Prolog sends a SQL 'select' query (which, typically, it has constructed dynamically) to the RDBMS;

- Prolog awaits the result relation (which it retrieves one tuple at a time), and returns them to the calling procedure (either one-at-a-time via backtracking or accumulated into a list).

In terms of the coupling architectures discussed above [§3.1], *DERIVE*'s interface is *hybrid*; and in terms of the tactical issues [§3.2] it:

- is a "dynamic" interface (requiring no build-time declarations or RDBMS accesses);
- maps the RDBMS data model into Prolog (not vice versa);
- supports arbitrary SQL *select* queries (not just table accesses);
- performs no caching (*DERIVE* applies this selectively);
- provides tuple-at-a-time delivery of results;
- is re-entrant;
- is cuttable.

All four techniques [§4] exploit this interface.

4 Practical Techniques for Term Indexing and Retrieval

We present practical techniques for implementing retrieval of terms which unify with a given query term by mechanically constructing SQL *select* queries.

---

[2]   ProData V2, from Keylink Computers [18]

4.1 Technique T1a: Retrieval of General Terms

Each distinct stored term is allocated (upon storage) a distinct identifier (a positive integer). This allocation is performed with an application front-end process, but the use of an RDBMS *sequence* [23] ensures global distinctness of allocated identifiers among all concurrent users.

Each node in the term is represented by a tuple (ID, KEY), where the KEY encodes the node's name and arity and its path from the root of the term. A path is a series of choices between sibling arguments, and each choice is encoded as an integer (and inserted between the name/arity components in the key [Fig. 8.]).

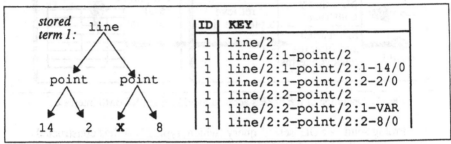

Fig. 8. Table of keys derived from an example item.

A node in a query term only matches a node in a stored term if they occupy the same respective positions (i.e. they have the same paths from the root of their terms) and their lines of ancestors (the functors on the path) are identical.

In our implementation [Fig. 9.], the keys are stored as hash function values, not as strings. The hash function which we use is an adaptation of the 32-bit cyclic redundancy check algorithm used for bigtext naming [26], and it yields a 32-bit integer which is more compact that the "string" keys (which can easily exceed the allowable field width for indexable ORACLE V6 columns).

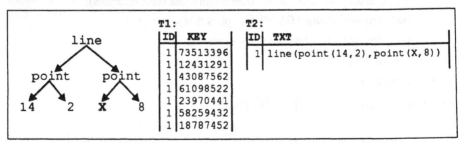

Fig. 9. RDBMS schema for general term indexing and retrieval.

It is impossible to reconstruct the original terms from the hashed keys (the hash function is non-invertible, since distinct key strings may hash to the same code), so we additionally store a flattened textual representation of each term in a separate table (T2 in [Fig. 9.]), keyed by the ID value.

We now consider an example of the most general case of term retrieval, in which the stored terms are possibly non-ground, and we wish to retrieve all those which are unifiable with an arbitrary non-ground query term.

We generate, recursively, a nested formula [Fig. 10.] from the query term, according to

```
query term:            matching condition:

        line            either  VAR
       /    \           or  (     line(_,_)
   point    fred        and  [similarly for point(X,14)
   /  \                 and  [similarly for fred]
  x    14               )
```

Fig. 10. Nested matching condition for general term (example).

a template [Fig. 10.].

```
either      the root node is matched by a stored variable
or  (       it is matched by a similar stored node
    and     the  first goal arg matches   first stored arg similarly
    and     the second goal arg matches second stored arg similarly
            [etc. for any further arguments]
    )
```

Fig. 11. Nested matching condition for general term (template).

This generates a formula which can be expressed as a Prolog goal [Fig. 10.] which, on

```
(       k( ID, 'var')
;       k( ID, 'line/2'),
    (       k( ID, 'line/2:1-var')
    ;       k( ID, 'line/2:1-point/2'),
        (       k( ID, 'line/2:1-point/2:2-var')
        ;       k( ID, 'line/2:1-point/2:2-14/0')
        )
    ),
    (       k( ID, 'line/2:2-var')
    ;       k( ID, 'line/2:1-fred/0')
    )
).
```

Fig. 12. Nested Prolog goal derived from term matching template.

backtracking, will bind ID to the unique identifier of each matching stored term successively).

Note that the query term's variable X gives rise to no condition in this formula, as any stored subterm at that position will match that variable.

Although the formula is illustrated with string keys (for clarity), our implementation trades off retrieval accuracy for storage economy by using hash codes instead of full string keys (as in [Fig. 9.]).

If the query term contains *shared* variables, e.g. line(A,A), then we

- construct a more general (complete but unsound) query with all distinct variables, e.g. line(A,B);

- reject any retrieved mismatches by unifying (within Prolog) each retrieved term with the original query term [Fig. 13.].

line(1,2)	= line(A,A)	*fails (retrieved term is rejected)*
line(1,1)	= line(A,A)	*succeeds (retrieved term is accepted)*

Fig. 13. Post-retrieval filtering of false drops where query term has shared variables.

The formula [Fig. 10.] is mechanically translated into SQL using established compiling techniques [14] [21] [6].

4.2 Technique T1b: Retrieval of Ground Terms

If it is known that all stored terms will be ground, then we can employ a simplification of the previous retrieval technique, since we need not consider the possibility that a node in the query term may be matched by a variable in the stored term.

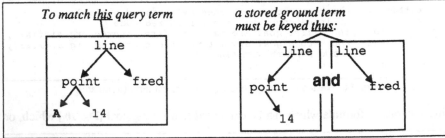

Fig. 14. Simplified retrieval condition where stored terms are known to be ground (example).

The generated formula is a conjunction of exactly as many index conditions as there are ground leaves in the query term (two, in this case: '14' and 'fred'). Hence the retrieval formula is:

```
k( ID, 'line/2:1-point/2:2-14/0'),
k( ID, 'line/2:1-fred/0').
```

As in technique T1a, the key strings may be replaced by hash codes.

This formula compiles into a SQL query which is a N-way join (when there are N ground leaves in the query term):

```
select ID
  from T1 T1a, T1 T1b
  where T1a.KEY = 'line/2:1-point/2:2-14/0'
    and T1a.ID  = T1b.ID
    and T1b.KEY = 'line/2:1-fred/0'
```

4.3 Technique T2(a,b): Storage and Retrieval of Maps

A (finite) map is a set of *key=value* pairs (wherein all keys are ground) [Fig. 15.].

```
[name=fred,suffix=c,text=#36]
```

Fig. 15. A finite map represented as a set of *key=value* pairs (example)

Configuration items in **DERIVE** are represented (abstractly) as maps, and although we employ a (rather complex) term encoding of maps for the purposes of rule interpretation (so that unification achieves *map union* [26]), we chose to define an independent relational representation for storage and retrieval purposes. Each representation suits its major operations: *unification* within Prolog, and *indexed retrieval* from the RDBMS. Within the database, each stored map is allocated a distinct integer ID (an SQL-conformant RDBMS will have a built-in provision for this), and exploded into individual *key=value* pairs [Fig. 16.] for the purpose of indexing.

T1:		
ID	**KEY**	**VAL**
1	name	fred
1	suffix	cpp
1	text	#36

Fig. 16. First Normal Form storage of a map within an RDBMS, to support unifiability tests.

In principle, maps can be reconstructed from this table of keys and values, but for the sake of efficiency, we (redundantly) store the maps in an additional table [Fig. 17.] as flattened text strings (also indexed by the **ID**).

T2:	
ID	**TXT**
1	[name=fred, suffix=cpp, text=#36]

Fig. 17. Denormalised storage of a map for efficient retrieval (by ID).

NB two maps are unifiable *if-and-only-if* for each key common to both they have unifiable values [Fig. 18.].

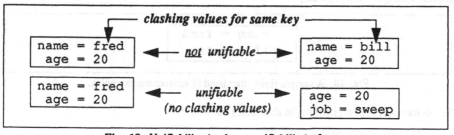

Fig. 18. Unifiability (and non-unifiability) of maps.

Map Retrieval from RDBMS. The retrieval of all maps which match some given query map proceeds in four stages.

- construct (within the front-end process) an SQL *select* query to compute the IDs of matching maps, and to retrieve their texts;

- send the query to the RDBMS for evaluation;

- retrieve into Prolog the flattened text of each matching map;

- unflatten each text into a term (using Prolog's built-in source-code parser).

We have developed two SQL algorithms for identifying matching maps:

- *match intersection* (T2a): for each attribute in the query map, compute the set of IDs of the matching maps, then retrieve the intersection of these sets;

- *clash subtraction* (T2b): compute the IDs of all the maps which clash, then retrieve *all other* maps.

Technique T2a: match intersection. The *match intersection* algorithm is close to the specification of unification: for each *key=value* attribute in the query map, a stored map matches [Fig. 19.] if

either it has the *same* value for that attribute key

or it has *no* value for that attribute key.

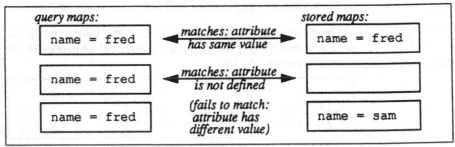

Fig. 19. Unifiability of map attributes

As an example, consider the algorithm applied to the retrieval of those maps which match a sample map [Fig. 20.].

```
        name = fred
        suffix = cpp
```

Fig. 20. A sample finite map used in subsequent examples.

Semi-formally, the algorithm (in this case) is:

```
retrieve each map's text if
        either     the map has    name    = 'fred'
        or         the map has no name    =
    and either     the map has    suffix  = 'cpp'
        or         the map has no suffix  =
```

In Prolog notation (using, as in all following examples, the schema illustrated in [Fig. 16.] and [Fig. 17.]):

```
retrieve( TXT) :-
    T2( ID, TXT),
    (      T1( ID, name, fred')          [ key has required value ]
    ;      \+ T1( ID, name, _)           [ ... or key is undefined ]
    ),
    (      T1( ID, suffix, 'cpp')        [ key has required value ]
    ;      \+ T1( ID, suffix, _)         [ ... or key is undefined ]
    ).
```

There are standard techniques [14] [21] [6] for translating predicate calculus formulae (or Prolog goals) into SQL, but they first transform the formula into *disjunctive normal form* (DNF). The example is in *conjunctive normal form*, i.e.

```
a • ( b + c̄ ) • ( d + ē )
```

where the literals correspond to simple goals thus:

```
a = T2( ID,  TXT)
b = T1( ID,  name,  'fred')
c = T1( ID,  name,  _)
d = T1( ID,  suffix,  'cpp')
e = T1( ID,  suffix,  _)
```

and this expands to DNF thus:

```
a•b•d + a•b•ē + a•c̄•d + a•c̄•ē
```

With N attributes in the query map, there will be 2^N conjunctions in the DNF formula, each of which denotes (at worst) a (N+1)-way join.

The mechanically-generated [6] SQL expression for the *match intersection* method (applied to the sample map in [Fig. 20.]) is:

```
        select    T2.TXT
        from      T2, T1 T1a, T1 T1b
        where     T2.ID    = T1a.ID
        and       T1a.KEY = 'name'
        and       T1a.VAL = 'crc'
        and       T2.ID    = T1b.ID
        and       T1b.KEY = 'suffix'
        and       T1b.VAL = 'cpp'
union
        select    T2.TXT
        from      T2, T1 T1a
        where     T2.ID    = T1a.ID
        and       T1a.KEY = 'name'
        and       T1a.VAL = 'crc'
        and       not exists
                  (    select    T1b.ID
                       from      T1 T1b
                       where     T1a.ID  = T1b.ID
                       and       T1b.KEY = 'suffix' )
union
        select    T2.TXT
        from      T2, T1 T1a
        where     t2.ID    = T1a.ID
        and       T1a.KEY = 'suffix'
        and       T1a.VAL = 'cpp'
        and       not exists
                  (    select    T1b.ID
                       from      T1 T1b
                       where     T1a.ID  = T1b.ID
                       and       T1b.KEY = 'name' )
union
        select    T2.TXT
        from      T2
        where     not exists
                  (    select    T1a.ID
                       from      T1 T1a
                       where     T2.ID   = T1a.ID
                       and       T1a.KEY = 'name' )
        and       not exists
                  (    select    T1b.ID
                       from      T1 T1b
                       where     T2.ID   = T1b.ID
                       and       T1b.KEY = 'suffix' )
```

The execution plan devised by ORACLE (V6) for the *match intersection* method is:

```
projection
 \--union
    \--union
       |  \--union
       |  |   \--sort(unique)
       |  |   |    \--nested loops
       |  |   |         \--nested loops
       |  |   |         |    \--table access(by rowid) T1
       |  |   |         |    |   \--index(range scan) T1_INDEX_2_3
       |  |   |         |    \--index(range scan) T1_INDEX_1_2_3
       |  |   |         \--table access(by rowid) T2
       |  |   |              \--index(range scan) T2_INDEX_1
       |  |   \--sort(unique)
       |  |        \--filter
       |  |             \--nested loops
       |  |                  \--table access(by rowid) T1
       |  |                  |   \--index(range scan) T1_INDEX_2_3
       |  |                  \--table access(by rowid) T2
       |  |                  |   \--index(range scan) T2_INDEX_1
       |  |             \--index(range scan) T1_INDEX_1_2
       |  \--sort(unique)
       |       \--filter
       |            \--nested loops
       |            |    \--table access(by rowid) T1
       |            |    |   \--index(range scan) T1_INDEX_2_3
       |            |    \--table access(by rowid) T2
       |            |        \--index(range scan) T2_INDEX_1
       |            \--index(range scan) T1_INDEX_1_2
    \--sort(unique)
         \--filter
              \--table access(full) T1
              \--index(range scan) T1_INDEX_1_2
              \--index(range scan) T1_INDEX_1_2
```

The execution plan takes into account available RDBMS indexes: the plan above is the simplest we could achieve by (generous) provision of indexes. We shall compare its cost to that of the next technique.

Retrieval algorithm T2b: clash subtraction. We illustrate an alternative algorithm, applied to the same query map [Fig. 20.]. An informal reading of the *clash subtraction* algorithm in this case is:

```
retrieve each map's text where that map
     neither     has a name other than 'fred'
     nor         has a suffix other than 'cpp'
```

Effectively, we initially consider all stored terms as candidates, then subtract all those with a key=value pair which clashes with a pair in the query term.

A Prolog definition of this example retrieval is:

```
retrieve( TXT) :-
     T2( ID, TXT),
     \+    (    T1( ID, name, VAL1),   VAL1 \== 'fred'
           ;    T1( ID, suffix, VAL2), VAL2 \== 'cpp'
           ).
```

An equivalent SQL query strongly resembles the Prolog version (above):

```
select     TXT
from       T2
where      ID not in
           (     select ID from T1
                 where     (KEY='name' and VAL!='fred')
                 or        (KEY='suffix' and VAL!='cpp')
           )
```

and Oracle's execution plan for this SQL query is:

```
filter
 \--table access(full) T2
 \--concatenation
     \--table access(by rowid) T1
     |   \--index(range scan) T1_INDEX
     \--table access(by rowid) TĪ
         \--index(range scan) T1_INDEX
```

In [Table 1] we compare the costs of the execution plans for techniques T2a and T2b.

	T2a (match intersection)	T2b (clash subtraction)
table access (full):	1	1
table access (by row id):	6	2
index (range scan):	11	2

Table 1. Total table and index accesses for each T2 algorithm (for example map)

From inspection of the formulae, the number of *table access (full)* operations will be constant, and the number of *table access (by row id)* and *index (range scan)* required by algorithm T2b is proportional to the number of attributes in the query term. Algorithm T2a, however, has a complexity which is exponential in the number of query term attributes (see the execution plan), and can be expected to cost more in every case.

4.4 Technique T3: Wild-card Retrieval of Ground Terms

This technique exploits the string-matching facilities of SQL, which are a small subset of *regular expression* operator. [13]. Terms are represented as character strings: in the

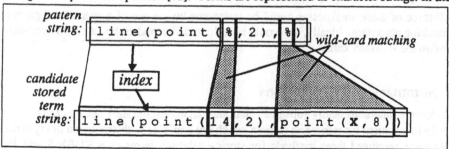

Fig. 21. Candidate stored terms with the required initial substring are found via an RDBMS index, then tested for wild-card matchability.

query term, each variable is replaced by the '%' meta-character, which (when interpreted by the SQL "LIKE" operation), matches a stored substring of any length.

Wild-card term retrieval [Fig. 21.] has these limitations:

* only *ground* terms will be retrieved correctly;

* if the query term contains many variables, the search may be expensive (the cost of naive wild-card matching algorithms is exponential in the

number of '%' patterns, although sophisticated techniques exist to reduce both the typical and worst-case costs);

- the flattened term must be short enough to fit into a matchable field in the RDBMS (a maximum of 255 characters in ORACLE V6).

It is advantageous to set up an uncompressed RDBMS index on the stored term string, as the initial sequence of literal characters (up to the first wild-card meta-character) will be used to drive a "range" retrieval of candidates [Fig. 21.]): this will reduce the number of wild-card string comparisons.

Meta-character remapping. SQL's wild-card meta-characters ('%' and '_') may also occur as object-level characters in both query and stored terms. We therefore map such occurrences onto other characters which have no meta-character meaning.

Under-specification of wild-card retrievals. The retrievals described above are under-specified in three ways.

Firstly, the meta-character remapping results in two object characters being overloaded. By choosing infrequently-occurring characters, the resulting false matches can be made negligible.

Secondly, wild-card string matching does not respect parenthesisation, and can yield false matches. These will be rejected within Prolog, when the reconstructed term fails to unify with the original query term.

Finally, as with the general (*exploded*) term retrieval mechanism, shared variables in the query term are treated as distinct variables during retrieval.

Ineligible matches, whatever their cause, will be rejected after retrieval by unification within Prolog. Overall retrieval is both sound and complete: the only impact of the under-specification is on performance.

All three of these weaknesses could be overcome by the use of a specialised pattern matching algorithm. Ideally, we would be able to define and embed such an operation within the RDBMS kernel.

5 Summary and Conclusions

Deductive databases neatly subsume relational databases, but they need a *clause* store and a mechanism for retrieving clauses which are *unifiable* with any given query term. We have presented three methods for storing arbitrary terms in a RDBMS and for retrieving not only unifiable stored terms but also *specialisations*, *generalisations* and *alphabetic variants* (not only for completeness. but also to serve meta-logical functions such as *memoisation* within our application). We also specialise one of these methods for storing (finite) *maps* (this abstract data type is of particular importance in our application).

The development of these techniques was not a goal in itself, but merely a necessary sub-task in the implementation of our *DERIVE* prototype. We have informally analysed the retrieval costs of the *map* storage techniques, and shown that one of them is (in some sense) linear in the size of the query term. Unlike some previously published schemes, we have striven to maximise the discrimination of candidate terms within the RDBMS, and minimise retrieval of invalid terms into Prolog.

Our experiences in using a proprietary RDBMS for such an unconventional purpose has led to the following "wish list":

- we wish to embed, within the RDBMS kernel, an application-specific comparison operations (for term-oriented string matching);

- we seek better support for caching RDBMS data within the application program (e.g. by the provision of an efficient test to determine whether a table has been updated since its contents were previously cached within the application);

- finally, we want better optimisation of SQL queries (our *match intersection* and *clash subtraction* formulae are equivalent, but give rise to execution plans of different complexities).

6 References

1. J. B. Bocca and P. J. Pearson, "On Prolog-DBMS Connections - A step forward from EDUCE", in [12], pp. 55-66 (1988).

2. J. B. Bocca, "MegaLog - A platform for developing Knowledge Base Management Systems", *Proceedings of the International Symposium on Database Systems for Advanced Applications*, Tokyo, Japan, pp. 374-380 (1991).

3. S. Ceri, G. Gottlob and G. Wiederhold, "Efficient Database Access from Prolog", *IEEE Transactions on Software Engineering*, vol. 15, pp. 153-164 (Feb 1989).

4. J. Chomicki and W. Grundzinski, "A database support system for Prolog", *Proceedings of the Logic Programming Workshop (Lisbon, Portugal)*, pp. 290-303 (1983).

5. R. M. Colomb, "Enhancing Unification in Prolog through Clause Indexing", *Journal of Logic Programming*, vol. 10, pp. 23-44 (1991).

6. C. Draxler, "A Powerful Prolog to SQL Compiler", *Report 92-61*, Centrum fur Informations- und Sprachverarbeitung, Universitat Munchen (1992).

7. H. van Emde Boas and P. van Emde Boas, "Storing and evaluating Horn-clause rules in a relational database", *IBM Journal of Research and Development*, vol. 30, no. 1 (1986).

8. M. Freeston, "Grid Files for Efficient Prolog Clause Access", in [12], pp. 188-211 (1988).

9. H. Gallaire and J. Minker (Eds.), "Logic and Databases", Proceedings of the Symposium on Logic and Databases (Toulouse, France, 1977), Plenum Press (New York, USA) (1978).

10. C. Garidis and S. Bottcher, "A Clustering Concept for Incremental Loading of Large Prolog Programs", *Proceedings of the 2nd PROTOS Workshop (Zurich)*, IBM Deutschland GmbH (Stuttgart) (1990).

11. P. M. D. Gray, "Logic, Algebra and Databases", Ellis Horwood (1984).

12. P. M. D. Gray and R. J. Lucas (Eds.), "Prolog and Databases: Implementations and New Directions", *Proceedings of the. Workshop on Prolog and Databases* (Warwick), Ellis Horwood (1988).

13.   J. E. Hopcroft and J. D. Ullman, "Introduction to Automata Theory, Languages and Computation", Addison-Wesley, Reading, Mass., USA (1979).

14.   M. Jarke, J. Clifford and Y. Vassiliou, "An Optimizing Prolog front-end to a Relational Query System", *Proceedings of the 1984 ACM SIGMOD Conference on Management of Data* (Boston, Mass., USA), pp. 296-306 (1984).

15.   H. Jasper, "Semantic Preserving Management of Accesses to Externally Stored Prolog Clauses", *Proceedings of the 1st PROTOS Workshop*, Sandoz AG (Basel), pp. 125-137 (1989).

16.   R. M. Keller and M. R. Sleep, "Applicative Caching", *ACM Transactions on Programming Languages and Systems*, vol. 8, no. 1, pp. 88-108 (Jan 1986).

17.   R. J. Lucas and G. Levine, "A Prolog-Relational Database Interface", in [12] (1988).

18.   R. J. Lucas, "ProData: Quintus Prolog / Oracle Interface V2", *Reference Manual*, Keylink Computers Ltd., UK (1990).

19.   K. Lunn and I. G. Archibald, "TREQL (Thornton Research Easy Query Language): an intelligent front-end to a relational database", in [12], pp. 39-51 (1988).

20.   G. Marque-Pucheu, J. Martin-Gallausiaux and G. Jomier, "Interfacing Prolog and Relational Data Base Management Systems", *New Applications of Databases*, Academic Press, London, pp. 225-244 (1984).

21.   R. Marti, C. Wieland and B. Wuethrich, "Adding Inferencing to a Relational Database Management System", *Proc. BTW '89 (T. Harder, Ed.)*, in Inf. Fachberichte, vol. 204, pp. 266-270 (1989).

22.   H. Nakashima, S. Tomura and K. Ueda, "What is a variable in Prolog?", *Proceedings of the International Conference on First Generation Computer Systems* (FGCS), pp. 327-332, ICOT (1984).

23.   "SQL Language Reference Manual (Version 6.0)", Oracle Corporation (1990).

24.   K. Rothermel, "An effective method for storing and retrieving Prolog clauses from a relational database", *Proceedings of the 3rd International Conference on Data and Knowledge Bases ("Improving Usability and Responsiveness")*, Jerusalem (1988).

25.   E. Sciore and D. S. Warren, "Towards an Integrated Database-Prolog System", *Proceedings of the 1st International Workshop on Expert Database Systems* (1986).

26.   P. Singleton, "Applications of Meta-Programming to the Construction of Software Products from Generic Configurations", *Ph.D. Thesis*, Computer Science Dept., Keele University (1992).

27.   W. F. Tichy, "Tools for Software Configuration Management", in [28] (1988).

28.   J. F. H. Winkler (Ed.), *Proceedings of the 1st International Workshop of Software Version and Configuration Control* (Grassau, FRG), published by B. G. Teubner (Stuttgart) for the German Chapter of the ACM (1988).

29.   K. F. Wong and M. H. Williams, "Design Considerations for a Prolog Database Engine", *Proceedings of the 3rd International Conference on Data and Knowledge Bases*, Morgan Kaufmann Inc (USA), pp. 111-119 (Jun 1988).

30.   Y. Zhang and P. Hitchcock, "Coupling Prolog to a Database Management System", *Information Systems*, vol. 15, no. 6, pp. 663-667 (1990).

Principles of Implementing
Historical Databases in RDBMS

Peter McBrien

Imperial College
Dept. of Computing
180 Queen's Gate
London SW7 2BZ

Tel: +44 71 589 5111
Fax: +44 71 581 8024
Email: pjm@doc.ic.ac.uk

Abstract. The issue of query languages for historical databases has received considerable interest in the database literature over the past decade. Recently temporal relational algebras have been described which provide a theoretical foundation for these languages in the same manner that the relational algebra provides for the SQL language. In this paper the issue of algorithms for the querying and updating of information for one such temporal algebra is discussed, in the specific context of implementing such algorithms on conventional database management systems (DBMS) based on the relational algebra. In so doing, we make apparent the extensions needed to make an RDBMS support any historical database query language with the expressive power of the temporal relational algebra.

Keywords: Historical Databases, RDBMS, Relational Algebra, Query Processing, Temporal Relational Algebra, US Logic

1 Introduction

The topic of adding the temporal dimension to the relational model has received considerable attention in the database literature, a recent survey of which may be found in [1]. Most of the historical databases systems described in the database literature, such as those of [2,13,11,9,6] assume specific methods for the storage of temporal information, and do not address the issue of providing a logic as the basis of the algebra. More recently work has been conducted to develop algebras for historical database querying, based on a conceptual data model called the *temporal structure* [14,5]. These algebras can be related to the *US Logic*, which is widely used for work in the temporal logic area [7,4]. This gives the temporal query languages based on these algebras a theoretical underpinning, allowing for the comparison of their expressive power, and sets a common framework for their implementation independent of the physical data model used.

This paper sets out to explore what are the requirements for changes to current

RDBMS in order that they support query languages based on the *temporal relational algebra* (*TRA*) described in [5]. This will be conducted by showing how the TRA queries may be translated into relational algebra queries on a relational encoding of the temporal structure. The extensions that it is necessary to make to the RA in order that it serves this role form the foundation of the extensions necessary to any RDBMS so that it can support queries of the TRA, or any TRA-based query language.

Section 2 describes some of the previous work which this paper develops upon, and justifies the method by which we choose to store historical data in a relational model. Section 3 describes a set of update primitives for historical data held in a relational model. Section 4 describes algorithms for the full implementation of the TRA in an RA extended with a set of higher-order functions. To give this work a practical perspective, the encoding of the algorithms in the Transact-SQL language of the Sybase RDBMS is presented where the expressive power of the latter makes this possible.

2 Background

The data model used by the TRA is the *temporal structure* introduced in [2], which describes any discrete linear bounded temporal model. In the temporal structure, a historical database D_τ (where τ is a natural number), is considered as a set of relational databases { $D_t \mid 0 \le t \le \tau$ }, where the subscript t denotes the time associated with the a particular database. Each D_t has the same schema as D_τ, a restriction natural in the context of databases since in practice we would hope to encode the various tuples contained in a relation R_t over time into a single relation R'. By restricting t to some finite subset of the natural numbers $0 \ldots \tau$ we achieve a bounded model, and using the usual ordering on the natural numbers achieve a linear model. As a shorthand, we will term each instance of t as a *tick*. The structure is extended in [5] to always include in D_τ a relation *TIME*, the single attribute of which represents the value of t in any particular D_t.

Example 1 : Example Temporal Structure

> For the rest of the paper we shall use the following temporal structure as the database on which example queries will operate. D_τ consists of the relations
>
> *TIME(T)*
> *EMP(NAME,SALARY)*
> *WORKS_FOR(NAME,MANAGER)*
>
> The table below shows tuples of the relations at the first few values of the tick time t

database	TIME	EMP	WORKS_FOR
D_0	(0)	(Peter,100) (Richard,90) (Ed,200)	(Peter,Ed) (Richard,Ed)
D_1	(1)	(Peter,110) (Richard,90) (Ed,200) (Dov,200)	(Peter,Ed) (Richard,Dov)
D_2	(2)	(Peter,110) (Richard,140) (Ed,200) (Dov,200)	(Peter,Dov) (Richard,Dov)
D_3	(3)	(Peter,140) (Richard,140) (Dov,200)	(Peter,Dov) (Richard,Dov)
D_4	(4)	(Peter,140) (Richard,140) (Ed,200) (Dov,200)	(Peter,Dov) (Richard,Dov)

As a shorthand, we may write tuples of a relation which hold at several ticks as the tuple followed by the set of ticks at which the tuple holds. For example, we may write the various instances of (Dov,200) being a member of *EMP* as (Dov,200) {1,2,3,4}. For a continuous series of ticks this set can be further simplified to an interval, which for the example results in (Dov,200) [1,4].

It should be noted that by associating real times with both the length of each tick and the time of tick 0, we may easily convert tick numbers to actual time values. For instance, if we choose a tick to be one minute, and tick 0 to be 11am 1st March 1991, then we know tick 120 is 1pm 1st March 1991, tick 1440 is 11am 2nd March 1991, etc.

The temporal structure may be queried using the *temporal relational algebra* (TRA), which consists of variants of the five RA operators, namely select σ, project π, Cartesian product $\times$, set difference − and union $\cup$, together with the temporal operators *since-product* S_x and *until-product* U_x. The semantics of the operators is defined by the following table, where q is the database tick time of the query.

TRA	Result for D_q
$R\,S_x\,S$	The product of all tuples from S at D_s with those from R at all D_t for which $s \leq t < q$
$R\,U_x\,S$	The product of all tuples from S at D_s with those from R at all D_t for which $q < t \leq s$
$R \cup_t S$	The union of tuples from R at D_q with those from S at D_q
$R \times_t S$	The product of tuples from R at D_q with those from S at D_q
$R -_t S$	The difference of tuples in R at D_q with those in S at D_q
$\pi_t R$	The projection of tuples from R at D_q
$\sigma_t R$	The selection of tuples from R at D_q

The evaluation of a *query* in the TRA can be made with respect to a database tick time q, in which case we write '*query* at q'. Alternatively the query can be made with respect to all times, the result for each D_q being '*query* at q'. Note that the five operators with names the same as the RA operators only produce output relations from input relations at the same D_q — that is taking the snapshot view of each time, the results produced by the operators are identical to those produced the RA operators. The new temporal operators produce output tuples in the 'current' database D_q from input relations in 'other' databases D_t (where $t \neq q$).

Example 2 : Some Results of TRA Queries on the Temporal Structure of Example 1

db	$EMP\,S_x\,TIME(0)$	$\pi_{NAME}\,EMP$	$EMP\,S\bowtie WORKS\_FOR$
D_0	$\varnothing$	(Peter) (Richard) (Ed)	$\varnothing$
D_1	(Peter,100) (Richard,90) (Ed,200)	(Peter) (Richard) (Ed) (Dov)	(Peter,100,Peter,Ed) (Richard,90,Richard,Ed)
D_2	(Richard,90) (Ed,200)	(Peter) (Richard) (Ed) (Dov)	(Peter,110,Peter,Ed) (Richard,90,Richard,Ed) (Richard,90,Richard,Dov)
D_3	(Ed,200)	(Peter) (Richard) (Dov)	(Peter,110,Peter,Ed) (Peter,110,Peter,Dov) (Richard,140,Richard,Dov)
D_4	$\varnothing$	(Peter) (Richard) (Ed) (Dov)	(Peter,140,Peter,Dov) (Richard,140,Richard,Dov)

Example 2 gives a table of results for each D_q of Example 1 for the following TRA queries:

- *EMP* S_x *TIME(0)* gives at each D_q the tuples of *EMP* which have always held in the past.

- π_{NAME} *EMP* gives for each D_q the projection of the *NAME* attribute of *EMP*.

- *EMP* $S_{\bowtie}$ *WORKS_FOR* gives the temporal natural *since-join* on the *NAME* attribute of *EMP* and *WORKS_FOR*, where

$$R\,S_{\bowtie}\,S = \pi_{i1,i2,...,im}\,\sigma_{R.A1=S.A1,...,R.An=S.An}\,(R\,S_x\,S),$$

and $A_1, A_2, ..., A_n$ are the shared attributes of R and S. This will return tuples which have held at all times in the past in the *EMP* relation since there was one in the *WORKS_FOR* relation with the same instance of the *NAME* attribute.

In [5] a method for storing and querying the temporal structure in a standard RDB was described, the resulting system being termed a *temporal relational database* *(TDB)*. In short, it proposed that tuples $(a_1,...,a_n)$ [start,end] of relation R are stored in an RDB as $R(a_1,...,a_n,start,end)$. To find if a tuple holds for the temporal structure at time q we only need ask the RDB query $\sigma_{start \leq q \leq end}\,R(a_1,...,a_n,start,end)$.

Adding the constraint that all such intervals are maximal gives the *temporal normal form (TNF)* of [9]. A fundamental premise of this paper is that all intervals stored in the RDB are maximal, a corollary of this is that for any tuple $R(a_1,...,a_n,start,end)$ there must be no other *matching* tuple $R(a_1,...,a_n,start',end')$ where the non-temporal attributes $a_1,...,a_n$ are identical, and the temporal attributes *overlap* by conforming to *start* $\leq$ *end'+1* and *end* $\geq$ *start'−1* (strictly speaking we are finding intervals which overlap or just touch each other). Also, to be a valid interval in the bounded model $0 \leq start \leq end \leq \tau$ must be satisfied. The effect of this restriction is that if we see $R(a_1,...,a_n,start,end)$ stored in the DB, then we know both $(a_1,...,a_n)[start-1]$ and $(a_1,...,a_n)[end+1]$ to be false. Since the notion of two intervals overlapping will be repeatedly referred to in the following discussions and definitions, we define a function here to determine if *overlap* holds for a pair of intervals.

function overlap([*start,end*],[*start',end'*])
    if *start* $\leq$ *end'+1* **and** *end* $\geq$ *start'−1* **then return true**
    else return false

The justification for choosing the TNF, against allowing overlapping intervals to be stored in the RDB, can be summarized as follows:

- It produces a more compact database, since the overlapping intervals of two tuples are replaced by a single interval for a single tuple.

- If the normal form were not chosen, then the primary keys of relations would be seen to have duplicates at some times. For example, if we have a relation R with a single attribute which is also its primary key, and we have stored in the database $R = \{ (1) [2,10] , (1) [10,20] \}$, then at tick 10 the primary key 1 is seen to be duplicated.

- The implementation of the query language would be complicated if we had to cater for an essentially continuous piece temporal of information being 'broken' across several tuples. For instance, if we want to find if $R(1)$ held for the interval [5,15], then in the TNF database one needs only check that $R(1)$ is stored in the database as holding for some interval which encloses [5,15], but in the non-TNF database we must merge all overlapping intervals to see if together they enclose [5,15].

Example 3 illustrates how the temporal structure may be encoded in relational form (the intervals are of course stored simply as two extra attributes of the *EMP* and *WORKS_FOR* relations).

Example 3 : TNF encoding of Example 1

EMP	WORKS_FOR
(Peter,100)[0,0]	(Peter,Ed)[0,1]
(Peter,110)[1,2]	(Peter,Dov)[2,4]
(Peter,140)[3,4]	(Richard,Ed)[0,0]
(Richard,90)[0,1]	(Richard,Dov)[1,2]
(Richard,140)[2,4]	
(Ed,200)[0,2]	
(Ed,200)[4,4]	
(Dov,200)[1,4]	

Obviously the operation of inserting or deleting tuples requires we maintain the TNF. This will complicate the implementation of these operations, since when inserting information we must now first check if this can be achieved by extending the interval of an existing tuple, and when deleting we must check if the tuple still holds for other ticks. This matter will be dealt with in Section 3.

In [5] the TRA' operators were partially implemented in the RA by performing arithmetic on the intervals of tuples. However, due to a lack of expressive power in the RA only a limited implementation could be achieved in this manner. Section 4 will describe an extension of the implementation which completely implements the TRA in the RA extended with a set of higher-order functions. This serves to make apparent what enhancements are necessary to RDBMS to fully implement query processing languages with the expressive power of TRA, one example being the Temporal-SQL.

3 Storing and Updating a Historical Database in an RDB

The encoding of the temporal structure using intervals has an obvious implementation in an RDBMS, where we need only add two extra attributes to a relation to store the intervals that each tuple is valid for. Using the Sybase Transact-SQL [12] as an example implementation language, if we have a relation R with a single integer attribute, then we need add start_time and end_time attributes to store the time stamp, to achieve the following definition of the relation:

```
CREATE TABLE R (
        arg1        int         not null,
        start_time  int         not null,
        end_time    int         not null)
```

We now shall consider how insertions to, and deletions from, the relations held in such a schema may be achieved.

3.1 Insertions into the TDB

To maintain the requirement that intervals stored in the RDB are maximal, we must not simply add new tuples to the database, but merge the tuple with any matching tuples in the database which have intervals overlapping. The addition of a tuple $t_{new} = (a_1,...,a_n)$ [start,end] of relation R may be achieved by the following procedure:

procedure insertTDB($R,(a_1,...,a_n)$ [start,end])

(i) $S = \{ (a'_1,...,a'_n)$ [start',end'] for_which $(a'_1,...,a'_n)$ [start',end'] $\in R$ and
    $a_1=a'_1, ... , a_n=a'_n$ and overlap([start,end],[start',end']) $\}$

(ii) **for_all** $t \in S$ **delete** t **from** R

(iii) $S' = S \cup (a_1,...,a_n)$ [start,end]

(iv) $start_{min} = $ **minimum** $\{ start$ for_which $[start,\_] \in S' \}$
    $end_{max} = $ **maximum** $\{ end$ for_which $[\_,end] \in S' \}$

(v) **insert** $(a_1,...,a_n)$ [$start_{min},end_{max}$] into R

Step (i) finds all tuples already stored in the relation that would violate TNF if the t_{new} were added. These are any tuples with the same attributes as the t_{new} and an associated interval which overlaps that of t_{new}. In step (ii) all these violating tuples are deleted, then in step (iii) t_{new} is added to the set so that we may compute in (iv) the maximum interval covering existing tuples and t_{new}. Step (v) then inserts a new tuple into R with the attributes of t_{new} and an interval extended to cover the period of existing tuples with the same attributes as t_{new}.

To implement this as a stored procedure in the Sybase Transact-SQL language is straight forward, but unfortunately the language does not allow a variable to hold a relation name (one may not say SELECT * FROM @R where @R is a variable), and thus we can only present here the format that the procedure can taken by giving an example for a specific relation R with a single integer attribute arg_1. The procedure begins by using a single SELECT statement to find the matching tuples in the database which overlap the one being added, and finding their minimum start, and maximum end time. If no such tuples are found we may add the new tuple in the database, otherwise we merge in the interval of the new tuple with the overlapping intervals just found, delete all the overlapping tuples, and then insert the new tuple. Note that it would be more efficient if we were able to delete the overlapping tuples as we found them with the initial SELECT, but this is not possible in Transact-SQL

```
CREATE PROCEDURE insertTDB_R
    @data1 int,
    @start int,
    @end int  AS

DECLARE @P int
DECLARE @Q int

SELECT @P=MIN(start_time),@Q=MAX(end_time)
FROM R
WHERE arg1=@data1 AND start_time<=@end+1
                AND end_time>=@start-1

IF @P IS NULL
   BEGIN
   INSERT INTO R VALUES (@data1,@start,@end)
   END
ELSE
   BEGIN
   IF (@P>@start) SELECT @P=@start
   IF (@Q<@end) SELECT @Q=@end
   DELETE FROM R
   WHERE arg1=@data1 AND start_time>=@P AND end_time<=@Q
   INSERT INTO R VALUES (@data1,@P,@Q)
   END
```

3.2 Deletions from the TDB

To remove a tuple over some interval of time requires that we *clip* all matching tuples in the RDB which have overlapping intervals. It fact we may narrow the overlapping criterion for two intervals [start,end] and [start',end'] to $start \leq end'$ and $end \geq start'$ since we are not interested in touching intervals (they could not clip each other). The removal of a tuple $t_{new} = (a_1,...,a_n)$ [start,end] of relation R may be achieved by the following procedure:

procedure removeTDB(R,t_{new})

(i) $S = \{ (a'_1,...,a'_n) [start',end'] \text{ for\_which } (a'_1,...,a'_n) [start',end'] \in R \text{ and}$
$a_1=a'_1, ... , a_n=a'_n \text{ and } start \leq end' \text{ and } end \geq start') \}$

(ii) **for_all** $t \in S$ **delete** t **from** R

(iii) $S' = S \cup (a_1,...,a_n) [start,end]$

(iv) $start_{min} = \text{minimum } \{ \ start \text{ for\_which } [start,\_] \in S' \}$
$end_{max} = \text{maximum } \{ \ end \text{ for\_which } [\_,end] \in S' \}$

(v)   **if** $start_{min} <$ start **then insert** $(a_1,...,a_n) [start_{min},start-1]$ **into** R
if $end_{max} >$ end **then insert** $(a_1,...,a_n) [end+1,end_{max}]$ **into** R

Save for the slight optimisation of the overlapping criterion, this algorithm is identical in steps (i) to (iv) to that for *insertTDB*. The only difference is in step (v), where we insert into the database the tuple for the times outside the interval specified for deletion, which is the complement of the interval we found in step (v) of the *insertTDB* algorithm.

As was the case for the insertion operation, the implementation of this procedure in Transact-SQL requires a separate procedure to be provided for each relation in the database. As an example of the form such procedures can take, the stored procedure definition for removing temporal information from a single argument relation R is given below.

```
CREATE PROCEDURE removeTDB_R
    @data1 int,
    @start int,
    @end   int   AS

DECLARE @P int
DECLARE @Q int

SELECT @P=MIN(start_time),@Q=MAX(end_time)
FROM R
WHERE arg1=@data1 AND start_time<=@end
            AND end_time>=@start

IF @P IS NOT NULL
    BEGIN
    DELETE FROM R
    WHERE arg1=@data1 AND start_time>=@P
            AND end_time<=@Q
    IF (@P<@start)
        INSERT INTO R VALUES (@data1,@P,@start-1)
```

```
IF (@Q>@end)
        INSERT INTO R VALUES (@data1,@end+1,@Q)
END
```

4 Querying the TDB

In this section we detail how the TRA operators may be implemented in terms of RA operators operating on the TDB encoding of the temporal structure, with the RA extended with two new higher-order functions.

4.1 Implementing the TRA in the RA

When making a query on the TDB, we expect an answer in the TNF. If this were not the case we might get incorrect results when the output relation from the query was as an input for another TRA operator, since each operator will be implemented to work on a database in the normal form. Relations are stored in TNF, so to ensure the result of a query is in TNF we need only consider that the implementation of all TRA operators results in an output relation which is in TNF. Each operator of the TRA will be given a definition in terms of a RA query on the TDB described in Section 1, and an estimate of the complexity of the execution of the operator will be made.

Select

Since a *select* serves only to reduce the number of tuples in a relation, the output from a *select* must be in TNF if the input relation R is. Thus we may use the RA *select* to implement directly the TRA *select*, and the complexity is of the order of the number of tuples in R.

$$\sigma_{t\,A,...}\,R = \sigma_{A,...}\,R$$

$$complexity(\sigma_t\,R) = O(N) \text{ where } N = \text{count}(R)$$

Project

In implementing *project*, we meet a problem concerning the maintenance of the TNF in the output from the operator, due to the *project* making what were distinct tuples at overlapping times become identical tuples at overlapping times, and thus violating the TNF. For example, the projection of the *NAME* attribute from the *EMP* relation if implemented using the RA *project* operator would give the following result:

$$\pi_{NAME}\,EMP = \text{(Peter) [0,0] (Peter) [1,2] (Peter) [3,3]}$$

which should be in TNF just (Peter) [0,3]. If we are to use the output from the RA *project* as the result of the TRA *project*, we need to define a higher-order function *coalesce* which removes such violations of the TNF. This may be achieved by sorting the relation on its attributes, and then merging all tuples which have the same attributes and overlapping intervals. A pseudo code algorithm for *coalesce* is defined below, which functions to filter the tuples returned by a sort of the relation to see if any two adjoining tuples in the sorted relation $t_1=(a_1,...,a_n)$ [*start,end*] and $t_2=(a'_1,...,a'_n)$ [*start',end'*] satisfy $a_1=a'_1, ... , a_n=a'_n$, *start'≤end+1*, in which case they should be replaced by a single tuple $t_{12}=(a_1,...,a_n)$ [*start,max(end,end')*]

function coalesce(R)
- (i) $R := R$ **order_by** $A_1,...,A_n$,START_TIME
  $R_C=\varnothing$
  size = count(R)
  $i = 1$
- (ii) **repeat**

  $(a_1,...,a_n)$ [*start,end*] = R_i
  while $(a'_1,...,a'_n)$ [*start',end'*] = R_{i+1} **and** $a_1=a'_1, ... , a_n=a'_n$
  and *start'≤end+1*

  end := max(*end',end*)
  $i := i+1$
  end_while
  insert $(a_1,...,a_n)$ [*start,end*] **into** R_C
  $i := i+1$
  while $i ≤ size$
- (iii) **return** R_C

The construct $(a_1,...,a_n)$ [*start,end*] = R_i in the above definition finds the *i*th tuple of relation *R*. Using the coalesce function we may define the TRA *product* in terms of the coalesce function being applied to the output of the RA *project*. The complexity of the TRA project is thus of order $N \ log(N)$, where N is the number of tuples in R, since the complexity of the coalesce function is $O(N \ log(N))$ due to the use of a sort in the function definition.

$$\pi_{t \ A,B,C} R = coalesce(\pi_{A,B,C,START\_TIME,END\_TIME} R)$$

$$complexity(\pi_t R) = O(N \ log(N)) \quad \textbf{where } N = \textbf{count}(R)$$

It is interesting to note that an operator called *contract*, with the same semantics as *coalesce*, was provided for in Sarda's algebra [10]. In [10] it was asserted that the operator was needed if the proposed algebra was to be considered expressively complete. This statement seems to be validated here by the need to introduce the operator in order to support the implementation of the TRA in the RA.

Product

From the definition of the TRA *product* operator, we see that the product of two tuples holds for all $\mathbf{D}_q$ in the temporal structure where both the tuples hold. Thus for the *product* to hold in the TNF, the intervals of the two tuples must overlap, and the period for which the product holds starts at the maximum of the start times of the two tuples, and ends at the minimum of the end times for each tuple. Providing the following functions to compute those *max* and *min* allows a definition of the TRA product to be given in terms of the RA *product* operator. The TRA *product* thus has the same complexity as the RA *product*.

function min(*x,y*)
    if $x \leq y$ **then return** *x*
    else return *y*

function max(*x,y*)
    if $x \geq y$ **then return** *x*
    else return *y*

$$R \times_t S = \pi_{R,S,\max(R.\text{START\_TIME},S.\text{START\_TIME}),\min(R.\text{END\_TIME},S.\text{END\_TIME})} \left(\sigma_{\text{overlap}(R,S)} \left(R \times S \right) \right)$$

$complexity(R \times_t S) = O(NM)$ **where** $N = \text{count}(R)$ **and** $M = \text{count}(S)$

Union

As was the case with *project*, the simple use of the RA *union* would result in an output relation violating TNF, since bringing two relations together can make a tuple from one relation overlap a relation in another. Thus we must use the *coalesce* function to merge the possibly overlapping intervals from the two relations.

$$R \cup_t S = \text{coalesce}(R \cup S)$$

$complexity(R \cup_t S) = O(N \log(N))$ **where** $N = \text{count}(R)+\text{count}(S)$

Difference

A peculiarity of using intervals for the encoding of the temporal structure is that the difference operator $R - S$ may result in more tuples than are present in R. For example, the query {(Dov,200) [1,4]} − {(Dov,200) [2,3]} results in two output tuples {(Dov,200) [1,1] , (Dov,200) [4,4]}. This leads to a re-implementation the relational *difference* operator, so that it reduces or splits the size of the interval R holds for as it searches the relation S. This procedure if defined by the following pseudo-code program.

function difference$(R,S)=RS\_$

(i) $RS\_ := \emptyset$

(ii) $\forall \ (a_1,...,a_n) \ [start,end] \in R$
     do $interval = \{ \ [start,end] \ \}$
              $\forall \ (a_1,...,a_n) \ [start',end'] \in S$ **do** $interval := interval - [start',end']$
              $\forall \ [start'',end''] \in S$ **do** $RS\_ := RS\_ \cup (a_1,...,a_n) \ [start'',end'']$

(iii) **return** $RS\_$

The function definition takes each tuple of R in turn, builds a set of intervals for which that tuple holds by iterating over tuples from S which overlap it. This set is initialized with the interval associated with the tuple in R, and has each of the intervals for which the same tuple is found in S removed. This generates a set of intervals for which the tuple is in R but not S, each of which is added to the output $RS\_$.

$$R -_t S \ = \ \text{difference}(R,S)$$

$$complexity(R -_t S) = O(NM) \text{ where } N = \text{count}(R) \text{ and } M = \text{count}(S)$$

Since-Product

From the definition of *since-product* working on the temporal structure given in Section 1, it can be seen that the following axioms hold for the operator when working on the encoding of the temporal structure as intervals (the axioms for *until-product* are the obvious 'reflections' in time):

(i)   The tuples of $R \ S_\times \ S$ hold for at least the interval $[s_{RS}+1,e_{RS}+1]$, where $[s_{RS},e_{RS}]$ is the interval that the tuples of $R \times S$ hold, due to the fact for any $\mathbf{D}_q$ in the temporal structure, $R \ S_\times \ S$ holds for all tuples that $R \times S$ holds for in $\mathbf{D}_{q-1}$.

(ii)   The tuples of $R \ S_\times \ S$ hold for the interval $[s_{RS}+1,e_R+1]$ when $s_R \leq e_{RS} \leq e_R$ where $[s_R,e_R]$ is the interval that the tuples of R hold, due to the fact that $R \ S_\times \ S$ always holds in $\mathbf{D}_q$ for all tuples that both R and $R \ S_\times \ S$ hold for in $\mathbf{D}_{q-1}$.

Figure 1 illustrates the result on the second axiom diagrammatically for a few of the tuples taken from Example 1. Clearly all that we need to evaluate a query $R\ S_\times\ S$ is to find the intervals over which R and S hold, then use the axioms listed above to create the interval for the *since-product*. The interval for axiom (i) is computed by a simple modification to that used to generate the intervals for $\times_t$, and then axiom (ii) is taken into account by making the end of the interval be that of R, not the maximum of R and S.

$$R\ S_\times\ S = \text{coalesce}(\pi_{R,S,\max(R.START\_TIME,S.START\_TIME)+1,R.END\_TIME+1}$$
$$\sigma_{\text{overlap}(R,S)}\ (R \times S)\ )$$

$$complexity(R\ S_\times\ S) = O(NM + (N+M)log(N+M))$$
$$\textbf{where } N = \textbf{count}(R) \textbf{ and } M = \textbf{count}(S)$$

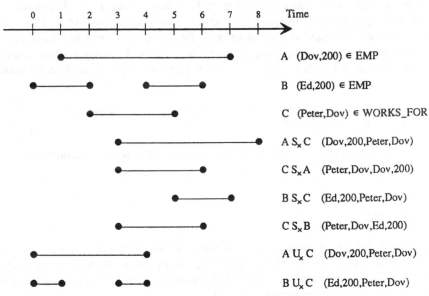

Figure 1 : Examples of intervals for which tuples hold

This use of the coalesce function is only necessary to remove 'extra' tuples of the form $(a_1,...,a_n)$ [start,end] where there is another tuple of the form $(a_1,...,a_n)$ [*start',end'*] for which *start'≤start≤end≤end'*. An example will make this point clear. In Figure 1 we illustrate some results of the *since-product* and *until-product* when we have EMP = { (Dov,200) [1,7], (Ed,200) [0,2], (Ed,200) [4,6] }, and $WORKS\_FOR$ = { (Peter,Dov) [2,5] }. Evaluating $WORKS\_FOR\ S_\times\ EMP$ using the above algorithm will return the tuples { (Peter,Dov,Ed,200) [3,6] , (Peter,Dov,Ed,200) [5,6] , (Peter,Dov,Dov,200) [4,8] } if no coalesce function is used. The tuple (Peter,Dov,Ed,200) is seen to have an 'extra' result as holding over [5,6]. Since the correct (maximal interval) result is also returned it may be realized that this is a problem of presentation. In a practical query language it would be sensible to allow the user to specify when the coalesce function is used, in the same manner that one can specify the use of DISTINCT in an SQL SELECT to remove duplicates [3].

Until-Product

From the definitions of the *since-product* and *until-product* it may be seen the latter operator is merely the 'reflection' of the former, working into the future instead of the past. We thus need only give the definition of the encoding here, using as justification the commentary given for the *since-product*.

$$R \ U_\times \ S = coalesce(\pi_{R,S,R.\text{START\_TIME}-1,min(R.\text{END\_TIME},S.\text{END\_TIME})-1} \\ \sigma_{overlap(R,S)} (R \times S))$$

$$complexity(R \ U_\times \ S) = O(NM + (N+M)log(N+M)) \\ \text{where } N = \textbf{count}(R) \text{ and } M = \textbf{count}(S)$$

4.2 Optimisations

The algorithms presented in the previous subsection make no attempt at optimizing the queries. It is not intended to cover this topic in any depth within this paper, but to indicate the directions in which future work may proceed. In very broad terms, we may divide the issues of query optimisation of the TRA queries into two categories:

(i) Structure of Query

The query may be the subject of some static analysis to determine the extent to which the TNF must be maintained in the output of each TRA operator that is a constituent of the query. For example:

- If a query is made with respect to a specific tick time, then we do not need to maintain the TNF in the output relation from principal operator of the query. Thus if we ask $\pi_t \ R$ at time(t) we can simplify the implementation of the project to $\pi \ \sigma_{\text{START\_TIME} \leq t \leq \text{END\_TIME}} \ R$.

- The coalesce function used in the definition of $S_\times$ is only needed if the output relation from the operator is not in the scope of another operator that uses *coalesce*. This is because the output of $U_\times$ and $S_\times$ without the application of *coalesce* only violates TNF by producing tuples with an interval which is a sub-interval of some other tuple. Thus they only violate the TNF by making some tuples appear to be duplicated are certain times, which can be ignored except for purposes of presenting results (or using aggregate operators such as

SUM which we do not consider here).

- The schema design should help to avoid the use of projects in queries, since the execution of projects in the TRA now has $O(N \log(N))$ complexity on the number of tuples in the relation.

- We can use the fact that the non-temporal operators can accept input in non-TNF, producing semantically correct answers as output, but still in non-TNF form. As can be seen from the table below, this allows us to use the RA implementation of an operator, excluding the use of coalesce for the majority of operations. Indeed, only operators that require TNF as input (i.e. S_x and U_x), and have the input produced by an operator which does not produce TNF (i.e. S_x, U_x, $\cup_t$ and π_t), need have coalesce applied.

TRA	non-TNF input?	Implement in RA?
S_x	✗	Yes (but produces 'subset' results)
U_x	✗	Yes (but produces 'subset' results)
$\cup_t$	✓	Yes (use *coalesce* to get TNF)
$\times_t$	✓	Yes
$-_t$	✓	No (entirely new algorithm used)
π_t	✓	Yes (use *coalesce* to get TNF)
σ_t	✓	Yes

(ii) Query Execution

The specification of the algorithms for coalesce, difference *etc* has been made external to the definitions of the algorithms for the RA operators. Since operators like product, since-product and until-product will be used to make a join, which will involve some sorting of the tuples from each relation involved, it is apparent that the TRA would much more efficiently implemented if these algorithms were more integrated.

(iii) Physical Data Model

Although we have used the data model of [9] as our implementation vehicle, this does not preclude the use of many different physical data models for the storage of the temporal information, which may give benefits in compactness when handling large amounts of information. The only requirement would be that the query processing be able to readily abstract the TNF form from the stored data without significant overhead. For instance, a common technique for overcoming the redundancy in the variation of a single attribute in a large tuple is to use *delta tuples*, where one records only the attribute that has changed together with its time-stamp. The results of this technique for the *EMP* relation of Example 3 is shown in Example 4. Clearly a database system supporting such delta tuples may be easily made to support the abstraction of 'full' tuples without great implementation overhead.

Example 4 : Delta tuple form of the *EMP* relation of Example 3

$$\Delta\,EMP$$

(Peter,100)[0,0]
Δ(110)[1,2]
Δ(140)[3,4]
(Richard,90)[0,1]
Δ(140)[2,4]
(Ed,200)[0,2]
(Ed,200)[4,4]
(Dov,200)[1,4]

Summary & Conclusions

This paper has presented methods by which a historical database may be stored and updated in a standard relational model, and queries of the TRA translated into an extended RA working on the relational model. The complexity of the TRA operators has been shown not to be significantly greater than that of their RA counterparts, with the exception of the TRA project which has complexity $O(N\,log(N))$ on the number of tuples in a relation. Design of database schemas to avoid the use of projects thus becomes important in the context of historical databases.

It has been shown that extending the RA with the *coalesce* and *difference* functions is all that is required in order to fully implement the TRA in the RA. By extending a RDBMS with these primitives we would allow for the implementation of any historical database query language with the expressive power of the TRA.

The techniques presented in this paper are currently being used as the foundation for the implementation of a Datalog-like temporal query language in the Tempora Esprit project, using the Sybase DBMS as the implementation platform. Future work will need to consider in greater depth the areas of query optimisation, looking at both static analysis, and at the integration of the algorithms detailed in this paper with existing techniques for the dynamic optimisation of RA queries, such as fast join algorithms. Future work will also consider how the techniques described may be extended to handle aggregate functions.

Acknowledgements

The work reported in this paper was partly funded by the EC under Esprit project number 2469. The author would like to thank all members of the project for their helpful involvement in numerous meetings, and in particular the contributions of M.Finger, D.Gabbay and R.Owens at Imperial College, and A.Conti, M.Niézette, F.Schumacker and P.Wolper at the University of Liège. The author would also like to thank M.Finger and R.Owens for much helpful advice during the preparation of this paper.

References

1. J.F.Allen: *Maintaining Knowledge about Temporal Intervals*, CACM Vol. 26, No. 11 pp 832-843, 1983.

2. J.Clifford & A.U.Tansel, *On An Algebra for Historical Relational Databases: Two Views*, Proc. ACM SIGMOD Conference 1985.

3. C.J.Date, *A Guide to the SQL Standard*, Addison-Wesley, 1989.

4. D.Gabbay, *The Declarative Past and Imperative Future*, Temporal Logic in Specification: Altrincham Workshop 1987, LNCS 398 pp 409-448, Springer-Verlag, 1989.

5. D.Gabbay & P.J.McBrien, *Temporal Logic and Historical Databases*, Proceedings of the 17th International Conference on Very Large Databases, Barcelona, 1991.

6. S.K.Gadia, *A Homogeneous Relational Model and Query Languages for Temporal Databases*, ACM TODS, Vol. 13, No. 4 pp 418-448, 1988.

7. H.Kamp, *On the Tense Logic and the Theory of Order*, PHD Thesis, UCLA, 1968.

8. L.E.McKenzie Jr. & R.T.Snodgrass, *Evaluation of Relational Algebra Incorporating the Time Dimension in Databases*, ACM Computing Surveys, Vol.23 No.4, December 1991.

9. S.B.Navathe & R.Ahmed, *TSQL - A Language Interface for History Databases*, Temporal Aspects of Information Systems, pp 109-122, *Ed.* C.Rolland, F.Bodart & M.Leonard, North-Holland, 1988.

10. N.Sarda, *Algebra and Query Language for a Historical Data Model.* Computing Journal, Vol 33, No. 1 pp 11-18, 1990.

11. R.Snodgrass, *The Temporal Query Language TQuel*, ACM TODS Vol. 12, No. 2 pp 247-298, 1987.

12. Sybase, *Transact-SQL User's Guide*, 9th October, 1989, Sybase Inc.

13. A.U.Tansel, *Adding Time Dimension to Relational Model and Extending Relational Algebra*, Information Systems Vol 11, No. 4, pp 343-355, 1986.

14. A.Tuzhilin & J.Clifford, *A Temporal Relational Algebra as a Basis for Temporal Relational Completeness*, Proceedings of the 16th International Conference on Very Large Databases, Brisbane, 1990.

Integrity Constraint Enforcement in the Functional Database Language PFL

Swarup Reddi

Department of Computer Science, Birkbeck College,
University of London, Malet Street, London WC1E 7HX

Abstract. The importance of the efficient enforcement of integrity constraints over deductive databases has long been recognised. Most of this work, however, has been done in the context of logic-based languages. In contrast, we here consider the specification and enforcement of constraints in the functional database language PFL. We show how an optimisation strategy developed for fast constraint enforcement in logic databases [8] can be adapted to the functional context and extended to support a wider class of constraints, including static aggregate constraints.

1 Introduction

An integrity constraint is a condition that a database must satisfy in order for the database to be in a valid state. It is the task of the database system to automatically reject any update that would result in the violation of an integrity constraint. The basic problem is not "how to enforce integrity constraints" but rather "how to enforce them efficiently". The early work considered integrity enforcement in relational databases. The problem of maintaining the integrity of a deductive database was first addressed by Nicolas and Yazdanian [10], and since then much work has been done on enforcing integrity constraints over logic databases [8,9,4,7,2,11]. The strategy underlying all the practical integrity maintenance methods (including ours) is to assume that the database is in a valid state before a given update and then to obtain a simplified or reduced set of integrity constraints such that if the database satisfies the reduced set of constraints then it is guaranteed to be in a valid state after the update.

But for a few exceptions such as [13], the majority of work on integrity maintenance in deductive databases has assumed a logic environment. However, the advantages of functional languages are now well documented (see for example [5,6]) and we consider the development of deductive database systems with a functional computation model to be a worthwhile endeavour. It is our intent in this paper to equip a functional database with at least the integrity enforcement capability that exists for logic databases. Lloyd and Topor [8,9] developed one of the first practical methods for integrity checking in a deductive database. The deductive rules in their database are defined as horn clauses and they assume the database, including the integrity constraints, to be range-restricted. The updates handled by their approach are insertions and deletions of clauses (both facts and deductive rules) and sets of such insertions and deletions. Upon a given update, a superset of the resulting cascaded updates is calculated. This superset is then used to select the integrity constraints requiring evaluation. It is basically this strategy we adapt to the functional environment of PFL. Although Lloyd and Topor's strategy does not enforce aggregate constraints [3], they are simply enforced in a functional environment [13] and we extend Lloyd and Topor's strategy to obtain an integrity maintenance system for PFL that enforces aggregate constraints.

One advantage of a logic language over a functional one is that in logic languages there is no necessity to specify which entities are input and which are output. Thus, before we can adapt a logic-based algorithm to a functional context we require a functional equivalent to invertible queries. In [14] it was shown how PFL contains an analogue to invertible queries over "facts" and how any stratified Datalog IDB predicate can be simulated by a PFL function. In this paper we introduce specific user-defined functions in order to formalise and extend the scheme presented in [14]. We describe how an integrity constraint, expressed in the form of a logic denial, can be translated into a PFL function and we show how constraints, that would require higher-order operators if expressed as logic formulae, can be specified in PFL. We also describe how integrity constraints can be efficiently implemented in PFL.

The remainder of this paper is organised as follows. In Section 2 we give a brief overview of PFL. In Section 3 we describe *extensional selectors*, the PFL functions that handle storage of bulk data and permit invertible queries over this bulk data. In Section 4 we define *intensional selectors* which are a syntactically restricted subset of user-defined functions that enable us to express invertible queries over rules. In Section 5 we describe how a logic rule can be expressed in terms of intensional selectors and how intensional selectors also allow us to express what would be higher-order operators in a logic language. In Section 6 we explain how integrity constraints are defined in terms of intensional selectors and in Section 7 we describe our integrity enforcement strategy and present the algorithms used to implement it. We make some concluding remarks in Section 8 and suggest a direction in which to extend this work.

2 Overview of PFL

We now provide a brief description of the aspects of PFL required by subsequent sections. More comprehensive descriptions can be found in [14,16]. PFL is a polymorphic, statically typed, persistent functional language. It provides a set of built-in types and facilities for the definition of new types and constants. Its functions are defined incrementally by the insertion and deletion of equations. The types of functions are inferred incrementally in the face of such updates. PFL's bulk data is stored in a class of function called *extensional selectors* which are the subject of the next section. In this section we sketch PFL's type system and show how types and constants are declared. We outline how functions are defined and explain what it means for one function to "depend on" another. We describe a particular type of expression termed a *list abstraction* [12] which is central to this paper. We conclude this section with a description of pattern-matching in PFL.

PFL's type system comprises three layers c.f. [1]. Firstly, there is the metalevel type `Type` which is the set of all types. Secondly, we have object-level types, both built-in and user-declared. These are also regarded as metalevel values of type `Type`. The third layer contains the values of each object-level type. The built-in types are `Str`,

`Int`, `Real` and `Char` which are initially populated by strings, integers, reals and characters. New constants, whether object-level or metalevel are declared using the command

```
> declare <constant> :: <type>
```

These constants are called *constructor functions* or *constructors* [12] since they construct values of the indicated types. In PFL, identifiers starting with an uppercase letter are constructors (metalevel or object-level) and identifiers starting with a lowercase letter are variables. For example, the statements

```
> declare Person :: Type
> declare Adam :: Person
> declare Any :: a
```

declare `Person` to be an object-level type, `Adam` to be an entity of type `Person` and `Any` to be a constant of every type. In general, constructors may take arguments. For example, we may declare a list constructor as

```
> declare List :: a -> Type
```

and we can declare 2-tuples and 3-tuples by

```
> declare Prod2 :: a->b->Type
> declare Prod3 :: a->b->c->Type
> declare Tuple2 :: a->b->(Prod2 a b)
> declare Tuple3 :: a->b->c->(Prod3 a b c)
```

For syntactic ease n-tuples are expressed using curly brackets. Thus, `{a,{b,c},d}` is shorthand for `(Tuple3 a (Tuple2 b c) d)`.

In PFL's syntax `=` is used for definitions and `==` is used for equality. Functions are defined by means of equations which are inserted using the syntax

```
> define <lhs> = <expression>
```

For example, we can define the 3-ary function `if` as follows:

```
> define if True x y = x
> define if False x y = y
```

Equations must be defined with unique left-hand sides and can be deleted using the syntax

```
> delete <lhs>
```

If evaluating a function `A` can result in a function `B` being evaluated, we say that function `A` *depends on* function `B`. More precisely, `A` depends on `B`, either directly, when `B` appears on the right hand side of an equation that defines `A`, or indirectly, when `B` appears on the right hand side of an equation that defines some function `C` and `A` depends on `C`. PFL maintains an internal graph of which functions depend on which and updates this graph each time an equation is added or removed by the `define` and `delete` commands.

A list abstraction is a list-valued expression where each element in the returned list is the result of evaluating some expression `E` that contains a number of variables as these variables are allowed to range over specified values. The values that the variables take are determined by a sequence of *generator* and *filter expressions* that are evaluated in order. The general syntax of a list-abstraction is

```
[ E | E1; E2; ... ; Ek]
```

where each `Ei` is either a generator expression or a filter expression. A filter expression is simply a boolean-valued expression. A generator expression assigns to a variable the value of each element in a specified list. For each such assignment, the filter expressions appearing to the right of the generator expression are evaluated. If any of the filter expressions evaluate to `False` that particular assignment is discarded. The syntax of a generator expression is

```
<pattern> <- <list-valued expression>
```

where the pattern and the elements of the list are of the same type. Thus, given the list of integers `int_list`, the list abstraction

```
[{x,y} | x <- int_list; y <- int_list; x > y]
```

defines the relationship "greater than" over the list `int_list`.

A facet of list abstractions that is significant in our use of them is that their syntax allows the use of a single symbol to represent more than one variable. We describe the semantics of this by example. Given the list-valued functions `f1` and `f3` and the boolean valued function `f2`, then the function `list_abs` defined by

```
> define list_abs x = [x | x <- f1 x; f2 x; x <- f3 x]
```

can equivalently be defined by

```
> define list_abs x0 = [x2 | x1 <- f1 x0; f2 x1; x2 <- f3 x1]
```

Retrieval of bulk data in PFL is done via pattern matching. We describe the pattern matching in terms of the predefined in-fix function $\sqsubseteq$, pronounced "matches", and the polymorphic "wildcard" `Any`. Given values `p` and `v`, the expression $(p \sqsubseteq v)$ yields `True` if `p` is identical to `v` except with respect to any occurrences of `Any` in `p`. For example, $\{1, \text{Any}, 3\} \sqsubseteq \{1, 2, 3\}$ returns `True` and $\{1, 2, 3\} \sqsubseteq \{1, \text{Any}, 3\}$ returns `False`. A precise definition of the semantics of $\sqsubseteq$ can be found in [16].

3 Extensional Selectors

In logic languages there is no necessity to specify which entities are input and which are output. In contrast, functional languages are *directional* [15], in that they require an explicit commitment as to which entities are input and which are output. For example, in a logic language, the base facts

$$parent(adam, abel) \quad parent(eve, abel) \quad parent(adam, cain) \quad parent(eve, cain)$$

allow us to identify the the parents of *cain* and the children of *eve* with the queries $parent(X, cain)$ and $parent(eve, X)$. A similar facility is provided in PFL by the use of *extensional selectors*.

In PFL storage of bulk data is handled by extensional selectors (e-selectors). These are single-argument list-valued functions. Each e-selector is associated with a relation. Retrieval of data from this relation is done via pattern matching. An e-selector function is declared by a statement of the form

```
> e_selector <name> :: <type> ->[<type>]
```
where <type> is a first-order type. When an e-selector is declared its associated relation is empty; the relation is physically stored in the database and the only way to add (or remove) elements to (or from) an e-selector's relation is by using the PFL commands include (or exclude). A statement of the form
```
> include <e-selector> <tuple>
```
inserts a tuple into an e-selector's relation, provided that the relation does not already contain the tuple. The command
```
> exclude <e-selector> <pattern>
```
deletes from an e-selector's relation any tuple <tuple> such that <pattern> ⊑ <tuple>.

An e-selector's relation is queried by applying the e-selector to a search pattern. The value obtained by applying an e-selector to a pattern,

　　　　<e-selector> <pattern>

is equivalent to

　　　　[x | x <- relation; <pattern> ⊑ x].

That is, when applied to an argument an e-selector returns a list containing all the tuples in its relation that are matched by that argument.

Consider, for example, the e-selector declared by
```
> e_selector parent :: {Person,Person} -> [{Person,Person}]
```
Assuming that Adam, Eve, Abel, Cain and Lilith are constructors of type Person and that the four statements
```
> include parent {Eve,Cain}
> include parent {Eve,Abel}
> include parent {Adam,Cain}
> include parent {Adam,Abel}
```
are the only updates to parent's relation, then the value returned by (parent Any), up to a permutation of elements, is the list

　　　　[{Eve,Abel}, {Eve,Cain}, {Adam,Abel}, {Adam,Cain}],

and the values of (parent {Eve,Any}) and (parent {Any,Lilith}), up to a permutation of elements, are respectively [{Eve,Abel}, {Eve,Cain}] and []．

If we now issue the single command
```
> exclude parent {Any,Abel}.
```
we delete all the tuples whose second element is Abel and the value returned by (parent Any) is now [{Eve,Cain}, {Adam,Cain}].

The above examples illustrate how the pattern-matching aspect of e-selectors can avoid the restrictions imposed by the input-output directionality of a functional language. Since each tuple in an e-selector's relation must be described and added explicitly, the information that can be expressed using e-selectors is analogous to the base facts of a logic database. Thus, e-selectors permit invertible queries over base facts. To obtain an analogue of invertible queries over rules, we now introduce *intensional selectors*.

4 Intensional Selectors

In logic languages, implied facts are derived from base facts using derivation rules. For example, we can define *grandparent* in terms of *parent* as follows:

$$grandparent(X,Y) \leftarrow parent(X,Z) \wedge parent(Z,Y)$$

Intensional selectors (i-selectors) undertake a similar role in PFL. An i-selector is similar to an e-selector in that it is a single-argument list-valued function whose type of the form `<type> -> [<type>]`, where `<type>` is a first order type. As with an e-selector, when applied to an argument, it returns a list of tuples, which are all matched by that argument.

Whereas an e-selector is associated with a physically stored relation that contains explicitly described tuples, an i-selector is only associated with a virtual relation whose tuples are defined in terms of other selectors (intensional or extensional). We note that an i-selector's relation does not physically exist and that i-selectors are simply a syntactically restricted subset of user-defined functions which we identify to facilitate fast implementation and the efficient enforcement of integrity constraints.

We now present a formal description of an i-selector and its syntax. An i-selector is defined in terms of a list valued expression we refer to as the i-selector's *s-list*. An i-selector `isel` with s-list L_s is defined by

```
> i_selector isel P_S = mkset L_S
```

where P_S is a tuple of variables and `mkset` is the function that removes duplicates from a list. We allow two types of s-list, T1 and T2, which are as follows:

T1) $L_S \equiv (s_1\ P_1)\ ++\ (s_2\ P_2)\ ++\ \ldots\ ++\ (s_n\ P_n)$

T2) $L_S \equiv [P_S|\ P_1' <-\ s_1 P_1;\ \ldots;\ P_l' <-\ s_l P_l;$
$x_{l+1} <-\ [F_{l+1}\ (s_{l+1}\ P_{l+1})];\ \ldots;\ x_m <-\ [F_m\ (s_m\ P_m)];$
$s_{m+1} P_{m+1} ==\ [];\ \ldots;\ s_n P_n ==\ [];$
$F_{n+1} P_{n+1};\ \ldots;\ F_N P_N]$

where

  $++$ is the function that concatenates two lists,
  s_i $(1 \leq i \leq n)$, are selectors (intensional or extensional),
  P_i $(1 \leq i \leq N)$ are patterns,
  x_i $(l < i \leq m)$ are variables that appear only in P_j $(n < j \leq N)$,
  F_i $(l < i \leq m)$, $(n < i \leq N)$ are functions that do not depend on any
      selectors (intensional or extensional),
  F_i $(n < i \leq N)$ are boolean valued functions and where
  P_i' $(1 \leq i \leq l)$ is the same as P_i except that it contains a variable anywhere P_i
      contains `Any`.

Thus, the T1 s-list is the concatenation of n sub-lists, each of which is the result of applying the selector s_i (extensional or intensional) to the pattern P_i. The T2 s-list is a list abstraction which permits only two forms of generator, G1 and G2, and two forms of filter, F1 and F2, namely,

G1)	$P_i' <-\ s_i\ P_i;$		F1)	$s_i\ P_i ==\ [];$
G2)	$x_i <-\ [F_i\ (s_i\ P_i)];$		F2)	$F_i\ P_i.$

Non-negated and negated predicates in a logic conjunction are expressed by G1 generator expressions and F1 filter expressions, respectively. How they do this is discussed in Section 5. F2 filter expressions are used to express built-in boolean operators such as *greater* and *equals*. A G2 generator expression assigns to the variable x_i the value returned by applying the function F_i to the list of tuples from s_i's relation that match the pattern P_i, where s_i is either an intensional or extensional selector. Thus, the F_i ($l < i \leq m$) allow us to express what would be higher-order operators in a logic formula. Intensional selectors defined in Sections 5 and 6 contain examples of both types of generator and both types of filter.

We next present an example of an i-selector in order to illustrate four points. Consider the i-selector `ancestor` which is defined as follows:

```
> i_selector ancestor {x,y} =
      mkset( (parent {x,y}) ++ (ancl {x,y}) )
> i_selector ancl {x,y} = mkset [{x,y} |
      {x,z} <- parent {x,Any}; {z,y} <- ancestor {z,y}]
```

Firstly, we note that `ancestor` allows us invertible queries. For example, antecedents and descendents of Abel can be obtained by evaluating

```
ancestor {Any,Abel} and  ancestor {Abel, Any},
```

respectively. We can see how this works by making the appropriate substitutions in the definitions of `ancestor` and `ancl`. Thus, omitting the `mkset`'s, we obtain for `ancestor {Any,Abel}`

```
(parent {Any,Abel}) ++
   [{x,y}|{x,z}<- parent {Any,Any}; {z,y}<- ancestor {z,Abel}],
```

and for `ancestor {Abel,Any}` we have

```
(parent {Abel,Any}) ++
   [{x,y}|{x,z}<- parent {Abel,Any}; {z,y}<- ancestor {z,Any}].
```

The second point to note is that both `ancestor` and `ancl` return lists of tuples that are matched by their arguments and that the tuples in `ancestor`'s relation are exactly those tuples in the list returned by applying `ancestor` to `{Any,Any}`. This follows from the semantics of using a single symbol to represent more than one variable. For example, the function `foo` defined by

```
> define foo x = [x | x <- s1 x; x <- s2 x],
```

where `s1` and `s2` are selectors (intensional or extensional), is equivalent to

```
> define foo x0 = [x2 | x1 <- s1 x0; x2 <- s2 x1].
```

If `s1` and `s2` are e-selectors it is clear that $x0 \sqsubseteq x1 \sqsubseteq x2$. That this is still true when `s1` and `s2` are i-selectors can be proved by induction. Thus, using P_s as the pattern on the left-hand side of an i-selector's definition as well as the pattern defining each element in the returned list (respectively, `x0` and `x2` in the `foo` example) guarantees that an i-selector returns a list of tuples that are matched by its argument.

The third point illustrated by the `ancestor` example is that there is no guarantee that evaluation of an i-selector will terminate. For example, if the relation of the e-selector `parent` contains the tuple `{Oedipus, Oedipus}`, then evaluating `ancestor`

{Oedipus, Any} will not terminate. This is the same as in Prolog where the evaluation of recursively defined predicates cannot be guaranteed to terminate.

Fourthly, we note that we could define an equivalent function in a single statement, as was done in [14], by replacing "ancl {x,y}" in the definition of ancestor by ancl's s-list. The only reason we have defined i-selectors to require the definition of both ancl and ancestor is that the explanation of our integrity enforcement strategy is much simplified by distinguishing between s-lists of type T1 and T2.

5 Expressing a Rule as an I-Selector

Preparatory to translating integrity constraints expressed as logic denials into functions, we show how a predicate that is defined as the conjunction of a number of predicates can be represented by an i-selector with an s-list of type T2. This is largely a formalisation of the method, presented in [14], for translating a Datalog IDB predicate into e-selectors and list abstractions. Henceforth, when it is immaterial whether a selector is intensional or extensional, we shall simply refer to it as a selector.

We denote the parameters for a predicate p, appearing in a logic formula F, by a vector which we refer to as the *argument vector*. For ease of notation, we define, for each argument vector $\overline{X}$, two patterns $\text{Tup}_{\overline{X}}$ and $\text{Arg}_{\overline{X}}$. $\text{Tup}_{\overline{X}}$ is basically $\overline{X}$ rewritten as a tuple. Its arity is the dimension of $\overline{X}$. Each of its components is either a variable or a constant, depending on whether the corresponding component of $\overline{X}$ is, respectively, a variable or a constant. $\text{Arg}_{\overline{X}}$ is determined by the formula F and the position of p within F, as well as by $\overline{X}$. $\text{Arg}_{\overline{X}}$ is the same as $\text{Tup}_{\overline{X}}$, except that any variable in $\overline{X}$ that has not previously been encountered (does not appear to the left of p in F) is replaced by Any. For example, consider the query *parent(eve,Y)*. The argument vector $\overline{X}$ is (eve,Y), $\text{Tup}_{\overline{X}}$ is {Eve,y} and $\text{Arg}_{\overline{X}}$ is {Eve,Any}. Applying the selector parent to {Eve,Any} returns the list of tuples corresponding to the set of substitutions that satisfy *parent(Eve,Y)*.

A predicate that is defined as the rectified [17] conjunction of a number of predicates can be represented by an i-selector with an s-list of type T2. To show this, we describe how to obtain the i-selector for a predicate $C(\overline{X}_C)$, defined by a rule of the form

R) $C(\overline{X}_C) \leftarrow p_1(\overline{X}_1) \wedge \cdots \wedge p_m(\overline{X}_m) \wedge \neg p_{m+1}(\overline{X}_{m+1}) \wedge \cdots$
$\cdots \wedge \neg p_n(\overline{X}_n) \wedge equals(L1,L2)$

where each p_i $(1 \leq i < n)$ is a predicate with argument vector $\overline{X}_i$ and where $\overline{X}_C$ is the argument vector for C and is made up from the range-restricted variables that appear in the $\overline{X}_i$. The final term, $equals(L1,L2)$, is present to compensate for the rectification of C. All the variables that would otherwise have been repeated make up the elements of the lists $L1$ and $L2$. For example,

$$CC(X,Y) \leftarrow p(X,X,X) \wedge q(Y,Y) \wedge \neg r(Z)$$

would be expressed as

$CC(X,Y) \leftarrow$
$\quad p(X,X1,X2) \wedge q(Y,Y1) \wedge \neg r(Z) \wedge equals([X,X1,Y],[X1,X2,Y1])$

For any predicate, $C(\overline{X}_C)$, whose definition is a rule of the form R it is possible to define a corresponding i-selector `isel`$_C$ by

```
> i_selector iselC Tupx̄c = LC
```

where `L`$_C$ is an s-list of type T2 which can be obtained by applying Algorithm A.

Algorithm A : to obtain the s-list of type T2 for the predicate $C(\overline{X}_C)$ whose definition is a rule of the form R and where each predicate p_i $(1 \leq i < n)$ has a corresponding selector s_i.

A1) For each positive literal p_i $(1 \leq i \leq m)$ appearing in R, we have the G1 generator
$$\text{Tup}\overline{x}_i \text{ <- } s_i \text{ Arg}\overline{x}_i;$$

A2) For each negated literal p_i $(m < i \leq n)$ appearing in R, we have the F1 filter
$$s_i \text{ Arg}\overline{x}_i \text{ == } [];$$

A3) We let T_{L1} and T_{L2} be the tuples whose components correspond to the elements of the lists $L1$ and $L2$, respectively. Then, for the term $equals(L1,L2)$, we have the F2 filter
$$T_{L1} \text{ == } T_{L2}$$

For example, the i-selector `anc1`, defined in Section 4, could be obtained by applying Algorithm A to

$$anc1(X,Y) \leftarrow parent(X,Z) \wedge ancestor(Z,Y)$$

We note that Algorithm A does not require generators of type G2. To illustrate the purpose of G2 generators we now present an example arising from SERC project GR/G 19596 where data pertaining to road accidents required validation.

Every casualty arising from a road accident is graded in terms of severity, ranging from 1 (slight) to 3 (fatal). The number of casualties involved in any given accident is recorded and the accident itself is also assigned a severity ranging from 0 to 3. The relevant subset of data is held in the relations:

accident(accident identifier, accident severity, number of casualties)
casualty(person's name, casualty severity, accident identifier)

It is required that

C0) The details of each casualty must be recorded.
C1) An accident has a severity of zero only if no associated casualty has a severity greater than 1.
C2) For each casualty the associated accident must be recorded.

Clearly C1 and C2 can be expressed by the formulae

$$\forall Z,W \; accident(Z,0,W) \rightarrow \neg \exists X,Y, \; casualty(X,Y,Z) \wedge greater(Y,1)$$
$$\forall X,Y,Z \; casualty(X,Y,Z) \rightarrow \exists V,W \; accident(Z,V,W)$$

However, we have a problem with C0 since we wish to check that the number of casualties specified in an accident record corresponds to the number of associated casualty records. Hence, C0 cannot easily be expressed as a first-order formula since it requires a higher-order operator to count an arbitrary number of casualty records. Given the selectors `accident` and `casualty`, corresponding to *accident* and *casualty* respectively, we can use a G2 generator to define the i-selector co whose relation contains the identifiers of the accidents that violate C0:

```
> i_selector c0 {z} = mkset [{z}| {z,v,w}<-accident {z,Any,Any};
    a <- [$(casualty {Any,Any,z})]; a != w ]
```

where $ is the function that returns the number of elements in a list. Thus, C0 can be expressed by

```
    c0 {Any} == [].
```

6 Integrity Constraints

We define an integrity constraint to be an i-selector that must have an empty relation. We term an i-selector that is also an integrity constraint to be a *constraint selector* or *c-selector*. Thus, c-selectors are analogous to constraints in logic systems that are expressed in the form of denials. An i-selector is declared to be a constraint selector by the PFL command constraint. For example, we can implement constraint C0 by declaring the already defined i-selector c0 to be a c-selector with the statement

```
> constraint c0
```

and thereafter any update that results in c0's relation not being empty is rejected.

As a further example of an integrity constraint consider the constraint C3 which is given by the logic formula

C3) $\forall X, Y \, a(X) \wedge b(X,Y) \rightarrow a(Y)$.

Constraints C1, C2 and C3, when written as denials, are expressed by the formulae F1, F2 and F3 respectively.

F1) $\leftarrow accident(Z,0,W) \wedge casualty(X,Y,Z) \wedge greater(Y,1)$
F2) $\leftarrow casualty(X,Y,Z) \wedge \neg accident(Z,V,W)$
F3) $\leftarrow a(X) \wedge b(X,Y) \wedge \neg a(Y)$

The formulae F1-F3 are all similar to the rule R, defined in Section 5, except that there is no left-hand side and, consequently, no argument vector $\bar{X}_C$. If for each F1-F3 we provide a predicate name and an argument vector for the left-hand side, then assuming that asel and bsel are the selectors corresponding to a and b, we can use Algorithm A to represent constraints C1, C2 and C3 with the following c-selectors

```
> i_selector c1 {x,y,z} = mkset [{x,y,z} |
    {z,0,w}<-accident {z,0,Any}; {x,y,z}<-casualty {x,y,z}; y>1]
> constraint c1
> i_selector c2 {x,y,z} = mkset [{x,y,z} |
    {x,y,z} <- casualty {x,y,z}; accident {z,Any,Any} == [] ]
> constraint c2
> i_selector c3 {x,y} = mkset [{x,y} |
    {x} <- asel {x}; {x,y} <- bsel {x,y}; asel {y} == [] ]
> constraint c3
```

We note that the choice of an argument vector $\bar{X}_C$, or equivalently the choice of the argument for which a c-selector is defined, is not unique.

Each i-selector `sel` is defined by a statement either of the form

> `i_selector sel P, = mkset L,`

where `P,` is a tuple of variables and `L,` is an s-list. For the sake of notational simplicity we introduce the wildcard `Any*` to represent, for any i-selector `sel`, the tuple that is the same as `P,`, except that `Any*` has `Any` everywhere `P,` has a variable. Examples of `Any*` are given in Table 1.

sel	P,	Any*
c0	{x}	{Any}
c1	{x,y,z}	{Any,Any,Any}
c2	{x,y,z}	{Any,Any,Any}
c3	{x,y}	{Any,Any}

Table 1: Examples of Any*

As described in Section 3, when applied to an argument, an i-selector returns a list of tuples, which are all matched by that argument. The most general argument that an i-selector can be applied to is `Any*`. Thus, the contents of a selector's relation are exactly those tuples returned by applying the selector to `Any*`. Hence, for integrity to be maintained, any c-selector when applied to `Any*` must return the empty list. For example, we can impose constraints C0-C3, once the c-selectors c_i ($0 \leq i \leq 3$) have been declared, by rejecting any update that would result in

c_i `Any* != [],`   for some i.

We now turn our attention to the *efficient* enforcement of constraints.

7   Efficient Enforcement of Integrity Constraints

Our strategy for enforcing integrity constraints is similar to the approach adopted by Lloyd and Topor [8]. The database is initially assumed to be in a valid state and, given a particular set of updates, the effects of those updates on the database are summarised and integrity constraints are only checked over those parts of the database that have altered and can potentially violate a constraint. In addition to restricting the domain over which a particular constraint is evaluated, efficiency is improved by not checking constraints that cannot possibly be affected by the given updates, and by avoiding checks that are subsumed by other checks.

We now introduce the notion of a *constraint set* which we use in order to check whether a given set of updates violates database integrity. A constraint set contains ordered pairs of the form (`csel`,P) where `csel` is a c-selector and P is a pattern. Given a set of updates U and a set S_U, we define S_U to be a constraint set for U if the statement "U does not violate any integrity constraints" is equivalent to

`csel P == []` $\forall$ (`csel`,P) $\in S_U$.

We now discuss constraint sets with reference to the examples of Sections 4 and 5. It is assumed that the only constraints we have are C0-C3 and that we have implemented them using the c-selectors `c0-c3`. We also assume that `accident`, `casualty`, `asel` and `bsel` are extensional selectors, that is, that they can only be updated by explicit use of the commands `include` and `exclude`. Consider the update $U1$ that represents the insertion of the fact that accident A0 is of severity 0 and that there are no casualties associated with it:

```
> include accident {A0,0,0}                                          U1
```

In order to check whether $U1$ violates any constraints we could use the constraint set S^*, defined by

$$S^* = \left\{ (c0,\text{Any*}),\ (c1,\text{Any*}),\ (c2,\text{Any*}),\ (c3,\text{Any*}) \right\},$$

since, the condition

$$ci\ \text{Any*} \ == \ [] \quad \forall\, (ci, \text{Any*}) \in S^*$$

is exactly the condition, described at the end of Section 5, for no constraint to be violated. In fact, S^* is a constraint set for any set of updates. However, $U1$ only affects information pertaining to accident A0 and we do not need to check the information regarding any other accident since it did not violate the integrity of the database before $U1$ and it has not changed. Thus we need check C0 and C1 only for accident A0. That is, we can determine whether $U1$ violates C0 or C1 by evaluating

```
c0 {A0} == []  and  c1 {Any,Any,A0} == [].
```

Since we assume that C2 was inviolate before $U1$, we can assume that none of the required accident records was missing prior to $U1$, and hence, since $U1$ does not delete any accident records, none of the required accident records can be missing after $U1$. Furthermore, constraint C3 clearly has nothing to do with the accident selector and cannot be affected by update $U1$. Thus, we do not need to check whether either C2 or C3 are violated by $U1$ and S_{U1} is a constraint set for $U1$, where

$$S_{U1} = \left\{ (c0,\{A0\}),\ (c1,\{\text{Any,Any,A0}\}) \right\}.$$

As a further example, we consider the update $U2$ that represents the addition of the fact that Abel was fatally injured in accident A0:

```
> include casualty {Abel,3,A0}                                       U2
```

As with $U1$, $U2$ cannot affect constraint C3 and we need only check whether C0 is violated by accident A0. By inspecting the definitions of the c-selectors c1 and c2 it can be seen that C1 and C2 need only be checked for the particular casualty {Abel,3,A0}. Thus, a constraint set for U2 is given by

$$S_{U2} = \left\{ (c0,\{A0\}),\ (c1,\{\text{Abel},3,A0\}),\ (c2,\{\text{Abel},3,A0\}) \right\}.$$

If we now combine $U1$ and $U2$ into a single transaction T, we can obtain S_T, a constraint set for T, simply by taking the union of constraint sets for $U1$ and $U2$:

$$S_T = S_{U1} \cup S_{U2}.$$

That is, we can check whether T invalidates the database by evaluating the four expressions

```
c0 {A0} == [],              c1 {Any,Any,A0} == [],
c1 {Abel,3,A0} == [],       c2 {Abel,3,A0} == [].
```

Note, however that the second expression makes the evaluation of the third expression unnecessary since any tuples generated by (c1 {Abel,3,A0}) will also be generated by (c1 {Any,Any,A0}). Thus, (c1,{Abel,3,A0}) is a redundant element of T's constraint set, S_T.

For any constraint set S_U for update U, we refer to the set of all the redundant elements of S_U as its *redundant set* and denote it by R_S. We define R_S as follows:

$$R_S = \left\{ (x,y) \in S_U \mid \exists\, (x,y1) \in S_U,\; y \neq y1,\; y1 \sqsubseteq y \right\}.$$

Thus, in order to determine whether an update U violates the integrity of the database we need only check

```
csel P == []   ∀(csel, P) ∈ S_U\R_S.
```

The above examples display our general approach to integrity enforcement. For a given update to a selector we identify the constraints that the update might compromise and we seek to restrict the domain over which a c-selector is evaluated. We make the argument of a c-selector more specific than Any* by comparing the tuple, with which we are updating the selector, with the pattern to which that selector is applied in the c-selector's definition. We summarise all the checks we need to make with a constraint set which we optimise by removing redundant elements .

It follows from inspecting T1 and T2, the definitions of i-selectors, that the only ways to affect the contents of an i-selector's relation are either to update an e-selector on which it depends or to update an ordinary function on which some F_i depends. If we change a function we can determine which c-selectors depend on that function and can then determine whether integrity has been violated by applying each of those c-selectors to Any*. Thus, updating a function f has a constraint set S_f defined by

$$S_f = \left\{ (\text{csel}, \text{Any*}) \mid \text{csel} \in CS,\; \text{csel} \leftarrow\!\sim f \right\},$$

where CS is the set of all c-selectors and where csel <~ f denotes the fact that csel depends on f. For any given function f we can easily determine which functions depend on it by locating the set of functions $\{f_1\}$ in whose defining equations it appears and recursively identifying the functions which depend on each f_1.

We note that S_f is a constraint set regardless of whether f is an ordinary function or an e-selector we have updated. When updating an ordinary function, although it is simple to identify the c-selectors that depend on the function, it is not generally possible to predict the effect of the update on the relations of those c-selectors and the only pattern guaranteed to match all the new tuples in a c-selector's relation is Any*. However, when updating an e-selector, we seek to find arguments that are less general than Any*. The rest of this section addresses the problem of deriving efficient constraint sets for updates to e-selectors.

Integrity maintenance is essentially concerned with ensuring that a given update does not cause tuples to be added to the relation of a c-selector. We generalise this problem by considering what happens to the relation of an i-selector lhs_sel when we update a selector sel (intensional or extensional) that appears in the s-list L_s of `lhs_sel`. An *update pattern* is a (non-unique) way of summarising the immediate effect of an update without having to list explicitly each tuple involved. We address the problem of cascaded effects, which we treat as a sequence of immediate effects, at the end of this section. If the update to `sel` results in tuples being added to `lhs_sel`'s relation, then the update pattern matches all those added tuples and is termed an *increment pattern*. Similarly, if the update to `sel` results in tuples being removed from `lhs_sel`'s relation, then the update pattern matches all those deleted tuples and is termed a *decrement pattern*. There is a third type of update pattern, called an *aggregate pattern*, which is only relevant to i-selectors with an s-list of type T2 and which we describe in greater detail below. We associate an update pattern with `lhs_sel` for each occurrence of `sel` in L_S. That is, (see definitions T1 and T2) there is a separate update pattern, UP_i for each i such that `sel` $==$ s_i. For example, if we were adding a tuple to `asel` then we would have two update patterns for `c3`, one arising from the generator `{x}<-asel{x}` and one resulting from the filter `asel{y} == []`.

In the above example with update $U1$ we argued that the only accident that could be affected by $U1$ was `A0` and consequently that we could check constraint c1 by applying the c-selector `c1` to the argument `{Any,Any,A0}`. Given that the argument of a selector matches all the elements in the returned list, any tuples added to `c1`'s relation would be matched by `{Any,Any,A0}`. Thus, `{Any,Any,A0}` is an increment pattern for `c1` arising from the update $U1$. Similarly, for the c-selector `c0`, the only possible addition to its relation after update $U1$ is `{A0}`, and consequently `{A0}` is an update pattern for `c0` generated by $U1$. In general, each pair in a constraint set S_U is a c-selector along with an increment pattern arising from the update U.

We now address the problem of constructing an update pattern UP_i for i-selector `lhs_sel` arising from the update to the selector `sel`. We assume that the update to `sel` can be summarised by its own update pattern U_{sel}. That is, if tuples are being inserted into `sel`'s relation then U_{sel} is an increment pattern and matches each of `sel`'s new tuples, or else, if tuples are being deleted from `sel`'s relation then U_{sel} is a decrement pattern and matches each of the deleted tuples. If tuples are being both added to and deleted from `lhs_sel`'s relation, we treat this as two separate updates; one for the insertions and one for the deletions.

We first consider the case where L_S, the s-list in which `sel` $= s_i$ for some i, is of type T1 (see Section 3). In this case L_S is simply the concatenation of a number of sub-lists. Clearly if tuples are added to one of those sub-lists then the effect on `lhs_sel`'s relation would be the inclusion of those added tuples that aren't duplicated in another sub-list. Similarly if tuples are being deleted from a sub-list then the effect on `lhs_sel`'s relation would be the removal of those deleted tuples that aren't duplicated in another sub-list. In either case U_{sel} matches all the tuples being added to, or deleted from, `lhs_sel`'s relation and is therefore an update pattern for `lhs_sel`. It is possible to obtain a more specific pattern for UP_i since any newly inserted or deleted tuple must also be matched by P_i, the pattern `sel` is applied to in L_S. Thus, UP_i is the most general pattern that is matched by both U_{sel} and P_i. Algorithm B provides a method for calculating UP_i.

Algorithm B : to obtain the update pattern UP_i for an i-selector `lhs_sel` defined by
> i_selector lhs_sel P_s = L_s
where

a) L_s is of type T1,

b) UP_i summarises the effect of an update to a selector `sel` that is equal to some s_i in L_s,

c) P_i is the pattern that s_i is applied to in the definition of L_s,

d) the update to `sel` can be summarised by the update pattern U_{sel}.

B1) If P_i has a component that is equal to a constant and the corresponding component of U_{sel} is equal to a different constant then the update to s_i cannot affect `lhs_sel` and UP_i does not exist.

B2) If U_{sel} is an increment pattern then UP_i is an increment pattern. If U_{sel} is a decrement pattern then UP_i is a decrement pattern.

The type enforcement of PFL ensures that UP_i, U_{sel} and P_i are all tuples of the same arity. We describe UP_i by describing its kth component, ui_k, in terms of u_k and p_k, the kth components of U_{sel} and P_i, respectively. Note that u_k must be either a constant or `Any` and that p_k is either a variable or a constant or `Any`. Thus we need only define ui_k in the following 3 cases:

B3) If p_k is some constant c_1 and u_k is some constant c_2 and $c_1 \neq c_2$, then UP_i does not exist. This is the case, described in B1, where the update to `sel` cannot affect `lhs_sel`.

B4) If p_k is some constant c and u_k is either c or `Any`, then $ui_k = c$.

B5) If p_k is either a variable or `Any`, then $ui_k = u_k$

We now obtain a method for constructing an update pattern for the i-selector `lhs_sel` when its s-list, L_s, is of type T2. What happens to `lhs_sel`'s relation as a result of an update to `sel` depends on two factors: whether `sel` is having tuples added or deleted and the type (G1, G2 or F1) of the expression in L_s that contains `sel`. We note that the only way to increase the number of elements returned by a list abstraction is either to increase the number of elements arising from a generator expression or to decrease the number of elements rejected by a filter expression. Conversely, to reduce the number of elements returned by a list abstraction we must either reduce the number of elements arising from a generator expression or increase the number of elements that are rejected by a filter expression. Thus, if we are adding tuples to `sel`'s relation then if `sel` appears in a G1 generator expression tuples can only be added to `lhs_sel`'s relation and if it appears in an F1 filter expression tuples can only be removed from `lhs_sel`'s relation. Similarly, if we are deleting tuples from `sel`'s relation then tuples can only be deleted from `lhs_sel`'s relation if `sel` appears in a G1 generator expression and tuples can only be added to `lhs_sel`'s relation if `sel` appears in an F1 filter expression. This is analogous to the effect, on the satisfiability of a logic formula, of adding/deleting facts that appear as positive/negative literals in that formula. However, it is not clear what effect updating a selector that appears in a G2 generator will have, since the expression generates a variable that occurs in the F2 filter and we can predict neither the change in the generated variable x_i (see definition T2) nor whether it will result in more or less tuples being rejected by the F2 filter. Our solution to the problem of deciding whether an update to a selector in a G2 generator results in an increment pattern or a decrement pattern is, effectively, to generate both increment and decrement patterns, regardless of whether U_{sel} is an update pattern or a decrement pattern. To simplify our algorithms we use the third type of update pattern, the aggregate pattern, to represent a pair of increment and decrement patterns resulting from a G2 generator expression.

Whatever the type of expression that `sel` appears in, the tuples affected by the update to `sel`, that is, tuples matched U_{sel}, can only affect `lhs_sel`'s relation if they are also matched by P_i, the pattern to which `sel` is applied in `lhs_sel`'s s-list. For example, consider the effect of update $U1$ on the relation of c-selector `c1`. In this case `sel`, U_{sel} and P_i are respectively `accident`, the increment pattern $\{A0,0,0\}$ and $\{z,0,Any\}$, the argument of `accident` in the definition of `c1`. The only way that $U1$ can affect `c1` is if $\{z,0,Any\} \sqsubseteq \{A0,0,0\}$, that is if z is set to `A0` or `Any`. It is by taking the more specific option and setting z to `A0` that we restrict the domain over which we evaluate `c1`. On the other hand, consider the update

> include accident {A1,3,2} $U3$

which corresponds to the adding the fact that accident `A1` has two casualties and is of severity 3. It is now impossible for P_i to match U_{sel}, that is, for $\{z,0,Any\}$ to match $\{A1,3,2\}$ and we can conclude that constraint C1 is unaffected by update $U3$. Algorithm C describes this method of computing an update pattern for an i-selector whose s-list is of type T2.

Algorithm C : to obtain the update pattern UP_i for an i-selector `lhs_sel` defined by
> i_selector lhs_sel P_S = L_S
where
    a) L_S is of type T2,
    b) UP_i summarises the effect of an update to a selector `sel` that is equal to some s_i in L_S,
    c) P_i is the pattern that s_i is applied to in the definition of L_S,
    d) the update to `sel` can be summarised by the update pattern U_{sel}.

C1) If P_i has a component that is equal to a constant and the corresponding component of U_{sel} is equal to a different constant then the update to s_i cannot affect `lhs_sel` and UP_i does not exist.

C2) UP_i is an aggregate pattern if s_i is in a G2 generator expression ($l < i \leq m$ in definition T2).

C3) UP_i is an increment pattern either if U_{sel} is an increment pattern and s_i is in a G1 generator expression ($1 \leq i \leq l$ in definition T2) or if U_{sel} is a decrement pattern and s_i is in an F1 filter expression ($m < i \leq n$ in definition T2).

C4) UP_i is a decrement pattern either if U_{sel} is an increment pattern and s_i is in an F1 filter expression or if U_{sel} is a decrement pattern and s_i is in a G1 generator expression.

C5) Transform the pattern P_S into the pattern p_1 by replacing each variable in P_S that also occurs in P_i as follows: If the variable, a say, is the the kth component of P_i then replace a in P_S by the kth component of U_{sel}.

C6) UP_i is obtained from pattern p_1 by replacing each variable by Any.

Given an update to an e-selector it is straightforward to identify all the i-selectors in whose s-lists the e-selector appears. Using Algorithms B and C it is then possible to construct the update patterns that summarise the changes to these i-selectors. This process can be recursively applied to these changing i-selectors thereby identifying all the i-selectors that are affected by the update while, at the same time, summarising the changes to them. Once this has been done, there will be, for every i-selector affected by the original update to an e-selector, a set of update patterns that identify all the possible changes to that i-selector. In particular all the c-selectors that might have tuples added to their relations (and thereby violate the integrity of the database) can be identified by their increment patterns. Thus we can construct a constraint set where each pair is made up of an increment pattern and the c-selector to which it belongs.

The previous paragraph provides the basic outline of our integrity enforcement strategy. However certain care must be taken to ensure that the process terminates. Each tuple in an e-selector's relation must be explicitly added with the include command and so an e-selector's relation must be finite. Since an i-selector's relation is constructed out of the relations of e-selectors, it too must be finite. Moreover, for a given tuple there are only a finite number of patterns that match it, that is, there are only a finite number of ways of replacing parts of that pattern with Any. Consequently, there are only a finite number of update patterns. Thus, the procedure, outlined in the previous paragraph, will terminate providing we avoid duplicating update patterns.

For the given update to an e-selector we summarise all the changes to i-selectors in a set of tuples we term the *transaction set*. Each tuple in the transaction set expresses an update to a selector. The tuple contains the name of the changing selector, an update pattern summarising changes to that selector's relation and whether the update pattern is increment, decrement or aggregate. There can be many tuples for any given i-selector in the transaction set and, as with constraint sets, there may be a certain amount of redundancy. For example, consider a transaction set that contains the two tuples

    {casualty,{Any,Any,A0},increment} and
    {casualty,{Abel,3,A0},increment}.

The first tells us that some tuples, which are matched by {Any,Any,A0}, may have been added to casualty's relation. The second tuple in the transaction set indicates that tuples that are matched by {Abel,3,A0} may have been added to the relation of the casualty selector. Any additions to casualty's relation that are described by the second tuple in the transaction set are also described by the first one and we regard the second tuple as redundant. Thus, we only insert a tuple into a transactions set if it is not redundant and if we do add a tuple to a transaction set we delete all the tuples it renders redundant.

Although, we only require the tuples in a transaction set to be of arity 3, we introduce another element that allows us to keep track of whether or not we have inspected a given tuple in the transaction set. Our method of obtaining a constraint set for an update to an e-selector is formalised in Algorithm D.

Algorithm D : to obtain a transaction set TS and a constraint set S_U for the update U where the e-selector `esel` has a tuple T either added to or deleted from its relation. That is, to obtain TS and S_U where U is either

> `include esel T`

or

> `exclude esel T,`

given that

    a) CS is the set of all c-selectors,

    b) the procedure *INSERT*()

        - adds data to a transaction set, provided the data is not redundant,

        - deletes all data in the transaction set made redundant by the new data.

D0)   Delete all elements from the set TS.

D1)   Let Update_0 = {unchecked, esel, T, *u_type*}, where *u_type* denotes the type of update and is either `increment` or `decrement`, depending on whether T is being `include`-ed or `exclude`-ed.

D2)   *INSERT*(Update_0, TS).

D3)   While ($\exists$ {unchecked, sel, U_{sel}, *update_type*} $\in TS$)   {

        For each i-selector `lhs_sel` with s-list L_S such that `sel` occurs in L_S {

            For each $s_i \in L_S$ such that $\text{sel} = s_i$ {

                if (L_S is of type T1)

                    use Algorithm B on {lhs_sel, L_S, s_i, U_{sel}} to create UP_i;

                else if (L_S is of type T2)

                    use Algorithm C on {lhs_sel, L_S, s_i, U_{sel}} to create UP_i;

                if (UP_i is an increment pattern or an aggregate pattern)

                    INSERT({unchecked, lhs_sel, UP_i, increment}, TS);

                if (UP_i is a decrement pattern or an aggregate pattern)

                    INSERT({unchecked, lhs_sel, UP_i, decrement}, TS);

            }

        }

        delete {unchecked, sel, U_{sel}, *update_type*} from TS;

        INSERT({checked, sel, U_{sel}, *update_type*}, TS);

    }

D4) $S_U = \left\{ \{\text{csel}, P\} \mid \{\text{checked}, \text{csel}, P, \text{increment}\} \in TS, \text{csel} \in CS \right\}.$

The use of the procedure *INSERT*() avoids duplication of update patterns for a given selector, thereby ensuring that Algorithm D terminates, even with recursively defined i-selectors. It also makes R_S, the redundant set for the constraint set S_U, empty. It is defined as follows:

$INSERT(\{a,b,c,d\}, T)$ || add $\{a,b,c,d\}$ to set T, removing redundant tuples ||
    if ($\neg\exists\ \{a1,b,c1,d\} \in T$ such that $c1 \sqsubseteq c$)   {
        For each $\{a2,b,c2,d\} \in T$ such that $c \sqsubseteq c2$
           delete $\{a2,b,c2,d\}$ from T;
        insert $\{a,b,c,d\}$ into T;
    }

We conclude this section by observing that Algorithm D is easily adapted to obtain a constraint set for a set of updates. After initialising TS in step D0, we simply repeat steps D1-D3 for each update to an e-selector. Then, after step D4, S_U will contain all the checks necessary to determine whether any of the updates to e-selectors compromise the integrity of the database. For each ordinary function f that iš updated we can generate the constraint set S_f. A constraint set for the entire set of updates is obtained by taking the union of every S_f and S_U.

8 Conclusions

In this paper we described how selectors allow us to mirror a logic-based integrity enforcement strategy [8] in a functional environment. Aggregate constraints, which are excluded from Lloyd and Topor's approach, are simply enforced in a functional environment [13]. However, the strategy described in [13] is limited in that it cannot enforce constraints over derived functions. Here, we have the best of both worlds and have equipped PFL with an integrity maintenance system that is equivalent to Lloyd and Topor's, enhanced with the ability to enforce aggregate constraints.

We note that, apart from knowing the actual e-selector and tuple involved in an update, the information about dependencies and the information required to compute update patterns are available when an i-selector is defined. Thus, it is possible to maintain tables that identify the i-selectors, `lhs_sel`, in whose definitions a given selector, `sel`, appears and to define simple functions, based on Algorithms B and C, that, given an update pattern, U_{sel}, for `sel`, return the appropriate update pattern, UP_i, for `lhs_sel`. This information, obtained once when an i-selector is defined, much simplifies the implementation of step D3 of Algorithm D, which is executed each time an e-selector is updated.

We also note that our integrity enforcement system does not require the database to be stratified and since, in the current implementation, i-selectors are simply a syntactically restricted subset of list-valued functions, it is possible to define i-selectors which, when evaluated against certain arguments, will not terminate. However, because an i-selector's relation is derived from the relations of e-selectors, which are finite, an i-selector's relation must also be finite. It should therefore be possible to implement i-selectors (for example, with magic sets) so that evaluating i-selectors could be guaranteed to terminate.

Acknowledgements

I am grateful to Carol Small and Alex Poulovassilis for their extensive help and advice. I would also like to thank Fefie Dotsika for the interesting discussions. This work has been carried out under SERC award GR/G 19596.

References

1. L. Cardelli, Types for data data-oriented languages, in *Advances in Database Technology (EDBT 88)*, LNCS 303. Springer-Verlag. 1988.

2. S.K. Das and H. Williams, A path finding method for constraint checking in deductive databases, *Data & Knowledge Engineering*, 1989. No. 4.

3. S.K. Das and M.H. Williams. Integrity checking methods in deductive databases: a comparative evaluation. *Proceedings of the 7th British National Conference on Databases*, CUP. 1989.

4. H. Decker, Integrity enforcement on deductive databases, *Proceedings of The First International Conference on Expert Database Systems*, Charleston, South Carolina. Edited by L. Kerschberg. 1986.

5. A.J. Field and P.G. Harrison, *Functional Programming*. Addison Wesley, 1988.

6. J. Hughes, Why functional programming matters. *The Computer Journal*. 1989. Vol. 32, No. 2.

7. R.A. Kowalski, F. Sadri and P. Soper, Integrity checking in deductive databases. *Proceedings of the 13th International Conference on Very Large Databases*, Brighton. 1987.

8. J.W. Lloyd and R.W Topor, A Basis for Deductive Database Systems. *Journal of Logic Programming*. 1985. No. 2.

9. J.W. Lloyd and R.W Topor, A Basis for Deductive Database Systems II. *Journal of Logic Programming*. 1986. No. 1.

10. J-M. Nicolas and K. Yazdanian, Integrity checking in deductive databases, in *Logic and Databases*, Edited by H. Gallaire and J. Minker. Plenum Press, 1978.

11. A. Olivé Integrity constraints checking in deductive databases. *Proceedings of the 17th International Conference on Very Large Databases*, Barcelona. 1991.

12. S.L. Peyton-Jones, *The Implementation of Functional Programming Languages*. Prentice Hall, 1987.

13. A. Poulovassilis, *The Design and Implementation of FDL, a functional database language*. Ph.D. Thesis, Birkbeck College, University of London. 1989.

14. A. Poulovassilis and C. Small, A functional programming approach to deductive databases. *Proceedings of the 17th International Conference on Very Large Databases*, Barcelona. 1991.

15. U.S. Reddy, On the relationship between logic and functional languages. in *Logic Programming, Functions Relations and Equations*, Edited by D. De Groot. Prentice Hall, 1986.

16. C. Small and A. Poulovassilis, An overview of PFL. *3rd International Workshop on Database Programming Languages*, Nafplion. 1991.

17. J.D. Ullman, *Principles of Database and Knowledge-base Systems*. Computer Science Press, 1988.

Implementation of a Version Model for Artists using Extended Relational Technology

Barry Eaglestone, Geoff Davies, Mick Ridley and Nigel Hulley.

Bradford University, Bradford, UK .
B.Eaglestone@comp.brad.ac.uk
Sound Information Technology Research Group (SITRG).

Abstract. Artists, like engineers, experience materials and process management problems. These are analysed, and a solution based upon adaptation of engineering design support technology is proposed. Our solution is a result of the TEMA project in which a composer's journal was analysed and an experimental database environment to support his style of composition was designed and prototyped. We describe in detail the main contribution of this project, an extended version model for use by artists. Two innovative features are a generalised workspace model, and a mechanism for the capture and reuse of process information. We also include notes on our experience of implementing the version model using the POSTGRES extended relational database system.

Key Words: database, version model, object-oriented, IPSE, design system, computer music, extended relational database, POSTGRES.

1 Introduction

Recent database research has focused on support for engineering design activities, such as CAD/CAM and software engineering. However, strong similarities between artists and engineers suggest to us that a transferral of design support technology for use in artistic applications will be of value [16]. The TEMA project [18] is part of our research towards this transferral. In TEMA we have analysed methods used by a composer, Tamas Ungvary, and prototyped an extended relational database environment to support his approach to composition. This paper describes the main contribution of TEMA: an artists' version model. Two innovatory features are:

- a generalised workspace model;
- process information capture and reuse.

The TEMA prototype was implemented using the POSTGRES extended relational database system [33]. We also relate our experiences with POSTGRES. A fuller discussion of our analysis of artistic design and support requirements can be found in [19].

2 Related Research

Our research into design systems for artists builds upon and complements the large body of engineering design system research.

Much of this related research has focuses on: design management and repository components of design systems; and support for process, version and configuration management. Process management is concerned with ensuring adherence to "good practice" rules or procedures. Languages and notations have been defined within which formal models of design processes can be represented and "enacted" [34]. "Process programs" are then used to constrain, guide and assist designers in carrying out the modelled processes [2]. In this way design knowledge can be reused. Version and configuration management are complementary to process management, and have been studied within the context of version model extensions to the repository. Version modelling can be viewed as a facet of temporal database [30, 15]. Version management issues include: capture of object histories, problems of changing type definitions, and concurrency control [6]. Configuration management [26] may be seen as a specific aspect of version management.

Version model requirements stem from the nature of the design task and are therefore closely related to process management. Version models support decomposition of design problems, and incremental refinement of component solutions, possibly to produce a range of designs to fit different situations. At a higher level, process management systems may constrain designers to use the version model in such a way as to ensure the integrity and quality of the evolving design. Semantic classifications of versions are used to model the status of design object within process models [25]. Various paradigms have been proposed, including version clusters [14], partitions [25], workspaces [11, 21], and types [23, 1]. However, these strategies are used primarily as a means of access and concurrency control and as such are devices for system management.

The retention of versions incurs obvious overheads, and so this facility is often made optional (e.g. as in [23] where "versioned" is a type, orthogonal to other types).

A versioned object represents a design object as an aggregation of its invariant properties (the generic object [14]) and versions of its variant properties (version history [21], version set [14], version graph [25], or refinement graph [22]). Ancestor/descendant relationships relate the versions, one of which is usually designated as current. The main derivation, principal path or default branch links the root to the current version. The version history is a directed graph, because it is possible for paths to merge forming a merged line of descent, reconciliation or consolidation [21]. References to a design object may be to a specific version (static), or to the most appropriate version (dynamic) [21, 25]. Problematic areas include: limiting the scope of version propagation and disambiguating dynamic references [5, 14, 24, 4] and change paths [1, 29]; and coping with intension difference between versions [24, 27].

Version models are a standard feature of third-generation database technologies [3, 31], but there is as yet no widely accepted architecture [6, 10, 25] or formal semantics. The confusion of concepts and terminology in the literature is partly resolved in [21].

3 Composers and Engineers

Similarities between engineers and composers [16] provided the motivation for the TEMA project [18]. TEMA is an experiment in the use of extended relational technology to support artistic design, and focuses on the repository of a design system for computer music [17].

Our reasoning was that composing, like engineering, is a design task in which requirements are transformed into a product through an iterative cycle of analysis, hypothesis, building and testing. Composers will therefore encounter problems similar to those of the engineers. Like the engineer, a composer must:

- track different versions of compositions, each component, and relationships between components;
- assemble, maintain and utilise archives of reusable materials;
- develop, maintain and utilise a toolkit of programs and techniques for using them;
- track the design process.

Composers will therefore often manage these problems by making informal use of engineering techniques, such as problem decomposition, phase-oriented design, and prototyping.

In TEMA we wished to test the extent of the above similarities, and to derive an artists' design system based on an adaptation of engineering design technology. Our aims were to derive a system which will:

- relieve composers of object and process management tasks;
- shield them from physical/implementation aspects of design objects and processes;
- provide a more intuitive and supportive environment for composition.

The design was derived through analysis of the journals of the composer, Tamas Ungvary, in which he documents the composition of a short piece (called TEMA) for tape and dance using the music-dance system NUNTIUS [35]. The journals provide a uniquely detailed description of computer music composition, and sharply illustrate associated object and process management problems that occur in the absence of design management support. The design environment, NUNTIUS, is a conventional file-oriented system.

It is, of course, impossible to generalise from the case study material how composers compose, or even how Ungvary composes music. Composers constantly seek new forms of individual expression, compositional philosophies, materials, tools, and methods (see [28] for a range of composers' perspectives on the use of computers in composition). However, we have attempted to provide a descriptive, flexible and open-ended design environment, rather than a prescriptive and constraining one as would be the norm in engineering applications. We believe we have achieved these objectives primarily through a generalised and extended version model.

We used the case study material in a way similar to that suggested in [12] for analyzing software engineering processes. We applied transformation analysis to identify objects, events and transformations. Activity descriptions in the journals were then generalised, and finally an object-oriented conceptual model was derived (using techniques in [13], but extended to include relative-time event sequences [15]). Completeness and consistency of the conceptual model was validated by re-representing the original transformation analysis as a time-sequence of instances of the conceptual model. In this way we derived a conceptual object model to act as a general framework for a particular style of composition.

The case study describes the composition of one minute of music, and involves manipulation of over fifty files and 150 Mbytes of data. The composer reused existing materials and techniques, and developed and subsequently reused new materials and techniques.

It was clear from the case study that intuition rather than methodology directed the composition process. However, Ungvary did make use of problem decomposition (the piece was composed in sections), and the design method was phase-oriented (sounds were assembled, then textured, and then reverberated). It was also apparent that transitions between object states were of interest as well as the objects themselves. Transitions constituted the composition techniques, and were reused when results were satisfactory. Particularly acute were the problems of managing multiple versions of sounds, each stored in a separate file, and of utilising inconsistent software tools.

In the absence of any higher-level object management support, file names were used to represent a wide range of information, including: associative names (e.g. ching, horn); descriptive names; originators; derivations; roles within the composition (e.g. INTRO, CODA, SLUT); object version identifiers; object types. These names were devised "on the fly" and did not adhere to any predefined conventions. File naming proved to be an inadequate system for representing such a range of information, much of which could have been captured and represented automatically. There was clearly a need for version and configuration management to be automated, but with facilities for the composer to annotate both objects and state transitions.

The analogy apparent in the case study was of the painter mixing materials to form new colours and textures and then applying them to the canvas to form the artwork. The composer's materials were stored, sampled and generated sounds, choreography, etc.. Mixing was done experimentally using software tools. The resulting materials were then combined experimentally (also using those tools) to form the art work, i.e. the composition. Manipulations of the materials were applications of the composer's techniques, which had been developed over the years through trial and error. All materials, tools and techniques are of potential reuse, but reuse was problematic in the file-based system because of object retrieval problems, insufficient documentation, and inconsistencies in the different tool interfaces.

The version, configuration and process management problems of composers are just those that design systems ease for engineers. However,we identified differences concerning the nature of the product requirements; the criteria used in testing and evaluating products; and the rigour and prescriptiveness of the process.

- Engineers work primarily to tangible, quantitative and testable requirements, and these form the basis of objective acceptance testing of the product. Similarly, there may be quantitative requirements and acceptance criteria for an artist, such as canvas size, composition length, orchestration constraints, libretto or choreographic requirements. However, the primary criteria for acceptance are subjective and are to do with aesthetics.
- The engineer will work within rules of good practice using prescribed methods and methodologies to ensure a quality-assured product. Artists also learn the techniques of past masters, but in addition will develop their own personal processes in order to achieve individuality of expression. "Good practice" rules, or "quality assured" design methods are therefore inappropriate. An artist may choose to work within rigid artistic forms (e.g. 12-tone sequences), but will always require freedom to break the rules. "Errors will often produce the most artistically interesting results!" [Ungvary, Personal communication].

These differences make current design systems unsuitable for use by artists.

4 Tema Version Model

An artists' design system should enable artists to develop their own ways of working, rather than impose standards, methods, and "good practice" rules. In this section, we define the TEMA version model, which is adapted in a way that satisfies this requirement. Our version model is described using terminology of Katz's "unified version model" [21], but with extensions to the concept of workspaces, and for capture and reuse of process information. The model is formally specified using Object-Z [9]. We chose Object-Z so as to define a database system-independent semantics for our generic object-oriented version model. The design technology we used [13] lacked the necessary formality and precision, and the "standard" formal object model we would ideally have liked to use does not yet exist. Object-Z was therefore chosen as a "stop gap" formalism. However, on the positive side: we found a clean mapping from our O*_model design to Object-Z; the generic class abstraction in Object-Z provided a natural formalism for the recursive generic structures of our version model; Object-Z supports functions as types, and lambda-expressions, which provide a promising basis for formalising behavioural semantics of the system, such as the derivation of objects. For brevity, operation specifications and type definitions are omitted.

4.1 Versioned Design Objects

The basic facility of a version model, i.e. representation and manipulation of design object histories, is a support requirement for Ungvary's composition method, since this method involves experimentation with design variants. However, we have made versioning of design objects optional. This is for both practical reasons, e.g. storage economy, and semantic reasons, i.e. better to represent a range of composition process models.

Relationships between design object versions are outlined in Figure 1. Figures 1, 2, 3 and 5 use the O*_model notation for describing structural relationships ("static schemas"). The objects are depicted by names, single-headed arrows represent is_a relationships (pointing from the specific to the general), double-headed arrows represent set structures (from element to set), and multi-tailed arrows represent aggregations of objects. Note that a versioned design object includes a set of design object versions, i.e. the design object history. Note also that the versioned design object and the individual design object versions are all specialisations of the design object.

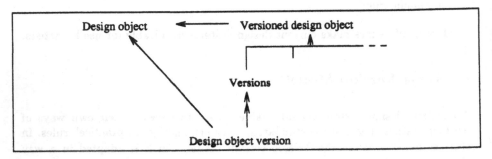

Fig. 1. Outline schema for versioned design object.

Each design object is uniquely identifiable by an object identifier (of type OBJECT_ID) and has a state (which is an instance of the generic type STATE). Therefore the definition of the database as a whole includes a partial function which maps object identifier to design object ($db : OBJECT\_ID \twoheadrightarrow design\_object[]$). The outline definition of the generic design object class is:

```
┌─ design_object[STATE] ──────────────────────────────────
│ state : STATE
│ ┌─ INIT ──────────────────────────────────
│ │ state = 'nil
│ ...
└──────────────────────────────────────────────
```

We represent a versioned design object and its versions as specialisations of design_object. The design object version history is a partial function which maps each version identifier (of type VERSION_ID) to the corresponding version, and a version graph which is a relation, mapping parent to child version identifiers.

Operations upon versioned design objects are:- create and derive (as in [1]), and version graph navigation functions (as in [5]).

Version histories, on their own, are inadequate, because composers are also interested in how design objects are created. Our model therefore also captures and represents database transformation functions. A versioned design object and each of its versions includes a derivation component in which is represented the time-stamped "message" (operation, argument objects, and other parameters) that caused that design object to come into being:

__ design_object_derivation _____

derivation = $TIME\_STAMP \times OPERATION \times$
$\quad \mathbb{P}\,OBJECT\_ID \times PARAMETERS$

An advantage of this representation of process information over the more conventional "tracing" of system use [10], is that dead-end experimentation and back-tracking are automatically omitted.

The invariant property of a composition design object (e.g. a sound) may be an intangible requirement, such as sounding aesthetically correct within a certain context. We therefore do not require predetermination of invariant properties. However, we do represent within a versioned design object, the version identifiers of the most recent and "current" versions; these are used for disambiguating generic references and for version numbering. Versioned design object state is therefore:

__ versioned_design_object_state[STATE] _____

most_recent_version : $VERSION\_ID$
current_version : $VERSION\_ID$
derivation : design_object_derivation
versions : $VERSION\_ID \nrightarrow design\_object\_version[STATE]$
version_graph : $VERSION\_ID \leftrightarrow VERSION\_ID$

---

where design object version is:

__ design_object_version[STATE] _____

design_object[STATE]

_____
version_derivation : design_object_derivation

_____
__ INIT _____
state = nil
derivation = $(system\_time, "new", \{\}, <>)$

Versioned design object is therefore defined as:

---
versioned_design_object[STATE] ———————————————————

design_object[versioned_design_object_state[STATE]]

  INIT ————————————————

    most_recent_version = nil and

    current_version = nil and

    derivation = {system_time,"new",{},<>} and

    version_graph = {}

  CREATE(creation_operation? : MESSAGE,
        first_version! : VERSION_ID)

  DERIVE(parent_version? : VERSION_ID,
        modification_operation? : MESSAGE,
        new_version! : VERSION_ID)

  FIRST_VERSION(first_version! : VERSION_ID)

  LAST_VERSION(last_version! : VERSION_ID)

  VERSION_SET(version! : ℙ VERSION_ID)

  GENERIC_INST(version? : VERSION_ID,
        object_id_of_versioned_object! : OBJECT_ID)

  SUCCESSORS(parent_version? : VERSION_ID,
        descendant_versions! : ℙ OBJECT_ID)

  IMMEDSUCCESSOR(parent_version? : VERSION_ID,
        child_version! : VERSION_ID)

  PREDECESSORS(child_version! : VERSION_ID,
        ancestor_versions! : ℙ VERSION_ID)

  IMMPREDECESSORS(child_version? : VERSION_ID,
        parent_versions! : ℙ VERSION_ID)

Different classes of design object (sound, dance, ...) are defined as instantiations of the generic design object, or generic versioned design object class, depending on whether or not they are versioned.

4.2 Workspaces

Workspace [21] and version classification, eg [1, 5], play a similar role; both are used to distinguish versions according to their status within the process model, and to implement process management functions such as change control. However, in most models, workspace frameworks and design object classifications are rigidly predefined, which prohibits a more general use.

Given the idiosyncratic nature of composers, we believe that the system administrator should be able to configure the system to support a range of process models. Our solution, in TEMA, is therefore to generalize workspace as a generic abstraction for modelling design object status within process models.

Relationships between workspaces and workspace elements are depicted in Figure 2. Note the recursive structure by which workspaces may be structured through nesting.

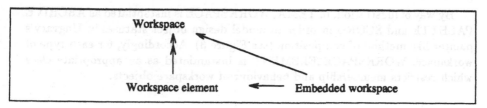

Fig. 2. Outline schema for workspace

Our approach is similar to the NF2 relational solution of [14] and [25], in which design objects are grouped within user defined clusters or partitions. However, our use of inheritance and recursively defined workspace structures provides a more flexible and expressive object-oriented solution to this problem. Our facility allows the specification of behavioural constraints (e.g. read only) which apply to all elements of a particular class of workspace, but also constraints which apply only to specific classes of element within a workspace (e.g. sounds within an archive workspace may be auditioned, but not modified). The recursive structure allows workspaces to be nested within other workspaces, thus providing a structured working environment.

We define workspace as a generic class, with a single generic parameter WORKSPACE_ELEMENT. The state is a named powerset of design objects, i.e.

```
_workspace_state_____
 ws_name : TEXT
 ws : P WORKSPACE_ELEMENT
```

and operations for adding, removing and accessing those elements:

```
_workspace[WORKSPACE_ELEMENT]_____
 design_object[workspace_state]
  _INIT_____
   ws_name = nil and ws = {}

 NAME_WORKSPACE(workspace_name? : TEXT)
 ADD(new_element? : OBJECT_ID)
 REMOVE(old_element? : OBJECT_ID)
 RETRIEVE(object_profile? : QUERY,
          retrieved_elements! : P OBJECT_ID)
```

Workspace can be instantiated for various roles within the process model. This is done by instantiating the generic parameter, WORKSPACE_ELEMENT, as a subclass of design object, possibly with modified or restricted operations. Class "history invariants" [9] may also be included, for example to impose access constraints.

By way of illustration, in TEMA, WORKSPACE is instantiated as ARCHIVE, PALETTE and SCORE in order to model design object statuses in Ungvary's painter-like method of composition (see Figure 3). Accordingly, for each type of workspace, WORKSPACE_ELEMENT is instantiated as an appropriate class which restricts membership and behaviour of workspace objects.

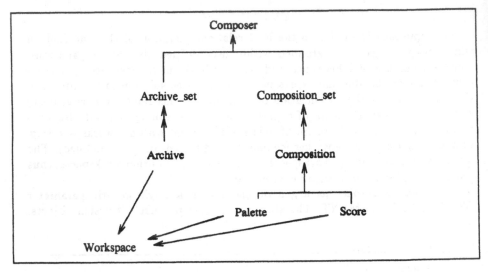

Fig. 3. Outline schema for TEMA workspace configuration

The ARCHIVE workspace, for example, is defined by replacing the generic WORKSPACE_ELEMENT type with ARCHIVE_ELEMENT, which is a sub-class of design object, i.e. the class of objects that may be archived:

```
_ ARCHIVE_ELEMENT[STATE] _____
  design_object[STATE]
```

Archive_Workspace == Workspace[ARCHIVE_ELEMENT[]]

Since all types of design object (including workspaces) may be archived, ARCHIVE_ELEMENT is specialised for each type of design object (archived_sound, archived_dance, archived_archive, ...). An archived design object is also a specialisation of the corresponding design object; archived_sound for example is a specialisation of both ARCHIVE_ELEMENT and sound (a specialisation of design_object). By re-definition or removal of operations the behaviour of archived design objects is restricted according to the requirements of the workspace. For instance, archived sounds may be auditioned, but may not be manipulated, and so archived_sound inherits the AUDITION operation of sound, but not the manipulation operations such as REVERBERATE and MIX:

```
__ archived_sound _____
  ARCHIVE_ELEMENT[]
  sound[remove REVERBERATE, remove MIX ...]
```

Palettes may include all types of object, and these may be manipulated to craft the components of a score. Palettes must support experimentation with individual design objects and so their component design objects are versioned. Thus, palette element is defined as a specialisation of the versioned design object class (rather than design object).

```
__ PALETTE_ELEMENTS[STATE] _____
  versioned_design_object[STATE]
```

Specific palette design object classes inherit from both PALETTE_ELEMENT and the corresponding design object in its versioned form.

Membership of a score is restricted in a similar way, to relative-time stamped event design objects [15], i.e. those which collectively define the composition. New versions of a score are created experimentally by adding, removing or repositioning elements within relative time. Therefore, the score itself is a versioned design object, rather than the component elements:

```
__ score _____
  versioned_workspace[SCORE_ELEMENT]
  __ INIT _____
    workspace.INIT

  ADD(new_score_element_state? : OBJECT_ID,
          position? : RELATIVE_TIME,
          new_score_element! : OBJECT_ID)
  REMOVE(old_score_element? : OBJECT_ID,
          new_position? : RELATIVE_TIME)
  REPOSITION(score_element? : OBJECT_ID,
          new_position? : RELATIVE_TIME)
```

where SCORE_ELEMENT is defined as:

```
__ SCORE_ELEMENT[STATE] _____
  design_object[STATE]
  relative_time_stamp : RTIME_STAMP
```

Workspaces are recursively defined, and this makes possible internal structuring. For example, a composer may choose to archive the palettes with which he or she created a particular composition, and later to add them to the palette for a new composition, so that the thematic and audio material and techniques may be reused. Therefore, one specialisation of ARCHIVE_ELEMENT is archived_palette, defined as:

```
 ┌─ archived_palette ─────────────────────────────────────────────
 │  palette
 │  ARCHIVED_ELEMENT[PALETTE_STATE]
 └────────────────────────────────────────────────────────────────
```

Similarly, scores may be structured into movements, each of which is represented as an embedded score.

We believe this approach has generality and that alternative methods of working can be accommodated by the system administrator through definition of different workspace specialisations.

4.3 Reuse of process information

The above configurable workspace model provides working environments which may be tailored to a composer's chosen method of working. However, additional support is also desirable to assist with effective use of tools. To this end we have developed a facility by which the composer may induce and reuse composition techniques from the derivation information captured within the repository.

This idea of process information induction has been researched in the field of software engineering. [20], for example, proposes induction of software engineering process knowledge from instances of problem solutions, and a system for fuzzy matching of problems so as to select and replay appropriate solution techniques; in this way design knowledge is captured and reused. Goldberg's strategy is to capture design decisions made when applying formal methods, initially expressed as the manual selection of transformation rules, and to replay them on specifications similar to the original. He states that this "transformation methodology supports design reuse in two interesting ways. First, the creation of transformations and tactics formalizes general design knowledge. Second, replay reuses design decisions made for related specifications."

In TEMA we have developed a similar approach, but consider it inappropriate to automate the selection of techniques for reuse. Our mechanism works in the following way:

As in Goldberg's system, design decisions are captured as manual selections of tools. For example, when a new sound is formed by mixing other sounds, details of the requested mix operation are stored as the "derivation" part of the new sound design object. Composers may access this derivation information to query how design objects were created. The query evaluation is in the form of a derivation graph which is constructed from the derivation components of the relevant design objects (see Figure 4).

We call a derivation graph a technique object because it embodies the composer's composition technique. A technique is a directed graph which connects design objects to other design objects that are derived from them. Edges are labelled with details of the transformation function.

Relationships between design objects, derivations and techniques are shown in Figure 5. A technique is a time-sequence of derivations, and can therefore characterise the user's way of working with the available tools.

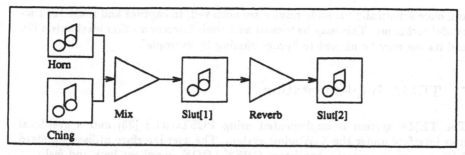

Fig. 4. Example derivation graph in which two sounds are mixed and then reverberated

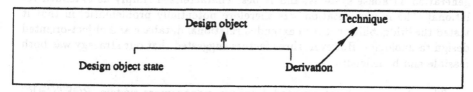

Fig. 5. Outline schema for design objects, derivations and techniques

A technique is defined as a set of triples (source object, transformation operations, result object):

$$TRANSFORMATION == CLASS \times OPERATION \times PARAMETERS$$

```
_ technique_state _____
  derivation_graph : ℙ(OBJECT_ID × TRANSFORMATION × OBJECT_ID)
```

```
_ technique _____
  design_object[technique_state]

  _ INIT _____
    derivation_graph = {}

  CREATE(design_object? : OBJECT_ID)
  EXTEND(add_object_derivation? : OBJECT_ID)
  CONTRACT(remove_object_derivation? : OBJECT_ID)
  EDIT(edit_details?)
  REPLAY(override_parameters?)
```

A derivation graph is incrementally constructed from the component derivation objects of design objects; the EXTEND operation will add the associated derivation triple to derivation_graph. The TECHNIQUE object may then be retained and may be replayed to replicate the sequence of processes represented in derivation_graph, but the user may override the parameters and argument object identifiers. This allows the composer, for example, to explore the effects that can be created using sound processing tools by experimenting with them, and once artistically valuable results are achieved, to capture and reuse the successful technique. This may be viewed as a tools interconnection mechanism [7], and its use may be likened to "programming by example".

5   TEMA Implementation

The TEMA system is implemented using POSTGRES [33] and a graphical user interface under the X-Window system. The user interface utilises standard XView routines to give a consistent OPEN LOOK compliant look and feel.

POSTGRES is one of the least strongly object-oriented of the emerging next generation database systems, and is best characterised simply as extended relational. The implementation was therefore potentially problematic, in that it tested the bridgability between extended relational database and object-oriented design technologies. However, three factors suggested that our strategy was both feasible and beneficial:

- Though not an object-oriented database management system, POSTGRES does meet the major criteria normally required such as those of providing object identity, inheritance and the facility to create user defined data types [32].
- In addition to its "object-oriented" features, which we knew we wanted from the design phase, POSTGRES, like relational systems, offers a powerful declarative, ad-hoc query language, POSTQUEL, which we believed would be a useful tool for system development through incremental prototyping.
- Analysis of the composer's journals suggested that retrieving sounds with common characteristics or performing the same transformations on groups of sound with some common feature was a very desirable facility for a compositional tool and one that had a "natural" formulation in a relational query language.

However, we know of no published data design methods for implementing an object-oriented conceptual model as a (POSTGRES) extended relational database schema. In this section we describe our design decisions and experiences, and present some general observations concerning this data design task.

Implementation of conceptual model objects, and is_a relationships between them, was generally straightforward using POSTGRES class and inheritance features. For instance, the POSTGRES system allowed direct implementation of the high-level design object, "design_object", as a POSTGRES class. This we were then able to specialise to create subclasses such as sound_object using the POSTGRES inheritance system. Multiple inheritance also allowed the sound_object class to inherit other generalized components or attributes, such as a composer, where composer itself is a particular specialization of the general POSTGRES class of PERSON.

Within the range of sound objects that we wished to model, mirroring the case study composition, were archive-, palette- and score-sounds. These were also implemented using the inheritance system to give different specialisations of sound_object and the corresponding general workspace element object classes.

Dragging sound objects between palette, archive and score workspaces using the graphical interface causes a copy of the object(s) to be made as palette_sound, archive_sound or score_sound, as appropriate. In the case of score_sound, relative start and stop times and channel attributes, inherited from the generic score_object class, are assigned values.

An advantage of the above implementation strategy is that it allows the system to be extended in a way that mirrors extensions to the conceptual model which incorporate new classes of design object. For example, we envisage using the above techniques to expand the system to include dance through specialisations which parallel those of sound.

However, implementation of Object-Z generic classes was less staightforward. We achieved generality for our Object-Z specification through extensive use of generic classes, but the POSTGRES typing system is very much weaker and provides no support for generics. We therefore had to rationalise our implementation; generic classes and their instantiations were implemented as classes/subclass hierarchies, using the POSTGRES inheritance mechanism.

The POSTGRES rule system gave us a straightforward means of implementing generic constraints on component objects. For example, we were able to implement the read-only feature of archive workspaces, at a correct system-wide level, using rules such as "on update of archive_sound do instead nothing".

POSTGRES allowed us to make extensive reuse of existing software. One physical design issue of the POSTGRES abstract data type for representing sound, was whether to use BLOBS (Binary Large ObjectS) or files external to POSTGRES to store the sounds themselves. In our prototype, we took the latter approach so as to achieve compatibility with existing software systems; our general design philosophy was to reuse software wherever possible. Sounds were represented using formats which are standard in computer music, and this has made possible the reuse of much public domain computer music software, such as the CARL library [8] and CSound [36]. However, the logical interface will be unchanged if at a future date we choose to change to the POSTGRES BLOB representation; the system depends only on specialized classes inheriting the sound data type irrespective of its internal structure.

The use of external storage structures can interfere with POSTGRES temporal features. One consequence of using external files for sounds is that the normal POSTGRES method of retrieving historical data can be invalidated. When creating a class, POSTGRES gives us options as to whether historic versions of the data will be stored and thus allows us the possibility of retrieving data as of a particular time point or period. If we reuse the same filename obviously we will not retrieve the correct sound whereas a BLOB implementation would ensure that historic versions were maintained.

The facilities for historic data in POSTGRES are good, but the version model is not as sophisticated as the one we require. The POSTGRES version system only allows us to keep alternative versions of entire classes rather than individual objects. It does this by maintaining classes of added and deleted tuples which are joined to the original class. We therefore had to provide alternative facilities for versions (or alternative histories).

Using the POSTGRES rule system it was straightforward for us to create our own alternative temporal features. Our alternative version and history facilities use our own version and time attributes rather than the system-provided ones. Each version or historic instance exists as a POSTGRES database object, together with an associated file. The object_id provides the file name. The system uses object_ids but all sounds are known to users by meaningful names, and there is also the option for users to give meaningful names to versions. The rule system gives a default name for versioned objects, where the user does not explicitly provide one. The rule system also completes the derivation component of versioned objects, which makes the objects effectively carriers of their own history information.

Our temporal facilities give us a unified system for versions and histories, which is orthogonal to the one provided by POSTGRES.

POSTGRES facilitated an incremental prototyping of the system. The POSTQUEL query language and the simple monitor interface to POSTGRES were both useful tools for testing and prototyping ideas. Prototyping via the monitor interface to POSTGRES also leads to a natural modularisation of the complete system where the interface to the database system becomes the embedded calls that were previously typed to the monitor.

The lack of a POSTGRES recursive retrieval facility created problems. The recursive retrieval features described in [33] are not implemented in the current version of the software. This can be overcome with looping structures in the host programming language, but at the cost of a less clean interface between the system's components and a less natural formulation of queries on nested objects. For example, we were unable to use the natural recursive formulation of the "unfold" operation on nested archives; unfold puts an archived archive onto a palette workspace so that a user can access all the component objects. Processing of chains of derivations would also be simpler with easily formulated recursive queries.

Navigation through POSTGRES inheritance hierarchies was difficult. Queries that traverse an inheritance hierarchy currently return inadequate information as to the positions within the hierarchy of the retrieved objects. Thus although we can query the system for all design_objects with a certain feature, having found them we do not know directly what kind of sounds they are, or even whether they are sound. We have overcome this problem by re-querying the system using the object_ids of the retrieved objects, but at a cost of an inelegant, unnatural and less efficient formulation.

6 CONCLUSIONS

A prototype of the TEMA system has been implemented using POSTGRES [33]. Initial experience suggests that our approach has validity, and more extensive evaluation is in progress.

Although the current implementation of POSTGRES did cause some problems, we found that the relational features were advantageous; the mapping from an object-oriented design was straightforward; and the ADT feature enabled us to make considerable reuse of existing 3GL software.

Other types of artistic design problem have similar characteristics to music composition. We therefore believe our results have some generality and apply to a range of artistic design problems.

7 ACKNOWLEDGEMENT

We wish to thank Tamas Ungvary and Iain Millns for their contribution to the design and implementation.

References

1. R.Ahmed, S.B. Navathe: Version Management of Composite Objects in CAD Databases. In: Proc of 1991 ACM SGMOD Int Conf on Management of Data. ACM SIGMOD Record 20(2) (June, 1991), pp 218-227.
2. V. Ashok, J. Ramanathan, S. Sarkar, V. Venugopal: Process Modelling in Software Environments. ACM SIGSOFT Engineering Notes 14(4) (June, 1989), pp 39-42.
3. M. Atkinson, et al: The Object-Oriented Database System Manifesto. In: Proc DOOD 89, Kyoto (1989), pp 223-240.
4. J. Banerjee, H-T. Chou, J.F. Garza, W. Kim, D. Woelk, N. Ballou: Data Model Issues for Object-Oriented Applications. ACM Trans on Office Info Systems 5(1) (January, 1987), pp 3-26.
5. D. Beech, B. Mahbod: Generalized Version Control in an ObjectOriented Database. In: IEEE Data Engineering: 4th Int Conf ,Los Angeles (Feb 19-22, 1988), pp 14-22.
6. A. Bjornerstedt, C. Hulten: Version Control in an Object-Oriented Architecture. In: W. Kim, F.H. Lokovskky (eds): Concepts, Databases and Applications. Addison-Wesley, Reading (1989).
7. A.W. Brown, M.H. Penedo: Bibliography on Integration in SE Environments. ACM SIFSOFT Software Engineering Notes 17(3) (July, 1992).
8. CARL Startup Kit. Computer Audio Research Laboratory, Center for Music Experiment, University of California, San Diego, CA (1985).

9. D. Carrington, D. Duke, P. King, G. Rose, G. Smith: Object-Z: An object-oriented extension to Z. Formal Description Techniques, II(FORTE'89), North-Holland (1990), pp 281-296.

10. E.E. Chan, D. Gedeye, R.H. Katz: The design and implementation of a Version Server for Computer-aided design data. Software Practice and Experience 19(3), Wile (March, 1989), pp 199-222.

11. H-T. Chou, W. Kim: A Unifying Framework for Version Control in a CAD Environment. VLDB, Kyoto (August, 1986), pp 336-344.

12. G. Chroust: Duplicate Instances of Elements of a Software Process Model. ACM SIGSOFT Software Engineering Notes 14(4) (June, 1989) , pp 61-64.

13. R. Colette, C. Corine, C. Priox: Methodology and Tool for Object-Oriented Database Design. 7th British National Conference on Database (BNCOD-7) (1989), pp 209-239.

14. K.R. Dittrich, R.A. Lorie: Version support for engineering data base systems. IEEE Trans Software Engineering 14(4) (April, 1988), pp 429-437.

15. B. Eaglestone: Keeping Time in a Music Database. 6th British National Conference on Database (BNCOD-6): Cambridge University Press (1988), pp 141-160.

16. B. Eaglestone, S. Oates: An IPSE for Sound Engineering. Computers in Music Research, Belfast (1991).

17. B. Eaglestone, A. Verschoor: An Intelligent Music Repository. International Computer Music Conference, Montreal (1991), pp 437-440.

18. B. Eaglestone, T. Ungvary, G.L. Davies: A Musical Experiment with Next Generation Database Technology. International Computer Music Conference, San Jose (1992), pp 376-377.

19. B. Eaglestone, G.L. Davies GL, T. Ungvary: A Extended Version Model for Artistic Design Applications. Accepted for inclusion in: 5th International Conference on Computing and Information, IEEE, Sudbury, Ontario, Canada (May 26-29, 1993).

20. A. Goldberg: Reusing Software Developments. ACM SIGSOFT Software Engineering Notes 15(6), Proc of the 4th ACM SIGSOFT Symposium on Software Development Environments, Ed Taylor RN, Irvine, Calif (Dec, 1990), pp 107-119.

21. R.H. Katz RH: Towards a Unified Framework for Version Modelling in Engineering Databases. ACM TODS 22(4) (Dec, 1990), pp 375-408.

22. M.V. Ketabchi, V. Berzins: Modelling and managing CAD databases. IEEE Computing Mag, 20(2) (February, 1987), pp 93-102.

23. W. Kim , N. Ballou, H-T. Chou, J.F. Garza JF, D. Woelk D: Features of the ORION Object Oriented Database System. In W. Kim, F.H. Lokovsky (eds): Object Oriented Concepts, Databases and Applications. ACM Press Frontier Series (1989).

24. W. Kim, J. Banerjee, H-T. Chou, J.F. Garza, D. Woelk D: Composite Object Support in an Object-Oriented Database System. OOPSLA, (1987) .

25. P. Klahold, G. Schlageter, W. Wilkes: A General Model for Version Management in Databases. VLDB 12th Int Conf, Kyoto (August, 1986), pp319-327.

26. A. Mahler, A. Lampen: Integrating Configuration Management into a Generic Environment. ACM SIGSOFT, Software Eng Notes 15(6) (Dec, 1990), pp 229-237.

27. S.R. Monk, I. Sommerville: A model for versioning of classes in object-oriented databases. Advanced Database Systems, 10th British National Conference on Databases, BNCOD 10. Lecture Notes in Computer Science 618. Berlin: Springer-Verlag (1992), pp 42-58.

28. Composers and the Computer. C. Roads (ed), W. Kaufmann Inc, Los Altos, California, USA (1985).

29. J. Rumbaugh: Controlling propagation of operations using attributes on relations. Proc OOPSLA '88 Conf, New York, ACM (September, 1988), pp 285-296.

30. R. Snodgrass: Temporal databases status and research directions. ACM SIGMOD RECORD 19(4) (Dec, 1990), pp 83-89.

31. M. Stonebraker, et al: Third Generation Data Base Manifesto. In: Proc 1990 ACM SIGMOD Int Conf on Management of Data, Atlanta (May, 1990), pp 31-44.

32. M. Stonebraker, L.A. Rowe, M. Hirohama: The Implementation of POSTGRES. IEEE Trans Knowledge and Data Engineering 2(1) (1990), pp 125-141.

33. M. Stonebraker: POSTGRES, a Next Generation Database Management System., CACM 34(10) (Oct, 1991).
[TI84] W.F. Tichy: RCS - A System for Version Control. Software Practice and Experience: John Wiley 15(7) (July, 1985).

34. C.J. Tully: Introduction to: Representing and Enacting the Software Process. Proc of the 4th Int Software Process Workshop. ACM SIGSOFT Software Eng Notes 14(4) (June, 1989).

35. T. Ungvary, S. Waters, P. Raijka: Nuntius: A computer system for the interactive composition and analysis of music and dance. Leonardo (Pergamon Press, Oxford) 1 (1992).

36. B. Vercoe: CSound: A Manual for the Audio Processing System Support Programs with Tutorial. MIT (1991).

Lecture Notes in Computer Science

For information about Vols. 1–615
please contact your bookseller or Springer-Verlag

Vol. 655: M. Bidoit, C. Choppy (Eds.), Recent Trends in Data Type Specification. X, 344 pages. 1993.

Vol. 656: M. Rusinowitch, J. L. Rémy (Eds.), Conditional Term Rewriting Systems. Proceedings, 1992. XI, 501 pages. 1993.

Vol. 657: E. W. Mayr (Ed.), Graph-Theoretic Concepts in Computer Science. Proceedings, 1992. VIII, 350 pages. 1993.

Vol. 658: R. A. Rueppel (Ed.), Advances in Cryptology – EUROCRYPT '92. Proceedings, 1992. X, 493 pages. 1993.

Vol. 659: G. Brewka, K. P. Jantke, P. H. Schmitt (Eds.), Nonmonotonic and Inductive Logic. Proceedings, 1991. VIII, 332 pages. 1993. (Subseries LNAI).

Vol. 660: E. Lamma, P. Mello (Eds.), Extensions of Logic Programming. Proceedings, 1992. VIII, 417 pages. 1993. (Subseries LNAI).

Vol. 661: S. J. Hanson, W. Remmele, R. L. Rivest (Eds.), Machine Learning: From Theory to Applications. VIII, 271 pages. 1993.

Vol. 662: M. Nitzberg, D. Mumford, T. Shiota, Filtering, Segmentation and Depth. VIII, 143 pages. 1993.

Vol. 663: G. v. Bochmann, D. K. Probst (Eds.), Computer Aided Verification. Proceedings, 1992. IX, 422 pages. 1993.

Vol. 664: M. Bezem, J. F. Groote (Eds.), Typed Lambda Calculi and Applications. Proceedings, 1993. VIII, 433 pages. 1993.

Vol. 665: P. Enjalbert, A. Finkel, K. W. Wagner (Eds.), STACS 93. Proceedings, 1993. XIV, 724 pages. 1993.

Vol. 666: J. W. de Bakker, W.-P. de Roever, G. Rozenberg (Eds.), Semantics: Foundations and Applications. Proceedings, 1992. VIII, 659 pages. 1993.

Vol. 667: P. B. Brazdil (Ed.), Machine Learning: ECML – 93. Proceedings, 1993. XII, 471 pages. 1993. (Subseries LNAI).

Vol. 668: M.-C. Gaudel, J.-P. Jouannaud (Eds.), TAPSOFT '93: Theory and Practice of Software Development. Proceedings, 1993. XII, 762 pages. 1993.

Vol. 669: R. S. Bird, C. C. Morgan, J. C. P. Woodcock (Eds.), Mathematics of Program Construction. Proceedings, 1992. VIII, 378 pages. 1993.

Vol. 670: J. C. P. Woodcock, P. G. Larsen (Eds.), FME '93: Industrial-Strength Formal Methods. Proceedings, 1993. XI, 689 pages. 1993.

Vol. 671: H. J. Ohlbach (Ed.), GWAI-92: Advances in Artificial Intelligence. Proceedings, 1992. XI, 397 pages. 1993. (Subseries LNAI).

Vol. 672: A. Barak, S. Guday, R. G. Wheeler, The MOSIX Distributed Operating System. X, 221 pages. 1993.

Vol. 673: G. Cohen, T. Mora, O. Moreno (Eds.), Applied Algebra, Algebraic Algorithms and Error-Correcting Codes. Proceedings, 1993. X, 355 pages 1993.

Vol. 674: G. Rozenberg (Ed.), Advances in Petri Nets 1993. VII, 457 pages. 1993.

Vol. 675: A. Mulkers, Live Data Structures in Logic Programs. VIII, 220 pages. 1993.

Vol. 676: Th. H. Reiss, Recognizing Planar Objects Using Invariant Image Features. X, 180 pages. 1993.

Vol. 677: H. Abdulrab, J.-P. Pécuchet (Eds.), Word Equations and Related Topics. Proceedings, 1991. VII, 214 pages. 1993.

Vol. 678: F. Meyer auf der Heide, B. Monien, A. L. Rosenberg (Eds.), Parallel Architectures and Their Efficient Use. Proceedings, 1992. XII, 227 pages. 1993.

Vol. 679: C. Fermüller, A. Leitsch, T. Tammet, N. Zamov, Resolution Methods for the Decision Problem. VIII, 205 pages. 1993. (Subseries LNAI).

Vol. 682: B. Bouchon-Meunier, L. Valverde, R. R. Yager (Eds.), IPMU '92 – Advanced Methods in Artificial Intelligence. Proceedings, 1992. IX, 367 pages. 1993.

Vol. 683: G.J. Milne, L. Pierre (Eds.), Correct Hardware Design and Verification Methods. Proceedings, 1993. VIII, 270 Pages. 1993.

Vol. 684: A. Apostolico, M. Crochemore, Z. Galil, U. Manber (Eds.), Combinatorial Pattern Matching. Proceedings, 1993. VIII, 265 pages. 1993.

Vol. 685: C. Rolland, F. Bodart, C. Cauvet (Eds.), Advanced Information Systems Engineering. Proceedings, 1993. XI, 650 pages. 1993.

Vol. 686: J. Mira, J. Cabestany, A. Prieto (Eds.), New Trends in Neural Computation. Procedings, 1993. XVII, 746 pages. 1993.

Vol. 687: H. H. Barrett, A. F. Gmitro (Eds.), Information Processing in Medical Imaging. Proceedings, 1993. XVI, 567 pages. 1993.

Vol. 688: M. Gauthier (Ed.), Ada - Europe '93. Proceedings, 1993. VIII, 353 pages. 1993.

Vol. 689: J. Komorowski, Z. W. Ras (Eds.), Methodologies for Intelligent Systems. Proceedings, 1993. XI, 653 pages. 1993. (Subseries LNAI).

Vol. 690: C. Kirchner (Ed.), Rewriting Techniques and Applications. Proceedings, 1993. XI, 488 pages. 1993.

Vol. 691: M. Ajmone Marsan (Ed.), Application and Theory of Petri Nets 1993. Proceedings, 1993. IX, 591 pages. 1993.

Vol. 692: D. Abel, B.C. Ooi (Eds.), Advances in Spatial Databases. Proceedings, 1993. XIII, 529 pages. 1993.

Vol. 693: P. E. Lauer (Ed.), Functional Programming, Concurrency, Simulation and Automated Reasoning. Proceedings, 1991/1992. XI, 398 pages. 1993.

Vol. 694: A. Bode, M. Reeve, G. Wolf (Eds.), PARLE '93. Parallel Architectures and Languages Europe. Proceedings, 1993. XVII, 770 pages. 1993.

Vol. 695: E. P. Klement, W. Slany (Eds.), Fuzzy Logic in Artificial Intelligence. Proceedings, 1993. VIII, 192 pages. 1993. (Subseries LNAI).

Vol. 696: M. Worboys, A. F. Grundy (Eds.), Advances in Databases. Proceedings, 1993. X, 276 pages. 1993.

Vol. 697: C. Courcoubetis (Ed.), Computer Aided Verification. Proceedings, 1993. IX, 504 pages. 1993.

Vol. 700: A. Lingas, R. Karlsson, S. Carlsson (Eds.), Automata, Languages and Programming. Proceedings, 1993. XII, 697 pages. 1993.